해커스 텝스
최신기출유형
실전모의고사
문제집

해커스 어학연구소

시험에 나올 문제를 미리 풀어보는
텝스 적중예상특강
해커스텝스 HackersTEPS.com

텝스 고득점 달성을 위한
나의 목표 달성기

목표 개수 _____ / 135개

달성 목표일 _____년 __월 __일

각 테스트를 마친 후 채점 결과를 아래의 <맞은 개수 표>에 기입합니다.
그 중 합계는 <실력 향상 확인 그래프>에 ■ 로 표시하여, 실력의 변화를 직접 확인해 보세요.

맞은 개수 표

영역 \ 회차	TEST 01	TEST 02	TEST 03	TEST 04	TEST 05	TEST 06
청해	/40	/40	/40	/40	/40	/40
어휘	/30	/30	/30	/30	/30	/30
문법	/30	/30	/30	/30	/30	/30
독해	/35	/35	/35	/35	/35	/35
합계	/135	/135	/135	/135	/135	/135

실력 향상 확인 그래프

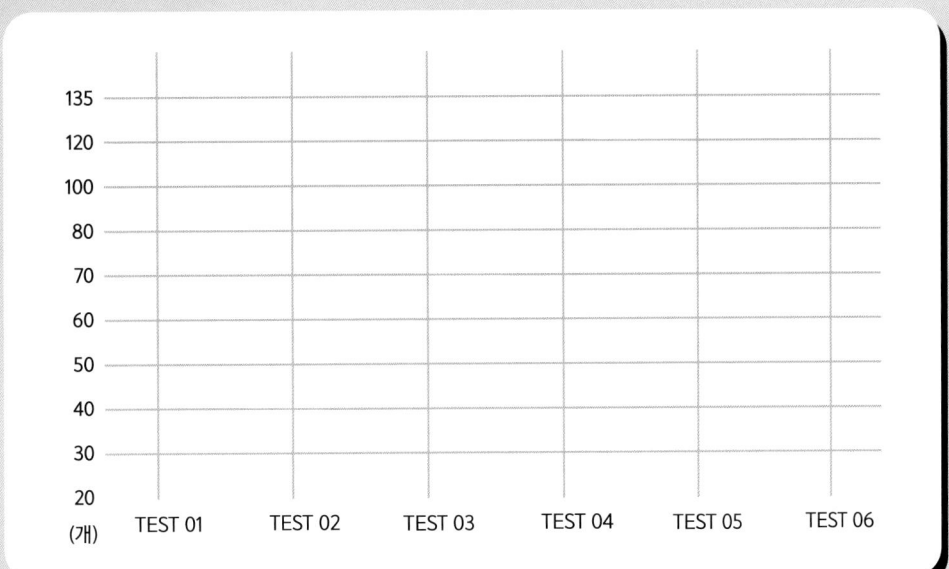

* 달성 목표일은 p.24의 '수준별 텝스 고득점 비법!'을 참고해서 정해 보세요.

텝스를 철저히 분석 반영한 마무리 실전서
해커스 텝스 최신기출유형 실전모의고사 문제집을 내면서

텝스 고득점을 목표로 하는 학습자들에게 목표 달성을 위한 가장 올바른 방향을 제시하고자 『해커스 텝스 최신기출유형 실전모의고사 문제집』을 출간하게 되었습니다. 『해커스 텝스 최신기출유형 실전모의고사』는 텝스 고난이도 문제로 구성된 고득점 달성을 위한 마무리 실전서입니다.

최신 텝스 출제경향을 철저히 분석하여 고난이도 문제에 대비할 수 있도록 하였습니다. 본 교재는 난이도가 높은 텝스 시험에 철저히 대비할 수 있도록 실전모의고사 6회분을 구성하였습니다.

고득점 달성을 위한 다양하고 철저한 학습관리 시스템을 수록하였습니다. 텝스는 자신에게 딱 맞는 학습 방법을 찾고 철저한 학습관리를 통해 '자신과의 싸움'에서 이겨내는 것이 중요합니다. 『해커스 텝스 최신기출유형 실전모의고사 문제집』에는 수준별 텝스 고득점 비법 및 셀프 체크리스트 등을 수록하여 학습자들이 철저한 자기관리를 통해 마지막까지 학습에 집중할 수 있도록 하였습니다.

텝스 문제 유형 파악 및 이해를 위해 정확한 해석·스크립트를 수록하였을 뿐 아니라 해설집을 별도로 출간하였습니다. 흔히 문제를 푸는 것보다 중요한 것은 이해하는 것이라고 말합니다. 문제집에 수록된 해석 및 스크립트뿐 아니라 『해커스 텝스 최신기출유형 실전모의고사 해설집』을 활용하여 문제에 대해 확실히 이해하고 넘어간다면, 최고의 학습 성과를 거둘 수 있을 것입니다.

더불어, 텝스 전문 커뮤니티 해커스텝스 사이트(HackersTEPS.com)에서 교재 학습 중 궁금한 점을 다른 학습자들과 나누고, 다양한 무료 텝스 학습 자료를 함께 이용한다면, 학습 효과를 더욱 높일 수 있을 것입니다. 또한, 실시간으로 공유하는 텝스 시험 정보를 통해 보다 효과적으로 시험에 대비할 수 있을 것입니다.

『해커스 텝스 최신기출유형 실전모의고사 문제집』이 여러분의 텝스 목표 점수 달성에 확실한 해결책이 되고 영어 실력 향상, 나아가 **여러분의 꿈을 향한 길에 믿음직한 동반자**가 되기를 소망합니다

해커스 어학연구소

CONTENTS

실전모의고사로 텝스 고득점 달성하기!   6
텝스 소개   10
텝스 전문가 해커스가 알려주는 영역별 공략법   12
수준별 텝스 고득점 비법!   24

TEST 01
LISTENING COMPREHENSION   31
VOCABULARY & GRAMMAR   37
READING COMPREHENSION   45

SELF-CHECK LIST   64

TEST 02
LISTENING COMPREHENSION   67
VOCABULARY & GRAMMAR   73
READING COMPREHENSION   81

SELF-CHECK LIST   100

TEST 03
LISTENING COMPREHENSION   103
VOCABULARY & GRAMMAR   109
READING COMPREHENSION   117

SELF-CHECK LIST   136

무료 단어암기장 & 단어암기 MP3
무료 정답녹음 MP3

해커스인강(HackersIngang.com)

해커스 텝스 최신기출유형 실전모의고사 문제집

TEST 04

LISTENING COMPREHENSION 139
VOCABULARY & GRAMMAR 145
READING COMPREHENSION 153

SELF-CHECK LIST 172

TEST 05

LISTENING COMPREHENSION 175
VOCABULARY & GRAMMAR 181
READING COMPREHENSION 189

SELF-CHECK LIST 208

TEST 06

LISTENING COMPREHENSION 211
VOCABULARY & GRAMMAR 217
READING COMPREHENSION 225

SELF-CHECK LIST 244

해석·스크립트

TEST 01 246
TEST 02 263
TEST 03 280
TEST 04 297
TEST 05 314
TEST 06 331

ANSWER KEYS 349
OMR 답안지 357

실전모의고사로
텝스 고득점 달성하기!

 **최신 텝스 시험 유형, 난이도를 반영한 실전모의고사로 완벽 대비!**

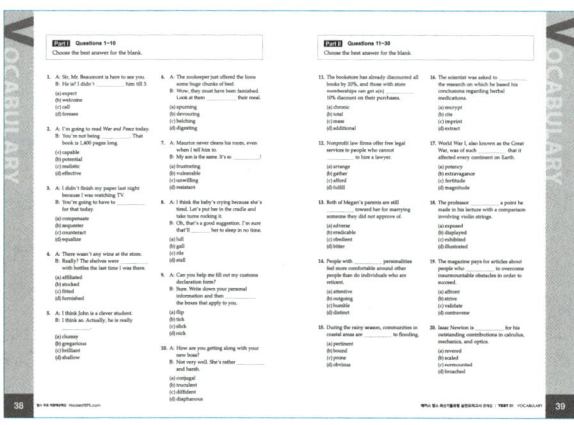

실전과 동일한 형태의 실전모의고사 6회분

최신 텝스 시험 난이도를 철저히 분석, 반영하여 총 6회분의 실전모의고사를 구성하였다. 특히, 난이도가 높은 시험에도 대비할 수 있는 고난도 문제들을 통해 어려운 문제에도 완벽하게 대비할 수 있어 텝스 고득점 달성이 가능하다.

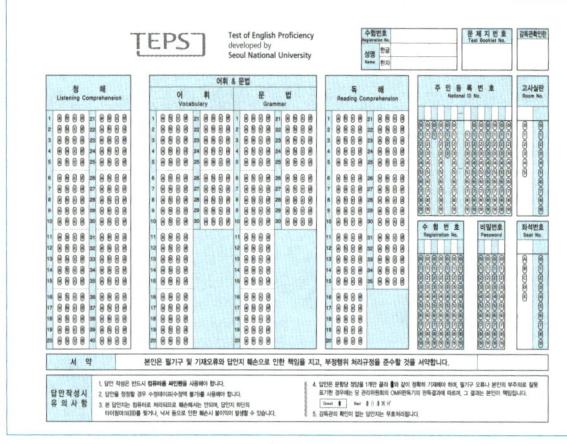

실전 연습이 가능한 OMR 답안지

실제 텝스 시험에 응시할 때 사용하는 답안지와 유사하게 디자인된 OMR 답안지를 테스트 별로 제공하였다. 실제 시험장에서처럼 문제를 풀고 마킹하면서, 시간 조절하는 연습을 할 수 있어 보다 철저하고도 완벽한 시험 대비가 가능하다.

해커스 템스 최신기출유형 실전모의고사 문제집

02 고득점 달성은 나의 것! **철저한 학습관리 시스템**

수준별 텝스 고득점 비법

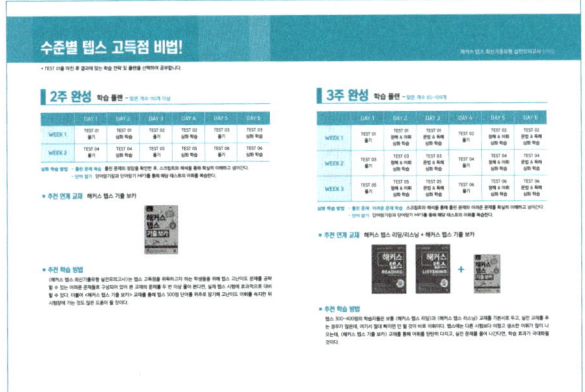

TEST 01의 맞은 개수에 따라 학습 플랜, 추천 연계 교재, 추천 학습 방법을 제시하였다. 자신의 수준에 맞는 교재 및 학습 플랜을 선택하여 공부한다면, 전략적인 텝스 고득점 달성이 가능하다.

셀프 체크리스트

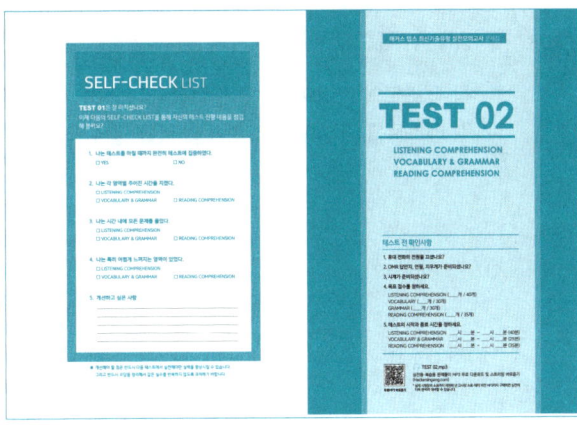

1회분의 테스트를 끝마칠 때마다 셀프 체크리스트 (SELF-CHECK LIST)를 통해 학습자들은 자신의 문제 풀이 자세를 점검하고, 마지막 테스트까지 목표 의식을 유지하며 학습에 전념할 수 있다.

실전모의고사로 **텝스 고득점 달성하기!**

 정확한 해석과 스크립트로 **텝스 문제 완전 분석!**

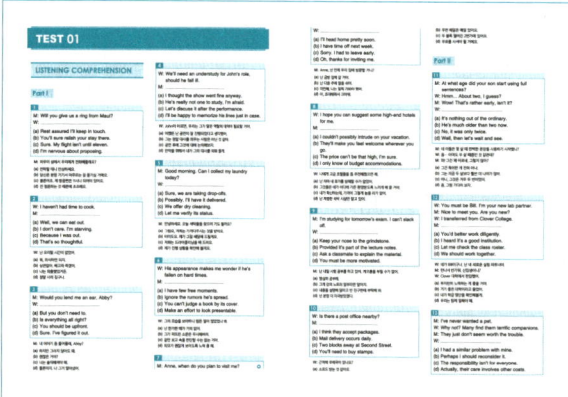

해석·스크립트

청해 영역 스크립트와 모든 영역의 지문과 문제에 대한 해석이 정확하게 제공되어, 학습자들은 문제를 정확히 확인하고, 이해하며 학습할 수 있다.

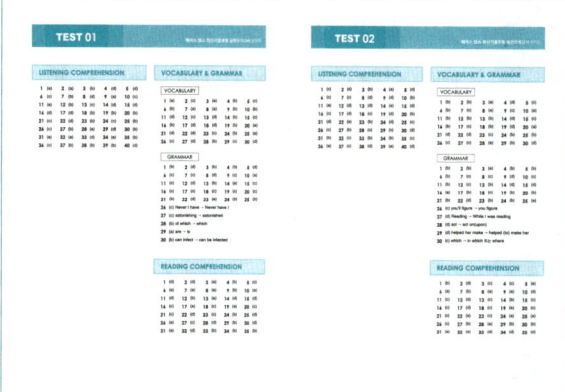

ANSWER KEYS

각 테스트의 정답이 한 곳에 정리되어 있어, 학습자들은 각 테스트를 마친 후 편리하게 채점을 할 수 있다.

04 해커스만의 노하우가 담긴 학습자료 200% 활용하기!

매일 새로운 텝스 무료 학습자료

해커스텝스 사이트(HackersTEPS.com)에서 무료로 제공되는 매일 텝스 풀기, 매일 텝스 어휘, 텝스 기출 보카 TEST 등을 통해 보다 빠른 텝스 목표 점수 달성이 가능하다.

들으면서 외우는 단어암기자료

교재에 수록된 핵심 단어들을 복습하고 암기할 수 있는 들으면서 외우는 단어암기자료를 해커스인강 사이트(HackersIngang.com)에서 무료로 이용할 수 있다. 단어를 듣고, 따라 읽으며 쉽고 재미있는 어휘 학습이 가능하다.

텝스 소개

TEPS란?

TEPS란 Test of English Proficiency developed by Seoul National University의 약자로, 서울대학교 언어교육원에서 개발하고 TEPS 관리위원회에서 주관하는 국내 개발 영어 인증 시험이다. 실제 활용하는 영어 능력을 평가함으로써, 기업체 및 공사, 고시 및 대학 입시 등 각종 자격 요건 평가시험으로 활용된다.

텝스의 구성

영역	파트	내용	문항 수	시간	배점
청해	Part I	질의 응답 (하나의 문장을 듣고 이어질 응답 고르기)	10	40분	240점
	Part II	짧은 대화 (3턴의 주고받는 대화를 듣고 이어질 응답 고르기)	10		
	Part III	긴 대화 (6~7턴의 주고받는 대화를 듣고 질문에 알맞은 답 고르기)	10		
	Part IV	담화문 (한 명의 화자가 말하는 긴 내용을 듣고 질문에 알맞은 답 고르기) (1지문 1문항)	6		
	Part V	긴 담화문 (한 명의 화자가 말하는 긴 내용을 듣고 질문에 알맞은 답 고르기) (1지문 2문항)	4		
어휘	Part I	구어체 (대화문의 빈칸에 가장 적절한 어휘 고르기)	10	25분	60점
	Part II	문어체 (단문의 빈칸에 가장 적절한 어휘 고르기)	20		
문법	Part I	구어체 (대화문의 빈칸에 가장 적절한 답 고르기)	10		60점
	Part II	문어체 (단문의 빈칸에 가장 적절한 답 고르기)	15		
	Part III	대화 및 문단 (어법상 틀리거나 어색한 부분 고르기)	5		
독해	Part I	빈칸 채우기 (빈칸에 가장 적절한 답 고르기)	10	40분	240점
	Part II	흐름 찾기 (한 단락의 글에서 내용 흐름상 어색한 부분 고르기)	2		
	Part III	내용 이해 (지문을 읽고 질문에 가장 적절한 답 고르기) (1지문 1문항)	13		
	Part IV	내용 이해 (지문을 읽고 질문에 가장 적절한 답 고르기) (1지문 2문항)	10		
14개 파트			135문항	105분	600점

* 각 문항의 난이도에 따른 반응 패턴을 근거로 평가하는 문항 반응 이론 적용

시험 응시 안내

1. 원서 접수
- 인터넷 접수: www.teps.or.kr로 접속한다. 사진 파일을 미리 준비해야 하고, 응시료는 신용카드 또는 계좌이체로 결제할 수 있다.
- 방문 접수: www.teps.or.kr의 시험 접수 → 접수처 안내에서 가까운 접수처를 확인한 후 방문하여 접수, 3*4 사진 한 장과 응시료가 필요하다.

2. 응시
- 응시일: 매달 토요일과 일요일 중 1~3회
  정확한 날짜는 www.teps.or.kr로 접속 → 시험 접수 → 시험일정 안내를 통해 확인
- 준비물: 규정에 맞는 신분증(주민등록증, 운전면허증, 청소년증 등이 인정되며, 자세한 신분증 규정은 www.teps.or.kr 에서 확인), 수험표, 컴퓨터용 사인펜(연필 불가), 수정테이프(수정액 사용 불가), 아날로그 손목시계
- 성적 확인: 휴대폰 문자 및 인터넷 확인 (성적 발표 일시는 시험 접수 시 확인 가능)

TEPS 응시 관련 Tips

1. 고사장 가기 전
- 준비물을 잘 챙겼는지 확인한다.
- 시험 장소를 미리 확인해 두고, 규정된 입실 시간에 늦지 않도록 유의한다.

2. 고사장 입구에서
- 수험표에 적힌 수험 번호가 배정된 고사실을 확인한다.

3. 시험 보기 직전
- 모든 영역의 시험이 끝날 때까지 휴식 시간이 없으므로 화장실은 미리 다녀온다.

4. 시험 시
- 답안을 따로 마킹할 시간이 없으므로 풀면서 바로 마킹한다.
- 연필이나 볼펜으로 먼저 마킹한 후 사인펜으로 마킹하면 OMR 카드에 오류가 날 수 있으니 주의한다.
- 정해진 영역을 푸는 시간에 다른 영역의 문제를 풀면 부정 행위로 간주되므로 주의한다.
- 대부분의 영역이 앞에는 쉬운 문제가, 뒤에는 어려운 문제가 나오므로 앞부분을 빨리 풀어 시간을 확보한다.
- 청해 시험 시 놓친 문제나 어휘 / 문법 / 독해 시험 시 풀기 어려운 문제에서 오래 머무르지 않아 다른 문제 풀 시간에 영향이 가지 않도록 한다.
- 문항 난이도, 변별도 및 영역별 특정 가중치에 따라 문항 배점이 다르므로, 어려운 문제를 많이 맞히면 높은 점수를 받을 확률이 더 높다.
- 청해 시험 시 문제지의 빈 공간에 조금씩 필기하는 것은 괜찮다.

텝스 전문가 해커스가 알려주는
영역별 공략법

청해 LISTENING COMPREHENSION

텝스 청해 영역의 Part I~III는 각각 10문항, Part IV는 6문항, Part V는 4문항을 풀도록 구성되어 있다. Part I~IV는 각 대화나 담화마다 한 문제가 출제되며, Part V는 한 담화에 두 문제가 출제된다. 순수하게 들어서 이해한 것만을 평가하기 위해 문제와 보기 모두 시험지에 인쇄되어 있지 않다.

■ 파트별 문제 유형

Part I 하나의 문장을 듣고 이어질 응답 고르기 (10문항, 1~10번)

W: What time are you coming here?
M: _____

(a) It's a quarter past three now.
(b) I'll be over in a little while.
(c) Thanks for sending me the invitation.
(d) I came down with the flu so I didn't go.

언제 올 예정인지 묻는 말에, 곧 갈 것이라고 대답한 (b)가 정답이다.

Part II 3턴의 주고받는 대화를 듣고 이어질 응답 고르기 (10문항, 11~20번)

M: What made you lease this apartment?
W: The location. It's next to the office.
M: That must save you time.
W: _____

(a) You're right. I guess I'll take it.
(b) Well, it was relatively cheap.
(c) That's what I like best about it.
(d) Because my hours were reduced.

사무실 근처에 집을 얻어서 시간이 절약되겠다는 의견에, 그 점이 가장 좋다고 대답한 (c)가 정답이다.

Part III 6~7턴의 주고받는 대화를 듣고 질문에 알맞은 답 고르기 (10문항, 21~30번)

Listen to a conversation between two friends.
M: You seem anxious. Aren't you excited to meet your old friend?
W: I'm apprehensive. Our last meeting was disastrous.
M: I take it you haven't met for a while?
W: No. Our relationship's deterioration has been difficult on both of us.
M: I get it. That's why you're nervous.
W: We used to be so close. I'm just hoping there's no leftover tension.

Q: What can be inferred from the conversation?

(a) The woman remains upset with her friend's actions.
(b) The woman and her friend had a falling out.
(c) The man thinks the woman shouldn't leave.
(d) The man and the woman's friend are mutual.

친구와의 관계 악화가 두 사람 모두를 힘들게 했다는 말을 통해, 두 사람에게 불화가 있었다는 것을 유추한 (b)가 정답이다.

Part IV 한 명의 화자가 말하는 긴 내용을 듣고 질문에 알맞은 답 고르기 (1지문 1문항) (6문항, 31~36번)

As copywriters, you should be aware that people have brief attention spans, so your ad campaigns should always use cleverly chosen words that catch the readers' attention. Long, tedious paragraphs bury the point of your advertisements and make people lose interest in what you've written. Make your headlines stand out by keeping them eye-catching while getting rid of superfluous information.

Q: What can be inferred about ad campaigns from the talk?

(a) They should be as informative as possible.
(b) They need to refrain from catchy mottoes.
(c) They should utilize graphics to communicate data
(d) They are more compelling when less verbose.

말이 길어지면 사람들의 관심이 떨어진다는 말을 통해, 광고 캠페인은 장황하지 않을 때 강력하다는 것을 유추한 (d)가 정답이다.

텝스 전문가 해커스가 알려주는 **영역별 공략법**

Part V 한 명의 화자가 말하는 긴 내용을 듣고 질문에 알맞은 답 고르기 (1지문 2문항) (4문항, 37~40번)

> The Laudner Hill Gallery is proud to announce that this year's Emerging Artists Exhibition will open on August 10. This year, the submission process began on June 1, and all artists were required to submit new two-dimensional art pieces on the theme "visibility." Having received work from more than 100 artists in each of our two categories, graphite and watercolor, it was certainly no easy task to narrow down our choices for the showcase. However, we're confident that our three winners, along with the two honorable mentions, are incredible talents that deserve the exposure this exhibition will offer them. Gallery hours are from 11 a.m. to 7 p.m., Tuesday to Saturday. The display will be open to the general public until September 25. Visit www.laudnerhillgallery.com for more information.
>
> Q1: What is the main topic of the talk?
>
> (a) An exclusive private event at a gallery
> **(b) An exhibition of new artistic works**
> (c) A submission deadline for an art contest
> (d) A ceremony honoring established artists
>
> Q2: Which is correct according to the talk?
>
> (a) The Emerging Artists Exhibition opened earlier than last year.
> **(b) The competition restricted the type of material artists could use.**
> (c) The exhibition will be made up of the work of three artists.
> (d) The tickets can be purchased on the Laudner Hill Gallery Web site.

Q1: 대회에서 우승한 예술가들의 새로운 작품들의 전시회에 대해 설명하고 있으므로, 새로운 예술 작품의 전시회라고 종합한 (b)가 정답이다.
Q2: 흑연과 수채화 두 가지 카테고리에서 작품을 받았다는 말을 통해, 대회는 예술가가 사용할 수 있는 재료의 종류를 제한했다고 언급한 (b)가 정답이다.

■ 파트별 공략법

Part I & II 공략법
1. 문제와 보기를 한 번씩만 들려주므로, 순발력과 빠른 판단력이 요구된다.
2. 구어 표현이 많이 출제되므로, 일상적인 대화 상황과 관련된 다양한 구어 표현을 외워둔다면, 고득점 달성에 많은 도움이 된다.
3. Part I의 경우 오답의 유형을 중점적으로 학습하고, Part II의 경우 전체적인 맥락을 파악하며 듣는 연습을 한다면, 답을 고르는 데 훨씬 도움이 된다.

Part III 공략법
1. 대화 상황 및 문제와 보기를 한 번씩만 들려주므로, 처음부터 끝까지 주의 깊게 들어야 한다.
2. 문제 유형의 배열이 정해진 편이므로, 21~23번은 중심 내용, 24~28번은 세부 정보, 29~30번은 추론 문제의 정답의 단서를 찾는 데 집중한다면, 효과적으로 문제를 풀 수 있다.
3. 대화에서 언급되는 모든 것이 정답의 단서가 될 수 있으므로, 문제지 여백에 특정 대상, 수치 등 자세한 내용까지 간단하게 메모하며 듣는다.

Part IV & V 공략법
1. 처음 들을 때는 주제와 문제 유형에, 두 번째 들을 때는 정답의 단서를 찾는 데 집중한다면, 효과적으로 문제를 풀 수 있다.
2. 세부 내용을 묻는 문제의 경우, 문제지 여백에 구체적인 지명, 수치 등을 간단하게 메모하며 듣는다. 단, 메모하는 것에 지나치게 집중하여 다른 내용을 놓치지 않도록 주의한다.

텝스 전문가 해커스가 알려주는 **영역별 공략법**

어휘 & 문법 VOCABULARY & GRAMMAR

텝스 어휘 & 문법 영역은 통합 25분 동안 어휘에서 30문항, 문법에서 30문항, 총 60문항을 풀도록 구성되어 있다. 어휘 영역은 상대적으로 문제 길이가 짧기 때문에 약 10분 정도의 시간을 할애하는 것이 권장되고, 문법 영역은 Part III에 상대적으로 길이가 긴 지문이 등장하는 것을 고려하여 약 15분의 시간을 분배하여 푸는 것이 권장된다.

어휘 (VOCABULARY)

텝스 어휘 영역은 Part I 에서 10문항, Part II 에서 20문항, 총 30문항을 풀도록 구성되어 있다. Part I 에서는 구어체, Part II 에서는 문어체를 통해 어휘 능력을 평가한다. 단어의 단편적인 의미보다는 문맥에서 쓰인 상대적인 의미를 더 중요하게 다룬다.

■ **파트별 문제 유형**

Part I 두 사람의 대화 중 빈칸에 적절한 단어 고르기 (10문항, 1~10번)

> A: Can we haggle for a lower price on this house?
> B: Sorry, the seller doesn't want to _____.
>
> (a) contemplate
> (b) evaluate
> (c) premeditate
> **(d) negotiate**

문맥상 빈칸에는 A의 haggle(흥정하다)과 유사한 의미의 단어가 와야 적절하므로, '협상하다'는 뜻의 (d)가 정답이다.

Part II 하나 또는 두 개의 문장의 빈칸에 적절한 단어 고르기 (20문항, 11~30번)

> The social _____ between the upper class and the lower class disturbs concerned citizens.
>
> (a) opposition
> (b) collision
> **(c) disparity**
> (d) distinction

문맥상 시민들을 불안하게 하는 것은 상류 계급과 하층 계급 사이의 '차이'일 것이므로 '차이'를 뜻하는 (c)가 정답이다.

■ 시간 배분 전략

앞부분 문제를 빠르게 풀고 뒷부분 문제에 시간을 할애한다.

어휘 영역은 문법 영역에 비해 상대적으로 문제 길이가 짧기 때문에 약 10분 정도의 시간을 할애하는 것이 권장된다. 이때, 각 파트의 앞부분 문제가 쉬운 편이고 뒷부분으로 갈수록 어려워지므로, 읽자마자 바로 정답을 체크하는 빠른 속도로 앞부분 문제를 풀어야, 뒷부분의 어려운 문제를 푸는 데 시간을 좀 더 사용할 수 있다.

■ 파트별 공략법

Part I & II 공략법

1. **문제 전체를 읽는다.** Collocation, 이디엄의 일부를 묻는 문제 등은 빈칸 앞과 뒤만 읽고도 답을 찾을 수 있으나, 대부분의 경우 대화와 문장의 일부만 읽고서는 정확하게 정답을 선택할 수 없다. 따라서 문장 전체를 빠르게 읽은 후 답을 찾는다.

2. **어휘의 쓰임을 중심으로 정답을 선택한다.** 우리말 의미로는 비슷하지만 제시된 문장에서의 쓰임에 적절하지 않아 답이 되지 않는 어휘들이 함께 보기로 출제되므로, 의미뿐만 아니라 쓰임에 근거해서 답을 찾는다.

3. **형태가 유사한 어휘들의 정확한 의미를 외워둔다.** 정답 어휘와 유사한 형태를 지닌 어휘들이 보기로 출제되므로, 정답을 쉽게 고를 수 있도록 형태가 유사한 어휘들의 의미 차이를 미리 외워두면 도움이 된다.

* 어휘는 고득점의 키를 잡고 있다고 할 정도로 중요하므로, 부족하다고 생각하는 학습자들은 〈해커스 텝스 기출 보카〉 교재로 어휘를 꼼꼼히 다지는 것을 추천한다.

텝스 전문가 해커스가 알려주는 **영역별 공략법**

문법 (GRAMMAR)

텝스 문법 영역은 Part I 에서 10문항, Part II 에서 15문항, Part III에서 5문항, 총 30문항을 풀도록 구성되어 있다. 구어와 문어 상황, 단문과 장문 등 다양한 상황과 길이의 문장을 통하여 문법 사항 이해도 및 활용도를 평가한다.

■ 파트별 문제 유형

Part I 두 사람의 대화 중 빈칸에 어법상 적절한 표현 고르기 (10문항, 1~10번)

> A: Don't you think this abstract painting expresses sadness?
> B: Honestly, I _____ modern art.
>
> (a) don't about anything understand
> **(b) don't understand anything about**
> (c) understand not about anything
> (d) understand anything not about

일반동사(understand)를 부정문으로 만들기 위한 don't, 일반동사 understand, 목적어 anything, 빈칸 뒤의 modern art라는 목적어를 받는 전치사 about을 어순에 맞게 나열한 (b)가 정답이다.

Part II 서술문의 빈칸에 어법상 적절한 표현 고르기 (15문항, 11~25번)

> The local shoe retailer works _____ hard to compete with the larger chains.
>
> (a) too
> **(b) very**
> (c) much
> (d) such

부사 hard를 꾸며주면서 '매우'란 뜻으로 자연스러운 문맥을 만드는 (b)가 정답이다.

Part III 긴 대화문이나 서술문에서 어법상 틀리거나 어색한 부분 고르기 (5문항, 26~30번)

> (a) A: Joe, would you like to join Kim and me for a movie later?
> (b) B: I don't think I have enough energy to go out tonight.
> (c) A: What's been making you feel so tired lately?
> **(d) B: Getting up at 6 am every day was really exhausting.**

요즘 피곤해 하는 이유를 묻는 질문에 '매일 일찍 일어나서 진이 빠진다'라는 현재시제 답변이 적절하므로, (d)에서 과거시제 was는 현재시제 is로 바뀌어야 맞다.

■ 시간 배분 전략

Part I, II 문제를 빠르게 풀고, Part III에 시간을 더 할애한다.
문법 영역은 Part III에 상대적으로 길이가 긴 지문이 등장하는 것을 고려하여 약 15분의 시간을 분배하여 푸는 것이 권장된다. 이때 Part I, II보다 Part III가 길고 어려운 편이므로, Part I, II는 빨리 풀고, Part III에는 좀 더 시간을 할애하여 꼼꼼히 풀도록 한다.

■ 파트별 공략법

Part I & II 공략법

1. **보기를 먼저 읽어 출제 포인트를 찾아 낸다.** 보기를 통해 문제의 문법 포인트가 무엇인지 먼저 파악하면, 문제를 보다 빠르고 정확하게 풀 수 있다.
2. **오답노트를 활용한다.** 문법의 경우, 오답패턴 분석과 문법 포인트를 암기하면 확실히 점수가 오를 수 있으므로 오답노트를 활용하여 오답과 정답을 꼼꼼히 분석하도록 한다.

Part III 공략법

1. **문맥을 파악하며 보기를 읽는다.** 문맥에 맞지 않는 시제나 조동사 찾기 등 해석을 해야만 풀 수 있는 문제가 많이 출제된다. 특히, 서술문의 경우 지문이 학술적인 내용으로 되어 있어 어렵게 느껴지므로, 모든 보기를 꼼꼼히 해석하여 문맥과 흐름을 파악하는 것이 좋다.
2. **한 단어, 한 단어 꼼꼼하게 확인한다.** 전치사, 조동사 등 작은 것 하나까지 문제로 출제될 수 있으므로 모든 단어가 어법상 맞는지 꼼꼼하게 확인하며 문제를 푼다.

텝스 전문가 해커스가 알려주는 **영역별 공략법**

독해 READING COMPREHENSION

텝스 독해 영역은 40분 동안 Part I에서 10문항, Part II에서 2문항, Part III에서 13문항, Part IV에서 10문항, 총 35문항을 풀도록 구성되어 있다. Part I~III은 보통 1개의 단락으로 이루어진 지문 한 개당 하나의 문제가 출제되고, Part IV는 2개 이상의 단락으로 이루어진 지문 한 개당 두 개의 문제가 출제된다. 지문은 편지/코멘트, 광고, 공지, 기사/논평 등의 실용문과 인문·사회·자연과학 등의 분야에 걸친 비전문적 학술문으로 구성되며, 일부 지문에는 실제를 반영하는 다양한 디자인이 적용된다.

■ 파트별 문제 유형

Part I 빈칸에 흐름상 적절한 내용 고르기 (10문항, 1~10번)

Wikis are Web sites where content can be changed or modified by anyone who has a computer and an Internet connection. They originated in 1995 and have since grown in popularity, spawning many popular wiki-based resources like the online encyclopedia Wikipedia, whose articles can be edited by any user. However, critics have pointed out that the "open content" platform of wikis leaves them open to vandals or to users who, unwittingly or not, fill a page with inaccurate or misleading information. Hence, the reliability of wikis _____.

(a) has been adequately tested by content experts
(b) was established as early as 1995
(c) can be preserved by letting users edit articles
(d) is considered a matter of debate

위키 웹사이트 정보는 누구나 수정 가능하여 정확하지 않은 정보가 제공될 수 있다고 했으므로 (d)가 정답이다.

Part II 한 단락의 글에서 흐름상 어색한 내용 고르기 (2문항, 11~12번)

Booking a tropical island vacation with your family might be due, as winter is just around the corner. (a) Before heading out to the nearest travel agent, there are several things that you should consider to ensure a memorable, stress-free vacation. (b) Research the place you want to go, as well as the activities that you want to do while on vacation, to make it easier for the travel agent to arrange your itinerary. **(c) Travel agencies usually offer family tour packages at a reduced rate if booked in advance.** (d) Having a concrete plan will help you avoid unwanted delays in the booking process.

가족 여행을 예약하기 전에 할 일에 대해서 알려주고 있다. 반면 (c)는 여행사의 패키지 상품에 대해서 설명하고 있으므로 (c)가 정답이다.

Part III 지문을 읽고 질문에 적절한 내용 고르기 (1지문 1문항) (13문항, 13~25번)

Ms. Bertinelli,

We at Max Games would like to apologize for the incident concerning your purchase. We have verified your complaint and found out that the MP3 player you were given had actually been returned by another customer earlier that day. The item had been returned with the packaging still intact, so our sales staff did not check it before placing the item in our stockroom. We were shocked to learn from your complaint that the packaging contained only a manual. Max Games accepts full responsibility for this incident. Should you wish, we are willing to ship a replacement item at no charge.

Sincerely,
Ceres Mallory

Q: Which of the following is correct about Ms. Bertinelli according to the letter?
(a) She returned the MP3 player she bought at Max Games.
(b) She was the victim of a scam targeting various retail stores.
(c) She asked for a complete refund on the MP3 player she bought.
(d) She was given a packaging missing an item.

Ms. Bertinelli가 받은 포장재 안에 MP3 플레이어가 없고 매뉴얼만 있었다고 했으므로 (d)가 정답이다.

텝스 전문가 해커스가 알려주는 영역별 공략법

Part IV 지문을 읽고 질문에 적절한 내용 고르기 (1지문 2문항) (10문항, 26~35번)

Supernova: The Death of a Star

The universe is full of mind-boggling phenomena, but there are few things as staggering as a supernova, the explosive death of a star. The immense blast of energy that constitutes a supernova emits enough light to obscure surrounding galaxies completely and causes a bright spot that can be visible from Earth for several days. The magnitude of these explosions propels debris through the universe at 10% of the speed of light, some of which provides the universe with its heavier atomic mass elements. Indeed, it is thought that many of the elements found on Earth may have come from supernovae.

The exact nature of a supernova can be difficult to determine, but astronomers have categorized these phenomena in two ways: those that are the result of a star running out of nuclear fuel and collapsing, and those that gain matter from another star in a binary system, leading to a nuclear reaction that destroys both stars. Although the exact figure is unknown, it is estimated that a supernova happens every fifty years in a Milky Way-sized galaxy, suggesting that they occur in the vicinity of Earth with astonishing regularity.

Q1: Which of the following is correct according to the passage?
(a) Supernovae are visible from Earth as a very brief explosion.
(b) All the atomic elements in the universe come from supernovae.
(c) Matter is expelled by supernovae 10% faster than the speed of light.
(d) Supernovae have contributed to the range of matter on Earth.

Q2: What can be inferred from the passage?
(a) The precise frequency of supernovae explosions is indefinite.
(b) A binary star system is more likely to result in a supernova.
(c) The Sun will one day run out of nuclear fuel and explode.
(d) Nearby supernova explosions pose a risk to life on Earth.

Q1: 지구에서 발견되는 물질의 대부분이 초신성으로부터 온다고 했으므로 (d)가 정답이다.
Q2: 초신성이 생겨나는 주기의 정확한 수치는 알려져 있지 않다고 했으므로 (a)가 정답이다.

■ 시간 배분 전략

1분에 한 문제씩 해결하고, 모르는 문제는 시간이 남을 때 해결한다.
주어진 40분의 시간 내에 35문제를 풀어야 하므로 약 1분에 한 문제를 풀어야 한다. 따라서 한 문제, 한 문제를 깊이 분석하려 하지 말고 속도감 있게 문제를 풀어가도록 한다. 주어진 시간이 많지 않으므로 모르는 문제는 일단 넘어가고, 풀 수 있는 문제에 집중해 시간을 현명하게 사용하도록 한다.

■ 파트별 공략법

Part I 공략법

1. **빈칸이 있는 문장을 먼저 읽는다.** 빈칸이 있는 문장을 읽어 어떤 내용을 빈칸에 넣을지 파악한 후 지문을 읽어야 지문을 읽는 내내 초점을 유지하며 답을 빨리 찾을 수 있다. 빈칸에 연결어를 넣는 9~10번은 주로 빈칸 바로 앞 문장과 뒤 문장에 정답의 단서가 있으므로 그 부분을 주의 깊게 읽는다.

2. **지문의 중심 내용을 파악하며 읽는다.** 지문의 중심 내용이 정답이 되거나 정답과 긴밀하게 연관된 경우가 많으므로 반드시 중심 내용을 파악하며 지문을 읽는다.

Part II 공략법

1. **첫 문장을 주의 깊게 읽는다.** 대부분 첫 문장이 주제문이며 그 주제와 관련이 없는 보기 문장이 정답이 되는 경우가 많으므로 반드시 첫 문장을 주의 깊게 읽고 그 내용을 기억하며 보기 문장을 읽는다.

2. **각 문장 간의 공통점과 차이점을 파악한다.** 각 보기 문장의 공통점과 차이점을 정리하며 지문을 읽으면, 전체적으로 일관성이 결여된 문장을 찾아내는 데 효과적이다.

Part III & IV 공략법

1. **지문의 중심 내용을 파악하며 읽는다.** 중심 내용 문제뿐 아니라, Correct 문제와 추론 문제의 경우에도 중심 내용이 정답인 경우가 많다. 중심 내용이 자주 나오는 첫 문장이나 마지막 문장, 또는 예시 앞 부분을 특히 주의하여 읽는다.

2. **지문의 내용이 paraphrase되어 정답으로 출제된다.** 정답은 지문에 있는 표현을 그대로 쓰기보다 다른 표현으로 paraphrase된 경우가 많다. 오답은 주로 지문에서 사용된 단어를 그대로 사용한다.

3. **보기를 먼저 읽고 지문을 읽는다.** Correct 문제와 육하원칙 문제의 경우, 보기를 먼저 읽고 지문을 읽으면, 보기의 내용을 지문에서 빠르게 찾아내어 대조할 수 있으므로, 시간을 절약할 수 있다.

4. **문제 유형을 파악하여 전략적으로 읽는다.** 특히, Part IV의 경우 지문의 길이가 길어 시간이 부족할 수 있고 어렵게 느껴지므로, 먼저 문제 유형과 질문 및 보기의 키워드를 파악하여 질문이 묻고 있는 내용을 위주로 읽는 것이 좋다.

수준별 텝스 고득점 비법!

* TEST 01을 마친 후 결과에 맞는 학습 전략 및 플랜을 선택하여 공부합니다.

2주 완성 학습 플랜 – 맞은 개수 110개 이상

	DAY 1	DAY 2	DAY 3	DAY 4	DAY 5	DAY 6
WEEK 1	TEST 01 풀기	TEST 01 심화 학습	TEST 02 풀기	TEST 02 심화 학습	TEST 03 풀기	TEST 03 심화 학습
WEEK 2	TEST 04 풀기	TEST 04 심화 학습	TEST 05 풀기	TEST 05 심화 학습	TEST 06 풀기	TEST 06 심화 학습

심화 학습 방법 – **틀린 문제 복습** 틀린 문제의 정답을 확인한 후, 스크립트와 해석을 통해 확실히 이해하고 넘어간다.
– **단어 암기** 단어암기장과 단어암기 MP3를 통해 해당 테스트의 어휘를 복습한다.

■ **추천 연계 교재** 해커스 텝스 기출 보카

■ **추천 학습 방법**
<해커스 텝스 최신기출유형 실전모의고사>는 텝스 고득점을 취득하고자 하는 학생들을 위해 텝스 고난이도 문제를 공략할 수 있는 어려운 문제들로 구성되어 있어 본 교재의 문제를 두 번 이상 풀어 본다면, 실제 텝스 시험에 효과적으로 대비할 수 있다. 더불어 <해커스 텝스 기출 보카> 교재를 통해 텝스 500점 단어를 위주로 암기해 고난이도 어휘를 숙지한 뒤 시험장에 가는 것도 많은 도움이 될 것이다.

3주 완성 학습 플랜 – 맞은 개수 85~109개

	DAY 1	DAY 2	DAY 3	DAY 4	DAY 5	DAY 6
WEEK 1	TEST 01 풀기	TEST 01 청해 & 어휘 심화 학습	TEST 01 문법 & 독해 심화 학습	TEST 02 풀기	TEST 02 청해 & 어휘 심화 학습	TEST 02 문법 & 독해 심화 학습
WEEK 2	TEST 03 풀기	TEST 03 청해 & 어휘 심화 학습	TEST 03 문법 & 독해 심화 학습	TEST 04 풀기	TEST 04 청해 & 어휘 심화 학습	TEST 04 문법 & 독해 심화 학습
WEEK 3	TEST 05 풀기	TEST 05 청해 & 어휘 심화 학습	TEST 05 문법 & 독해 심화 학습	TEST 06 풀기	TEST 06 청해 & 어휘 심화 학습	TEST 06 문법 & 독해 심화 학습

심화 학습 방법 - **틀린 문제·어려운 문제 학습** 스크립트와 해석을 통해 틀린 문제와 어려운 문제를 확실히 이해하고 넘어간다.
- **단어 암기** 단어암기장과 단어암기 MP3를 통해 해당 테스트의 어휘를 복습한다.

■ **추천 연계 교재** 해커스 텝스 리딩/리스닝 + 해커스 텝스 기출 보카

■ **추천 학습 방법**

텝스 300~400점의 학습자들은 보통 〈해커스 텝스 리딩〉과 〈해커스 텝스 리스닝〉 교재를 기본서로 두고, 실전 교재를 푸는 경우가 많은데, 여기서 절대 빠지면 안 될 것이 바로 어휘이다. 텝스에는 다른 시험보다 어렵고 생소한 어휘가 많이 나오는데, 〈해커스 텝스 기출 보카〉 교재를 통해 어휘를 탄탄히 다지고, 실전 문제를 풀어 나간다면, 학습 효과가 극대화될 것이다.

수준별 텝스 고득점 비법!

4주 완성 학습 플랜 – 맞은 개수 84개 이하

	DAY 1	DAY 2	DAY 3	DAY 4	DAY 5	DAY 6
WEEK 1	TEST 01 풀기	TEST 01 청해 심화 학습	TEST 01 어휘 & 문법 심화 학습	TEST 01 독해 심화 학습	TEST 02 풀기	TEST 02 청해 심화 학습
WEEK 2	TEST 02 어휘 & 문법 심화 학습	TEST 02 독해 심화 학습	TEST 03 풀기	TEST 03 청해 심화 학습	TEST 03 어휘 & 문법 심화 학습	TEST 03 독해 심화 학습
WEEK 3	TEST 04 풀기	TEST 04 청해 심화 학습	TEST 04 어휘 & 문법 심화 학습	TEST 04 독해 심화 학습	TEST 05 풀기	TEST 05 청해 심화 학습
WEEK 4	TEST 05 어휘 & 문법 심화 학습	TEST 05 독해 심화 학습	TEST 06 풀기	TEST 06 청해 심화 학습	TEST 06 어휘 & 문법 심화 학습	TEST 06 독해 심화 학습

심화 학습 방법 – 모든 문제 복습 스크립트와 해석을 통해 모든 문제를 확실히 복습한다.
　　　　　　　– 틀린 문제·어려운 문제 학습 틀린 문제와 어려운 문제를 스크립트와 해석을 통해 확실히 이해하고 넘어간다.
　　　　　　　– 단어 암기 단어암기장과 단어암기 MP3를 통해 해당 테스트의 어휘를 복습한다.

■ 추천 연계 교재 해커스 텝스 베이직 리딩/리스닝 + 해커스 텝스 중급 문법

  +

■ 추천 학습 방법

텝스는 기초가 중요한 만큼, 기초를 탄탄히 다지고 실전문제를 푼다면 그 효과가 배가 될 수 있다. 특히, 문법의 경우에는 〈해커스 텝스 베이직 리딩〉이나 〈해커스 텝스 중급 문법〉 교재로 기본 개념을 2회 이상 정리한다면, 어려운 문제를 푸는 데 필요한 기초를 충분히 다질 수 있을 것이다.

시험에 나올 문제를 미리 풀어보는
텝스 적중예상특강
해커스텝스 HackersTEPS.com

해커스 텝스 최신기출유형 실전모의고사 문제집

TEST 01

LISTENING COMPREHENSION
VOCABULARY & GRAMMAR
READING COMPREHENSION

테스트 전 확인사항

1. 휴대 전화의 전원을 끄셨나요?
2. OMR 답안지, 연필, 지우개가 준비되셨나요?
3. 시계가 준비되셨나요?
4. 목표 점수를 정하세요.
   LISTENING COMPREHENSION (____개 / 40개)
   VOCABULARY (____개 / 30개)
   GRAMMAR (____개 / 30개)
   READING COMPREHENSION (____개 / 35개)
5. 테스트의 시작과 종료 시간을 정하세요.
   LISTENING COMPREHENSION ___시 ___분 ~ ___시 ___분 (40분)
   VOCABULARY & GRAMMAR ___시 ___분 ~ ___시 ___분 (25분)
   READING COMPREHENSION ___시 ___분 ~ ___시 ___분 (35분)

무료MP3 바로듣기

🎧 TEST 01.mp3
실전용·복습용 문제풀이 MP3 무료 다운로드 및 스트리밍 바로듣기
(HackersIngang.com)

* 실제 시험장의 소음까지 재현해 낸 고사장 소음·매미 버전 MP3까지 구매하면 실전에
  더욱 완벽히 대비할 수 있습니다.

Listening Comprehension

DIRECTIONS

1. In the Listening Comprehension Section, the content will be presented in oral rather than written form.
2. There are five parts in this section, and you will receive separate instructions for each. Listen to the instructions carefully, and choose the best answer for each question from the available options.

Part I **Questions 1~10**

You will now hear ten statements or questions, and each will be followed by four responses. Choose the most appropriate response.

Part II **Questions 11~20**

You will now hear ten conversation fragments, and each will be followed by four responses. Choose the most appropriate response.

Part III Questions 21~30

You will now hear ten complete conversations. Before each conversation, you will hear a short description of the situation. Then you will hear the conversation and its corresponding question, both of which will be read only once. Next, you will hear four options, which will also be read once. Choose the option that best answers the question.

Part IV Questions 31~36

You will now hear six monologues. For each item, you will hear a monologue and its corresponding question, both of which will be read twice. Then you will hear four options which will be read only once. Choose the option that best answers the question.

Part V Questions 37~40

You will now hear two longer monologues. For each item, you will hear a monologue and two corresponding questions, all of which will be read twice. Then you will hear four options for each question, which will be read only once. Choose the option that best answers each question.

Vocabulary & Grammar

DIRECTIONS

These two parts of the exam test your vocabulary and grammar skills. You will have a total of 25 minutes to answer 60 questions. There will be 30 from the Vocabulary section and 30 from the Grammar section. Make sure to follow the directions given by the proctor.

Part I Questions 1~10
Choose the best answer for the blank.

1. A: Sir, Mr. Beaumont is here to see you.
   B: He is? I didn't _____ him till 3.
   (a) expect
   (b) welcome
   (c) call
   (d) foresee

2. A: I'm going to read *War and Peace* today.
   B: You're not being _____. That book is 1,400 pages long.
   (a) capable
   (b) potential
   (c) realistic
   (d) effective

3. A: I didn't finish my paper last night because I was watching TV.
   B: You're going to have to _____ for that today.
   (a) compensate
   (b) sequester
   (c) counteract
   (d) equalize

4. A: There wasn't any wine at the store.
   B: Really? The shelves were _____ with bottles the last time I was there.
   (a) affiliated
   (b) stocked
   (c) fitted
   (d) furnished

5. A: I think John is a clever student.
   B: I think so. Actually, he is really _____.
   (a) clumsy
   (b) gregarious
   (c) brilliant
   (d) shallow

6. A: The zookeeper just offered the lions some huge chunks of beef.
   B: Wow, they must have been famished. Look at them _____ their meal.
   (a) spurning
   (b) devouring
   (c) belching
   (d) digesting

7. A: Maurice never cleans his room, even when I tell him to.
   B: My son is the same. It's so _____!
   (a) frustrating
   (b) vulnerable
   (c) unwilling
   (d) resistant

8. A: I think the baby's crying because she's tired. Let's put her in the cradle and take turns rocking it.
   B: Oh, that's a good suggestion. I'm sure that'll _____ her to sleep in no time.
   (a) lull
   (b) gall
   (c) rile
   (d) stall

9. A: Can you help me fill out my customs declaration form?
   B: Sure. Write down your personal information and then _____ the boxes that apply to you.
   (a) flip
   (b) tick
   (c) slick
   (d) nick

10. A: How are you getting along with your new boss?
    B: Not very well. She's rather _____ and harsh.
    (a) conjugal
    (b) truculent
    (c) diffident
    (d) diaphanous

Part II Questions 11~30

Choose the best answer for the blank.

11. The bookstore has already discounted all books by 20%, and those with store memberships can get a(n) _____ 10% discount on their purchases.

    (a) chronic
    (b) total
    (c) mass
    (d) additional

12. Nonprofit law firms offer free legal services to people who cannot _____ to hire a lawyer.

    (a) arrange
    (b) gather
    (c) afford
    (d) fulfill

13. Both of Megan's parents are still _____ toward her for marrying someone they did not approve of.

    (a) adverse
    (b) eradicable
    (c) obedient
    (d) bitter

14. People with _____ personalities feel more comfortable around other people than do individuals who are reticent.

    (a) attentive
    (b) outgoing
    (c) humble
    (d) distinct

15. During the rainy season, communities in coastal areas are _____ to flooding.

    (a) pertinent
    (b) bound
    (c) prone
    (d) obvious

16. The scientist was asked to _____ the research on which he based his conclusions regarding herbal medications.

    (a) encrypt
    (b) cite
    (c) imprint
    (d) extract

17. World War I, also known as the Great War, was of such _____ that it affected every continent on Earth.

    (a) potency
    (b) extravagance
    (c) fortitude
    (d) magnitude

18. The professor _____ a point he made in his lecture with a comparison involving violin strings.

    (a) exposed
    (b) displayed
    (c) exhibited
    (d) illustrated

19. The magazine pays for articles about people who _____ to overcome insurmountable obstacles in order to succeed.

    (a) affront
    (b) strive
    (c) validate
    (d) contravene

20. Isaac Newton is _____ for his outstanding contributions in calculus, mechanics, and optics.

    (a) revered
    (b) scaled
    (c) surmounted
    (d) broached

21. Melanie and her coworkers no longer have time to go to the gym because of their _____ schedule at work.

    (a) sedentary
    (b) deliberate
    (c) explicit
    (d) hectic

22. To increase women's safety, transportation authorities have proposed the _____ of certain subway cars by gender.

    (a) infiltration
    (b) disengagement
    (c) procurement
    (d) segregation

23. Writers _____ their characters to suit the plots, themes, and messages of their stories.

    (a) contaminate
    (b) eradicate
    (c) manipulate
    (d) precipitate

24. The board members are concerned about how the _____ value of their stock will affect the financial status of the company.

    (a) stooping
    (b) plummeting
    (c) veering
    (d) pivoting

25. Hospitals are subject to an annual assessment of their _____ with governmental health and safety regulations.

    (a) compliance
    (b) fabrication
    (c) solidarity
    (d) solicitation

26. Getting an insufficient amount of sleep can be detrimental for children as it affects hormone production, which in turn can _____ growth.

    (a) infiltrate
    (b) alleviate
    (c) stunt
    (d) admonish

27. It would be _____ to call Leonardo da Vinci a mere artist; he was highly gifted in multiple fields.

    (a) jovial
    (b) obtuse
    (c) sloppy
    (d) remiss

28. Alzheimer's disease is a(n) _____ condition that develops without any apparent symptoms.

    (a) conspicuous
    (b) insidious
    (c) nondescript
    (d) incongruent

29. The politician's reputation was damaged when he revealed that he had been having _____ meetings with CIA operatives.

    (a) commodious
    (b) facetious
    (c) clandestine
    (d) dilatory

30. Emma believed her child to be _____ when he began reading encyclopedias at the age of three.

    (a) preliminary
    (b) pristine
    (c) proprietary
    (d) precocious

정답 p. 350 / 해석 p. 255

The Vocabulary section is complete. Please move on to the Grammar section.

Part I Questions 1~10

Choose the best answer for the blank.

1. A: Did your boss give you that promotion you had asked for?
   B: Yeah, and he _____ gave me a large bonus.
   (a) so
   (b) even
   (c) much
   (d) rather

2. A: How can I get my daughter to settle down at bedtime?
   B: Read her a story. By the time you finish, she _____.
   (a) calmed down
   (b) would calm down
   (c) will be calming down
   (d) will have calmed down

3. A: Have you ever tried Thai cuisine before?
   B: Yes. I'm particularly fond of _____ type of food.
   (a) the
   (b) that
   (c) such
   (d) some

4. A: If I don't leave in five minutes, I may miss my flight.
   B: OK. Make sure _____ once you arrive in Toledo.
   (a) call
   (b) to call
   (c) calling
   (d) for calling

5. A: The food was fantastic, wasn't it?
   B: Yeah, but the experience would've been more enjoyable if the tables outside _____ available.
   (a) is being
   (b) will be
   (c) has been
   (d) had been

6. A: I heard the national swimming team has a rigid practice schedule.
   B: Yes, their coach _____.
   (a) trains for six hours every day for them
   (b) for them trains every day six hours
   (c) trains them for six hours every day
   (d) for them trains six hours every day

7. A: Congratulations. I heard your dog just gave birth to a litter of puppies.
   B: That's right, and all _____ have very light fur.
   (a) new offspring
   (b) a new offspring
   (c) the new offspring
   (d) some new offspring

8. A: Do you have any idea why Alice is still working at the factory?
   B: I don't know. She _____ easily find a better job.
   (a) must
   (b) may
   (c) needs to
   (d) could

9. A: Wow, I don't believe I've ever seen your kitchen this clean.
   B: _____ could be, I spent hours tidying it up.
   (a) Being as filthy as
   (b) Being as filthy as it
   (c) It being as filthy as
   (d) It was as filthy as

10. A: Is it true that the Webbers are in the hospitality industry?
    B: Yes. Their business _____ of several successful hotels.
    (a) consists
    (b) is consisted
    (c) is consisting
    (d) has been consisted

Part II Questions 11~25

Choose the best answer for the blank.

11. _____ a daily dose of antibiotic medicine should not be necessary, since there has been no trace of a fever.

    (a) Take
    (b) Took
    (c) Taking
    (d) Having taken

12. Members of the development team should regularly communicate with _____ for efficient project execution.

    (a) them
    (b) the other
    (c) another
    (d) one another

13. This program provides support to fourth grade students _____ an unusual amount of difficulty with reading at the appropriate level.

    (a) have
    (b) having
    (c) to have
    (d) been having

14. Those with food allergies must keep in mind which _____ in order not to suffer an allergic reaction.

    (a) food products must be avoided
    (b) must food products avoided be
    (c) food must be products avoided
    (d) must be avoided food products

15. _____ thoroughly, the towels will dry on a line outside as quickly as the rest of the clean laundry.

    (a) Wring
    (b) Wringing
    (c) Wrung
    (d) Having wrung

16. To avoid impulse buying, you should think about _____ you need to purchase before going shopping.

    (a) whose
    (b) which
    (c) what
    (d) however

17. The assistant _____ that information on the project should remain confidential.

    (a) had been aware long
    (b) aware had long been
    (c) had long been aware
    (d) aware long had been

18. The hurricane destroyed virtually everything in the town, _____ the hospital, which, fortunately, was left intact.

    (a) between
    (b) about
    (c) except for
    (d) through

19. _____ his wife's suggestion to start his own venture, Mr. Lee would have probably lived his life from paycheck to paycheck.

    (a) Not had been it for
    (b) For it had been not
    (c) Had it not been for
    (d) If it not for had been

20. Substance abuse among _____ commonly occurs as a result of stressful life experiences.

    (a) the adolescents
    (b) the adolescent
    (c) adolescents
    (d) adolescent

21. The most popular of George Gershwin's compositions _____ "Rhapsody in Blue" and "An American in Paris," according to a recent radio poll.

    (a) is
    (b) are
    (c) was
    (d) being

22. The company specializes in the development of new technology _____ physicians can more quickly detect the onset of cancer.

    (a) what
    (b) that
    (c) for whom
    (d) with which

23. _____ finished her preparations for a two-hour lecture than her associate called to notify her of its postponement.

    (a) No sooner had Amanda
    (b) No sooner Amanda had
    (c) Had no sooner Amanda
    (d) Had Amanda no sooner

24. Water bottles made of polycarbonate, a tough plastic material, _____ now available in different colors and sizes.

    (a) is
    (b) are
    (c) has been
    (d) have been

25. _____ will help scientists better comprehend the nature of space.

    (a) The galaxy in detail observed
    (b) Observing the galaxy in detail
    (c) The galaxy observed in detail
    (d) Observing in the detailed galaxy

Part III Questions 26~30

Identify the option that contains an awkward expression or an error in grammar.

26. (a) A: Were you able to get tickets for Sarah Donnell's concert last night?
(b) B: I was. My favorite part was when she performed her rendition of "Make Believe."
(c) A: Me too. Never I have heard anyone sing that song so well.
(d) B: I agree. Her version of that ballad was a real improvement upon the original.

27. (a) A: Have you noticed what George does when he plays tennis?
(b) B: Yes. I've seen him switch the hand that's holding the racket during games.
(c) A: I was really astonishing to find out he's ambidextrous.
(d) B: It does explain why he continues to win against everyone he plays.

28. (a) Several students at Baybridge High School have reported having problems with malfunctioning computers in the library. (b) They claimed that some of the computers of which had only been purchased recently suddenly shut down without warning. (c) The school has informed the manufacturers of this problem and a technical team will be sent to check on the matter. (d) To avoid further damage, the affected computers will not be used until all issues have been resolved.

29. (a) Physics, defined as the study of matter and motion, are used in the development of new technologies. (b) Many concepts that were once nothing more than fictional musings have come into being as a result of advances in physics. (c) Because of scientists' understanding of physics, modern devices such as the television and microwave were able to be created. (d) Moreover, space travel would not have been possible had it not been for advances made by physicists.

30. (a) First identified in Saudi Arabia in 2012, Middle East Respiratory Syndrome coronavirus (MERS-CoV) poses a significant risk to humans. (b) Although MERS has been primarily circulating in dromedary camels, humans can infect through contact with animals stricken with the virus. (c) Infected people may display a wide range of symptoms and complications such as high fever and muscle aches, but some who contract the virus exhibit no symptoms at all. (d) Judicious personal hygiene is recommended since MERS is potentially fatal, resulting in death in up to 40% of cases.

The Vocabulary and Grammar sections are complete. Do NOT start the Reading Comprehension section until instructed to do so. You are NOT allowed to open any of the other sections of the exam.

Reading Comprehension

DIRECTIONS

This part of the exam tests your ability to understand reading passages. There will be 35 questions in 40 minutes. Make sure to follow the proctor's instructions.

Part I Questions 1~10

Read the passage. Then choose the option that best completes the passage.

1. Over the years, experts have debated _____. Much attention has been given to the possibility that sleep plays a role in regulating children's growth. A study in last month's *Journal of Pediatrics* refutes this hypothesis, however, by revealing that babies who sleep half of the day are on average no taller than those who sleep only at night. Doctors believe that genes and a proper diet play a more crucial role in helping young children achieve their full growth potential.

   (a) why sleeping is important
   (b) what vitamins young kids require
   (c) why babies sleep during the day
   (d) what fuels infant physical development

2. Searching for _____? Let Swift Tailors help you. Our expertise in making all kinds of ready-to-wear and custom-tailored apparel will ensure that you stand out from the crowd. With the help of our in-house staff, we can also handle your suit and gown orders for any formal occasion. In fact, if you are in a rush, we offer an expedited tailoring service that can get your garments altered and delivered within 72 hours. Looking good is a breeze with Swift Tailors.

   (a) the top-selling clothing available
   (b) the newest in brand-name formal wear
   (c) a reliable dry cleaner for luxury goods
   (d) the right shop for fancy dresses

3. The Catholic Church maintains that instructing high school students about sex will lead to more permissive attitudes toward the subject among adolescents, but very little evidence supports this claim. In fact, in countries where sex education is taught in schools, the incidence of pregnancy and rape among teens is about 30 percent lower than in countries where the discussion of sex is left to the discretion of parents. From this, it can be inferred that _____.

   (a) teaching teens sex education is beneficial
   (b) teenagers can learn about sex from others
   (c) the church does not trust state education
   (d) parents find the topic uncomfortable

4. Since ancient times, boats have been the means of transportation used to explore distant lands. As international exchange flourished, a means of allowing foreign sailors and local crews to effectively exchange messages when docking a ship was sought. A series of multicolored flags was settled upon, and ships raised and lowered these flags in various configurations depending on the message. Rather than needing a working knowledge of the languages in such far-flung places as Micronesia, Croatia, and Madagascar, seafarers could _____.

(a) communicate while far offshore
(b) rely upon a universal signal system
(c) conduct business in a common language
(d) focus on destinations closer to home

5. Judging a figure skating performance requires a delicate balancing act between recognizing artistry and assessing technical merit. Merely paying attention to the visual aspects of a routine doesn't do justice to the technical skills skaters must demonstrate. Similarly, judges can't simply take difficulty into account, as jumps are only a small part of a tightly integrated routine. To effectively evaluate a performance, judges _____.

(a) ought to have experience creating a routine
(b) should be able to rate skaters by technical skill
(c) need to consider it from multiple perspectives
(d) should regard it as a critic does a work of art

6. If not for _____, Sir William Herschel would not have become an astronomer and discovered the planet Uranus in 1781. Early in life, he played in a band before eventually becoming a music teacher and composer. An avid learner, Herschel came across a book during his self-directed academic study entitled *A Complete System of Optics*, which led him to create his own telescopes with mirrors composed of copper, tin, and antimony. He produced telescopes of tremendous quality that were far superior to those used at the Greenwich Observatory, which had been considered the finest optical instruments created up to that point.

   (a) a book on telescope construction
   (b) his access to literature on astronomy
   (c) his experience at a world-class observatory
   (d) the influence of England's scientific establishment

7.
   Dear Mr. President,

   I watched in horror as you signed into law a bill that grants foreigners unlimited land ownership rights in our country. This sets a dangerous precedent, because poor citizens may be denied access to land in favor of foreign nationals with deeper pockets. Such a state of affairs will surely exacerbate economic inequalities. Instead of making this decision unilaterally, it would have been wiser to have taken the public's opinion into account through a referendum. I can assure you that the majority of us want _____.

   Sincerely,
   Scott Thompson

   (a) our territory to be under the control of citizens
   (b) the rich to cease their exploitation of the poor
   (c) to reduce foreign influence on our native culture
   (d) a reduction in the severity of land ownership regulations

8. There was a time when scientists were pessimistic about _____, but research is giving them a newfound sense of hope. Studies of extreme environments on Earth have revealed that organisms can survive in almost any environment. For example, it was discovered that life exists in deep-sea vents at temperatures over 150 degrees Celsius, which leads scientists to speculate that, if creatures can exist in such conditions on Earth, they might also survive Mars' harshness.

   (a) the suitability of the Martian atmosphere for sustaining life
   (b) finding extreme environments on the Earth's surface
   (c) encountering life at the bottom of the ocean
   (d) the adaptability of organisms to fluctuating conditions

9.

Biz Report

Rainbow Roller Skating Rink is running circles around the competition through an ingenious marketing approach. Of course, the rink did what was expected in creating an effective PR strategy for its target audience: 18-to 30-year-olds. But it didn't stop there—the rink also executed a dedicated ad campaign to an entirely different consumer base. _____, it tapped into the often-overlooked senior citizen demographic, encouraging their patronage by evoking their nostalgia for roller skating as an activity of their youth.

(a) Even though
(b) Particularly
(c) That being said
(d) Alternatively

10. The Supreme Court of the Republic of Chango is in disarray after seven justices of the fifteen-member court died in an explosion at the national courthouse late yesterday afternoon. Chango's president attempted to allay citizens' fears by stating that the government would conduct a speedy investigation of the incident and that new justices would be appointed soon to replace those killed. _____, the situation is creating an atmosphere of uncertainty and paranoia, as residents are afraid to leave their homes for fear of further attacks.

(a) Even so
(b) Therefore
(c) On the contrary
(d) In fact

Part II Questions 11~12

Read the passage. Then identify the option that does NOT belong.

11. Are you still looking for a dream house that can stay in your family for generations to come? (a) Look no further, as Bradley Homes is here to turn your dreams into reality. (b) Our pool of top-notch architects and engineers will help you design your house from scratch. (c) If you prefer ready-made units, our spacious and energy-efficient home designs offer striking ambiance in a modern setting. (d) Please visit our Web site to submit your architectural designs and portfolio of past work.

12. People have long explored spirituality as a possible means of curing addiction. (a) One such individual was the cofounder of Alcoholics Anonymous, Bill Wilson, who believed that alcoholism cannot be conquered without divine help. (b) He developed the Twelve Steps program to help alcoholics permanently conquer their addiction in a supportive environment. (c) Wilson thought that sober alcoholics who had kicked their habit by relying on their religious faith would make good role models for struggling addicts. (d) He hoped alcoholics would seek their own spiritual conversion and use it as the foundation for an eventual recovery.

Part III Questions 13~25

Read the passage and the question. Then choose the option that best answers the question.

13. Exceeding its own performance in previous quarters as well as the economic forecasts for January to March of 2015, India's economy swelled by 7.5% in the first three months of the year. Such a figure puts India ahead of China in terms of economic expansion, but financial analysts caution that the statistics may not be so clear-cut. India has implemented a new method for assessing growth, which has been derided by some as exaggerative. Experts point out that the figures furnished by this method do not line up with other indicators of economic growth, such as factory and industrial production.

    Q: What is the passage mainly about?

    (a) India's reported economic growth may not be accurate.
    (b) Old methods of assessing growth are outdated and vague.
    (c) Factory and industrial production are adversely impacting the economy.
    (d) There may be unintended side effects to India's swift expansion.

14. Polar bears have subcutaneous layers of fat, not to mention thick fur, and hairy soles so they can endure the freezing temperatures of the Arctic regions. Besides having to combat the cold on land, they also must be capable of doing so in the water in order to dig through ice to feed on marine mammals like ringed seals. As a result, polar bears have acquired the ability to use their front limbs to swim and have developed sharp claws for ice digging.

    Q: What is the passage mainly about?

    (a) Common activities polar bears perform
    (b) The physical development polar bears undergo
    (c) The feeding habits that polar bears possess
    (d) Attributes that help polar bears survive

15. Thanks to new research, math teachers in the city's high schools are gaining insights into why so many students are uninterested in the subject. According to the study, students do not believe that the mathematical concepts discussed in the classroom have any application in their day-to-day lives. Furthermore, the researchers found that many topics that are covered in high school math like algebra and calculus are highly abstract. Students prefer subjects applicable to the concrete situations they encounter in their lives.

Q: What is the main topic of the passage?

(a) Why teachers need to challenge math students
(b) Why mathematical instruction is crucial
(c) Why math is taught in theoretical ways
(d) Why students consider mathematics unappealing

16. Before the 20th century, poets were counted on to create poetry that rhymed and followed a metrical pattern. However, there were those who disregarded the traditional structure used by many and chose instead to write in free or blank verse. Free verse lacks any noticeable pattern, while blank verse maintains meter but does not rhyme. By using and popularizing these unstructured forms, they inspired other poets to exercise greater liberty with their works and motivated those who were previously intimidated by strict rules to write freely.

Q: What is the passage mainly about?

(a) Writers who preferred free verse over blank verse
(b) Differences between metered and rhyming poetry
(c) Poets who introduced new approaches to their craft
(d) Unique elements of unstructured poetry

17. More than for the ships he was commissioned to design by Britain's navy, Hubert Booth is remembered for later revolutionizing the way people cleaned their carpets. His suction-type vacuum cleaner contained long plastic tubes and an air pump mounted on a modified carriage. His invention became so popular that clients would ask for transparent tubes to be installed so they could watch the machine extracting dust from carpets. Booth's vacuum cleaner dominated the market for the first half of the 20th century before yielding to the Hoover vacuums of the 1950s.

Q: Which is correct about Hubert Booth according to the passage?

(a) He previously worked with the British military.
(b) He invented a carriage to make vacuums portable.
(c) He created covers for transparent vacuum tubes to hide dust from view.
(d) He developed the suction-type vacuum cleaner in the 1950s.

18.
Dear Alfred,

I'm pleased to hear that your condition has improved and you're no longer undergoing physical therapy. In light of your recovery, I guess we can now push through with the vacation that we've been planning. I'll send you an email about the vacation spots I have in mind and a list of airlines that are offering discounted fares. I'd appreciate it if you could give me your input on possible locales so that I can get the ball rolling with my travel agent.

Always,
Cristina

Q: Which of the following is correct according to the letter?

(a) Alfred just learned of Cristina's injury.
(b) Alfred needs to book tickets with a travel agent.
(c) Cristina would like to make a mutual decision.
(d) Cristina wants to choose the cheapest trip.

19. After besting other nominees at the Oryx Awards, sprinter Archie Barnes became the first person honored as Athlete of the Year in two consecutive years. Barnes received a majority of the votes from members of the Oryx Awards nomination committee, which included several previous awardees. His latest success has put him on par with two-time winners like legendary Olympic swimmer Mark Smythe, and makes him the most heavily decorated sprinter since Jesse Jones. The event is held annually to recognize athletes who make the biggest contributions to the athletic world.

Q: Which of the following is correct about Barnes according to the passage?

(a) He has attained a feat never before accomplished.
(b) He received the trophy two years ago.
(c) He was voted for unanimously by the selection committee.
(d) He is considered a more accomplished athlete than Mark Smythe.

20.
Look Sharp All the Time with EZ-Iron!

EZ-Iron is an innovative clothes iron designed with functionality and convenience in mind.

- Say goodbye to cords that get in the way! EZ-Iron's cordless design makes it easy to use anywhere, anytime.
- Have a lot of ironing to do? EZ-Iron's battery lasts for up to an hour on a full charge.
- Never damage your clothes again! EZ-Iron's specially coated base does not stick to fabric, making it less likely that you will burn your clothes.

To achieve professional results every time you iron, choose EZ-Iron. Visit www.eziron.com to learn more.

Q: What problem does the EZ-Iron prevent through its features?

(a) The coating needing to be regularly replaced
(b) Fluctuations in the temperature of the metal
(c) Fabric being damaged by the bottom of the device
(d) An unreasonably long charging time for the battery

21. When brain cells are damaged due to a head injury, stroke, or tumor, it is possible for a person to develop dementia. Communication problems and memory loss are two typical manifestations of this condition, and depression may also indicate the onset of dementia. Dementia commonly occurs in people aged 75 and above; however, it may also affect the young. Although manageable, dementia is generally untreatable, but has been known to reverse itself in rare cases.

Q: Which of the following is correct about dementia according to the passage?

(a) It may damage brain cells and lead to strokes.
(b) It only affects those who are advanced in age.
(c) It influences a person's linguistic ability.
(d) It is a rare but curable degenerative disease.

22.
> Dear Customer,
>
> We are grateful for your acquisition of the new IN1933 mobile phone. Before using the phone, please inspect its facade for scratches or visible defects. Damaged phones should be shipped back to us using the prepaid mailing label found inside the package. Rest assured that all IN1933 phones come with a one-year warranty that covers all replacements and repair work. If your phone becomes defective within a year of purchase, we will exchange it for one in mint condition free of charge. Enjoy your new phone!
>
> The IN1933 Sales Team

Q: Which of the following is correct about IN1933 according to the letter?

(a) It is not covered by warranty if repaired.
(b) It has a lifetime warranty on all major parts and services.
(c) It will automatically be replaced after one year.
(d) It can be shipped back at no cost if defective.

23.

Opinions > Politics

Government Cronyism in Action

Appointing a chief supporter of the Liberal Party as the chairwoman of the National Cultural Committee proves how pervasively political debts of gratitude are infiltrating our government. Clearly, a small kickback or a campaign endorsement is no longer sufficient remuneration for those in one's inner circle. Giving a political crony a post historically held by esteemed artists and intellectuals shows that this administration is more enthusiastic about cementing its grip on power than running the country.

Q: Which statement would the writer most likely agree with?

(a) The Liberal Party must try to reach out to political rivals.
(b) Giving positions of power to allies makes government more efficient.
(c) The current National Cultural Committee chair is not qualified for the job.
(d) Political allies are better off getting monetary favors from the government.

24. Dark matter is one of the most groundbreaking concepts in modern astronomy and cosmology. Since Vera Rubin substantiated its existence in the 1970s, dark matter has become the most widely accepted justification for the anomalies observed in the universe. Dark matter theory has disproved the conjecture that the expansion of the universe has been decelerating since the Big Bang. Rather, dark matter has been shown to continuously impel objects in space further apart, thus hastening the universe's expansion rate.

Q: What can be inferred from the passage?

(a) Astronomers and cosmologists interpret dark matter's function differently.
(b) Dark matter has changed perceptions of the development of the universe.
(c) The expansion of the universe is being impeded by dark matter.
(d) The expansion rate of the universe will eventually plateau.

25.

ATTENTION: Service Employees Union Meeting

Members of the Service Employees Union are invited to attend a brainstorming session on a proposal to change the organization's bylaws, including those pertaining to retired members.

Union bureaucrats will discuss proposals of policy amendments regarding membership contributions and benefits, along with substantive amendments to regulations governing the responsibilities of members.

An open forum will follow the discussions and participants are encouraged to ask questions. The organization anticipates introducing the bylaw changes during next year's officer elections, so your suggestions now will help us in focusing future efforts.

Q: What can be inferred from the passage?

(a) Participants will be asked to contribute a donation.
(b) Bylaws will be amended following the appointment of new officers.
(c) Union benefits are the sole focus of the discussion.
(d) Policy revisions will not be implemented at the meeting.

Part IV Questions 26~35
Read the passage and the questions. Then choose the option that best answers each question.

Questions 26-27

Construction Inspector Wanted

Hansen & Lin Incorporated is seeking a qualified construction inspector for routine assessments of underground water utilities infrastructure in the Indianapolis area. The successful candidate will inspect all work done by contractors to ensure that it is in compliance with safety requirements and client requests. He or she will notify contractors of any problems and keep clients updated on the status of projects.

For nearly 80 years, Hansen & Lin Incorporated has undertaken a wide array of projects involving urban water management. We have won multiple industry awards for engineering excellence and have very high expectations for anyone in our employ. Therefore, candidates must have:
- a bachelor's degree in civil engineering
- a minimum of five years of relevant experience
- a Public Infrastructure Inspection License

Candidates will have to travel locally for 5 to 10 hours per week, so they must have a vehicle and a driver's license. Also, a 12-hour workplace safety class must be taken within 30 days of starting in the position. Call 555-8824 for more information.

26. Q: Which of the following is correct according to the passage?

   (a) The job will involve communicating with clients about the progress of work.
   (b) Candidates who have won an engineering award are preferred.
   (c) Hansen & Lin Incorporated has done work in multiple industries.
   (d) Hansen & Lin's headquarters has been in Indianapolis for 80 years.

27. Q: What will happen soon after a candidate is hired?

   (a) An agreement to keep company information confidential will be signed.
   (b) A licensing exam on water infrastructure inspection will be given.
   (c) A course on safety in work environments will be completed.
   (d) A vehicle from the company's fleet will be assigned.

Questions 28-29

Lisa Groves [11:40 a.m.]

Hi, Trevor.
I forgot to tell you that I'll be dropping by your office later today to pick up the sales brochures. I really need to get them as soon as possible since I am supposed to hand them out at a trade fair tomorrow morning. I'll be there at 3 p.m. if that's OK with you. I was hoping to come by sometime this morning, but I got a call from a client in San Mateo. Unfortunately, it lasted longer than I expected.

Trevor Drake [12:15 p.m.]

Hi, Lisa.
The brochures are all packed up and ready to go. I have to pick up a coworker from the airport after lunch, so I won't be back in the office until about 3:30 p.m. Any time after that is perfectly fine as I don't have any other appointments. In fact, we can even grab a coffee when you come. There's a nice café really close to the office that we can check out.

28. Q: Why did Lisa write a message?

  (a) She wants to change the layout for some booklets.
  (b) She wants some advice about dealing with potential customers.
  (c) She wants to take a business trip to a nearby city.
  (d) She wants to collect some leaflets for an upcoming event.

29. Q: Which of the following is correct according to the conversation?

  (a) Lisa will meet a client this afternoon near Trevor's office.
  (b) Trevor will be out of the office at 3 p.m.
  (c) Lisa plans to print some documents for a trade fair today.
  (d) Trevor needs to reserve a flight for a coworker.

Questions 30-31

Indian independence leader Mahatma Gandhi developed the concept of satyagraha to express his philosophy of nonviolent resistance to Britain's colonization of India. Unlike other forms of civil disobedience, the notion of satyagraha was imbued with metaphysical significance. The term satyagraha literally means "holding firmly to truth" in Sanskrit, and Gandhi defined it as the "force which is born of truth." He believed that truth represented the essential nature of the world, and that the independence movement embodied the forces of truth, which would inevitably win out over those of falsehood — the British colonizers.

Satyagraha reflected Gandhi's dual status as a spiritual figure and political leader in India, which helped him inspire religious fervor among the Indian populace. When carrying out satyagraha, Gandhi instructed independence campaigners to harbor no anger against their opponents, to avoid any form of retaliation, and to voluntarily submit to arrest. In practice, this led to peaceful protests against British rule on a massive scale, bringing the colonial economy to a standstill. As the British often responded to these tactics with violence, their claims about the advantages of the status quo were easily disproven.

30. Q: What is the main topic of the passage?

   (a) The conflict between Gandhi's role as a political thinker and as an independence leader
   (b) The importance of leadership for the success of a protest movement
   (c) The spiritual significance of Gandhi's teachings in British society
   (d) Gandhi's philosophical concept of peaceful resistance to colonial rule

31. Q: What can be inferred from the passage?

   (a) Britain justified its rule of India as beneficial to the native people.
   (b) Indian independence campaigners did not always stick to Gandhi's precepts of nonviolent protest.
   (c) Gandhi's concept of satyagraha was intended to appeal mainly to devout Hindus in India.
   (d) Satyagraha was adopted as a political tactic in various countries following Indian independence.

Questions 32-33

The Planet's Magnetic Reversal

Earth's magnetic field stretches far into space from the center of the planet. Generated by electric currents emanating from the planet's molten core, this field deflects solar wind from the Sun and thereby protects the ozone layer, allowing life on Earth to exist. It has also become an important means of navigation for humans, who have used it to stay correctly oriented, using compasses, since the 12th century AD. However, what few people realize is that this field occasionally flips, so that north and south are interchanged.

Through studying the geological record, researchers discovered that this flip happens every 200,000 to 300,000 years, although it takes thousands of years to complete. During this process, the magnetic poles move gradually, causing them to emerge in strange locations at various times. Currently, the magnetic north pole is moving about 40 miles northward per year, suggesting that a switch is imminent, if not under way. What causes this is unclear, but some theorists believe that tectonic plates are a factor. Their movements could alter the flow of iron in Earth's core and instigate a flip. Whatever the cause may be, these reversals appear to have had no significant impact on flora and fauna on the planet.

32. Q: What is the writer's main point about Earth's magnetic field?

   (a) It is a phenomenon generated by solar heat.
   (b) It causes the annual reversal of the north and south poles.
   (c) It has been decreasing in strength for several centuries.
   (d) It has been found to be capable of inversion.

33. Q: What can be inferred from the passage?

   (a) Magnetic reversals occur on every planet in the universe.
   (b) Earth's iron flow influences the magnetic field's orientation.
   (c) The movement of the poles speeds up as they reverse.
   (d) The most recent magnetic flip took place in the last century.

Questions 34-35

The Monthly Standard

Column: *The National Electronics Industry*

By Hugh Chang

As many economists will tell you, maintaining a trade deficit can have a negative impact on a country's economic growth. Over the past decade, we developed a deficit with regard to electronics, importing an average of $5 billion in electronic goods annually, more than double the $2 billion we exported. Thankfully, this trend abruptly changed last year, as the value of high-tech imports and exports started to balance out. Imports plummeted to $2.2 billion while export volume increased to $2.5 billion.

There are two main reasons for this shift, the first being the government's proactive decision to raise tariffs on foreign products, which gave the domestic electronics industry a boost, allowing it to be more competitive. Secondly, trade agreements reached with several nations over the past few years increased electronics exports. Experts are hopeful that the boom will continue as the growth of this sector could bring a range of benefits to our economy. Continued government action is therefore required to ensure that the value of the nation's electronics exports overtakes that of imports, and that the trade deficit is wiped out.

34. Q: Which of the following is correct according to the article?

    (a) Manufacturers have begun operating facilities in several other countries.
    (b) There has been an increase in the value of electronics exports.
    (c) Exports over the past 10 years have totaled $5 billion.
    (d) Most buyers prefer imported electronics to locally made goods.

35. Q: Which statement would the writer most likely agree with?

    (a) Increasing taxes on imported electronics would make the market less competitive.
    (b) The government has been influential in increasing sales of domestic products.
    (c) Trade deficits are often necessary for the growth of an economy.
    (d) Most nations attempt to stick to trade agreements with other countries.

정답 p. 350 / 해석 p. 257

The Reading Comprehension section of the exam is complete. Please stay in your seat until the proctor tells you to leave. You are NOT allowed to open any of the other sections of the exam.

시험에 나올 문제를 미리 풀어보는
텝스 적중예상특강
해커스텝스 HackersTEPS.com

SELF-CHECK LIST

TEST 01은 잘 마치셨나요?
이제 다음의 SELF-CHECK LIST를 통해 자신의 테스트 진행 내용을 점검해 볼까요?

1. 나는 테스트를 마칠 때까지 완전히 테스트에 집중하였다.
   ☐ YES   ☐ NO

2. 나는 각 영역별 주어진 시간을 지켰다.
   ☐ LISTENING COMPREHENSION
   ☐ VOCABULARY & GRAMMAR   ☐ READING COMPREHENSION

3. 나는 시간 내에 모든 문제를 풀었다.
   ☐ LISTENING COMPREHENSION
   ☐ VOCABULARY & GRAMMAR   ☐ READING COMPREHENSION

4. 나는 특히 어렵게 느껴지는 영역이 있었다.
   ☐ LISTENING COMPREHENSION
   ☐ VOCABULARY & GRAMMAR   ☐ READING COMPREHENSION

5. 개선하고 싶은 사항
   _____
   _____
   _____
   _____
   _____

■ 개선해야 할 점은 반드시 다음 테스트에서 실천해야만 실력을 향상시킬 수 있습니다.
그리고 반드시 오답을 정리해서 같은 실수를 반복하지 않도록 유의하기 바랍니다.

해커스 텝스 최신기출유형 실전모의고사 문제집

TEST 02

LISTENING COMPREHENSION
VOCABULARY & GRAMMAR
READING COMPREHENSION

테스트 전 확인사항

1. 휴대 전화의 전원을 끄셨나요?
2. OMR 답안지, 연필, 지우개가 준비되셨나요?
3. 시계가 준비되셨나요?
4. 목표 점수를 정하세요.
   LISTENING COMPREHENSION (____개 / 40개)
   VOCABULARY (____개 / 30개)
   GRAMMAR (____개 / 30개)
   READING COMPREHENSION (____개 / 35개)
5. 테스트의 시작과 종료 시간을 정하세요.
   LISTENING COMPREHENSION ___시___분 ~ ___시___분 (40분)
   VOCABULARY & GRAMMAR ___시___분 ~ ___시___분 (25분)
   READING COMPREHENSION ___시___분 ~ ___시___분 (35분)

 TEST 02.mp3
실전용·복습용 문제풀이 MP3 무료 다운로드 및 스트리밍 바로듣기
(HackersIngang.com)
* 실제 시험장의 소음까지 재현해 낸 고사장 소음·매미 버전 MP3까지 구매하면 실전에
  더욱 완벽히 대비할 수 있습니다.

무료MP3 바로듣기

LISTENING COMPREHENSION

DIRECTIONS

1. In the Listening Comprehension Section, the content will be presented in oral rather than written form.
2. There are five parts in this section, and you will receive separate instructions for each. Listen to the instructions carefully, and choose the best answer for each question from the available options.

Part I Questions 1~10

You will now hear ten statements or questions, and each will be followed by four responses. Choose the most appropriate response.

Part II Questions 11~20

You will now hear ten conversation fragments, and each will be followed by four responses. Choose the most appropriate response.

Part III Questions 21~30

You will now hear ten complete conversations. Before each conversation, you will hear a short description of the situation. Then you will hear the conversation and its corresponding question, both of which will be read only once. Next, you will hear four options, which will also be read once. Choose the option that best answers the question.

Part IV Questions 31~36

You will now hear six monologues. For each item, you will hear a monologue and its corresponding question, both of which will be read twice. Then you will hear four options which will be read only once. Choose the option that best answers the question.

Part V Questions 37~40

You will now hear two longer monologues. For each item, you will hear a monologue and two corresponding questions, all of which will be read twice. Then you will hear four options for each question, which will be read only once. Choose the option that best answers each question.

Vocabulary & Grammar

DIRECTIONS

These two parts of the exam test your vocabulary and grammar skills. You will have a total of 25 minutes to answer 60 questions. There will be 30 from the Vocabulary section and 30 from the Grammar section. Make sure to follow the directions given by the proctor.

Part I Questions 1~10

Choose the best answer for the blank.

1. A: Did the manager approve the proposal?
   B: No, he _____ it. He thinks the budget for the project is unrealistic.
   (a) endorsed
   (b) rejected
   (c) disproved
   (d) advised

2. A: Can I _____ your class, professor?
   B: I'm sorry, but undergraduates aren't allowed to sit in on law courses.
   (a) submit
   (b) audit
   (c) assign
   (d) listen

3. A: I'm surprised you don't like fries.
   B: Well, I tend to get _____ when I eat greasy food.
   (a) queasy
   (b) ravaging
   (c) sickening
   (d) rigorous

4. A: Do you think we should carry our passports around?
   B: No, let's leave them in the hotel room safe. We need to _____ caution so that we don't lose them.
   (a) dissuade
   (b) satisfy
   (c) dodge
   (d) exercise

5. A: Did you ask Crystal to go to the movies with you tonight?
   B: That was my plan, but I wasn't able to _____ the courage.
   (a) knock off
   (b) get across
   (c) work up
   (d) run up against

6. A: I shouldn't have put the wine glasses in that box.
   B: The movers won't be _____. I marked it as fragile.
   (a) tacky
   (b) rough
   (c) tactless
   (d) naughty

7. A: My computer is having trouble starting up.
   B: It might be due to a _____ hard drive.
   (a) scrawny
   (b) skimpy
   (c) faulty
   (d) pathetic

8. A: Erin drove her father's car without permission and backed up into a tree.
   B: Oh, that's not good. Her father is going to _____.
   (a) go through the roof
   (b) get the inside track
   (c) paint the town red
   (d) bark up the wrong tree

9. A: Wow, Cindy sure wore out her welcome last night.
   B: _____. She lingered until way past my bedtime.
   (a) You're pulling my leg
   (b) You make me laugh
   (c) You can say that again
   (d) You reap what you sow

10. A: The boss was _____ through my cabinet this morning.
    B: Really? What could he have been looking for?
    (a) rummaging
    (b) tampering
    (c) petitioning
    (d) manipulating

Part II Questions 11~30

Choose the best answer for the blank.

11. Hazmat suits are designed to protect against injury following spills of substances that behave in a(n) _____ manner, such as sulfuric acid.

    (a) obstructive
    (b) corrosive
    (c) predictive
    (d) coercive

12. The German dictator Adolf Hitler acquired power in his country after _____ the confidence of nationalists through his speeches.

    (a) issuing
    (b) gaining
    (c) striving
    (d) requesting

13. People who say things in haste often _____ not having thought twice before speaking.

    (a) contract
    (b) regret
    (c) obtain
    (d) endure

14. Soon after the powerful offshore earthquake occurred, the tide ebbed, signifying that a tsunami was _____.

    (a) horrific
    (b) subsistent
    (c) forceful
    (d) imminent

15. One of the girls invited to the party decided not to go because she didn't have a(n) _____ dress to wear.

    (a) extreme
    (b) strict
    (c) decent
    (d) familiar

16. The newly hired sales manager will _____ the company's marketing operations in the region.

    (a) overlook
    (b) oversee
    (c) underlie
    (d) underscore

17. For many parents, raising a child can be a lifelong _____.

    (a) fiddle
    (b) scuffle
    (c) struggle
    (d) hustle

18. Readers are encouraged to _____ their views about the magazine's content by writing to the editor.

    (a) recount
    (b) voice
    (c) comment
    (d) notify

19. Mr. Baker was hired for the position because of his keen _____ into market research and strategy.

    (a) concepts
    (b) aspects
    (c) regards
    (d) insights

20. The film was about a man who _____ to be a millionaire but ended up living off the charity of others.

    (a) aspired
    (b) envisioned
    (c) motivated
    (d) projected

21. The wine shop's patrons generally prefer the _____ flavor of red wine over the sweet taste typical of white wine.

    (a) meager
    (b) paltry
    (c) caustic
    (d) robust

22. The giant wave that struck Thailand was particularly _____ because it wiped out much of the coastal population.

    (a) tedious
    (b) benign
    (c) opaque
    (d) devastating

23. Prices are known to _____ often, going up when demand increases and declining when it decreases.

    (a) expedite
    (b) accumulate
    (c) fluctuate
    (d) coalesce

24. Despite their rivalry in basketball, Alexander and Christian remained _____ with one another.

    (a) fastidious
    (b) congenial
    (c) irate
    (d) palatable

25. Due to its _____ ratings, Harry Acton's talk show on the LNB Network will probably be cancelled.

    (a) stirring
    (b) faltering
    (c) sobering
    (d) beguiling

26. Universities were given a _____ of resources to assist them in the proper enforcement of alcohol regulations on campus.

    (a) colloquium
    (b) syllabus
    (c) compendium
    (d) curriculum

27. The speaker was accused of _____ trouble when members of the audience became furious, but he insisted it was not his purpose.

    (a) placating
    (b) disgracing
    (c) instigating
    (d) mortifying

28. The president will _____ the details of his health care program on live television.

    (a) promulgate
    (b) protract
    (c) proliferate
    (d) protrude

29. To achieve global unity, societies around the world must condemn _____.

    (a) abstention
    (b) bigotry
    (c) quandary
    (d) flamboyance

30. The thick morning mist that covered the town was _____ by the rising sun.

    (a) sprawled
    (b) abated
    (c) subsided
    (d) dispersed

정답 p.351 / 해석 p.272

The Vocabulary section is complete. Please move on to the Grammar section.

Part I Questions 1~10

Choose the best answer for the blank.

1. A: Dave, it's your turn to do the dishes.
   B: But I _____ them last time and the time before that.
   (a) wash
   (b) washed
   (c) have washed
   (d) had washed

2. A: There is no better player on the football team than George.
   B: I agree. I marvel _____ his speed and dexterity.
   (a) for
   (b) at
   (c) in
   (d) from

3. A: What can I use to post up this flier?
   B: Either thumbtacks or some tape _____ what you need.
   (a) is
   (b) are
   (c) has been
   (d) have been

4. A: Do you know where Hal's Bakeshop is?
   B: It's _____ beside the entrance to the train station.
   (a) only
   (b) right
   (c) quite
   (d) very

5. A: How will I know when my package is expected to go out?
   B: You _____ after it's been shipped.
   (a) will notify
   (b) will be notified
   (c) will have notified
   (d) will have been notified

6. A: Do you think you'll be able to attend Ada's party on Saturday night?
   B: No, because _____ at the office this weekend.
   (a) a late-night conference at I have
   (b) I have a late-night conference
   (c) I have a conference late-night
   (d) a conference I have at late-night

7. A: Were your parents happy you got engaged?
   B: Yeah. They were _____ to congratulate me.
   (a) first one
   (b) first ones
   (c) the first ones
   (d) some first ones

8. A: Did you see the speech the president made last night?
   B: Yes, I saw it. He addressed one of the most _____ issues in the country.
   (a) debate
   (b) debating
   (c) debated
   (d) to debate

9. A: I thought your flight was supposed to get in at eight.
   B: Had it not been for the snowstorm, the plane _____ as late as it did.
   (a) have not been arrived
   (b) was not arriving
   (c) would not arrive
   (d) would not have arrived

10. A: How can you be certain Bob is the culprit?
    B: There's no question. He confessed to _____ the money.
    (a) embezzle
    (b) embezzled
    (c) embezzling
    (d) be embezzled

Part II   Questions 11~25
Choose the best answer for the blank.

11. Hardly any of the seminars had been attended, _____ the organizers grew worried about the outcome of the convention.
    (a) if
    (b) so
    (c) but
    (d) while

12. Foreign visitors who use the rail system for the first time often find themselves _____.
    (a) to perplex
    (b) perplex
    (c) perplexed
    (d) perplexing

13. A study has found that companies using aggressive marketing experience faster financial growth than _____ that don't.
    (a) another
    (b) those
    (c) theirs
    (d) one

14. In an interview, the actor offered a public apology, explaining that his remarks _____ as a joke.
    (a) meant
    (b) has been meant
    (c) had meant
    (d) had been meant

15. Those who are caught discarding _____ in areas that are not designated for waste disposal must pay a fine.
    (a) a litter
    (b) the litters
    (c) litters
    (d) litter

16. _____ the new handheld console became a big hit worldwide was a surprise to everyone in the gaming industry.
    (a) That
    (b) Yet
    (c) But
    (d) As

17. Anyone with a Kroogle email account _____ no longer worry about privacy, as Kroogle now enforces tougher security measures.
    (a) could
    (b) need
    (c) would
    (d) might

18. _____ for millions of years, the mammoth skeleton provided paleontologists with new evidence about the species.
    (a) Having preserved
    (b) To be preserved after
    (c) Having been preserved
    (d) To have been preserved

19. _____ with retiree medical benefits.
    (a) Have done away not all companies
    (b) Not all companies have done away
    (c) Companies not all have done away
    (d) All companies not have done away

20. _____ the firm suffered losses last year due to a production shortfall, it was able to recover some ground this year.
    (a) Because
    (b) Though
    (c) Once
    (d) Until

21. With the votes _____, the news anchor announced the final results of the presidential election.

    (a) tally
    (b) tallied
    (c) tallying
    (d) to be tallied

22. Because there _____ no explanation for the recent outbreak of influenza as yet, the officials advise people to get vaccinated.

    (a) be
    (b) had been
    (c) been
    (d) has been

23. The TV studio on the third floor is renowned for _____ of producing award-winning documentaries.

    (a) extensive history
    (b) an extensive history
    (c) the extensive history
    (d) any extensive history

24. Skipping meals to lose weight, which _____, is as ineffective as it is unhealthy.

    (a) it is not advisable in no way
    (b) is in no way advisable
    (c) it in no way it is advisable
    (d) is not advisable in no way

25. Much to Jill's dismay, the play _____ before she and her husband arrived at the theater.

    (a) had started
    (b) have started
    (c) will be starting
    (d) have been starting

Part III Questions 26~30

Identify the option that contains an awkward expression or an error in grammar.

26. (a) A: I was told that you're in charge of organizing and running the workshop this weekend.
    (b) B: Yes, I'm under a lot of pressure. I have so many things left to deal with.
    (c) A: Well, let me know once you'll figure things out. I need to send the schedule to the other staff members.
    (d) B: Sure. When things are set, you'll be the first to know.

27. (a) A: Are you ready to submit that report you've been toiling over all week?
    (b) B: Unfortunately, I have to start over from scratch.
    (c) A: But you were almost ready to turn it in the last time I spoke with you.
    (d) B: Reading over the draft, my finger slipped and I accidentally deleted everything.

28. (a) Last March, Singapore witnessed yet another wave of mass fish deaths, with thousands of carcasses washing up on a jetty. (b) A plankton bloom, in which plankton suddenly and swiftly multiply, was identified as the cause. (c) Monitoring the health of the waters, authorities had actually anticipated the bloom and warned fish farmers to move their stocks into protected areas. (d) However, most did not act this warning quickly enough as they underestimated the speed and intensity of the bloom.

29. (a) One of the most prominent members of the United States Ski Team is Lindsey Vonn, a four-event ski racer. (b) At just 24, Vonn is the first female American to have won two consecutive World Cup overall titles. (c) Aside from her World Cup wins, she has four World Championship medals and several Olympic medals. (d) These feats have helped her make the most successful woman in American ski racing history.

30. (a) Elephants are large land-dwelling mammals characterized by their long snouts and ivory tusks. (b) Only three of the hundreds of elephant species that once existed remain at this time, namely, savanna, forest, and Asian elephants. (c) The only two continents which these surviving species can be found are Africa and Asia. (d) Climate change, habitat loss, and human intrusion have contributed to the elephant's status as an endangered animal.

정답 p.351 / 해석 p.273

The Vocabulary and Grammar sections are complete. Do NOT start the Reading Comprehension section until instructed to do so. You are NOT allowed to open any of the other sections of the exam.

Reading Comprehension

DIRECTIONS

This part of the exam tests your ability to understand reading passages. There will be 35 questions in 40 minutes. Make sure to follow the proctor's instructions.

Part I Questions 1~10

Read the passage. Then choose the option that best completes the passage.

1. A savings account can help you attain financial freedom. At first, maintaining the discipline to keep a positive account balance can be challenging. The most important thing to remember is not to give in to material desires and to save as much as you can. During the first few months, try to allocate 10 percent of your total earnings to savings, increasing this proportion as putting away money every month becomes instinctual and requires progressively less effort. After a few years, you'll realize that having a savings account is _____.

   (a) a necessary lifestyle change
   (b) a simple task to manage
   (c) a vital tool for purchases
   (d) a place to keep large deposits

2. Mutualism, or the beneficial association between two different species, is exhibited by acacia ants and the bull-horn acacia tree. The acacia provides food and shelter to the ants, while the ants ward off leaf-eating animals. Such a mutually beneficial relationship undoubtedly exists between ants and people, yet most are unaware of it because the tiny creatures' link with humans is not readily apparent. Instead, humans consider ants to be pests. This leads to _____.

   (a) mutualism between ants and people
   (b) people protecting trees from ants
   (c) more people studying ants
   (d) ants being exterminated by people

3. As I toured the Chinese countryside, it dawned on me how _____. In every town I visited, the charming view of rows of ancient stone buildings was marred by concrete and glass monstrosities that housed fast food restaurants and convenience stores. It is good that these sleepy rural towns are showing signs of progress towards modernity, but I'm concerned that these rural communities are effacing their heritage just to become copies of soulless cities.

   (a) progress alters the lifestyle of people
   (b) the landscape has progressively changed
   (c) urbanization can destroy an area's identity
   (d) urban and rural architecture are different

4. A private organization is taking on the challenge of _____.
   As proof of its commitment to the project, the institution has acquired 12 acres of land, where several tenements will be constructed to free an estimated 1,000 homeless families from the daily struggle they face living on the streets. In addition, the institution has convinced several businesses to donate appliances with which to furnish the homes. Lastly, the institution has vowed to bear the financial burden of maintaining the dwellings even after they are occupied.

   (a) distributing appliances to the homeless
   (b) rebuilding the homes of accident victims
   (c) providing permanent residences for the less fortunate
   (d) helping the poor with their employment prospects

5. Here at InfoTech Managed Solutions, our clients have generally responded with positive feedback with respect to our technical support and data management services, but they have raised concerns over the attitude of some of our customer service staff. To address this, human resources has initiated a customer service retraining course for all personnel. Furthermore, management is planning to institutionalize workshops on the latest customer service technology as part of our employee development program. It is expected that these measures will _____.

   (a) improve how we interact with our customers
   (b) deflect attention from our customer service staff
   (c) lead to improved hiring standards for new personnel
   (d) highlight the importance of customer service retraining courses

6. The reign of Sheikh Sabah, emir of Kuwait from 1977 to 2006, was _____ _____. From his first days at the country's helm, the Sheikh's policies were opposed by members of the parliament. In response to their interference, he dissolved parliament in 1986 and imposed press censorship to quell dissent. Amidst domestic turmoil, Kuwait was invaded by Iraq in 1990, which forced the Sheikh to seek exile in Saudi Arabia. He returned once the Iraqis were vanquished by a multinational military operation, but opposition to his rule limited his political clout.

    (a) marked by political unrest and armed conflict
    (b) established as a result of military victory
    (c) solidified when the parliament was dissolved
    (d) interrupted by the invasion of Saudi Arabia

7.
    Dear Mr. Peeves,

    The department has considered your request to receive course credit for working at a communications firm. As you know, undergraduate internships that are eligible for course credit are posted before the start of every semester. Modifications to this arrangement may be made on a case-by-case basis when students have found an opportunity relevant to their field of study, but approval must be granted before the internship commences. It is impossible for such permission to be retroactively granted, as in the case of your request. As such, _____.

    Sincerely,
    Mr. Roy Culler
    Dean, College of Mass Communication

    (a) a leave of absence to seek employment is granted
    (b) your experience will not appear on your academic record
    (c) student apprentices must wait until next semester
    (d) you must select an alternative course this semester

8. In celebration of Women's Month, the National Commission on Women is sponsoring a festival that will showcase the talents of up-and-coming vocalists. All proceeds will be used to fund social programs that help domestic abuse victims. Despite the progress that has been made in eradicating some remnants of male chauvinism from society, females are still physically harmed by male family members and domestic partners. It is only by taking a stand together that this problem can be solved. Attend the concert to show that you _____ _____.

    (a) support ending violence against women
    (b) encourage women's rights activists
    (c) are aware domestic abuse affects both genders
    (d) know gender discrimination no longer exists

9. Prince Carl of Denmark ascended to Norway's throne after the country regained independence from Sweden. Upon assuming control, he took the Old Norse name of Haakon, becoming Haakon VII. This show of respect for the importance tradition plays in Scandinavian life endeared him to his people, and during World War II, King Haakon VII further earned his subjects' admiration when he resisted requests that he abdicate his throne, despite pressure to do so from leaders as powerful as Adolf Hitler. _____, it is not surprising that when he died in 1957, hundreds of thousands mourned the loss of a sovereign who truly understood his people.

   (a) Hence
   (b) Conversely
   (c) Granted
   (d) Moreover

10. Conceived in honor of democracy and freedom, Beethoven's Symphony No. 3 was originally a tribute to Napoleon, and titled "Buonaparte," since the composer saw the French ruler as embodying these ideals. Beethoven was horrified, then, when Napoleon declared himself emperor, a move that he feared would limit individual rights and lead to tyranny. _____, the composer renamed the symphony and dedicated it to his patron Lobkowitz so as not to allow any vestige of Napoleon to tarnish the intent of the work.

    (a) On the other hand
    (b) Put another way
    (c) Admittedly
    (d) Accordingly

Part II **Questions 11~12**
Read the passage. Then identify the option that does NOT belong.

11. Alexander Graham Bell's background was critical in bringing his invention of the telephone to fruition. (a) His father and brothers were leading authorities in speech communication, which provided Bell with training in sound production from his earliest years. (b) His dream of transmitting sound through electricity was spurred by the hearing impairments afflicting his mother and wife. (c) Bell went on to work in the Vocal Physiology department at Boston University and also had a lucrative private practice in audiology. (d) Those closest to Bell gave their continuous support and encouraged him to seek a patent for his device.

12. In the past, individual fishermen would go out to sea and catch fish using simple tools. (a) A fishnet was typically used, and the catch provided just enough for a family's needs, barring a few leftovers that might be sold. (b) However, these days, most seafood is caught using complex, large-scale commercial fishing methods. (c) Modern procedures utilize powerful deep-sea vessels and sophisticated mechanical equipment that are a far cry from what traditional fishermen employed. (d) Today, many small-scale fishermen complain of a diminished catch because most areas are pillaged by commercial fishermen at the earliest opportune moment.

Part III Questions 13~25

Read the passage and the question. Then choose the option that best answers the question.

13.

Dear Ms. Pan,

As you requested when I inquired previously about a cost estimate, I have enclosed some pictures of my kitchen. It was constructed back in the 1980s, so natural wear and tear have taken their toll. The style could certainly use an update, too. Seeing the kitchen's rundown condition, I hope that you can provide an estimate of the expenses I'd incur to have it remodeled. I look forward to your speedy reply.

Sincerely,
Sharon Gorman

Q: What is the email mainly about?

(a) An agreement to renovate a kitchen
(b) A criticism of the kitchen's poor condition
(c) A request for the cost of remodeling a kitchen
(d) A real estate deal with a homeowner

14.

Science Review

New brain research has shed light on the function of sleep. Scientists have observed that interstices in the brain expand during sleep, widening pathways through which toxins can be expelled. These spaces form a plumbing system of sorts, known as the glymphatic system, which is what allows cerebrospinal fluid to flow throughout the brain. Slumber effectively opens up this network of channels and crevices, allowing the fluid to clear out toxic materials much more quickly than it does during waking hours. This indicates that sleep functions as kind of protective measure against damage and deterioration.

Q: What is the writer's main point?

(a) Sleep shuts down the brain so that toxins cannot cause damage.
(b) A brain system flushes harmful entities from the brain during sleep.
(c) The glymphatic system only activates when the brain goes to sleep.
(d) Sleep floods the brain with fluids that widen the areas between brain cells.

15. In ancient Rome, those aspiring to join the legislative assemblies had to hold Roman citizenship. Typically, it was granted at birth to legitimate children of Roman citizens, but in other cases, those who were not born as Romans but were loyal to Rome were given naturalized citizenship. It was also possible for freed slaves to acquire citizenship. Still, Roman citizenship was useless to those seeking a political voice but living outside Rome, as assemblies were held exclusively in the capital.

Q: What is the passage mainly about?

(a) The granting of legitimacy to children of Roman citizens
(b) The selection of Rome as the seat of governance
(c) The means of gaining Roman citizenship
(d) The election system of Rome's assemblies

16. Local policymakers want to pass a bill that will require the media to publicize a response from people criticized in editorials, believing it will ensure accurate reporting. How would this bill affect the press, however? Media companies would lose full editorial control over the content of their publications or broadcasts, and might censor themselves to avoid eliciting a negative response. I believe that the suggested bill would stifle the freedom of the press and may force it to withhold information from the public.

Q: What is the main idea of the passage?

(a) Lawmakers must guarantee that media reports are truthful.
(b) The press needs to address allegations of biased reporting.
(c) The media should be free from external interference.
(d) Media practitioners are advised against criticizing public figures.

17.
> Dear Mr. Kowalski,
>
> Welcome to the company! As president of the workers union, I would like you to know how happy I am with your appointment to the company's top office. I look forward to establishing a satisfactory relationship with you, and I pledge my cooperation in helping the company grow. Furthermore, the union is fully committed to nurturing a more harmonious work environment. That being said, as the new CEO, the employees expect you to deliver on your promise to settle the issues left unresolved by the previous management.
>
> Respectfully,
> Stanley Malkovich

Q: Which of the following is correct according to the letter?

(a) Mr. Kowalski promised to help Mr. Malkovich manage the company.
(b) Stanley Malkovich helped appoint new company leadership.
(c) Union members are demanding better compensation packages.
(d) Mr. Malkovich hopes the CEO will deal with unsettled issues.

18. In a developing human embryo, the first organ to begin its formation is the heart. Only three weeks post conception, a vague heart tube develops. This sign is soon followed by the appearance of a prenatal heartbeat, typically one month after fertilization has occurred. Blood vessels begin to appear soon after, which kick-start the growth of the embryo's other organ systems. When the heart begins beating, an embryo measures less than a centimeter, but a growing circulatory system allows the embryo to double and then redouble its length in the coming weeks.

Q: Which of the following is correct according to the passage?

(a) The heart is the only organ to fully form before birth.
(b) An embryo doubles in length in the first month.
(c) Development of the heart tube precedes a heartbeat.
(d) The heart tube will transform into a blood vessel.

19.

> ### Reduce Your Waste Output With Green Bin
>
> Green Bay EcoTechnologies is proud to introduce the Green Bin. For only $300, this deluxe composter will take care of all your biodegradable kitchen and garden waste, allowing you to reduce the amount of garbage you produce by up to 70 percent.
>
> What's more, with the Green Bin, you can have free homemade fertilizer for your home garden! The device accelerates the composting process, and allows you to increase your garden's yields in just twenty-one days. More efficient gardening and greater yields mean lower grocery bills.
>
> *All of these can be yours with the Green Bin.*

Q: Which of the following is correct according to the passage?

(a) Composting can make gardening more productive.
(b) Green Bay manufactures products designed for farms.
(c) The Green Bin eliminates the need to recycle food waste.
(d) The Green Bin is meant for homes with large kitchens.

20. At an Indonesian zoo, a large female Komodo dragon, a venomous species of lizard, has become an object of intense curiosity after it laid twenty eggs despite having no contact with a male counterpart. Reports say that Audrey, the reptile, could become the first female Komodo dragon to yield offspring without the benefit of male companionship. An alert zoo attendant inadvertently came across the eggs while he was feeding Audrey in her enclosure. Another female Komodo dragon was reported to have reproduced asexually five years ago, but none of its eggs ever hatched.

Q: Which of the following is correct about Audrey the Komodo dragon according to the passage?

(a) Its popularity at the Indonesian zoo has long been established.
(b) It has attracted little notice since it was not the first to reproduce asexually.
(c) Its eggs were stumbled upon unexpectedly.
(d) It is the first Komodo dragon to lay an egg asexually.

21. A common misconception is that water is a good conductor of electricity, yet in its ideal form it should act as an effective insulator. Water molecules are merely oxygen and hydrogen, neither of which contributes any electrical charge by way of loose ions. The water encountered in nature, or even from a bottle, however, is never entirely unadulterated and contains contaminants in the form of solutes. The solutes—typically salts—have an electrical charge and are easily dissolved in water. The water thereby becomes conductive and any contact between it and electricity poses an electrocution risk for humans.

Q: Which of the following is correct according to the passage?

(a) The addition of solutes removes ions from water.
(b) Bottled water contains fewer solutes.
(c) Water is conductive because of impurities within it.
(d) Water found in nature acts as a good insulator.

22. Many of William Faulkner's contemporaries praised his ability to write intricate stories, but others criticized his use of needlessly complex vocabulary. Ernest Hemingway was one such detractor. When Faulkner won the Nobel Prize in 1949, Hemingway cynically said that Faulkner's next novel was doomed to fail, as no one had written a definitive masterpiece after winning. The sniping continued to intensify, and when Faulkner criticized Hemingway's penchant for monosyllabic words, the latter purportedly asked, "Poor Faulkner, does he really think big emotions come from big words?"

Q: Why did Hemingway disparage Faulkner?

(a) He thought Faulkner used unnecessarily difficult words.
(b) He believed that Faulkner's books were too long.
(c) He could not compete with Faulkner's literary success.
(d) He considered the themes in Faulkner's stories too cynical.

23.

Meet the Authors

You are invited to the exclusive book signing of *When the Game Was Ours* by basketball legends David Bronson and Lyle Hart at:

Powell's Books
2373 Fairview Lane
Long Beach, CA 90803

Saturday, November 13, 1 p.m. – 4 p.m.

Don't miss your chance to meet two former greats! Hear them recount the fierce rivalry that developed when they played against each other in the 1980s state championships, and learn how they overcame their grudges 20 years after retiring and finally coauthored a memoir about it.

Visit www.powellsbooks.com to buy a ticket.
Each ticket purchased comes with a copy of *When the Game Was Ours*.

Q: What can be inferred about Bronson and Hart from the passage?

(a) They began playing against one another in childhood.
(b) They were members of the same basketball team.
(c) They became closer after their sports careers ended.
(d) They worked on the autobiography in Long Beach.

24. In the corporate realm, there exists a type of contract known as a golden parachute. Given to vital executives, golden parachutes grant sizeable benefits—generous cash bonuses and stock options are not uncommon—should the executive be terminated in the wake of a company merger. Of the several arguments in favor of the practice, one of the most compelling is that golden parachutes discourage CEOs from blocking mergers that, while being of benefit to the company, would jeopardize their own standing.

Q: Which statement about golden parachutes would the writer most likely agree with?

(a) They allow recipients to make more objective business decisions.
(b) They work best when offered in the aftermath of a merger.
(c) They offer early indication to executives of their imminent dismissal.
(d) They can inadvertently encourage executives to resign prematurely.

25.

Visit Derm Beauty Salon for a Chance to Win!

This April marks Derm Beauty Salon's 10th anniversary, and we're having a raffle to celebrate!

Participation is easy. For every $5 you spend on any of our beauty services and products between April 1 and April 30, you'll get a raffle ticket. The prizes are from our in-store boutique!

  First Prize: One year's supply of Strength Vita shampoo
  Second Prize: Six months' supply of Wave Goodbye hair dye
  Third Prize: One box of Ultra-Shine conditioner

Winners will be notified by telephone on May 1.
Prizes cannot be exchanged for cash.

Q: What can be inferred from the advertisement?

(a) The beauty salon sells hair products in its shop.
(b) The salon is opening an in-store boutique in April.
(c) The price of treatments will be lowered during the promotion.
(d) The customer with the most tickets will win first prize.

Part IV Questions 26~35

Read the passage and the questions. Then choose the option that best answers each question.

Questions 26-27

Job Opportunity

The Grand Wilmington Hotel, a luxury establishment located on the outskirts of Franklin, is seeking an experienced, dynamic, hard-working individual to fill the role of hotel manager.

What Will Your Duties Be?
As hotel manager, you will be responsible for handling day-to-day operations. These include scheduling, budgeting, delegating tasks, and responding to guest inquiries. You will also recruit, interview, and train staff members in the necessary skills for their jobs.

What Are We Looking For?
In order to carry out these duties to the high standards of the Grand Wilmington, it is vital that you have a minimum of three years' experience managing a five-star hotel with 200 or more rooms. You must also hold a degree from a fully accredited hospitality school, be capable of directing multiple teams of workers, and be fluent in both English and Spanish.

Qualified candidates are encouraged to forward their résumés along with the contact information of two former employers to jobs@grandwilmington.com no later than August 5.

26. Q: What is one of the hotel manager's duties?

 (a) The completion of regular safety checks throughout the hotel
 (b) The creation of the marketing schedule for hotel promotions
 (c) The training of new workers in the abilities required for their roles
 (d) The collection of guests' opinions of the hotel during their stays

27. Q: Which of the following is correct according to the advertisement?

 (a) Applicants must submit two letters of reference from past employers.
 (b) Proficiency in multiple languages is a requirement for the position.
 (c) Applicants must send a completed application form after August 5.
 (d) The manager is responsible for multiple branches of the Grand Wilmington.

Questions 28-29

Few American writers have epitomized their generation to the same degree as F. Scott Fitzgerald, whose novels and short stories captured the spirit of the Jazz Age, a time when young Americans upturned traditional social mores. Fitzgerald's debut novel, *This Side of Paradise*, became an instant sensation for its depiction of the youth of the time. Published 14 years later, his final completed work, *Tender is the Night*, portrayed the escapism and decadence of the American expatriates who lived on the French Riviera. The book initially sold poorly and was criticized for failing to keep up with the times, but modern critics now consider *Tender is the Night* to be Fitzgerald's masterpiece.

However, his most-read book is not *This Side of Paradise* or *Tender is the Night* but *The Great Gatsby*. In this novel, Fitzgerald explores two sides of American society through its characters. Jay Gatsby, the main character, has risen from an ordinary background by achieving the American Dream, but has become morally compromised. On the other hand, the narrator, Nick Carraway, has lived a life of upper class privilege, affording him the luxury of upright values. *The Great Gatsby* resonates with readers today for its expression of the excitement and wildness of the Jazz Age, and also for what it reveals about American culture.

28. Q: Which of the following is correct about F. Scott Fitzgerald?

    (a) His last full novel did not receive popular acclaim.
    (b) He resisted the trends set by leading members of the Jazz Age.
    (c) His book *This Side of Paradise* was about people who moved abroad.
    (d) He tended to portray the optimism of young Americans.

29. Q: What is the writer mainly saying in the second paragraph?

    (a) *The Great Gatsby* does not successfully describe the time in which it took place.
    (b) *The Great Gatsby* offers insights into the social realities of the US.
    (c) *The Great Gatsby* can be read as an autobiographical novel.
    (d) *The Great Gatsby* has elicited controversy because of its provocative scenes.

Questions 30-31

American alligators are well known for their long life spans, with many living as long as humans. Given their immense size, it was thought that they continued to grow throughout their lives, but new research has revealed that this may not be true. A study conducted at a wildlife center in Georgetown, South Carolina, collated 35 years' worth of data on alligators and found that many of the creatures achieved their maximum size between 25 and 35 years of age. This mirrors the growth pattern of similar species, such as freshwater crocodiles.

Perhaps more surprisingly, the team discovered that female alligators can continue to reproduce for years after they stop growing. One specimen in the study even produced a healthy batch of eggs at the age of 68. This also overturned long-held ideas about alligators, as scientists had previously believed that they were most fertile around middle age. These findings are significant because they come from an area in South Carolina in which alligator hunting is prohibited. Data from these protected alligators therefore reveal natural patterns of growth and aging. Additionally, by comparing this information to that of unprotected creatures in the rest of the state, researchers can get a better understanding of the impact of hunting on the species in general.

30. Q: What is the main topic of the passage?

    (a) The similarities between various species of alligator and freshwater crocodile
    (b) The findings of a study on the life cycle of the American alligator
    (c) The discovery that alligators continue to grow late in life
    (d) The attempt to conserve alligator populations in South Carolina

31. Q: What can be inferred from the passage?

    (a) Hunting alligators is allowed in some areas of South Carolina.
    (b) Many alligator species are on the list of endangered creatures.
    (c) Alligator species lay eggs at least once a year.
    (d) Alligators are difficult to study because of their size.

Questions 32-33

http://www.edugazette.com/society/university-fee-hikes

Edu Gazette

University Fee Hikes

READERS' COMMENTS
Joey185 | 3 hours ago

You don't seem fully aware of the problems with the university fee hikes. Your analysis of the issue fails to mention that even though fees are rising drastically, the quality of education is not. Many colleges have raised tuition fees, saying it is because of government budget cuts. But they should not be doing this at the same time as paying their administrators such exorbitantly high salaries. Some presidents of universities that announced tuition hikes reportedly receive salaries and bonuses totaling over a million dollars a year, which I find absolutely outrageous. A college's resources should benefit the students as well as the employees.

Furthermore, while students' financial burdens are increasing, many universities have reduced the number of courses that they offer in order to save money and use it for other purposes. This limits the number of academic options available to students and deprives them of vital learning opportunities. It's unreasonable for institutions to raise fees without enhancing the overall learning experience. Universities throughout the country not only suffer from subpar teaching, but are also blighted by poor IT systems and limited library resources, not to mention abysmal facilities. An increased windfall from higher fees should be used to rectify these faults, rather than lining the pockets of administrators.

32. Q: What is the writer mainly trying to do?

   (a) Point out that rising student fees only benefit university employees
   (b) Justify the budget cuts suffered by most university programs
   (c) Suggest a compromise for meeting the needs of professors and students
   (d) Draw attention to unfair practices carried out by college admission offices

33. Q: Why have universities begun offering fewer courses?

   (a) They are unable to find instructors trained in certain disciplines.
   (b) They have limited funds for outfitting classrooms with electronic equipment.
   (c) They want to provide students with practical skills for finding employment.
   (d) They want to spend money on things other than teaching.

Questions 34-35

The Struggle for Equality throughout the Years

Motivated by the popularity of liberal ideas during the Age of Enlightenment in Europe, members of the feminist movement in the mid to late 1800s pushed for reforms that would grant women the same political, social, and economic opportunities available to men. Their efforts called attention to the injustices inflicted upon their gender by a predominantly patriarchal society. They asked that women be allowed to vote, study, work, and own property. They wanted to be treated as intelligent beings with certain inalienable rights rather than members of a weaker sex who needed male protection.

While these early feminists succeeded in many respects, feminism had almost entirely disappeared by the 1950s, when women were encouraged to support their husbands and families as housewives. Then in the 1960s, there was a resurgence of feminist activity, often referred to as second-wave feminism. It was influenced immensely by author Betty Friedan, who said women were limiting their possibilities by staying at home. Another prominent figure of the period was journalist Gloria Steinem, who called for a revolution of women against their male exploiters. She was a proponent of a society without gender roles that would allow a woman to pursue a career if she chose to do so.

34. Q: Which of the following is correct about the feminist movement of the 1800s?

    (a) It began as a means of resisting male violence.
    (b) It appeared once women were allowed to attain political office.
    (c) It was intended to give women an equal say in marriage.
    (d) Its proponents wanted women to be treated as individuals with full social rights.

35. Q: What can be inferred about Gloria Steinem?

    (a) She said gender roles were often influenced by the media.
    (b) She significantly altered how men viewed the abilities of women.
    (c) She was a proponent of using violence to revolt against exploitation.
    (d) She believed women should seek fulfillment in the workforce.

정답 p. 351 / 해석 p. 274

The Reading Comprehension section of the exam is complete. Please stay in your seat until the proctor tells you to leave. You are NOT allowed to open any of the other sections of the exam.

시험에 나올 문제를 미리 풀어보는
텝스 적중예상특강
해커스텝스 HackersTEPS.com

SELF-CHECK LIST

TEST 02는 잘 마치셨나요?
이제 다음의 SELF-CHECK LIST를 통해 자신의 테스트 진행 내용을 점검해 볼까요?

1. 나는 테스트를 마칠 때까지 완전히 테스트에 집중하였다.
   ☐ YES   ☐ NO

2. 나는 각 영역별 주어진 시간을 지켰다.
   ☐ LISTENING COMPREHENSION
   ☐ VOCABULARY & GRAMMAR   ☐ READING COMPREHENSION

3. 나는 시간 내에 모든 문제를 풀었다.
   ☐ LISTENING COMPREHENSION
   ☐ VOCABULARY & GRAMMAR   ☐ READING COMPREHENSION

4. 나는 특히 어렵게 느껴지는 영역이 있었다.
   ☐ LISTENING COMPREHENSION
   ☐ VOCABULARY & GRAMMAR   ☐ READING COMPREHENSION

5. 개선하고 싶은 사항
   _____
   _____
   _____
   _____

■ 개선해야 할 점은 반드시 다음 테스트에서 실천해야만 실력을 향상시킬 수 있습니다.
그리고 반드시 오답을 정리해서 같은 실수를 반복하지 않도록 유의하기 바랍니다.

해커스 텝스 최신기출유형 실전모의고사 문제집

TEST 03

LISTENING COMPREHENSION
VOCABULARY & GRAMMAR
READING COMPREHENSION

테스트 전 확인사항

1. 휴대 전화의 전원을 끄셨나요?
2. OMR 답안지, 연필, 지우개가 준비되셨나요?
3. 시계가 준비되셨나요?
4. 목표 점수를 정하세요.
   LISTENING COMPREHENSION (____개 / 40개)
   VOCABULARY (____개 / 30개)
   GRAMMAR (____개 / 30개)
   READING COMPREHENSION (____개 / 35개)
5. 테스트의 시작과 종료 시간을 정하세요.
   LISTENING COMPREHENSION   ____시 ____분 ~ ____시 ____분 (40분)
   VOCABULARY & GRAMMAR   ____시 ____분 ~ ____시 ____분 (25분)
   READING COMPREHENSION   ____시 ____분 ~ ____시 ____분 (35분)

무료MP3 바로듣기

🎧 TEST 03.mp3
실전용·복습용 문제풀이 MP3 무료 다운로드 및 스트리밍 바로듣기
(HackersIngang.com)
* 실제 시험장의 소음까지 재현해 낸 고사장 소음·매미 버전 MP3까지 구매하면 실전에 더욱 완벽히 대비할 수 있습니다.

LISTENING COMPREHENSION

DIRECTIONS

1. In the Listening Comprehension Section, the content will be presented in oral rather than written form.
2. There are five parts in this section, and you will receive separate instructions for each. Listen to the instructions carefully, and choose the best answer for each question from the available options.

Part I Questions 1~10

You will now hear ten statements or questions, and each will be followed by four responses. Choose the most appropriate response.

Part II Questions 11~20

You will now hear ten conversation fragments, and each will be followed by four responses. Choose the most appropriate response.

Part III Questions 21~30

You will now hear ten complete conversations. Before each conversation, you will hear a short description of the situation. Then you will hear the conversation and its corresponding question, both of which will be read only once. Next, you will hear four options, which will also be read once. Choose the option that best answers the question.

Part IV Questions 31~36

You will now hear six monologues. For each item, you will hear a monologue and its corresponding question, both of which will be read twice. Then you will hear four options which will be read only once. Choose the option that best answers the question.

Part V Questions 37~40

You will now hear two longer monologues. For each item, you will hear a monologue and two corresponding questions, all of which will be read twice. Then you will hear four options for each question, which will be read only once. Choose the option that best answers each question.

Vocabulary & Grammar

DIRECTIONS

These two parts of the exam test your vocabulary and grammar skills. You will have a total of 25 minutes to answer 60 questions. There will be 30 from the Vocabulary section and 30 from the Grammar section. Make sure to follow the directions given by the proctor.

Part I Questions 1~10

Choose the best answer for the blank.

1. A: Have you paid the electric bill yet?
   B: Sorry, I forgot. Please _____ me about it tomorrow.

   (a) memorize
   (b) remind
   (c) infer
   (d) warn

2. A: I'm glad the hotel staff is warm and accommodating.
   B: Yeah, they're definitely _____.

   (a) usable
   (b) liable
   (c) hospitable
   (d) appreciable

3. A: How much do you expect from the sale of your jewelry?
   B: I have no idea. It hasn't been _____ yet.

   (a) appraised
   (b) mortgaged
   (c) depreciated
   (d) reckoned

4. A: Nikki never arrives on time for her appointments.
   B: Yeah, she's consistently _____.

   (a) tacky
   (b) tardy
   (c) snappy
   (d) naughty

5. A: This is the third night we've done overtime. I'm tired of this.
   B: It's peak season. There's no point _____ about it.

   (a) criticizing
   (b) regretting
   (c) roaring
   (d) grumbling

6. A: It's discouraging how the coach always finds fault in our performance.
   B: I know. He's too _____ of us.

   (a) vindictive
   (b) detached
   (c) painful
   (d) critical

7. A: Helen loves to meddle in our affairs and I just hate it!
   B: I agree. She can be really _____ sometimes.

   (a) tepid
   (b) prudent
   (c) nosy
   (d) standoffish

8. A: Does this road go to the county library?
   B: It does, but you need to turn right where it _____.

   (a) veers
   (b) forks
   (c) halts
   (d) cracks

9. A: I have a student in class who is very _____.
   B: Well, there should be a way to get him to talk.

   (a) ingenious
   (b) profound
   (c) reticent
   (d) ambiguous

10. A: Did the doctor give you the information you needed?
    B: Yes, he _____ the potential side effects of the medicine he wanted me to take.

    (a) quarantined
    (b) enumerated
    (c) pulverized
    (d) chastened

Part II Questions 11~30

Choose the best answer for the blank.

11. Details of the investigation were _____ by the police at a press conference.
    (a) excavated
    (b) assured
    (c) disclosed
    (d) pleaded

12. Critics warn that the Internet, where posts filled with discriminatory language and graphic violence are commonplace, is normalizing _____ behavior.
    (a) deviant
    (b) redundant
    (c) ascendant
    (d) reluctant

13. Malaria is _____ from one person to another through infected Anopheles mosquitoes.
    (a) scattered
    (b) captured
    (c) transmitted
    (d) gained

14. The valedictorian's graduation speech depicted her _____ of a society where truth and justice reign.
    (a) ideal
    (b) medium
    (c) insight
    (d) approach

15. The current economic _____ has resulted in the loss of thousands of jobs, particularly in manufacturing and trade.
    (a) emission
    (b) recession
    (c) exposition
    (d) reprehension

16. Having seen her drunk before, Greg warned Lydia to limit her alcohol intake because she could be a _____.
    (a) loose cannon
    (b) paper tiger
    (c) fifth wheel
    (d) shrinking violet

17. Leah stopped working to _____ her time to being a mother after she gave birth to her son.
    (a) devote
    (b) offer
    (c) refute
    (d) challenge

18. China has more than 1.3 billion _____, making it the most populous nation in the world.
    (a) allies
    (b) inhabitants
    (c) objects
    (d) personas

19. Skydiving is an extreme sport that can put you in great _____ if you don't have the proper training.
    (a) scheme
    (b) peril
    (c) impunity
    (d) decadence

20. Cats were once considered _____ animals by the Egyptians and were thus worshipped as divine beings.
    (a) sacred
    (b) devout
    (c) ascetic
    (d) pious

21. Many science fiction novels feature aliens that come to Earth in order to observe _____ life.

    (a) celestial
    (b) existential
    (c) terrestrial
    (d) torrential

22. The beautiful white house lit by the morning sun was _____ high on the slope of a hill.

    (a) straddled
    (b) perched
    (c) sauntered
    (d) affixed

23. Some paints contain chemicals that _____ the skin upon contact.

    (a) pique
    (b) irritate
    (c) seize
    (d) tantalize

24. Scientists theorize that the underlying reason plants not _____ to an area become invasive involves mechanisms within the ecosystem.

    (a) incipient
    (b) susceptible
    (c) indigenous
    (d) exhaustive

25. A company in California offers Pacifica visitors a(n) _____ ride on the Segway, an electric-powered two-wheeled vehicle.

    (a) reverberant
    (b) poignant
    (c) miscreant
    (d) exhilarating

26. Not even the _____ rumblings of the volcano could persuade residents in the vicinity to evacuate.

    (a) ominous
    (b) disparaging
    (c) exuberant
    (d) sanguinary

27. Both parties came to an agreement on all of the _____ points stipulated in the contract.

    (a) ambient
    (b) salient
    (c) laconic
    (d) insipid

28. The task may have been given at the last minute, but the director did not expect it to be handled in such a _____ manner.

    (a) cursory
    (b) transient
    (c) defiant
    (d) tactful

29. Senator Hurst was _____ by rumors that she was involved in a political scandal.

    (a) clattered
    (b) placated
    (c) rattled
    (d) appeased

30. Michael often relates experiences that are so unbelievable that everyone thinks he _____ them.

    (a) concocted
    (b) conjugated
    (c) accreted
    (d) atoned

정답 p. 352 / 해석 p. 289

The Vocabulary section is complete. Please move on to the Grammar section.

Part I Questions 1~10
Choose the best answer for the blank.

1. A: No matter when I go to bed, I can't fall asleep at night.
   B: Maybe you should drink beverages that contain _____ caffeine.
   (a) few
   (b) less
   (c) least
   (d) fewest

2. A: I heard that new drama is terribly sad and moving.
   B: I saw it, and everyone in the theater, both children and adults, _____.
   (a) has wept
   (b) have wept
   (c) was weeping
   (d) were weeping

3. A: Is Carrie new to the company as well?
   B: No. By the time December comes, she _____ here for a year.
   (a) is working
   (b) was working
   (c) has been working
   (d) will have been working

4. A: The book club members want me to host our meetings at my house.
   B: If I were you, I'd _____.
   (a) be reluctant to
   (b) be reluctant to do
   (c) be reluctant to be
   (d) be reluctant to be doing

5. A: Is everyone from the office coming on the weekend retreat?
   B: All agreed to participate _____ one: Marcia from accounting. She can't come.
   (a) amid
   (b) against
   (c) beyond
   (d) save

6. A: Your laptop doesn't seem to be in the den.
   B: My sister _____ be using it in the kitchen.
   (a) will
   (b) need
   (c) must
   (d) would

7. A: Why did Madeline come to work after lunch today?
   B: She said she _____ the doctor's office this morning.
   (a) is visiting
   (b) was visiting
   (c) has been visiting
   (d) will have been visiting

8. A: What do you think of our expansion plan?
   B: It seems like it will be _____ a difficult project.
   (a) very
   (b) quite
   (c) way
   (d) so

9. A: Did Natalie quit her job last week?
   B: Yes. It's because she _____ more than two months' worth of pay but never received it.
   (a) is owed
   (b) is owing
   (c) had owed
   (d) was owed

10. A: Did Althea tell you about her engagement?
    B: Yeah. She called me right away, _____ about the news.
    (a) thrill
    (b) thrilling
    (c) thrilled
    (d) to thrill

Part II Questions 11~25

Choose the best answer for the blank.

11. She hadn't noticed the red light; otherwise she _____ sooner.
    (a) stopped
    (b) had stopped
    (c) will stop
    (d) would have stopped

12. All lease contracts must be approved before prospective residents can take _____ of their apartments.
    (a) occupancy
    (b) occupancies
    (c) an occupancy
    (d) the occupancy

13. It was surprising that the movie _____ to win any awards at the recently concluded film festival.
    (a) fails
    (b) failed
    (c) is failing
    (d) was failing

14. The chemicals used in the laboratory, many _____ are highly volatile, must be stored in their appropriate containers.
    (a) which
    (b) that
    (c) of which
    (d) of what

15. As another publisher put out Jay Bard's earlier novels, releasing the series as a whole _____ under consideration.
    (a) is not
    (b) are not
    (c) is not being
    (d) are not being

16. The psychology department _____ scholarships to five students who conducted research on child behavior.
    (a) were presented
    (b) is presented
    (c) presented
    (d) present

17. After delivering the TV, the technician offered _____ it free of charge.
    (a) installing
    (b) to install
    (c) for installing
    (d) to be installing

18. Scanning the computer's entire database, the virus program did not show the results of its search until it _____.
    (a) will finish
    (b) finishes
    (c) was finished
    (d) has been finishing

19. The largest empire of the ancient world was established in 550 BC in _____ is now Iran.
    (a) who
    (b) what
    (c) which
    (d) where

20. Helen Keller would have remained isolated from the world around her _____ for Anne Sullivan's guidance.
    (a) has it not
    (b) were it not
    (c) has it not been
    (d) had it not been

21. By no means _____ _____ research that involved experimenting on animals.

    (a) was the funding intended to support
    (b) the funding was intending to support
    (c) the funding was supporting to intend
    (d) was the support intending to fund

22. The electrical crew did not have _____ idea why the lighting was malfunctioning.

    (a) every
    (b) one
    (c) any
    (d) some

23. Bread turns brown when toasted due to the Maillard reaction, _____ the sugar and protein molecules in bread chemically interact.

    (a) although
    (b) therefore
    (c) whereby
    (d) while

24. Fewer married couples are seeking housing in urban apartments, whose rent prices are known to be _____.

    (a) those higher than of other locations
    (b) higher than those of other locations
    (c) higher than of other locations
    (d) those of other locations higher

25. The contractors were able to obtain _____ by conciliar means to renovate the property that had at one point been a recreation center.

    (a) permission
    (b) permissions
    (c) a permission
    (d) the permissions

Part III Questions 26~30

Identify the option that contains an awkward expression or an error in grammar.

26. (a) A: Which lessons do you think will appear on our civics exam?
    (b) B: You were absent when the teacher announced that it will be chapters three and four.
    (c) A: Oh no! I'll end up fail the exam if I don't review those chapters.
    (d) B: As long as you read them thoroughly, you should do fine.

27. (a) A: Isn't it a bit too cold today for you to be wearing such a light jacket?
    (b) B: Are you saying you'd rather I didn't wear this jacket anymore?
    (c) A: Don't get wrong, it looks great. I'm just concerned for your health.
    (d) B: Your concern is appreciated, but to tell the truth, this jacket is warmer than it looks.

28. (a) Asian carp are an invasive species in North American waters, and they have many environmentalists concerned. (b) Their growing numbers pose a significant threat to those aquatic ecosystems. (c) The carp are known to eat up vast amounts of small organisms, such as plankton, leaving none for the native species to consume. (d) In order for the native species in the area to survive, the carp population has to be held consistent in check.

29. (a) Before setting out to colonize the Americas, Christopher Columbus spent much time seeking ways to fund his expedition. (b) Columbus was eventually granted an audience with the king and queen of Spain after lobbying and negotiating for two years. (c) He explained what provisions are needed them to grant him in order for his journey to be successful. (d) Most of his demands were met, although no one expected that he would ever return from his voyage.

30. (a) Twenty-two-year-old Aktarer Zaman found himself embroiled in a lawsuit with United Airlines last November. (b) The airline sued Zaman after he built a website that let air travelers find "secret" affordable fares. (c) Only after the popularity of his site exploded he did get into trouble, and he was hauled into court. (d) He was relieved when the judge ultimately threw out the case, although he expects the airline will continue to pursue legal action against him.

The Vocabulary and Grammar sections are complete. Do NOT start the Reading Comprehension section until instructed to do so. You are NOT allowed to open any of the other sections of the exam.

Reading Comprehension

DIRECTIONS

This part of the exam tests your ability to understand reading passages. There will be 35 questions in 40 minutes. Make sure to follow the proctor's instructions.

Part I Questions 1~10

Read the passage. Then choose the option that best completes the passage.

1. People today are no longer satisfied with just buying products. They want to feel as though their purchases are going to support a good cause. Recognizing this, most multinational companies are now adopting "responsible" marketing practices in order to appeal to the benevolent side of consumers. What is meant by "responsible marketing" is the blending of sales promotions with philanthropic activities. For instance, a few major bottled water companies bankroll the causes of celebrities who endorse their products. Companies _____ _____ certain nongovernment organizations and charitable foundations.

   (a) give promotional advice to
   (b) feel a social responsibility for
   (c) likewise lend monetary support to
   (d) capitalize on the proceeds available from

2.
   Dear Olive,

   Although this mountaineering expedition has been exhilarating, I realize I made a serious mistake in my planning. Weeks before leaving on the trip, I stopped at an outdoor supplier to purchase all the gear I would need, including new boots. However, after the first day of climbing, my feet developed painful blisters and became so swollen that I could barely stand up and had to postpone the remainder of my climb. I'm still having a ball, but it's not nearly the fun I would have had on a climb. I should have _____.

   Take care,
   Brooke

   (a) gone on a more relaxing vacation
   (b) acclimated my feet to the new gear first
   (c) wasted less money on unnecessary equipment
   (d) prepared for the physical demands of the trip

3. I finally convinced my father, who has been an independent proprietor for longer than I've been alive, to begin compiling his transaction records in a computerized spreadsheet. He was reluctant to transition away from a ballpoint pen and paper, but inputting the data into the computer soon became second nature. This decision proved important, as just last month a fire in his shop destroyed nearly all of the documents stored there. Fortunately, his accounting data was safely backed up off-site, but this near miss made it clear to my father that he ____ _____.

   (a) ought to prepare for another calamity
   (b) should solicit the business advice of family
   (c) would continue to track transactions on paper
   (d) made a timely decision in changing accounting methods

4. No matter their gender, many people _____. They dedicate time and attention to this not only for aesthetic purposes, but for hygienic reasons as well, because the nails safeguard the delicate tissue of the tips of the fingers. Fingernails tend to trap dirt beneath them, so proper care is important in preventing the spread of bacteria when the hands are brought in the vicinity of the mouth or nose. Additionally, keeping one's cuticles well groomed prevents the formation of hangnails and other unsightly occurrences.

(a) occasionally encounter hangnail problems
(b) grow their nails long as a fashion
(c) wash their hands for various reasons
(d) take meticulous care of their nails

5. Today, people still marvel at what was, from 1889 to 1929, the _____ _____. The Eiffel Tower reaches 300 meters above the streets of Paris and is made of an interlocking series of wrought-iron beams. Before 1929, nothing remotely approaching its magnitude had ever been built. It was twice as lofty as the dome of St. Peter's Basilica in Rome and the Great Pyramid of Giza. The tower was erected in only two years, which amazed people even more than its enormous stature.

(a) biggest dome-topped structure in existence
(b) quickest such tower ever constructed
(c) loftiest man-made edifice in the world
(d) grandest memorial designated to honor Eiffel

6. As a 23-year-old, I enlisted with the Peace Corps and was deployed to Malawi, an African nation. Our objective was to build a municipal sewage system to adequately dispose of waste that had begun contaminating local waterways. We were taken with the cooperation and support given by the locals, and I was convinced that in developing countries, citizens had the desire but not the means to make material improvements to their communities. Driven by this realization, I chose to dedicate my life to those people and figuring out _____.

   (a) how they can best control water contamination
   (b) how sewage problems could best be tackled
   (c) how they can escape from abject poverty
   (d) how to provide the requisite material support

7. Outcome-focused initiatives such as No Child Left Behind transformed American education. The heightened stringency applied to gauging how well children learned also turned the spotlight on how well teachers instructed. In effect, student test scores became the benchmark by which to measure teacher effectiveness. While such a method tidily quantifies teacher performance, its accuracy remains suspect. After all, a single score can scarcely furnish a comprehensive perspective on a teacher's ability. Given how complex and varied a profession teaching is, it seems patently misguided that _____.

   (a) there is no way to ensure the standards are being upheld
   (b) we expect all students to thrive under such a strict system
   (c) teachers single out their students by their test scores
   (d) a teacher's success should have its basis wholly in students' achievement

8. No Sweat Center's award-winning fitness program is finally here and as a part of the chain's regional expansion, the first 100 people to enroll in our home-based conditioning program will receive a 25 percent markdown on their monthly fee. No Sweat offers personal training at home or in your office at an affordable price, so there's no excuse for those with densely packed schedules not to burn away belly fat, build a stronger torso, or sculpt their biceps and triceps with No Sweat's special regimen. If you long for _____, dial 702–NO–SWEAT.

   (a) the most comprehensive athletic club
   (b) a fitness program with a flexible schedule
   (c) exercise machines you can operate at home
   (d) an inexpensive gym membership

9.

Historical Insights into Antibiotic Resistance

Due to the overuse of antibiotics, many bacteria have become resistant to drugs. A case in point is the tuberculosis bacterium, which had become untreatable by common antibiotics by the 1980s. Others, like Staphylococcus aureus, started developing defenses against antibiotics as early as the late 1940s. By the 1950s, 40 percent of patients infected with the bacterium stopped responding to penicillin, a common treatment. _____, an outbreak of resistant Enterococcus faecalis spread in the US, which led to thousands of infected individuals developing life-threatening heart diseases and bladder infections.

(a) Meanwhile
(b) Especially
(c) In effect
(d) For example

10. Since its inception thousands of years ago, Homer's classic epic *The Odyssey* has been probed and dissected by readers the world over. Each chapter of the ancient poem contains a variety of themes and experimental elements, which has led to multiple different interpretations and elaborate discussions of the work's esoteric content. _____, not only the common man but also the well-versed scholar of literature is often compelled to seek out and study the many topics related to this masterpiece.

(a) In addition
(b) Alternatively
(c) Otherwise
(d) Therefore

Part II Questions 11~12

Read the passage. Then identify the option that does NOT belong.

11. In Chinese culture, the image of a portly Buddha holding a big bag is known to signify wealth and triumph. (a) Buddha's large satchel symbolizes treasure, more specifically the spoils of victory. (b) The deity's laughing countenance, meanwhile, denotes the joy of triumph amidst the adversities that challenge us in our lives. (c) Revered in many cultures throughout Asia, Buddha is sometimes depicted as a thin, ascetic man. (d) Such a representation reflects a quote attributed to Buddha that success comes only to those who endure pain.

12. Art critics are of differing opinions on just what is depicted in Jan van Eyck's masterpiece *The Arnolfini Portrait*. (a) The portrait depicts a merchant-class couple and is thought by some to symbolize marriage and fertility. (b) That the woman in the portrait sports a noticeable bulge in her midsection, indicating a pregnancy, substantiates this view. (c) However, such a perspective takes no account of how the painter struggled to accurately render the female form. (d) But some critics reject this interpretation, claiming that the woman is merely holding her skirts up around her torso, as was the fashion of the times, and is not with child.

Part III Questions 13~25

Read the passage and the question. Then choose the option that best answers the question.

13. Debate has raged among engineers for decades about which engine is superior: diesel or gasoline. However, the facts speak for themselves. Gasoline engines convert a respectable 30% of the energy from fuel into actual power. Diesel bests that by 20%. Their reliability is also without match. The sputtering that hounds gasoline engines when a spark plug fails is a nonissue for diesel engines since the latter uses compression rather than a spark to ignite fuel. Lastly, diesels have the edge on efficiency, running cooler and cleaner than their gasoline counterparts

Q: What is the writer's main point about diesel engines?

(a) Their 20% rate of fuel conversion is one area in which they fall short.
(b) They outperform gasoline engines in several respects.
(c) They are less powerful but more reliable than gasoline engines.
(d) Their reliance on spark plugs gives them a significant advantage.

14.
Middleton Children's Library

The Middleton Children's Library is a project of the Middleton Baptist Church. The library, which also holds reading classes for preschool children and ESL students, is funded entirely through proceeds from the church's Sunday mass collections. With today's rising costs, however, the library has been encountering difficulties with its operating budget. Middleton Church is counting on the increased support of its parishioners to keep the library open and well maintained.

Q: What is the main point of the advertisement?

(a) The library will be opening more ESL classes.
(b) The library requires an increase in funding.
(c) The library has been trying to cut operating costs.
(d) The library will now offer fee-based classes.

15.

Obesity Studies

Locating risk factors and causes of obesity has become a cause célèbre within science, and new research published by the American Psychological Association pinpoints a source: character.

Individuals whose disposition veers toward neuroticism and away from conscientiousness are most likely to struggle with excess weight, according to the study. In particular, impulsivity was identified as one of the key characteristics that drive people to succumb to temptation and abandon weight-loss efforts at the first sign of difficulty.

Q: What is the writer's main point?

(a) Being overweight can have adverse effects on one's personality.
(b) Individuals who are both neurotic and conscientious tend to overeat.
(c) Evidence shows that dieting is even more difficult than previously thought.
(d) Research suggests that personality traits are a key determinant of obesity.

16. The solstice is an event that happens twice a year when, depending on the season, the Sun's position at zenith relative to the horizon is at either its highest or lowest point. Depending on the tilt of Earth's axis, areas close to the poles alternately experience extremely long days and nights. When a pole is tilted toward the Sun, the Sun stays above the horizon for 24 hours. Meanwhile, the exact opposite is happening at the pole tilted away from the Sun. There, the Sun is not seen above the horizon at any time of day.

Q: What does the passage mainly discuss?

(a) The solstice's effect on seasonal change
(b) The relationship between the Sun and Earth at solstice
(c) How the solstice shifts the position of Earth's axis
(d) What role the Sun plays in determining day length

17.
> ### Replace Your Personal Computer with a PMC-300 Tablet!
>
> A lightweight tablet with a 10.5-inch LCD screen, the PMC-300 is ideal for watching movies, surfing the Internet, or catching up on work.
>
> Features:
>
> - **128 gigabytes of internal storage**
>   (expandable to 256 gigabytes with inclusion of a PMC-G256 memory card)
> - **a large-capacity quick-charging battery**
>   (able to last for up to 18 hours)
> - **high-definition front and rear-facing cameras**
> - **comes with the photo editing program Blue Oceans**
>
> The PMC-300 is available at electronics stores nationwide and retails for only $489.99. Get yours while supplies last!

Q: Which of the following is correct about the PMC-300 according to the passage?

(a) It is intended for use in offices.
(b) It requires an external device to store files.
(c) It comes in two different versions.
(d) It includes software for image manipulation.

18. Gustave Flaubert was put on trial for immorality after releasing *Madame Bovary* in 1857. The story follows Emma Bovary, a middle-class woman who engages in adulterous relationships in her quest for love, wealth, and social status. Flaubert was acquitted thanks to his lawyer Marie-Antoine-Jules Senard's argument that the novel actually warns of the dangers of immorality. Senard added that it merely exhibited the predicament faced by women of Emma's class who were obsessed with their own fantasies of a perfect life. The work was meant to be a critical commentary on society's problems.

Q: Which of the following is correct about Flaubert's *Madame Bovary*?

(a) The working class acclaimed it upon publication.
(b) It makes a statement about the dangers of uncontrolled ambition.
(c) Senard got it banned on the grounds of immorality.
(d) Flaubert wrote it following the death of a woman named Emma.

19. Although bathing is now a major part of daily hygiene, it was not nearly as commonplace a practice in late medieval times. Sixteenth-century Europeans believed that water carried diseases. That belief was reinforced after many people were killed by frequent occurrences of the bubonic plague, thought to have been caused by water-borne contaminants. People avoided taking baths for fear that it would have an adverse effect on their health. Bathing became a hygienic practice only after doctors in the nineteenth century introduced the idea that disease-causing germs could be neutralized by washing the body with soap and water.

Q: Which of the following is correct according to the passage?

(a) Water purification was used as a remedy against the bubonic plague.
(b) Nineteenth-century doctors promoted bathing as a healthy habit.
(c) Regular bathing was practiced in sixteenth-century Europe.
(d) The bubonic plague is a disease that is caused by contaminated water.

20. Folic acid is vital to a healthy pregnancy, but unfortunately, many women neglect to consume the vitamin in sufficient amounts. Serious birth defects affecting the neural tube, such as spina bifida and anencephaly, can be prevented by adequate folic acid levels obtained either through diet or supplements. The neural tube, from which the spine and brain develop, forms within the first month of pregnancy, so women who start taking the supplement after becoming pregnant may not be able to reap the benefits of folic acid. This is why doctors urge women to begin taking folic acid before trying to conceive.

Q: Which of the following is correct according to the passage?

(a) Ample folic acid intake is incidental to a successful pregnancy.
(b) Taking supplements is considered an inferior way to obtain folic acid.
(c) Neural tube defects emerge only in the final stages of pregnancy.
(d) Prime folic acid levels must be achieved before conception for maximum benefit.

21.
> Dear Principal Watkins,
>
> The winners of our third annual amateur art competition will be chosen on March 28. There will be an exhibit of all submitted paintings three days prior to the award ceremony. Kindly inform your students that for their entries to be considered for the final selection process, they need to turn in their work before March 25. The date for the announcement of the winners has not been finalized, but it will definitely be either March 29 or 30.
>
> Sincerely,
> Claire Fuentes
> Young Artists Foundation

Q: Which of the following is correct according to the letter?

(a) Students should submit their work on March 28.
(b) Winners will be declared no later than March 30.
(c) The exhibition is held on the same day as the ceremony.
(d) Winning entries will be determined before March 25.

22. Pressure cookers, which have often been maligned as dangerous, are actually among the most reliable and useful cooking devices. The unfair reputation derives from early-generation malfunctions, but nowadays, safety innovations like release valves prevent accidents from occurring and permit consumers to safely enjoy the swiftness with which the devices can cook everyday meals. The contraptions are sealed, so pressure buildup within them creates higher temperatures than a pan on a stovetop, due to the fact that pressure and temperature are directly correlated.

Q: Which of the following is correct about pressure cookers?

(a) They had defective valves when first introduced.
(b) They are valuable for accelerating food preparation.
(c) They use a heating element to maximize temperature.
(d) They remain popular despite carrying some risk of injury.

23.

Dear Mr. Mayor,

I am perturbed that many business establishments in our city do not issue official receipts for cash transactions. Each time I request one, I am met with a curious stare. I want to exercise my rights as a consumer by demanding the mandated official receipt, but shopkeepers often seem bothered by my request because other customers don't ask for one. By not giving a receipt, businesses are able to underreport the sales tax revenue they owe. Why does the government enact laws if they are not going to be enforced?

Respectfully,
Ernest Daz

Q: What can be inferred from the letter?

(a) Shop owners are guilty of deceiving their customers.
(b) Business owners in the city find cash transactions inconvenient.
(c) Most store clerks are unaware they must provide a receipt.
(d) Businesses may make more money when purchase receipts are not given.

24.

News > Politics

Brookes Island Mayor in Trouble

The mayor of Brookes Island was slapped with an impeachment complaint yesterday by various nonprofit groups. The complainants said that the mayor betrayed the public's trust and violated some laws of the island city. His detractors allege that the mayor is not doing his job of preserving peace and order on the island.

The Brookes Island City Council, which is responsible for investigating the complaint, should immediately determine if the mayor has indeed been negligent in his duties because the public's confidence in the government is at stake.

Q: Which statement would the writer most likely agree with?

(a) A speedy investigation will serve the city's best interest.
(b) The mayor became corrupt upon coming to power.
(c) The city council should reject the impeachment request.
(d) A new mayor must be appointed by the city council.

25. When moving to another town or city, you should be aware that differences may crop up. Being insensitive to the existing norms of a community can lead to many social problems. In the city, young couples out on a date are commonplace, but in conservative cities like Eureka, older residents will publicly admonish girls and boys who are alone together, especially during nighttime. Furthermore, the parents of "misbehaving" teenagers may be threatened with expulsion from the community if their children do not correct their behavior.

Q: What can be inferred from the passage?

(a) People avoid Eureka because of its strict social norms.
(b) Each community sets its own ethical standards.
(c) People who move to new places need not follow social norms.
(d) Cultural norms ensure similar behavior from place to place.

Part IV Questions 26~35

Read the passage and the questions. Then choose the option that best answers each question.

Questions 26-27

Calling All Bird Lovers

If you are interested in taking up bird-watching as a hobby, consider In Flight, a special introductory course offered by the Pennsylvania Wildlife Institute.

The three-hour class begins with an overview of the bird species native to our region. After that, you'll have a chance to examine some actual nests built by local bird species in our facility's enclosure. Then, you'll listen to some recorded bird calls and practice making them yourself. Finally, the entire group will head out for an afternoon of bird-watching in the countryside. Our expert guide will lead you and the other participants to an area with a large bird population. He'll provide you with photographs of local birds to help you identify the ones you see. All you need is a pair of binoculars to get up close and personal with our feathered friends.

The cost of the course is $35 per person. To sign up, visit www.pwi.com and click on the registration link.

26. Q: What is the passage mainly about?

(a) An educational video about the social behavior of birds
(b) A program that provides the knowledge needed by novice bird-watchers
(c) The best methods for locating native bird species in Pennsylvania
(d) Measures that are being taken to protect some endangered wildlife

27. Q: What will the guide give participants?

(a) A pair of binoculars
(b) A pamphlet of instructions
(c) Images of local wildlife
(d) Some audio files

Questions 28-29

To: kowalski19@greymail.com
From: donation@mercianimal.com

Subject: Thank you for your donation - Mercy Animal Farm

Dear Mr. Kowalski,

Thank you for investing in the work of the Mercy Animal Farm. Your donation of $1,000 provides valuable support especially at a time when charity revenue has been in decline. Contributions like yours help us maintain our vital feeding and rehabilitation programs and allow us to rescue more retired animals. As you know, we are often required to purchase animals outright when they might otherwise be destined for slaughter. We also try to rescue abandoned pets that have been deposited with nearby shelters.

As a gesture of thanks, you will be receiving a free T-shirt in the mail. The shirt was designed by local artist Elizabeth Mason. I'd also like to take this opportunity to remind you that there are other ways you can help. We provide volunteer opportunities that can last anywhere from a few hours to several days. Volunteers are welcome to stay on the property or at a neighboring hotel. We would also appreciate it if you directed your friends to our social media page where we share photos of the farm and other information.

Sincerely,
Misha Campbell
Director of operations

28. Q: What will some of Mr. Kowalski's donation be used for?

(a) The procurement of animals that are going to be killed
(b) The establishment of a second shelter for abandoned pets
(c) The rehabilitation of a farm that produces animal products
(d) The maintenance of a program for tourists visiting a facility

29. Q: Which of the following is correct about Mr. Kowalski?

(a) He represents a charitable institution aimed at animal welfare.
(b) His friends will match his contribution to the charity.
(c) He will be sent a specially designed article of clothing.
(d) His donation entitles him to a free stay at a hotel.

Questions 30-31

A Battle for Feudal Supremacy

In 1590, the Japanese feudal lord Toyotomi Hideyoshi led a siege on the Hojo clan, which he viewed as a great threat to his power. However, very little fighting actually occurred when Hideyoshi's troops surrounded the Hojo castle at Odawara and set up camp. They simply blocked everything and everyone from going in or out of the castle. After three months, the Hojo had used up their food supply, and, realizing they were significantly outnumbered by Hideyoshi's soldiers and samurai warriors, they surrendered.

Following this, the Hojo lands were bequeathed to Hideyoshi's top general, while the head of the Hojo clan, Ujinao, and his wife were exiled to Mount Koya. To make sure that the Hojo clan was completely decimated, Hideyoshi insisted on the suicide of Ujinao's father and uncle. Ujinao died of a disease the following year, and that, along with the deaths of the eldest males in his family, allowed Hideyoshi to effectively prevent the Hojo clan from ever regaining power. Thus, the biggest potential obstacle to Hideyoshi's rule was permanently removed and he was able to further solidify his control over much of Japan.

30. Q: Which of the following is correct about Hideyoshi's army?

   (a) It fought numerous battles against the Hojo at Odawara.
   (b) It used starvation to force the Hojo clan to surrender.
   (c) It contained a larger number of samurai than soldiers.
   (d) It split up the lands it conquered after the castle siege.

31. Q: What can be inferred from the passage?

   (a) Ujinao was spared from death because he betrayed his father and his uncle.
   (b) A family dispute prior to the siege contributed to the downfall of the Hojo clan.
   (c) Ujinao's relatives had plans to overthrow Hideyoshi so that they could take control.
   (d) Forced suicide was used as a means of securing Hideyoshi's control over the Hojo clan.

Questions 32-33

The Amazon rainforest is in danger of being completely destroyed. In Brazil alone, the need for additional farmland has led to nearly 150,000 square kilometers of rainforest being leveled over the last six years. Agricultural ventures such as cattle ranching and crop production may have jump-started the country's export industry, but they have also contributed significantly to the destruction of the rainforest. Landowners and farmers have cleared forested land in order to meet overseas demand for cattle, soybeans, and maize.

In addition to the loss of plant life, deforestation is putting pressure on the region's animal populations, as their habitats are being destroyed. With their numbers in decline, more Amazon species are now on the endangered list than ever before. The need for more farmland is also having a negative impact on humans. Native people are being driven out of their traditional homelands by large corporations and, at times, government officials. This dispersal puts native cultures in peril, since their languages and traditions are lost as indigenous communities are split up and assimilated into mainstream culture. Though the effects of deforestation are seen everywhere in the Amazon region, relatively little is being done to curb further losses.

32. Q: What is the best title for the passage?

(a) The Increase in Animal Populations Due to Rainforest Loss
(b) The Impact of Deforestation on Life in the Amazon Rainforest
(c) The Advantages of the Amazon for Brazil's Agricultural Industry
(d) The Rapid Disappearance of Rare Amazonian Plant Species

33. Q: Which of the following is correct about the Amazon rainforest?

(a) It is home to more endangered species than any other forest.
(b) Close to 150,000 square kilometers of it were destroyed last year.
(c) Global agricultural demand is a factor in its deforestation.
(d) It is being leveled to build homes for people moving to farms.

Questions 34-35

The Contemporary Crisis of Homelessness

By Tara Jones

I believe that homelessness in major urban areas urgently needs to be addressed. As housing costs continue to skyrocket, more and more people are being priced out of accommodation in many of the largest cities in the country, including New York, Los Angeles, and Chicago.

Take San Francisco, where the median rental cost is about 50 percent of average monthly income, as an example. Most people can't afford to pay that much, of course. Unsurprisingly, many homeless people in the city actually have jobs, but don't make enough money to pay for an apartment.

In order to increase the housing supply and lower prices, cities should ease building restrictions that limit the construction of new homes or apartments. Furthermore, working people should be given more assistance when requesting loans to purchase residences.

The most significant step the government could take, however, is to build cheaper housing for people with lower incomes. Rather than constructing more temporary homeless shelters that only serve to perpetuate the problem, building affordable homes would provide many homeless people with a way to get off the street. Even though the problem of homelessness might seem hopeless, it could be solved if politicians had the will to do so.

---

34. Q: Why are some people in San Francisco homeless?

(a) They are unable to find employment within the city center.
(b) Their incomes are insufficient to cover living expenses in the city.
(c) They are restricted from living in some locations by the government.
(d) They lost their homes during the recent financial downturn.

35. Q: What is NOT asserted by Tara Jones?

(a) The government should reduce the level of building regulations.
(b) More accommodations that low-wage earners can afford should be built.
(c) Help should be offered to those who want to borrow money.
(d) The authorities should construct more shelters for homeless people.

정답 p.352 / 해석 p.291

The Reading Comprehension section of the exam is complete. Please stay in your seat until the proctor tells you to leave. You are NOT allowed to open any of the other sections of the exam.

시험에 나올 문제를 미리 풀어보는
텝스 적중예상특강
해커스텝스 HackersTEPS.com

SELF-CHECK LIST

TEST 03은 잘 마치셨나요?
이제 다음의 SELF-CHECK LIST를 통해 자신의 테스트 진행 내용을 점검해 볼까요?

1. 나는 테스트를 마칠 때까지 완전히 테스트에 집중하였다.
   ☐ YES   ☐ NO

2. 나는 각 영역별 주어진 시간을 지켰다.
   ☐ LISTENING COMPREHENSION
   ☐ VOCABULARY & GRAMMAR   ☐ READING COMPREHENSION

3. 나는 시간 내에 모든 문제를 풀었다.
   ☐ LISTENING COMPREHENSION
   ☐ VOCABULARY & GRAMMAR   ☐ READING COMPREHENSION

4. 나는 특히 어렵게 느껴지는 영역이 있었다.
   ☐ LISTENING COMPREHENSION
   ☐ VOCABULARY & GRAMMAR   ☐ READING COMPREHENSION

5. 개선하고 싶은 사항
   _____
   _____
   _____
   _____
   _____

■ 개선해야 할 점은 반드시 다음 테스트에서 실천해야만 실력을 향상시킬 수 있습니다.
그리고 반드시 오답을 정리해서 같은 실수를 반복하지 않도록 유의하기 바랍니다.

해커스 템스 최신기출유형 실전모의고사 문제집

TEST 04

LISTENING COMPREHENSION
VOCABULARY & GRAMMAR
READING COMPREHENSION

테스트 전 확인사항

1. 휴대 전화의 전원을 끄셨나요?
2. OMR 답안지, 연필, 지우개가 준비되셨나요?
3. 시계가 준비되셨나요?
4. 목표 점수를 정하세요.
   LISTENING COMPREHENSION (____개 / 40개)
   VOCABULARY (____개 / 30개)
   GRAMMAR (____개 / 30개)
   READING COMPREHENSION (____개 / 35개)
5. 테스트의 시작과 종료 시간을 정하세요.
   LISTENING COMPREHENSION   ___시 ___분 ~ ___시 ___분 (40분)
   VOCABULARY & GRAMMAR   ___시 ___분 ~ ___시 ___분 (25분)
   READING COMPREHENSION   ___시 ___분 ~ ___시 ___분 (35분)

 TEST 04.mp3

실전용·복습용 문제풀이 MP3 무료 다운로드 및 스트리밍 바로듣기
(HackersIngang.com)

무료MP3 바로듣기

* 실제 시험장의 소음까지 재현해 낸 고사장 소음·매미 버전 MP3까지 구매하면 실전에 더욱 완벽히 대비할 수 있습니다.

Listening Comprehension

DIRECTIONS

1. In the Listening Comprehension Section, the content will be presented in oral rather than written form.
2. There are five parts in this section, and you will receive separate instructions for each. Listen to the instructions carefully, and choose the best answer for each question from the available options.

Part I Questions 1~10

You will now hear ten statements or questions, and each will be followed by four responses. Choose the most appropriate response.

Part II Questions 11~20

You will now hear ten conversation fragments, and each will be followed by four responses. Choose the most appropriate response.

Part III Questions 21~30

You will now hear ten complete conversations. Before each conversation, you will hear a short description of the situation. Then you will hear the conversation and its corresponding question, both of which will be read only once. Next, you will hear four options, which will also be read once. Choose the option that best answers the question.

Part IV Questions 31~36

You will now hear six monologues. For each item, you will hear a monologue and its corresponding question, both of which will be read twice. Then you will hear four options which will be read only once. Choose the option that best answers the question.

Part V Questions 37~40

You will now hear two longer monologues. For each item, you will hear a monologue and two corresponding questions, all of which will be read twice. Then you will hear four options for each question, which will be read only once. Choose the option that best answers each question.

Vocabulary & Grammar

DIRECTIONS

These two parts of the exam test your vocabulary and grammar skills. You will have a total of 25 minutes to answer 60 questions. There will be 30 from the Vocabulary section and 30 from the Grammar section. Make sure to follow the directions given by the proctor.

Part I Questions 1~10

Choose the best answer for the blank.

1. A: Careful! You nearly spilled wine on my dress!
   B: I'm sorry. I _____ my balance.
   (a) missed
   (b) wasted
   (c) lost
   (d) dropped

2. A: I've never seen a more _____ performer than Brandon.
   B: Yes, he's an actor, comedian, and singer all rolled into one.
   (a) resilient
   (b) contentious
   (c) versatile
   (d) malleable

3. A: I moved the weekly meetings to Fridays.
   B: No problem. That _____ me.
   (a) agrees
   (b) fits
   (c) solves
   (d) suits

4. A: I've been receiving so much junk mail lately.
   B: That can be irritating. Just _____ it.
   (a) release
   (b) ignore
   (c) desert
   (d) excuse

5. A: I hear your daughter's getting high grades.
   B: Yes. Hiring a personal tutor has _____.
   (a) filled in
   (b) made up
   (c) smoothed out
   (d) paid off

6. A: I heard Pam passed out due to heat exhaustion.
   B: Yeah, she was _____ for a minute.
   (a) incapable
   (b) inaccessible
   (c) unavailable
   (d) unconscious

7. A: Why do I have to get a flu shot?
   B: It will make you become _____ to the virus.
   (a) definite
   (b) immune
   (c) desperate
   (d) infectious

8. A: I hope the board approves our funding request for the project.
   B: I have some good news. They've already agreed to _____ it.
   (a) sustain
   (b) endorse
   (c) placate
   (d) rebuke

9. A: I found Helen's comment about Sally's clothes quite rude.
   B: It probably came out wrong. I'm sure she meant it to be _____.
   (a) blunt
   (b) corpulent
   (c) garrulous
   (d) innocuous

10. A: The problem with mileage cards is you're forced to fly with just one airline.
    B: Actually, you can _____ mileage when you use the airline's partner carriers.
    (a) accrue
    (b) assemble
    (c) integrate
    (d) consolidate

Part II Questions 11~30

Choose the best answer for the blank.

11. The alternatives the company is weighing to avoid filing bankruptcy will be _____ at the meeting.
    (a) arranged
    (b) composed
    (c) discussed
    (d) managed

12. The hotel has launched a new _____ in an effort to boost its occupancy rate.
    (a) promotion
    (b) market
    (c) stock
    (d) turnover

13. Management at headquarters hired a consultant to _____ potential problems at the new branch.
    (a) transport
    (b) pinpoint
    (c) detach
    (d) pronounce

14. Dr. Richland received _____ for his medical research from several private organizations.
    (a) interest
    (b) profits
    (c) funding
    (d) access

15. Mercury thermometers should be _____ because they taint water sources when improperly disposed of.
    (a) banned
    (b) sealed
    (c) dismissed
    (d) discharged

16. The president reads major newspapers and magazines to keep _____ of social, political, and economic issues.
    (a) deviant
    (b) intimate
    (c) consummate
    (d) abreast

17. Members are requested to _____ financially to support the organization's ongoing projects.
    (a) convey
    (b) distribute
    (c) transmit
    (d) contribute

18. This company _____ diversity and employs individuals regardless of their ethnicity, gender, or sexual identity.
    (a) prohibits
    (b) overpowers
    (c) confronts
    (d) embraces

19. Because society has become more politically correct, many words once used to refer to minorities are now considered _____.
    (a) reverberant
    (b) pejorative
    (c) garrulous
    (d) impractical

20. People who have trouble relating to others and are alienated from society as a whole tend to _____ from social contact.
    (a) defend
    (b) withdraw
    (c) distract
    (d) suspend

21. The suspect claims that he was _____ by the police into admitting that he stole the vehicle.

    (a) devastated
    (b) immured
    (c) coerced
    (d) ousted

22. When ready to give birth, pregnant women may request a local _____ to ease the pain.

    (a) anesthetic
    (b) euthanasia
    (c) autopsy
    (d) panacea

23. For centuries, astronomers have _____ the existence of life forms on other planets.

    (a) generated
    (b) waived
    (c) accorded
    (d) contemplated

24. In Norse _____, the Valkyries were maidens sent by the god Odin to choose the bravest warriors among those who had died.

    (a) lore
    (b) aphorism
    (c) vernacular
    (d) axiom

25. More than 70,000 people _____ at the Pyeong Chang Olympic Stadium in Korea during the 2013 Special Olympics.

    (a) configurated
    (b) conglobated
    (c) convoluted
    (d) congregated

26. A parent should not pay too much attention when a child _____ because it only reinforces the negative behavior.

    (a) ebbs and flows
    (b) throws a tantrum
    (c) cuts to the chase
    (d) sits on the fence

27. The diplomat used his negotiating skills to _____ officials into releasing the backpackers who had crossed a borderline.

    (a) finesse
    (b) assuage
    (c) beleaguer
    (d) pacify

28. After the final confrontation at the end of the novel, the fate of the characters was revealed in the _____.

    (a) ellipsis
    (b) excerpt
    (c) denouement
    (d) anecdote

29. The boxer's victory was _____ when allegations that he had taken prohibited drugs before the fight were confirmed.

    (a) recouped
    (b) rescinded
    (c) recanted
    (d) rectified

30. Many innocent civilians were arrested and _____ for the duration of the war.

    (a) incarcerated
    (b) repatriated
    (c) obliterated
    (d) coagulated

The Vocabulary section is complete. Please move on to the Grammar section.

Part I Questions 1~10

Choose the best answer for the blank.

1. A: Did you read Todd Farmer's new mystery novel?
   B: Yes, but it fell so _____ below my expectations.
   (a) right
   (b) far
   (c) much
   (d) very

2. A: Where's Jennifer? She's supposed to lead today's rally.
   B: That's not good. Most of the attendees _____ on her.
   (a) are really relying
   (b) are really being relied
   (c) had really been relying
   (d) has really been relied

3. A: How's your report coming along?
   B: I don't think I can meet the deadline at this pace, so I am going to need _____ from you.
   (a) assistance
   (b) assistances
   (c) an assistance
   (d) the assistances

4. A: Did you see Mandy's presentation this morning?
   B: No, I had a meeting. I really regret _____ it.
   (a) miss
   (b) to miss
   (c) having missed
   (d) to have missed

5. A: Isn't Joe running a business with _____?
   B: Yes. He and Mark co-own a restaurant.
   (a) that friend of his old
   (b) that old friend of his
   (c) his friend of that old
   (d) his old friend of that

6. A: How do you think your interview went?
   B: It was OK, but I wasn't sure _____ to say when asked about my future prospects.
   (a) how
   (b) what
   (c) when
   (d) which

7. A: It's too expensive to buy new furniture.
   B: I saw some _____ couches on the street that seemed to be in good condition.
   (a) to discard
   (b) discarding
   (c) discarded
   (d) discard

8. A: Do we need to prepare anything for the first aid course?
   B: No, the instructor is supposed to provide all of _____ we'll need.
   (a) equipment
   (b) equipments
   (c) an equipment
   (d) the equipment

9. A: How did you get onto the dance squad?
   B: Apparently, they spotted me _____ at a local competition.
   (a) break-dance
   (b) break-dancing
   (c) having break-danced
   (d) doing break-dance

10. A: The students have worked hard on this project.
    B: Yes, _____ it their best.
    (a) plain seeing they're given to have seen it's plain
    (b) they're plain to see to have given
    (c) seeing them it's plain having given
    (d) it's plain to see they've given

Part II Questions 11~25

Choose the best answer for the blank.

11. Before starting his new job, Jeremy signed a non-disclosure agreement stipulating that he _____ certain information confidential.

    (a) keep
    (b) keeps
    (c) kept
    (d) be kept

12. Analysts predict that between the two juices, consumers will prefer _____ has more health benefits.

    (a) which
    (b) that
    (c) whomever
    (d) whichever

13. Mike Sullivan is broadcasting live on the hurricane sweeping the east coast and _____ doing so for the past few hours.

    (a) is
    (b) was
    (c) has been
    (d) had been

14. An increased quantity _____ carbohydrates in one's diet may lead to negative health effects.

    (a) of
    (b) for
    (c) within
    (d) among

15. Because they _____ the championship game, the team will surely be in a gloomy mood today.

    (a) didn't win
    (b) had not won
    (c) haven't been winning
    (d) have not been won

16. The marketing team realized that their attempt _____ customers with discounts was a bad idea.

    (a) lure
    (b) lured
    (c) to lure
    (d) luring

17. To stay more alert, people who spend the day in front of a computer monitor _____ get at least seven hours of sleep per night.

    (a) will
    (b) might
    (c) should
    (d) would

18. A steady trend of rising ocean acidity levels _____ by numerous professionals in the field.

    (a) are noted
    (b) will be noted
    (c) has been noted
    (d) will have been noted

19. The writers finished the article, _____ not up until five minutes before the deadline.

    (a) as
    (b) but
    (c) nor
    (d) any

20. The CTG Electric Corporation will conduct monthly inspections of its plants, _____ to state safety regulations.

    (a) conforms
    (b) conformed
    (c) it conformed
    (d) conforming

21. Although not technically a partner in the firm, Roger Habbs has long been acknowledged as _____ due to his generous donations.

    (a) it
    (b) him
    (c) this
    (d) one

22. Illegal _____, people still do it when in a hurry.

    (a) it is on sidewalks parking may be
    (b) may be as parking on sidewalks
    (c) as parking on sidewalks may be
    (d) parking may be on sidewalks

23. As a new recruit on the St. Louis police force, Henry encountered a little more danger than _____ expected in his line of work.

    (a) was to be
    (b) has been
    (c) were to be
    (d) have been

24. In order to succeed _____, today's leading corporations need to distinguish themselves from their competitors through effective advertising.

    (a) an increasing in competitive market
    (b) in an increasingly competitive market
    (c) an increasingly a competitive market
    (d) in a market in competitive increase

25. Four zoologists in New Zealand have located the nest of a rare species of insect they _____ for since first observing the insect months ago.

    (a) look
    (b) was looking
    (c) has looked
    (d) had been looking

Part III Questions 26~30

Identify the option that contains an awkward expression or an error in grammar.

26. (a) A: Would you call the store to follow up on our order?
    (b) B: I already did. They promised to deliver the supplies for a short while.
    (c) A: What's been taking them so long? The supplies should have arrived hours ago.
    (d) B: Well, they thought the delivery was actually scheduled for tomorrow.

27. (a) A: Hey, Jackson. Did you hear about the outreach program that our university is offering this summer?
    (b) B: Yes, I heard it's in Cambodia. Because of safety issues, there aren't as many volunteers as expected.
    (c) A: I also think finding applicants who are willing to give up their holidays are not easy.
    (d) B: I agree. That's actually one reason I'm hesitant about signing up.

28. (a) Antelopes are grazing mammals with slender limbs, small cloven hooves, and pointed hollow horns. (b) These graceful animals comprise 90 species, in which the majority can be found in Africa. (c) Because antelopes look like deer, many people might think the two are very closely related. (d) However, antelopes belong to the family Bovidae and not Cervidae, to which deer belong.

29. (a) Astronomers are delighted that the *Philae Lander*, a European space probe, has begun transmitting information back to Earth. (b) The probe landed on a comet but ran out of power in November 2014. (c) To function again after environmental conditions on the comet changed, the probe started sending data packets on June 13, 2015. (d) It is hoped that scientists will be able to recover all of the stored data that has accumulated in the probe.

30. (a) Of late, 3-D technology has seen a resurgence among electronics companies, particularly those centered around the entertainment industry. (b) Specialists in film, TV, and more are harnessing the technology to provide new and innovative means of experiencing visual media. (c) When people were surveyed about what features are expected entertainment to provide in the future, most chose greater immersion. (d) As a result, companies are striving to take audiences to that future by utilizing 3-D technology to offer more stimuli.

정답 p.353 / 해석 p.307

The Vocabulary and Grammar sections are complete. Do NOT start the Reading Comprehension section until instructed to do so. You are NOT allowed to open any of the other sections of the exam.

Reading Comprehension

DIRECTIONS

This part of the exam tests your ability to understand reading passages. There will be 35 questions in 40 minutes. Make sure to follow the proctor's instructions.

Part I Questions 1~10

Read the passage. Then choose the option that best completes the passage.

1. Researchers have always known that basking sharks seasonally varied the depth at which they dwelled. What puzzled experts, though, was some of the sharks' complete disappearance during winter. Determined to know more, marine biologists monitored several sharks using hi-tech tracking devices. The study showed that most of the sharks migrated to the tropical waters near South America. The researchers believe the findings could help determine why basking sharks _____.

   (a) decide to migrate periodically
   (b) avoid warmer tropical waters
   (c) are not detected by tracking devices
   (d) stay near the ocean's surface

2. When driving in extreme weather conditions, it's crucial that you adhere to traffic laws. Inclement weather understandably makes you want to get to your destination expediently, but excessive haste will multiply the probability of an accident, especially on slick roads or if visibility is compromised due to fog. Responsible drivers should remain composed in inclement weather and abstain from taking unnecessary risks. Therefore, make an effort to _____.

   (a) avoid driving in severe weather
   (b) exercise caution by observing speed limits
   (c) seek out skidproof roads
   (d) ensure the safety of passengers

3. The heiress to the fortune of Charles and Ray Eames, the iconic American furniture designers, has halted an auction of their work. The dispute stems from the Eames' relationship with Marilyn and John Neuhart, who the Eames entrusted with much of their collection while alive. Lucia Eames, a granddaughter and executor of the Eames' estate, feels the Neuharts have no right to permanent possession of the property and are taking advantage of their relationship with the designers. The Neuharts disagree with the insinuation that _____, and have stated their willingness to bequeath the art to a museum.

   (a) they are unfairly trying to capitalize off of the Eames
   (b) Charles and Ray Eames disapproved of their decision
   (c) Lucia Eames originally owned the property in question
   (d) they should sell their collection to the Eames' family

4. For decades, medical professionals have contended that people who smoke are more likely to pass away at a young age because of the detrimental effects of tobacco. The case of the Italian city of Milan is surprising in that the city _____. In fact, 130,000 of the two million residents of Milan are aged 75 and above. When taken into consideration that a large proportion of Milanese are tobacco users, the city's large geriatric population is particularly astounding.

(a) has a plethora of young nonsmokers
(b) encourages its senior citizens to quit smoking
(c) seems to contradict this supposition
(d) has a considerable proportion of smokers

5.
Dear Diego,

I can't stop singing the praises of _____. The cutting-edge experiments I and Dr. Anand, my adviser, are conducting could have a substantial impact on molecular biology. Although I work 60-hour weeks as a mere apprentice and only receive a small stipend, the passion I feel for our research makes it worthwhile. I am currently editing a journal article under both our names for submission to a major journal. In fact, I must quit procrastinating and get back to typing. Take care!

Love,
Dora

(a) my academic research internship
(b) life as a university biology professor
(c) the apprentices on my research team
(d) the scientific journal I currently work for

6. As the personnel director for a medium-sized advertising company, I lament the demise of the liberal arts in universities. Subjects like philosophy, history, and logic are very necessary in developing the skills I look for in prospective employees. Critical reasoning ability is paramount in any sort of office milieu, not to mention the clarity and concision with which students studying these subjects are forced to present their ideas in written form. These days, students can breeze through four years of an undergraduate program _____.

   (a) studying subjects necessary for business
   (b) while remaining unprepared for collaboration
   (c) overwhelmed by liberal arts courses
   (d) without developing sufficient intellectual rigor

7. Despite a decrease in overall net profit, Perfect Palette _____.
   Sales statistics tabulated by the Department of Investment and Trade showed Perfect Palette ahead of the pack, accounting for 45 percent of all house paints purchased last year. Industry insiders credited the company's masterful marketing techniques and the product's enhanced durability for Perfect Palette's robust sales. Former top seller Pigments Inc. has been relegated to the second spot this year, comprising a mere 25 percent share of the market.

   (a) has doubled its overall production
   (b) has earned record revenue for shareholders
   (c) has reached the pinnacle of its market segment
   (d) has released environmentally safe paints

8. *The Hitchhiker's Guide to the Galaxy* TV series originally aired in 1981—three years prior to the advent of the first Internet service providers, or ISPs. At the time of the show's inception, the Internet _____. The Hitchhiker's show, which featured an "electronic book" that conveyed information on any subject, presaged today's ubiquitous wireless Internet-enabled laptops. Using a home PC to access multimedia content on a remote server finally became feasible with the creation of the Web browser in the early 1990s, but a decade would elapse before the Internet adoption rate among consumers became commercially significant.

   (a) had started to commandeer market share
   (b) was first emerging as an entertainment medium
   (c) had yet to penetrate the public consciousness
   (d) was freely accessible to those with computer literacy

9. State legislator Yuri Yusuf has been formally arraigned on bribery charges by the Anti-Corruption Task Force and, if found guilty, could face 15 to 20 years in prison. He allegedly received $90,000 from businessman Gerry Reno in a transaction caught on tape by a surveillance team during a money laundering investigation. The prosecutor filed charges exactly a week after the evidence was captured. _____, a witness has submitted a declaration stating that Yusuf accepted "cash gifts" on several other occasions.

(a) Granted
(b) Consequently
(c) Nonetheless
(d) Furthermore

10. Contrasting sensory elements can complement the dramatic impression of a movie scene. In *The Godfather*, for example, the sound abruptly drops out at the moment the lead character cries out in anguish over his daughter's demise. The absence of sound evokes the enormity of the character's grief and symbolizes his isolation, creating a poignant representation of this distraught individual. _____, the scene acquires a depth that intensifies its effect on viewers.

(a) Accordingly
(b) For instance
(c) On the contrary
(d) Alternatively

Part II Questions 11~12

Read the passage. Then identify the option that does NOT belong.

11. The "Golden Age" of the American film industry lasted from 1927 to the late 1950s, with several cinematic milestones having been achieved during the period. (a) The first "talking" film, *The Jazz Singer*, was released in 1927, ending the era of silent movies. (b) Film studios created several silent films after 1927, but this genre of movie was eventually phased out. (c) *Snow White and the Seven Dwarfs* became the first animated film when it was created in 1937. (d) Two years later saw the release of *Gone with the Wind*, the highest-grossing film in history when earnings are adjusted for inflation.

12. The concept of a "success story" usually applies to disadvantaged people who achieve financial success through sheer determination. (a) However, the role of luck is something we cannot understate when it comes to achievement. (b) History is replete with examples of those who, lacking good fortune, remained mired in poverty despite their determination. (c) Faith in a bright future is lacking among the impoverished, who perceive far less of a chance than others to advance their social standing. (d) Hence, as most daily wage earners can attest, a mix of providence and determination is indispensable in becoming successful.

Part III Questions 13~25

Read the passage and the question. Then choose the option that best answers the question.

13.
> **No Time to Shop? Try Robertson's VIP Service!**
>
> Robertson's VIP Service will make your life easier and free up your time.
>
> Simply:
> 1. Visit our location at Pinehill Mall.
> 2. Drop your grocery list off at our customer service counter.
> 3. Wait for a text message letting you know your groceries are ready to be picked up and paid for.
>
> Why waste time searching for items and waiting in the checkout line when you can have everything done for you? To learn more about this service, visit Robertson today!

Q: What is mainly being advertised?

(a) A shop's automated checkout counter
(b) A special discount for VIP customers
(c) A mall's package delivery service
(d) A store's assisted shopping system

14. Popular novels will be auctioned off next month at the Comenius University library. The event is being spearheaded by university alumnus Ivan Tomka, who is the current president of the National Book Club. Proceeds from this fundraising activity will be allocated to the ongoing refurbishment of the library. For more information on how to participate in the auction, please visit the university information center at Moritz Hall or log on to www.nbclub.com.sk.

Q: What is the main topic of the passage?

(a) The opening of a new library at an educational institute
(b) The establishment of a literacy program by a university graduate
(c) An effort to raise money for the renovation of a facility
(d) An activity to promote a recent publication by an academic

15. In a race like the 100-meter dash, several key elements affect finishing times. To run most efficiently, an ideal stride length must be achieved, which a coach can determine with an analysis of a runner's physique. Additionally, to maintain maximal speed, runners must keep their upper bodies perpendicular to the track and pump their arms in rhythm with their strides. Finally, a quick reaction to the starting gun is critical to exploding from the blocks ahead of the other competitors.

Q: What is the main topic of the passage?

(a) What body types are best for running
(b) What techniques runners use to start quickly
(c) How sprinters can achieve a peak performance
(d) How coaches analyze a runner's stride

16.
Wonders of the Stars

At City Planetarium, our primary goal is to educate the public about the wonders of astronomy. The planetarium's hemispheric domed ceiling is used as a screen onto which images of stars, planets, and other celestial objects are projected. The planetarium uses the latest top-of-the-line digital projector system equipped with fish-eye lenses and laser projection devices, so images are crystal clear. Daily sky shows commence at one and end at four in the afternoon. They will surely fascinate children and adults alike.

For more details about our sky show, please visit our website at www.cityplanetarium.org.

Q: What is the passage mainly about?

(a) City Planetarium's schedule of upcoming events
(b) Planned upgrades to City Planetarium's equipment
(c) Various educational activities for children at City Planetarium
(d) The facilities and services available at City Planetarium

17.

Dear Mr. Gordon,

The Smock Institute of Fashion Design will be holding a fashion show to exhibit the innovative creations of its students. The event will be held at the institute's auditorium on Thursday, July 23, at five o'clock in the afternoon. This year, we thought it would be beneficial to invite some of the institute's graduates to critique the designs being exhibited, and the committee would like you to serve as one of the critics. We hope that you can oblige and help our students hone their craft.

Truly yours,
Robin Jackson

Q: Which of the following is correct about the fashion show according to the invitation?

(a) It will showcase the work of the institute's graduates.
(b) It is attempting to bring alumni and students together.
(c) It will exhibit the outstanding creations of Mr. Gordon.
(d) Its main objective is connecting students with career opportunities.

18. From the 1970s until the 1990s, most computer data was stored on floppy disks. The floppy disk was invented by IBM in 1967 and made available to the public in 1971. It remained the most advanced portable storage medium until the optical disk was introduced in the 1980s. As laser technology was utilized to encode information on an optical disk, it could store hundreds or thousands of times the amount of data a floppy disk could. Optical disk technology formed the backbone of inventions like the CD and recordable DVD, making it an important step in the advancement of technology.

Q: What happened in 1971?

(a) IBM began developing a revolutionary new computer system.
(b) A portable storage device became widely purchasable.
(c) Optical disks began to be used for recording data.
(d) The floppy disk was replaced by superior technology.

19. American filmmakers in the 1940s invented a movie genre that would eventually earn the appellation of "film noir." The films of this genre are characterized by the use of high-contrast lighting and flashbacks recounted by omniscient narrators. The heroes of film noir movies are morally ambiguous and cynical about the actions of the people around them. Today, six decades after the introduction of the genre, the popularity of film noir has yet to completely wane. Many recent movies have incorporated film noir techniques, in particular period pieces that evoke an earlier decade.

Q: Which of the following is correct about film noir according to the passage?

(a) It is distinguishable by its tightly chronological storylines.
(b) It is typified by a narrator who brings past events to light.
(c) It fell out of favor due to its morally off-putting heroes.
(d) It is not a common style among modern film directors.

20. A recent study revealed that the Internet aids teenagers in developing social and technical skills, disputing the common belief of parents that the Internet is a detriment to their children. The researchers questioned over 800 teens and their parents and spent over 1,000 hours observing young people on social networking sites, documenting their Web surfing habits. They found that young people enhance their social skills and take in new information while online. Still, many parents contend that the Internet is dangerous and that it detracts from academic performance.

Q: Which of the following is correct according to the passage?

(a) Over 1,000 teens and their parents were interviewed for the study.
(b) Many parents think that the Internet helps their children's development.
(c) The researchers interviewed teenagers about their online activities.
(d) Young people acquire unhealthy social habits from online activities.

21.

> **Enjoy French Cuisine in Jackson's Bistro**
>
> A mainstay of Boston's historic Bay Village district, Jackson's Bistro is launching a full-scale celebration of French food.
>
> For two weeks, the beloved local restaurant will serve a menu of French delicacies, thoughtfully paired with wines from a variety of regions across France and expertly crafted by visiting guest Chef Jacques Papillon.
>
> At the vanguard of contemporary French cuisine for over a decade, Chef Papillon boasts an impressive résumé of stints at five-star hotels. Jackson's couldn't be more thrilled to have him take over the kitchen for this highly anticipated event.

Q: Which of the following is correct according to the passage?

(a) A restaurant is holding a promotion with a high-profile French chef.
(b) Chef Papillon is opening a new bistro in Boston's historic district.
(c) Jackson's Bistro will reopen its doors for a limited time.
(d) Chef Papillon was at the vanguard of French cuisine for a short time.

22. Bugs Bunny, a character created in 1938, remains a staple of popular weekend cartoon shows. He was created the same year Adolf Hitler began his attempt at conquering Europe. Bugs' popularity soared during World War II and he was portrayed in cartoons battling Hitler, Benito Mussolini, and other villains and scapegoats of the time. After the war, a new generation of converts was wowed by Bugs, who started appearing not only in short films, but also in full-length features. Today, seven decades after his creation, Bugs still captivates children and adults alike.

Q: Which of the following is correct about Bugs Bunny according to the passage?

(a) His popularity waned temporarily during World War II.
(b) His cartoons are still appreciated by modern audiences.
(c) He reached the zenith of his popularity on TV in 1938.
(d) He was created after the war had reached an end.

23. By the end of World War II, trepidation had increased regarding the potential harm of Soviet Russia's political intentions to American interests. As a result, America launched a program to decode Soviet intelligence messages, which eventually led to the discovery that Russia was trying to obtain information about America's nuclear program. Among the suspected spies for Russia were Julius and Ethel Rosenberg, a Jewish couple living in New York City. Although Ethel's participation was minimal, and lethal punishment was a severe reprisal, both were convicted of espionage and executed.

Q: What can be inferred from the passage?

(a) Jewish Americans were sympathetic towards Soviet Russia.
(b) Ethel Rosenberg's death sentence was unwarranted.
(c) The US military prevented Russians from receiving information.
(d) Russia never found out about the United States' nuclear weapons.

24. No longer a lone rogue working for mere bragging rights, the modern hacker is of a far different breed than what most people envision. Today's hackers belong to a complex and intricate criminal ecosystem, working in tandem with each other to exploit vulnerabilities in software. Moreover, those responsible for thwarting hacks are finding it increasingly perplexing to identify malicious invasions by these masterminds. Since these gatekeepers are only capable of detecting attack strategies they are familiar with, new and innovative tactics are nearly impossible to discern before it's too late.

Q: Which statement would the writer most likely agree with?

(a) Staying ahead of hacking attempts is relatively straightforward.
(b) Hacking invasions are obvious while they are being executed.
(c) Contemporary hackers tend to be isolated and aimless individuals.
(d) The public is at greater risk due to the evolving sophistication of hackers.

25.

Health & Medical News

Mosquito Warning

Because mosquitos act as carriers for diseases that can become terminal, public health officials must be conscientious of their capacity to spread disease. These nuisance creatures can transmit parasites between humans through contact with their blood by way of a mosquito's syringe-like appendage. These insects are usually found in tropical and subtropical regions because they are incapable of regulating their internal temperature. As a consequence, mosquito-borne diseases have traditionally plagued the tropics, but the veracity of this statement may soon come into question as some tropical species of mosquito have genetically adapted to temperate climates.

Q: What can be inferred from the passage?

(a) Most ailments caused by mosquitoes lead to death.
(b) Mosquito populations have grown due to genetic adaptation.
(c) Global climate changes have allowed mosquitoes to resist cold.
(d) Tropical diseases may appear outside of tropical countries.

Part IV Questions 26~35

Read the passage and the questions. Then choose the option that best answers each question.

Questions 26-27

> **Full-Time Position Available:**
>
> The Recovery Road Foundation is searching for an executive fund-raiser. Our organization was founded in 1984 by Sam Jackson to teach disabled people skills that can help them earn a living. Many of Recovery Road's beneficiaries have launched successful businesses. By selling various crafts, they have managed to attain a degree of financial independence.
>
> - The successful applicant will solicit support from individuals as well as companies.
> - The duties will include organizing fund-raising events, attending meetings with current and potential sponsors, and managing a promotional team at our head office. Establishing and maintaining a network of donors is also a vital part of the role.
>   *The funds raised will be used to hire teachers, purchase craft supplies and equipment for our classes, and cover operating expenses.
> - Experience with digital marketing is needed. Related tasks will include managing our social networking sites.
> - Those who have held a similar position with a charity or NGO are preferred, and all applicants must have a master's degree in a relevant field.

26. Q: What was the intent of the founder of the Recovery Road Foundation?

   (a) He wanted to encourage corporate executives to give classes about financial independence.
   (b) He wanted to teach disabled people things they can use to support themselves.
   (c) He wanted to set up a market for crafts made in the local community.
   (d) He wanted to develop a social networking site for digital marketers.

27. Q: What can be inferred from the passage?

   (a) The successful candidate will serve on a voluntary basis.
   (b) Beneficiaries are given grants to start a small business.
   (c) The foundation makes use of the Internet as a promotional tool.
   (d) Events are held to celebrate the conclusion of training sessions.

Questions 28-29

Animal World

Things You Never Knew About Reindeer

Among the many ways that reindeer have adapted for survival in the Arctic, one of the most unique is the seasonal change that occurs in their eyes. Because reindeer live at high latitudes, they are exposed to great variations in light levels. In the summer, daylight shines uninterruptedly for weeks; however, in the frigid winters, the sun never rises, so they must cope with darkness for a long period. In response to the lack of light, reindeer's eyes actually grow more sensitive in the winter. Though their vision does not become especially precise, they are able to see more of what is going on around them. This helps them flee from predators.

Interestingly, the change that allows a reindeer's vision to remain acute year round is related to the hue of the eye. A part of their eyeballs is golden in the summer, but it becomes dark blue in the winter. Consequently, less light is reflected from the retina and more information about the animal's surroundings is captured. The change from gold to blue is linked to the pressure that occurs when the eye dilates to allow in the maximum amount of light over an extended period. This pressure squeezes the tissue behind the retina, allowing a reindeer's eye to better reflect the shorter wavelengths of blue light in the Arctic winter.

28. Q: Which of the following is correct according to the passage?

(a) Reindeer migrate to higher latitudes during the warmer part of the year.
(b) Places located at high latitude experience seasonal variations in sunlight.
(c) Behavioral changes help species in the Arctic avoid dangerous weather.
(d) A lack of light causes some animals' vision to deteriorate.

29. Q: What is mainly discussed in the second paragraph?

(a) The colors that allow reindeer to mask their presence from predators
(b) The longer wavelength of the blue light during the Arctic winter
(c) The way in which light reflects through the reindeer's retina
(d) The color shift that allows the reindeer's sight to adjust

Questions 30-31

Martha [2:30 p.m.]

Hi, Raymond.
How have you been? I didn't see you at the writing class last weekend. I'm not sure if you heard the news yet, but the submission date of our university's poetry contest has changed. If anyone in our poetry club wishes to participate, they must submit their entries prior to September 28, not October 1. The poetry committee of professors will review the submissions, and the winners will be announced on October 7. There will also be a poetry reading event to celebrate the winners on that day.

Raymond [2:51 p.m.]

Hello, Martha.
I'm doing well, thanks. I was in Oahu Island visiting my grandmother last week. I was supposed to get back to town last weekend and attend the class, but there were no flights because of an unexpected typhoon. Anyway, thanks for letting me know about the date change. I will tell everyone in our group about it when we have our next poetry club meeting on September 17. Many of our members plan on entering the competition. Actually, I plan on making a submission too.

30. Q: When will the poetry reading be held?

   (a) September 17
   (b) September 28
   (c) October 1
   (d) October 7

31. Q: Why did Raymond not attend the writing class?

   (a) He was visiting his friends out of the town for the weekend.
   (b) He was delayed due to a sudden change in the weather.
   (c) He had a meeting with his classmates about a poetry competition.
   (d) He was writing poems for publication in a university newspaper.

Questions 32-33

The age at which children start formal schooling differs around the world, ranging from five in the United Kingdom to eight in Norway. Studies of the benefits of starting school later have been largely inconclusive, but new research suggests that it has a positive behavioral impact. Researchers at Stanford University surveyed children from Denmark and found that those who started compulsory education a year later had much better levels of self-control, implying that spending time in an unstructured environment plays an important role in the development of children's mental health.

In the study, researchers tracked the progress of two groups of children from the age of six. One group went into formal schooling, and the other was sent to a day care center for a year, where they were encouraged to express themselves in unrestricted play. By the age of 11, the latter group displayed a significantly lower rate of inattention and hyperactivity than the former group. Moreover, these children developed a level of maturity that helped them control their impulses and focus once they entered a classroom environment. The researchers believe that over the long-term school entry age could be related to the ability to ignore distractions later in life.

32. Q: What is the passage mainly about?

(a) The characteristics of impulse displayed by Danish students
(b) The academic benefits of starting school at a young age
(c) The influence that a later start to formal education has on conduct
(d) The effects that compulsory education can have on lifelong learning

33. Q: What can be inferred from the passage?

(a) Children are less hyperactive if they engage in more uncontrolled play.
(b) Students who received their schooling at home quickly adapt to university life.
(c) Kindergarteners tend to distract each other during educational sessions.
(d) Children that start school sooner have fewer problems with their attention span.

Questions 34-35

The Accidental Hero: Alexander Fleming

Sir Alexander Fleming, the famed Scottish scientist and recipient of a Nobel Prize in 1945, was a lowly London shipping clerk before being a doctor of biology. He eventually became a professor at St. Mary's Hospital Medical School and then served in the Royal Army Medical Corps during World War I, working as a bacteriologist. He studied the wounds of soldiers and found that the antiseptics being prescribed to fight infections were actually more harmful than curative.

Following the war, he became the head of the inoculation department at St. Mary's. It was there that he had his first research success, which was discovering lysozyme, a mild antiseptic produced by the body.

But probably the most widely recognized of Fleming's many contributions to medicine, and the reason he gained worldwide recognition, was the discovery of penicillin. This natural extraction is a potent antibiotic that can be used to fight off a vast variety of infections. Since Fleming stumbled upon penicillin in 1928, we have used it to treat diseases like syphilis, meningitis, and pneumonia. Nowadays, antibiotics have become one of the most frequently administered forms of medicine throughout the world.

34. Q: Which of the following is correct about Sir Alexander Fleming according to the passage?

   (a) He moonlighted as a shipping clerk in London while he was a professor at St. Mary's.
   (b) He became head of the biology department at St. Mary's following World War I.
   (c) He achieved international acclaim for his discovery of the antibiotic properties of penicillin.
   (d) He cured a range of diseases with a potent, naturally occurring antiseptic called lysozyme.

35. Q: What is the main purpose of the passage?

   (a) To introduce the anecdotes of a war hero who saved millions of lives
   (b) To point out the problems created by overusing penicillin
   (c) To contrast traditional and modern medical treatments for infections
   (d) To describe the career of a historic figure in medicine

정답 p.353 / 해석 p.308

The Reading Comprehension section of the exam is complete. Please stay in your seat until the proctor tells you to leave. You are NOT allowed to open any of the other sections of the exam.

시험에 나올 문제를 미리 풀어보는
텝스 적중예상특강
해커스텝스 HackersTEPS.com

SELF-CHECK LIST

TEST 04는 잘 마치셨나요?
이제 다음의 SELF-CHECK LIST를 통해 자신의 테스트 진행 내용을 점검해 볼까요?

1. 나는 테스트를 마칠 때까지 완전히 테스트에 집중하였다.
   ☐ YES   ☐ NO

2. 나는 각 영역별 주어진 시간을 지켰다.
   ☐ LISTENING COMPREHENSION
   ☐ VOCABULARY & GRAMMAR   ☐ READING COMPREHENSION

3. 나는 시간 내에 모든 문제를 풀었다.
   ☐ LISTENING COMPREHENSION
   ☐ VOCABULARY & GRAMMAR   ☐ READING COMPREHENSION

4. 나는 특히 어렵게 느껴지는 영역이 있었다.
   ☐ LISTENING COMPREHENSION
   ☐ VOCABULARY & GRAMMAR   ☐ READING COMPREHENSION

5. 개선하고 싶은 사항
   _____
   _____
   _____
   _____
   _____

■ 개선해야 할 점은 반드시 다음 테스트에서 실천해야만 실력을 향상시킬 수 있습니다.
그리고 반드시 오답을 정리해서 같은 실수를 반복하지 않도록 유의하기 바랍니다.

해커스 텝스 최신기출유형 실전모의고사 문제집

TEST 05

LISTENING COMPREHENSION
VOCABULARY & GRAMMAR
READING COMPREHENSION

테스트 전 확인사항

1. 휴대 전화의 전원을 끄셨나요?
2. OMR 답안지, 연필, 지우개가 준비되셨나요?
3. 시계가 준비되셨나요?
4. 목표 점수를 정하세요.
   LISTENING COMPREHENSION (____개 / 40개)
   VOCABULARY (____개 / 30개)
   GRAMMAR (____개 / 30개)
   READING COMPREHENSION (____개 / 35개)
5. 테스트의 시작과 종료 시간을 정하세요.
   LISTENING COMPREHENSION ___시 ___분 ~ ___시 ___분 (40분)
   VOCABULARY & GRAMMAR ___시 ___분 ~ ___시 ___분 (25분)
   READING COMPREHENSION ___시 ___분 ~ ___시 ___분 (35분)

🎧 TEST 05.mp3
실전용·복습용 문제풀이 MP3 무료 다운로드 및 스트리밍 바로듣기
(HackersIngang.com)
* 실제 시험장의 소음까지 재현해 낸 고사장 소음·매미 버전 MP3까지 구매하면 실전에 더욱 완벽히 대비할 수 있습니다.

무료MP3 바로듣기

Listening
Comprehension

DIRECTIONS

1. In the Listening Comprehension Section, the content will be presented in oral rather than written form.
2. There are five parts in this section, and you will receive separate instructions for each. Listen to the instructions carefully, and choose the best answer for each question from the available options.

Part I Questions 1~10

You will now hear ten statements or questions, and each will be followed by four responses. Choose the most appropriate response.

Part II Questions 11~20

You will now hear ten conversation fragments, and each will be followed by four responses. Choose the most appropriate response.

Part III Questions 21~30

You will now hear ten complete conversations. Before each conversation, you will hear a short description of the situation. Then you will hear the conversation and its corresponding question, both of which will be read only once. Next, you will hear four options, which will also be read once. Choose the option that best answers the question.

Part IV Questions 31~36

You will now hear six monologues. For each item, you will hear a monologue and its corresponding question, both of which will be read twice. Then you will hear four options which will be read only once. Choose the option that best answers the question.

Part V **Questions 37~40**

You will now hear two longer monologues. For each item, you will hear a monologue and two corresponding questions, all of which will be read twice. Then you will hear four options for each question, which will be read only once. Choose the option that best answers each question.

Vocabulary & Grammar

DIRECTIONS

These two parts of the exam test your vocabulary and grammar skills. You will have a total of 25 minutes to answer 60 questions. There will be 30 from the Vocabulary section and 30 from the Grammar section. Make sure to follow the directions given by the proctor.

Part I Questions 1~10

Choose the best answer for the blank.

1. A: Why are you at home instead of the office today?
   B: I've _____ the flu.
   (a) come down with
   (b) put in for
   (c) kept on about
   (d) cut down on

2. A: Hi. I'd like to rent a 20-foot moving van for this weekend.
   B: That should be _____. We have a few on hand.
   (a) spacious
   (b) accurate
   (c) feasible
   (d) convenient

3. A: That documentary about climate change was enlightening.
   B: I agree, it was very _____.
   (a) absolute
   (b) adequate
   (c) fundamental
   (d) informative

4. A: Why are you moving out?
   B: I couldn't pay the loan installments, so I have to _____ the house.
   (a) vacate
   (b) detour
   (c) discard
   (d) substitute

5. A: Is the university sending Derek to the debate championship?
   B: Yes. He's never been _____, so we hope his streak of victories continues.
   (a) caught
   (b) beaten
   (c) acquired
   (d) arrested

6. A: Only Sid can get a party arranged on such short notice. That's _____ organizing.
   B: I know. He must have a lot of experience.
   (a) blatant
   (b) adroit
   (c) chintzy
   (d) awkward

7. A: The last time I ordered items from a foreign website, I ended up paying way too much!
   B: Well, it's because of the government's recent _____ of higher duties on imports.
   (a) austerity
   (b) compromise
   (c) repatriation
   (d) imposition

8. A: That's a _____ meal you're eating. You'll be hungry again soon.
   B: I have a stomachache and don't want to eat much.
   (a) skinny
   (b) slender
   (c) skimpy
   (d) sterile

9. A: Bobby took my car without permission.
   B: That boy is _____. Let's have a long talk with him.
   (a) finicky
   (b) incorrigible
   (c) meritorious
   (d) scrupulous

10. A: Was Taylor kicked out of his apartment?
    B: No, he wasn't _____. He left voluntarily.
    (a) disconnected
    (b) transported
    (c) evacuated
    (d) evicted

Part II **Questions 11~30**

Choose the best answer for the blank.

11. The prisoners at St. Andrews State Prison are _____ to harsher punishment than is allowed by the government.
    (a) inspired
    (b) committed
    (c) exhibited
    (d) subjected

12. The Australian marsupial Gilbert's Potoroo is a(n) _____ that was believed to be extinct before it was rediscovered in Albany.
    (a) variety
    (b) species
    (c) offspring
    (d) objective

13. The scientists Francis Crick and James Watson were given _____ for the discovery of the double helix structure of DNA.
    (a) blessing
    (b) veto
    (c) merit
    (d) credit

14. The hospital _____ about 5,000 patients annually for cardiac surgery.
    (a) admits
    (b) permits
    (c) approves
    (d) administers

15. A government official has proposed _____ a tax on junk food to curtail the large amounts being consumed.
    (a) deviating
    (b) instituting
    (c) mitigating
    (d) brandishing

16. The _____ old man seemed to become even grumpier with each passing year.
    (a) cantankerous
    (b) florid
    (c) affable
    (d) cordial

17. Researchers say some herbs, such as chamomile, have a calming and _____ effect on an upset stomach.
    (a) seething
    (b) soothing
    (c) reassuring
    (d) tempting

18. Although hailed by critics, the movie was only _____ successful at the box office.
    (a) marginally
    (b) virtually
    (c) typically
    (d) expectedly

19. Bedbugs are persistent creatures that can _____ long periods of starvation.
    (a) withstand
    (b) disregard
    (c) prolong
    (d) thwart

20. Penny's nervousness about speaking in front of audiences causes her to _____ her words out.
    (a) stammer
    (b) pledge
    (c) mesmerize
    (d) penetrate

21. The present political _____ in Iran was largely caused by the recent controversial presidential election.

    (a) turmoil
    (b) vigor
    (c) civility
    (d) repose

22. A group of people were arrested the other day for the illegal activity of _____ movies.

    (a) cloning
    (b) defrauding
    (c) pirating
    (d) emulating

23. Producing nearly 900 paintings in only 10 years, Van Gogh was _____ despite his short artistic career.

    (a) redundant
    (b) benevolent
    (c) prolific
    (d) hectic

24. Do not attempt to delete or _____ with the files in the system folder, or your computer's operating system may not start.

    (a) redeem
    (b) tamper
    (c) conjecture
    (d) absolve

25. Retailers _____ shoppers with eye-catching window displays, markdowns, and special events.

    (a) lure
    (b) stalk
    (c) baffle
    (d) fray

26. _____ the bodies of the thousands who died in the earthquake seemed the best way to reduce health risks.

    (a) Undertaking
    (b) Embodying
    (c) Cremating
    (d) Enshrining

27. Daryl is known to _____ until the last minute before he begins working on a project.

    (a) encroach
    (b) falter
    (c) procrastinate
    (d) estrange

28. The judges became aggravated when the rejected contestant _____ them for a second chance.

    (a) deplored
    (b) hindered
    (c) pandered
    (d) importuned

29. To cut back on his monthly expenses, Simon rides his bicycle to work and _____ on food.

    (a) fritters
    (b) scrimps
    (c) gnaws
    (d) defrays

30. Jim tends to _____ when he has chores, which is why his family calls him lazy and irresponsible.

    (a) protract
    (b) denigrate
    (c) harangue
    (d) dawdle

The Vocabulary section is complete. Please move on to the Grammar section.

Part I Questions 1~10
Choose the best answer for the blank.

1. A: Why don't you like attending parties?
   B: Well, _____ introverted, I'd rather stay at home than mingle with people.
   (a) I am
   (b) to be
   (c) being
   (d) has been

2. A: Brittany's apartment was really classy, wasn't it?
   B: That's because she spends _____ too much on decorating.
   (a) quite
   (b) way
   (c) fairly
   (d) pretty

3. A: James says he doesn't know if he can attend the book club tonight.
   B: Well, tell him he _____ always just drop by for half an hour or so.
   (a) will
   (b) must
   (c) could
   (d) should

4. A: Why are you throwing out that shaving razor?
   B: It felt too rough _____ my skin.
   (a) off
   (b) against
   (c) beneath
   (d) among

5. A: Did Ted return from his vacation yet?
   B: Yes. Julie and I passed him _____ through the park today.
   (a) stroll
   (b) to stroll
   (c) strolling
   (d) strolled

6. A: Did you just wake up? It's already 10:30.
   B: I _____ so late if I hadn't done so much hiking yesterday.
   (a) won't sleep
   (b) wouldn't sleep
   (c) won't have slept
   (d) wouldn't have slept

7. A: Are you heading to Pete's party on Saturday?
   B: No, my friend can't make it, and I detest _____ parties alone.
   (a) attend
   (b) to attend
   (c) attending
   (d) having attended

8. A: How disappointing that Sandra can't compete in the dance competition.
   B: I know. _____ just before the first round.
   (a) Only if she wasn't twisted her ankle
   (b) Only if she hadn't twisted her ankle
   (c) If only she didn't twisted her ankle
   (d) If only she hadn't twisted her ankle

9. A: The staff is debating over which piece to feature as the main article.
   B: _____ with such a dilemma, I would consent to whichever most people are in favor of.
   (a) Confronted
   (b) Confronting
   (c) To be confronting
   (d) Having confronted

10. A: I heard you're planning to backpack across Europe.
    B: Yeah. It will take four weeks to cover _____ of the journey.
    (a) length
    (b) a length
    (c) the length
    (d) any length

Part II Questions 11~25

Choose the best answer for the blank.

11. After the political scandal, the governor _____.

    (a) announced by choosing his resignation
    (b) chose his resignation to announce
    (c) announced his resignation by choosing
    (d) chose to announce his resignation

12. Hippocrates was a Greek physician _____ established a code of ethics for the medical profession.

    (a) who
    (b) what
    (c) how
    (d) which

13. About two-fifths of the coastal city's population _____ foreign-born.

    (a) is
    (b) are
    (c) has been
    (d) are being

14. Jamie didn't think _____ to work since there was bound to be a lot of traffic.

    (a) taking it a taxi to be smart
    (b) it smart take a taxi
    (c) to take a taxi smart
    (d) it smart to take a taxi

15. *Model Gadget Magazine* is designed to inform and update those _____.

    (a) to keep unable up with new technology
    (b) of technology unable to keep up
    (c) unable to keep up with new technology
    (d) keeping new technology unable up to new

16. Lemonte Company's stock has risen _____ approximately 60 percent since last quarter.

    (a) with
    (b) to
    (c) for
    (d) by

17. _____ oil prices have skyrocketed over the past week, consumption of petroleum is at an all-time high.

    (a) For
    (b) Once
    (c) Whereas
    (d) Even though

18. _____, the protestors assembled downtown to voice their outrage over the department's misconduct.

    (a) With anti-police sentiment mounting
    (b) Anti-police sentiment mounts
    (c) Mounting with anti-police sentiment
    (d) Anti-police sentiment to be mounting

19. Simon _____ a message on his phone when his car crashed into the one in front of him.

    (a) types
    (b) was typing
    (c) has typed
    (d) will be typing

20. Carbon dioxide, water, and sunlight are the basic components _____ plants need in order to survive.

    (a) that
    (b) whom
    (c) whose
    (d) what

21. Over the years, thousands of animal species _____ extinct due to human activity.

    (a) go
    (b) will go
    (c) are going
    (d) have gone

22. Researchers found a vaccine for measles improved immunity when Vitamin A was administered in conjunction with _____.

    (a) it
    (b) one
    (c) some
    (d) each

23. By the time the mayor conducted an interview about the scandal, his role in the affair _____.

    (a) had been reported already widely
    (b) had already been widely reported
    (c) widely had already been reported
    (d) widely had been reported already

24. Sir Isaac Newton was the scientist who calculated _____ first, having measured its effects on various objects.

    (a) gravity
    (b) a gravity
    (c) the gravity
    (d) a few gravity

25. It is imperative that executives managing multiple offices of a company _____ a certain amount of control over their operations.

    (a) exert
    (b) exerted
    (c) is exerting
    (d) be exerted

Part III Questions 26~30

Identify the option that contains an awkward expression or an error in grammar.

26. (a) A: I was hoping I could borrow a book from you.
    (b) B: Sure, I'll loan you whatever you want. Is there a particular title you have in mind?
    (c) A: Do you have any of Jane Austen's works by any chance?
    (d) B: I only have an old tattered copy of *Pride and Prejudice*, but I'd be happy to lend to you.

27. (a) A: Why do you look like you're in such a bad mood?
    (b) B: I was woken up at 3 am by loud music from an upstairs neighbor.
    (c) A: That's rather irritating. I also get grumpy when I awaken like that.
    (d) B: Yeah. Some people are very inconsiderate and should be taught manners!

28. (a) Before it was eradicated in the 20th century, people greatly feared smallpox, an infectious disease. (b) This was understandable, considering the high death rate and lack of available treatment at the time. (c) However, in 1796, an experiment performed by Edward Jenner unearthed a vaccine for smallpox. (d) It had not been for Jenner's initiatives, the world might not have been freed from the fatal disease.

29. (a) The mammal known as the rhinoceros, comprising five different species, is at risk of extinction. (b) Hunting and poaching have caused the rhino's numbers to plummet due to demand for its horn. (c) As a result, manywildlife organizations are striving to protect the threatening species from further decimation. (d) However, at the rate that human activity and poaching have progressed, it may be impossible to effectively save the rhino.

30. (a) Construction workers in Turkey's Cappadocia region found something they didn't intend to do. (b) While working on a housing project, the workers unearthed an underground city. (c) Though a large-scale investigation has yet to occur, the size and major features of the area indicate that it is a significant site. (d) It is possible the underground city could have housed as many as 20,000 inhabitants.

The Vocabulary and Grammar sections are complete. Do NOT start the Reading Comprehension section until instructed to do so. You are NOT allowed to open any of the other sections of the exam.

Reading
Comprehension

DIRECTIONS

This part of the exam tests your ability to understand reading passages. There will be 35 questions in 40 minutes. Make sure to follow the proctor's instructions.

Part I **Questions 1~10**

Read the passage. Then choose the option that best completes the passage.

1. Searching for _____? Why not take your special someone to the Promenade at Maiden's Hill Hotel? For only $100, you and your companion can have a sumptuous romantic dinner in a private booth. You can enjoy a spectacular sunset view of the city while being serenaded by our string quartet, and we'll even present your loved one with a box of luxury chocolates and a bouquet of roses. Call for reservations now!

   (a) a memorable place for a rendezvous
   (b) a budget dining experience
   (c) lodging for you and your sweetheart
   (d) the best venue for viewing the city

2. Irish doctors have concluded from an experiment that babies who used walkers _____. The finding reinforces the beliefs of some mothers that baby walkers, contrary to manufacturers' claims, do not help babies walk, because infants get used to the devices aiding them. The experts asked parents of children at several day care centers to answer questions regarding their babies' use of baby walkers and how early the infants were able to walk. The results showed that baby walkers can delay the onset of locomotion in infants.

   (a) were emotionally attached to the devices
   (b) experienced more productive physical development
   (c) began walking later than other infants did
   (d) could be left unattended longer than others

3. Residents of Mexico City are distressed as a result of _____. In late 2006, the enormous tectonic plate sliding under Mexico abruptly reversed its trajectory and is now shifting four times more rapidly than before the adjustment. Increased precision in GPS measurements grants scientists the capability to detect miniscule plate movements imperceptible by humans. Technology, no matter how advanced, is no help in ascertaining whether the erratic behavior indicates increased seismic activity, as it is the first time scientists have witnessed a reversal of such significance.

   (a) the limitations of seismic activity detection
   (b) earthquakes that are becoming more severe
   (c) serious dangers from drifting tectonic plates
   (d) geological events that remain inexplicable

4. Linking our bottom line with that of every worker's pay ensures employees will _____. With this in mind, the following memorandum has been distributed to describe the profit-sharing plan the firm has recently implemented. Our goal in initiating this program is twofold. First, we want workers to feel a sense of ownership and responsibility at the office. Second, we wish to encourage employees to conserve company resources and minimize expenditure while maximizing revenue.

   (a) not be the major expenditure for the firm
   (b) endeavor to help the company succeed
   (c) not lapse when it comes to working together
   (d) earn more than they are entitled to

5. EagleVision, the most advanced security system on the market, is here to protect your valuable stock against larceny. With computer-controlled cameras and an automated alert mechanism, EagleVision will secure the premises of your establishment while you concentrate on making your business grow. It is equipped with a wireless intercom ideal for emergency situations, and the system records and organizes security video footage in an easy-to-access database. EagleVision lets you _____.

   (a) identify customers through facial recognition
   (b) manage the company's inventory system
   (c) maintain productivity and stay safe
   (d) control video cameras from any computer

6. Ancient Greek astronomers relied purely upon rough geometric formulas and rudimentary readings done with the naked eye to estimate magnitude and distance. Although the methods employed resulted more often than not in imprecise figures, it should be borne in mind that the Greeks _____. Mathematics and scientific inquiry were embryonic disciplines, and what the epoch's greatest minds lacked capability-wise was made up for with ingenuity. Their burgeoning understanding of the cosmos influenced astronomical thought for nearly two millennia.

   (a) accomplished astounding feats with limited resources
   (b) influenced all areas of intellectual development
   (c) invented geometry for use in calculations of space
   (d) possessed an accurate perception of the universe's scale

7. Many inventions humankind takes for granted _____.
   The military introduced cutting-edge advancements for use only by the armed forces, and because these developments were shrouded in secrecy, private citizens were oblivious to their existence. However, once a piece of military technology became known to the public, defense contractors often brainstormed ways to tailor it for peacetime operation. In antiquated times, chariots and wheelbarrows first found prominence for their expediency in battle; in our postindustrial age, many innovations used for leisure and recreation have a military pedigree, like satellite television and flight simulation games.

   (a) are employed by the armed forces as well
   (b) are rooted in ancient military practice
   (c) were not expected to gain such prominence
   (d) were not initially intended for civilian use

8. The proliferation of smartphones and mobile applications has introduced a heretofore unfathomable level of convenience to our lives. But these technological godsends are not without their drawbacks. In a rush to deliver their latest offerings into the hands of consumers, tech companies tend to release products riddled with bugs and defects, which customers rightly take exception to. Diminished battery life and sluggish performance are just two of the many issues that arise from bugs. The onus is on companies to _____.

   (a) seek customer feedback about the features they most desire
   (b) address these glitches that are sapping their products' utility
   (c) adapt their services to be compatible with mobile devices
   (d) be timely about releasing the latest versions of their gadgets

9.
Safety in Cheerleading

Cheerleading troupes perform with very little regulatory oversight from sports committees. Compared to other sports, there have been relatively few incidences of serious injury attributed to cheerleading, even as routines have become progressively more perilous and intricate. _____, school administrators have been calling for stricter guidelines for cheerleading activities. To address their concerns, the National Collegiate Athletic Association has endorsed an upper threshold on the difficulty of stunts performed during competition.

(a) In fact
(b) After all
(c) Consequently
(d) Nevertheless

10. For many centuries, the "untouchables," or low-caste Hindu groups in India, were subjected to social restrictions that forbade them from entering many schools and temples. _____, the election of Kocheril Raman Narayanan as president of India in 1997 was an indication of how much things had changed. Narayanan, an "untouchable" himself, was elected by the National Parliament and state assemblies, whose members have typically come from upper castes.

(a) For all that
(b) In effect
(c) In addition
(d) Given that fact

Part II Questions 11~12

Read the passage. Then identify the option that does NOT belong.

11. The first television set we had at our family's home was a 14-inch black-and-white monitor encased in a large, wooden box. (a) It changed our lives dramatically because we suddenly had a new form of entertainment with which to occupy our time. (b) It had a big plastic knob that could be twisted to change the channel, and smaller knobs to adjust the volume and picture quality. (c) The speakers, tinny and scratchy as they were, sat behind carved wooden screens that were almost as wide as the monitor. (d) The TV casing even had two folding doors, which hid the monitor when the TV set was not in use.

12. Communication Hub does not currently offer mobile phone subscriptions of less than twelve months. (a) Only those customers willing to sign a year-long contract will be eligible for our plans, which include a monthly billing feature. (b) Communication Hub, however, offers short-term prepaid packages for mobile phone users who have a tight budget. (c) Clients can choose from three-month or six-month prepaid packages without needing to show income statements or certification of good credit standing. (d) Applicants for our contract-based plans must pass an in-store credit check conducted in the shop in order to qualify.

Part III Questions 13~25

Read the passage and the question. Then choose the option that best answers the question.

13.
> **Notice**
>
> Graduating students who are defending their theses must coordinate with the college secretary to reserve the conference room. As a rule, scheduled times must be strictly adhered to in order to avoid the disruption of other activities that have been planned. Although the conference rooms are available free of charge to students, a fee will be charged to individuals who fail to arrive on time or who use the facility beyond the duration of time they've been granted.
>
> Administration Office

Q: What is the announcement mainly about?

(a) The penalty fee for canceling a reservation
(b) The necessity of observing reservation times
(c) The available venues for thesis presentations
(d) The process of making a reservation for the conference room

14. In her 1959 play *A Raisin in the Sun*, African-American playwright Lorraine Hansberry portrayed black characters, themes, and conflicts in a manner that had never been seen in a Broadway production. She addressed many issues in 1950s America, including the growing domestic and racial tensions beneath the economic prosperity that characterized the US in the years following World War II. For Hansberry, the rising affluence experienced by white Americans in the 1950s could not hide the discrimination still being perpetrated against black people.

Q: What is the main topic of the passage?

(a) What social conflicts Hansberry predicted
(b) How black people were portrayed in Broadway productions
(c) How greater affluence affected postwar American literature
(d) What Lorraine Hansberry's groundbreaking play discusses

15.

Dear Mr. Alexander,

We've received your request for the cancellation of your satellite television service. Please be informed, however, that the service contract you entered into with our company is binding for two years, and an early termination fee of $300 is stipulated if you wish to cancel your service. If you do not wish to pay this fee, our company will continue billing you at the agreed-upon monthly rate, exclusive of taxes and surcharges, and you will continue to receive programming. Please inform us of your intentions regarding this matter.

Sincerely,
William Johnston

Q: What is the main purpose of the letter to Mr. Alexander?

(a) To inform him that he needs to sign a contract with the company
(b) To confirm his request to terminate his satellite television service
(c) To ask that he pay his outstanding balance as soon as possible
(d) To inquire whether or not he wishes to update his satellite package

16. British anatomist and paleontologist Richard Owen proposed the term "dinosaur" in 1842 to name the large, extinct reptiles whose bones had been recently unearthed in England. He observed that the unknown creatures had five vertebrae in their hips, whereas most known reptiles have two. Additionally, rather than holding their limbs sprawled out like lizards' legs, the newly discovered reptiles held their limbs under the body. Hence, Owen believed that they should be classified as their own group of reptiles.

Q: What is the main idea of the passage?

(a) Dinosaurs were believed to have evolved into reptiles over time.
(b) The field of paleontology developed as a formal science in England.
(c) Dinosaurs and lizards were discovered to have similar characteristics.
(d) Owen was the first to recognize dinosaurs as a distinct reptile category.

17.

Seeking Experienced Server

Mughal Palace, one of Trenton's oldest Indian food restaurants, is seeking an experienced server to work lunch and dinner shifts from Tuesday to Sunday.

The main duties of the position are taking orders and serving food. However, additional tasks—including setting up our buffet counter, mixing drinks, and helping with food preparation—may be assigned. Candidates must have at least six months' experience working as a server in a fine-dining establishment and should be familiar with Indian food.

To apply, send your résumé to mughalpalace@joynet.org. Include two professional references. Salary depends on applicant.

Q: What information is NOT included in the advertisement?

(a) The type of experience required
(b) The amount the server will be paid
(c) The responsibilities of the employee
(d) The contact information of the restaurant

18. During the last 300 years, two major innovations have enabled spectacular progress in crop yields. The first innovation was a higher-level conceptualization of genetics, as a result of which hybridization and selective breeding continually augment the homogeneity and hardiness of crops. Furthermore, the invention of apparatuses like the combine and the tractor boosted labor productivity. A single cultivator can now seed, thresh, and harvest unprecedented quantities of grain. These agricultural advances are central to farmers' ability to nourish the world's population.

Q: Which of the following is correct according to the passage?

(a) Advancements in technology have made farmers less essential.
(b) Agricultural science developed approximately 300 years ago.
(c) Food supplies were insufficient prior to mechanization.
(d) Research in genetics has led to hardier plants.

19.

> To Whom It May Concern:
>
> I wish to file a grievance regarding the service I received at your airport location. After landing late in the evening, I confirmed my rental car reservation and was directed to the storage lot. The agent there noted that there was damage to the fender, but confirmed that I would not be charged for it as it did not occur while the vehicle was in my possession. Lo and behold, upon returning the car at the agreed-upon time, the agent inspecting the vehicle held me liable for repairs. I hope we can come to an understanding before I am driven to seek legal representation.
>
> Sincerely,
> Tom Johnson

Q: Which of the following is correct according to the letter?

(a) The writer is responsible for the vehicle's condition.
(b) The writer received conflicting statements from staff members.
(c) The writer's insurance is unwilling to cover damages to the vehicle.
(d) The writer has contacted a lawyer to manage his side of the dispute.

20. Since the 1990s, work opportunities for Americans in the manufacturing and customer service fields have grown scarce, with most positions being outsourced overseas. American workers are competent and highly educated but also highly paid; by relocating abroad, companies can reduce labor costs to the point where investment in new facilities is quickly recovered. Davidson Industries, for example, bases some of its more cost-sensitive departments in India. As a result of this trend, the American job market has been shaken up.

Q: Why are American companies setting up operations in other countries?

(a) Foreign workers have more experience working in production plants.
(b) The cost of labor abroad is often much cheaper.
(c) The US labor market is saturated with overqualified workers.
(d) The US job market is unstable due to policy changes.

21.

National > Politics

Furlong Loses Support

Prime Minister Rod Furlong has suffered a debilitating political setback after several members of his Far Left Party defected to the opposition Conservative Party over the past fortnight. The switch in party affiliation occurred just days after inside sources leaked word of a rift brewing among leaders of the ruling party to media sources.

Some of the deserters were associates in Furlong's Cabinet, including Economy Minister Reggie Galveston. The grumblings in the administration mounted after the Far Left Party was humiliated by its rivals in the midterm elections, which convened several months ago.

Q: Which of the following is correct about the Far Left Party according to the passage?

(a) It gained new members following defections from other parties.
(b) It is in disarray after an electoral defeat.
(c) It disintegrated after Prime Minister Furlong was defeated.
(d) It is currently engaged in a conflict with some media entities.

22.

James Cook University Presents
The 12th Annual Creative Writing Conference
February 22-24

Details:
- A keynote speech by author Christopher Noble at the Student Union Center that explores how novice writers can overcome challenges
- Seminars and workshops on a variety of writing genres, all of which will be held in various buildings around campus; visit www.jamescookuniversity.com/englishdept for a detailed schedule and list of venues
- A closing ceremony and networking event at Pottsville Community Center

Please note that seating for each seminar will be limited, so early registration is recommended. Register before February 1 to get a 15 percent discount on the ticket price.

Q: Which of the following is correct according to the advertisement?

(a) The closing ceremony will be hosted by a renowned author.
(b) People who register for multiple seminars will pay less.
(c) The conference can only be attended by published writers.
(d) The events will be held at several different venues.

23. Often considered the most accomplished scribe in English literature, William Shakespeare is best known for being a dramatist. However, few people know that he could not subsist exclusively by being a poet and a playwright. Shakespeare was reportedly also a schoolmaster in England and a soldier in Northern Europe. If not for such diversions, many literary critics wonder what other masterpieces Shakespeare might have produced had he concentrated solely on writing plays and poems.

Q: What can be inferred about Shakespeare from the passage?

(a) His dramas were better received than his poems.
(b) He was a soldier before beginning his writing career.
(c) His literary pursuits did not provide sufficient income.
(d) Critics believe other pursuits improved his writing ability.

24. A new study suggests that an early ancestor of humans may have adapted physiological changes to survive extreme climates. Scientists who conducted the study say that a *Homo erectus* whose fossils were discovered in China in the 1920s may have undergone physiological evolution that allowed more blood to flow to his extremities. Experts estimate that Peking Man, as this particular *Homo erectus* is known, lived during the glacial age, about 770,000 years ago, when fire had yet to be discovered. The scientists believe their hypothesis can explain how Peking Man survived the conditions of the era.

Q: What can be inferred from the passage?

(a) Peking Man used clothing made from fur to keep him warm.
(b) China was the coldest place on earth during the glacial age.
(c) *Homo erectus* was the first human ancestor to make fire.
(d) Peking Man survived frigid temperatures without an external heat source.

25. Organ transplantation is laden with moral and ethical implications. However, a unique form of regenerative medicine invented by Dr. Anthony Atala at the University of North Carolina may circumvent such ramifications. The imaginative procedure uses specially modified ink-jet printers and printer cartridges that eject cells in an alternating pattern along with a special gel. Once the gel evaporates, the cells grow together and can be laid across an organ-shaped scaffold. A fully grown organ grows within the scaffolding, and can then be safely transplanted into a patient without risk of rejection.

Q: Which statement would the writer most likely agree with?

(a) Parallels can be drawn between cell creation and printer functionality.
(b) Scientific advancements will one day make organ transplants unnecessary.
(c) Dr. Atala's technique has brought to light philosophical concerns.
(d) Technological adaptations can potentially create medical breakthroughs.

Part IV Questions 26~35

Read the passage and the questions. Then choose the option that best answers each question.

Questions 26-27

Mother's Day Celebration Competition: "Dear Mom" Video Submissions

CommunityWeb is celebrating Mother's Day with a video competition. We're inviting sons and daughters to submit a video message dedicated to their mother. Contestants may sing a song for their mother, read a poem for her, or tell a story involving her. Or they may opt for a more creative approach. We'll upload the best entries on our "Dear Mom" page, and the creator(s) of the most popular video will win a cruise to the Bahamas for up to five family members (two adults and three children).

Guidelines:
- The videos must be submitted as either AVI or MP4 files. Files larger than 25MB won't be accepted.
- The messages should be from children, but a parent can step in if the child is too young.
- We cannot accept music or video clips that are under copyright.
- Profanity is not allowed.

Send the video to dearmom@communityweb.com by May 10. If the file size exceeds 10MB please use a zip program.

26. Q: Which of the following is correct?

(a) All video files must be compressed before they are sent.
(b) Only AVI files will be published on the "Dear Mom" page.
(c) Videos must be copyrighted to be eligible for the competition.
(d) There is a size limit for the video submissions.

27. Q: What can be inferred from the advertisement?

(a) The cruise to the Bahamas will begin on Mother's Day.
(b) CommunityWeb sells products that are designed for young children.
(c) A recording device can be operated by one of the parents.
(d) Participants are not allowed to vote for their own submission.

Questions 28-29

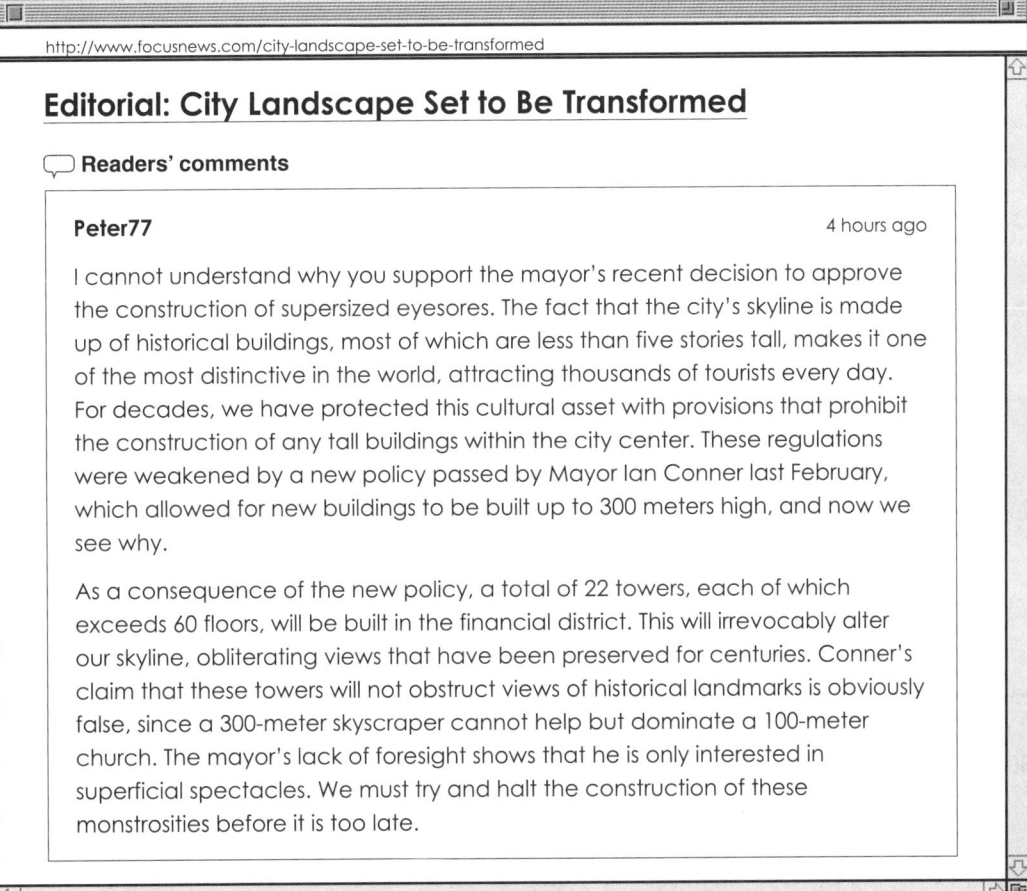

28. Q: What is the main purpose of the comment?

(a) To demand that Mayor Ian Conner step down from his office
(b) To request that the design of the planned buildings be altered
(c) To highlight the poor state of the city's historical buildings
(d) To challenge the choice of the mayor to build new skyscrapers

29. Q: Which statement would the writer most likely agree with?

(a) The new policy should be removed to preserve the city's assets.
(b) The new skyscrapers will only benefit the rich in society.
(c) The decision to allow new tall buildings proves the mayor is corrupt.
(d) The mayor should stop all construction in the city centre.

Questions 30-31

Egalitarianism is the belief that most societal discord stems from the unequal distribution of wealth. Economic inequality usually results from governments giving preferential treatment to members of society's upper classes. Such a practice is interpreted as an affront to the rights of the poor, resulting in a tense struggle between the haves and the have-nots. Hence, egalitarians aim to erase favoritism and promote greater equality among social classes, thereby providing citizens with more balanced economic opportunities. Advocates believe that only when this has occurred will society be free of civil conflict.

People often confuse egalitarianism with communism because these two schools of thoughts share many basic tenets. For example, these ideologies oppose the existence of a social elite that controls the majority of available financial resources and favor reducing the number of poor people. In addition, both agree with the idea that individuals should receive social and economic benefits based solely on ability. However, communism advocates the elimination of social classes, while egalitarianism does not argue that this is necessary.

30. Q: What is a belief of egalitarians?

   (a) Building a strong economy is the best way to ensure the rights of the poor are protected.
   (b) Favoritism is considered an effective means of creating a fairer and more just society.
   (c) Providing equal economic opportunities for all classes of people could eliminate social conflict.
   (d) Promoting the growth of the middle class will help get rid of societal corruption.

31. Q: What is NOT a way that egalitarianism is similar to communism?

   (a) It opposes the holding of excessive wealth by one social group.
   (b) It argues that the poverty level should be substantially reduced.
   (c) It advocates for individuals to be rewarded based on merit.
   (d) It supports the complete elimination of all classes within society.

Questions 32-33

The Nations of the Island of Hispaniola

The Dominican Republic and Haiti, despite sharing the Caribbean island of Hispaniola, differ in several respects. For one thing, the former is more suited to agriculture, with abundant pastures and thick soil, than the latter. However, during the 17th century, Haiti initially outpaced its counterpart in terms of economic development. One reason for this was that Haiti had been colonized by France, while the Dominican Republic was controlled by an ailing Spain. France had the resources to send more slaves, upping Haiti's population and productivity, while simultaneously hastening the deforestation and soil erosion that squandered the nation's agricultural capital.

Today, it is a very different story, as the Dominican Republic has grown into the largest economy in the Caribbean. Rather than continue being so dependent on the export of agricultural produce, the country diversified and has growing service and manufacturing industries. Unlike its neighbor, the Dominican Republic has also attained a level of political stability in recent years, which has allowed its economy to prosper. Haiti, on the other hand, has suffered from a series of devastating earthquakes that have decimated its agricultural base. It is now one of the most impoverished places on the planet, lacking even the most basic infrastructure.

32. Q: What is the passage mainly about?

(a) The economic development of a Caribbean island during the colonial period
(b) The historical reasons Hispaniola was occupied by France and Spain
(c) The distinct histories of two neighboring former European colonies
(d) The decline of agricultural production in various Caribbean countries

33. Q: What can be inferred about Haiti from the passage?

(a) It lacks political stability in comparison to the Dominican Republic.
(b) It relies heavily on the Dominican Republic for financial and humanitarian aid.
(c) It has suffered several natural disasters due to widespread deforestation.
(d) It has restored the majority of its public services in recent years.

Questions 34-35

Breaking News   Updated 3 hours ago

State Senator Eyes Higher Office

By Alice Merton

    Jean Stein, a state senator from Pennsylvania, has officially announced her candidacy for president at the state's Conservative Party Headquarters. Senator Stein is the third candidate to register for New Hampshire's upcoming primary election, following the current president Carson McCullers and Alabama governor Austin Bates. During her two terms in office, Stein has become a symbol of innovation and fired up young conservatives who are fed up with politicians with narrow-minded, outdated views. According to recent polls, she is neck and neck with McCullers, the most likely candidate, and her candidacy is gaining both popularity and momentum.

    Stein's popularity across the nation is believed to be due to her outspoken criticism of the current president and his administration's financial scandals. Unlike McCullers, who is considered a lobbyist's dream, Stein has few corporate connections, and is funding her campaign solely through individual donations. She has also proposed a ban on congressional lobbying and has suggested that politicians should only accept contributions from private citizens. Meanwhile, McCullers, seeking to outflank Stein, has proposed that candidates all receive the same amount of funding during each election. Although many doubt Stein's chances, her presence has already shaken up the status quo.

34. Q: What is the main topic of the news report?

   (a) The progress of the reelection campaign of President Carson McCullers
   (b) The corruption of a potential candidate in a primary election
   (c) A local politician who is gaining support in a nationwide race
   (d) The system of political lobbying and corporate donations in Congress

35. Q: Which of the following is correct according to the news report?

   (a) Stein has proposed that all lobbyists be banned from seeking office.
   (b) McCullers is renowned for his resistance to the influence of vested interests.
   (c) Stein is funding her campaign through totally anonymous contributions.
   (d) McCullers has suggested that financing be equal among all the candidates.

The Reading Comprehension section of the exam is complete. Please stay in your seat until the proctor tells you to leave. You are NOT allowed to open any of the other sections of the exam.

시험에 나올 문제를 미리 풀어보는
텝스 적중예상특강
해커스텝스 HackersTEPS.com

SELF-CHECK LIST

TEST 05는 잘 마치셨나요?
이제 다음의 SELF-CHECK LIST를 통해 자신의 테스트 진행 내용을 점검해 볼까요?

1. 나는 테스트를 마칠 때까지 완전히 테스트에 집중하였다.
   ☐ YES   ☐ NO

2. 나는 각 영역별 주어진 시간을 지켰다.
   ☐ LISTENING COMPREHENSION
   ☐ VOCABULARY & GRAMMAR   ☐ READING COMPREHENSION

3. 나는 시간 내에 모든 문제를 풀었다.
   ☐ LISTENING COMPREHENSION
   ☐ VOCABULARY & GRAMMAR   ☐ READING COMPREHENSION

4. 나는 특히 어렵게 느껴지는 영역이 있었다.
   ☐ LISTENING COMPREHENSION
   ☐ VOCABULARY & GRAMMAR   ☐ READING COMPREHENSION

5. 개선하고 싶은 사항
   _____
   _____
   _____
   _____
   _____

■ 개선해야 할 점은 반드시 다음 테스트에서 실천해야만 실력을 향상시킬 수 있습니다.
그리고 반드시 오답을 정리해서 같은 실수를 반복하지 않도록 유의하기 바랍니다.

해커스 텝스 최신기출유형 실전모의고사 문제집

TEST 06

**LISTENING COMPREHENSION
VOCABULARY & GRAMMAR
READING COMPREHENSION**

테스트 전 확인사항

1. 휴대 전화의 전원을 끄셨나요?
2. OMR 답안지, 연필, 지우개가 준비되셨나요?
3. 시계가 준비되셨나요?
4. 목표 점수를 정하세요.

   LISTENING COMPREHENSION (____개 / 40개)
   VOCABULARY (____개 / 30개)
   GRAMMAR (____개 / 30개)
   READING COMPREHENSION (____개 / 35개)

5. 테스트의 시작과 종료 시간을 정하세요.

   LISTENING COMPREHENSION ___시 ___분 ~ ___시 ___분 (40분)
   VOCABULARY & GRAMMAR   ___시 ___분 ~ ___시 ___분 (25분)
   READING COMPREHENSION   ___시 ___분 ~ ___시 ___분 (35분)

 TEST 06.mp3

실전용·복습용 문제풀이 MP3 무료 다운로드 및 스트리밍 바로듣기
(HackersIngang.com)

* 실제 시험장의 소음까지 재현해 낸 고사장 소음·매미 버전 MP3까지 구매하면 실전에
  더욱 완벽히 대비할 수 있습니다.

무료MP3 바로듣기

Listening Comprehension

DIRECTIONS

1. In the Listening Comprehension Section, the content will be presented in oral rather than written form.
2. There are five parts in this section, and you will receive separate instructions for each. Listen to the instructions carefully, and choose the best answer for each question from the available options.

LISTENING COMPREHENSION

Part I Questions 1~10

You will now hear ten statements or questions, and each will be followed by four responses. Choose the most appropriate response.

Part II Questions 11~20

You will now hear ten conversation fragments, and each will be followed by four responses. Choose the most appropriate response.

Part III Questions 21~30

You will now hear ten complete conversations. Before each conversation, you will hear a short description of the situation. Then you will hear the conversation and its corresponding question, both of which will be read only once. Next, you will hear four options, which will also be read once. Choose the option that best answers the question.

Part IV Questions 31~36

You will now hear six monologues. For each item, you will hear a monologue and its corresponding question, both of which will be read twice. Then you will hear four options which will be read only once. Choose the option that best answers the question.

Part V Questions 37~40

You will now hear two longer monologues. For each item, you will hear a monologue and two corresponding questions, all of which will be read twice. Then you will hear four options for each question, which will be read only once. Choose the option that best answers each question.

Vocabulary & Grammar

DIRECTIONS

These two parts of the exam test your vocabulary and grammar skills. You will have a total of 25 minutes to answer 60 questions. There will be 30 from the Vocabulary section and 30 from the Grammar section. Make sure to follow the directions given by the proctor.

Part I **Questions 1~10**

Choose the best answer for the the blank.

1. A: Come visit me again soon, OK?
   B: I will. Thanks for _____ me today!

   (a) taking
   (b) having
   (c) acquiring
   (d) noticing

2. A: What's this stuff on your garage floor?
   B: Don't worry. I'm throwing all that _____ away.

   (a) junk
   (b) volume
   (c) rebuff
   (d) debris

3. A: You're always late for class.
   B: I know. I need to be more _____.

   (a) variable
   (b) current
   (c) delicate
   (d) punctual

4. A: Why didn't you tell me you were moving away?
   B: Sorry. I didn't have time to _____.

   (a) bring it up
   (b) call it out
   (c) make it up
   (d) set it up

5. A: Can't we stay here another week?
   B: I'd like that myself, but we have no _____.

   (a) opportunity
   (b) precedence
   (c) replacement
   (d) alternative

6. A: Why is Sam mad? I gave him my honest opinion of his art.
   B: Well, _____ won't encourage him to improve.

   (a) putdowns
   (b) comedowns
   (c) blowouts
   (d) callouts

7. A: To save time, we must keep all email correspondence _____.
   B: OK, I'll let the staff know.

   (a) blunt
   (b) avid
   (c) succinct
   (d) keen

8. A: Did you comprehend Robert's article on social change?
   B: I'd like to say I did, but it was _____.

   (a) inalterable
   (b) indisputable
   (c) impervious
   (d) inscrutable

9. A: I feel pity for the union leaders who are on a hunger strike.
   B: I know. Their faces look so _____.

   (a) docile
   (b) gaunt
   (c) jocular
   (d) errant

10. A: That manager shows a _____ disregard for the employees' dignity.
    B: You're absolutely right. They ought to fire him.

    (a) flailing
    (b) flagrant
    (c) flaccid
    (d) flamboyant

Part II Questions 11~30

Choose the best answer for the blank.

11. During peak season, _____ booking is recommended to ensure a seat on your desired flight.
    (a) imperative
    (b) premature
    (c) advance
    (d) forward

12. A characteristic that _____ the training regimen of athletes from that of amateurs is intensity.
    (a) compares
    (b) withdraws
    (c) distinguishes
    (d) commits

13. To avoid litigation, citizens in Michigan are turning to community mediators to _____ the dispute.
    (a) whimper
    (b) evade
    (c) detach
    (d) resolve

14. Although donations to relief organizations have decreased, the number of volunteers has not _____.
    (a) soared
    (b) expanded
    (c) immersed
    (d) dwindled

15. The institute _____ scholarships to needy students who wish to pursue a university education.
    (a) grants
    (b) sources
    (c) transfers
    (d) delivers

16. Daphne _____ a small amount of concealing cream on her face to cover up her blemishes.
    (a) smacked
    (b) tapped
    (c) dabbed
    (d) nipped

17. The hotel's presidential suite is _____ with several pieces of handcrafted furniture.
    (a) adorned
    (b) savored
    (c) tarnished
    (d) buffed

18. Government contributions to workers' pensions will be _____ beginning next month to reduce federal spending.
    (a) demoted
    (b) deferred
    (c) tilted
    (d) capped

19. Eating spicy dishes can cause _____ abdominal pain for people with ulcers.
    (a) excruciating
    (b) convivial
    (c) monotonous
    (d) tedious

20. Tony was _____ from military service because of a heart condition.
    (a) mandated
    (b) acquitted
    (c) exempted
    (d) exiled

21. Air traffic controllers are given training to help them _____ encrypted messages used during flights.

    (a) contradict
    (b) terminate
    (c) decipher
    (d) contend

22. About 150,000 kilometers of tropical rain forest in Brazil were _____ by illegal logging.

    (a) diffused
    (b) accredited
    (c) eradicated
    (d) implanted

23. Some politicians with a tarnished reputation still manage to _____ voters because of their charisma.

    (a) court
    (b) jostle
    (c) spur
    (d) kindle

24. The patient's arms were so badly injured that the doctors think it will take two years to _____ them.

    (a) rehabilitate
    (b) inspect
    (c) encounter
    (d) confront

25. The lawyers successfully _____ their client from charges that he embezzled millions from investors.

    (a) alienated
    (b) exonerated
    (c) ostracized
    (d) incarcerated

26. Carl thinks it is all right to _____ less-important duties when he is working on a major project.

    (a) scour
    (b) meander
    (c) besmirch
    (d) shirk

27. The upstanding company is very _____ when it comes to conducting business deals, doing everything by the book.

    (a) propitious
    (b) punctilious
    (c) ostentatious
    (d) duplicitous

28. High school teachers commonly encounter students who display _____ behavior that is often difficult to handle.

    (a) magnanimous
    (b) subordinate
    (c) ebullient
    (d) idiosyncratic

29. The newspaper columnist exposed the tendency of even volunteer organizations to become _____ by fraud.

    (a) enervated
    (b) extenuated
    (c) vitiated
    (d) undulated

30. News stations have devoted excessive coverage to the two firms _____ in a copyright dispute.

    (a) triggered
    (b) disconcerted
    (c) pilfered
    (d) enmeshed

The Vocabulary section is complete. Please move on to the Grammar section.

Part I Questions 1~10

Choose the best answer for the blank.

1. A: Would you like to have lunch on Friday?
   B: I _____, but I have a dental appointment that day.
   (a) would love
   (b) would love to
   (c) would love to do
   (d) would have loved to

2. A: How did your shopping for a new dress go?
   B: I didn't like any of them, _____ I bought a purse instead.
   (a) yet
   (b) for
   (c) or
   (d) so

3. A: Have you replaced the flat tire on my car?
   B: Yes, I _____.
   (a) am
   (b) was
   (c) have
   (d) did

4. A: This is my first time visiting LA.
   B: How about we go for _____ around the city?
   (a) drive
   (b) a drive
   (c) the drive
   (d) some drive

5. A: Is your family still planning to convert your garage into a studio?
   B: Yes, but we _____ until May.
   (a) didn't renovate
   (b) aren't renovating
   (c) haven't renovated
   (d) hadn't renovated

6. A: If you're interested, I have a second ticket for Vienna.
   B: Sure. I haven't gone _____ yet this year.
   (a) none
   (b) nowhere
   (c) somewhere
   (d) anywhere

7. A: Look out. The paint on that bench hasn't fully dried yet.
   B: Thanks, I nearly _____ on it.
   (a) sat
   (b) will sit
   (c) was sitting
   (d) have sat

8. A: No one's buying these flowers. They're just too expensive.
   B: They would sell a lot better _____.
   (a) were we to lower the price
   (b) were if we to lower the price
   (c) we were to lower the price
   (d) if we were lower to the price

9. A: What did you do to make this French toast so delicious?
   B: I added _____ powdered sugar for extra flavor.
   (a) little
   (b) few
   (c) a little
   (d) a few

10. A: Why didn't you include this song in your newly released album?
    B: _____ could be, it was a poor fit that had to be abandoned.
    (a) As pedestrian as
    (b) Being as pedestrian as
    (c) Having been as pedestrian as
    (d) It was as pedestrian as

Part II Questions 11~25

Choose the best answer for the blank.

11. The Great Pyramid of Giza is _____ ancient structures.
    (a) certainly one of the most remarkable
    (b) certainly the most remarkable one
    (c) one the most remarkable certainly
    (d) one of the certainly most remarkable

12. The newest flavor of Jamaican Blue Mountain coffee tastes less bitter than _____ coffee flavors.
    (a) such other
    (b) the others
    (c) other
    (d) another

13. Jean _____ the requirements necessary to receive a master's degree by the end of this module.
    (a) is fulfilled
    (b) has fulfilled
    (c) has been fulfilling
    (d) will have fulfilled

14. People normally begin developing _____.
    (a) childhood during relationships with peers
    (b) relationships with peers during childhood
    (c) during childhood relationships with peers
    (d) with peers of childhood during relationships

15. According to scholars, early Chinese poetry _____ as some of the finest literature from the ancient era.
    (a) cite
    (b) is citing
    (c) is cited
    (d) are cited

16. Cliff Davis was prepared to pay _____ it cost to defend himself against the plagiarism lawsuit.
    (a) however
    (b) whatever
    (c) whenever
    (d) whichever

17. The mayor of Durham, together with several ranking members of the city council, _____ their mission to expand local health care benefits.
    (a) is proclaimed
    (b) has proclaimed
    (c) are proclaimed
    (d) have been proclaimed

18. _____ for driving while intoxicated on multiple occasions, Steve had his license indefinitely revoked.
    (a) Been reprimanded
    (b) To reprimand
    (c) To have been reprimanded
    (d) Having been reprimanded

19. The judge found _____ which parent would receive custody of the children to be problematic.
    (a) arbitrates
    (b) arbitrating
    (c) arbitrated
    (d) to arbitrate

20. Similar to the behavior of _____, female bees are most particular when finding a place to build a nest.
    (a) people
    (b) peoples
    (c) a people
    (d) the people

21. Last night, the Hawks defeated the Pirates _____ sports analysts say was one of the biggest upsets in the league's history.

    (a) that
    (b) which
    (c) in what
    (d) of which

22. When reporting any technical difficulties or making inquiries, the system administrator _____ by dialing extension 952.

    (a) is reaching
    (b) can be reached
    (c) is being reached
    (d) can be reaching

23. _____ to stay contemporary with customers' prevailing tastes, Bradford's wares are updated periodically.

    (a) It was designed
    (b) Be designed
    (c) Designing
    (d) Designed

24. Throughout history, swarms of locusts _____ known to annihilate crops and pastureland.

    (a) are
    (b) were
    (c) had been
    (d) have been

25. _____ of the break-in at the city treasury that police had to seal off the premises for weeks.

    (a) So exhaustive was the investigation
    (b) The investigation was so exhaustive
    (c) Was so exhaustive the investigation
    (d) Exhaustive was the investigation so

Part III Questions 26~30

Identify the option that contains an awkward expression or an error in grammar.

26. (a) A: Have you ever read the book *Tuesdays with Morrie*?
    (b) B: It happens to be one of the best books I've ever read.
    (c) A: I agree. I've never been such moved by a story before.
    (d) B: Although it's very inspiring, the way it was written was what engaged me.

27. (a) A: The kitchen faucet is turned off proper, but it's still dripping.
    (b) B: Oh, it hasn't stopped doing that since the plumber last tried to fix it.
    (c) A: I can take a look and see what I can do about it if you'd like.
    (d) B: It's OK. We're going to have the entire system repaired sometime next week.

28. (a) Recent studies show that people who adopt a Western diet increase their risk of heart disease. (b) This type of diet mainly consists of processed meats and foods that are high in fat and sodium content. (c) Unhealthy foods like these can cause high blood pressure and clog the arteries. (d) To prevent this, health experts stress that people need modify their diets and eat more fiber.

29. (a) Launched in 1971, the Mariner 9 became the first spacecraft to orbit another planet. (b) The space vehicle had been designed to survey Mars and study the planet's atmosphere. (c) Through the Mariner 9 space probe, scientists were able to identify the natural landscape features of the so-called Red Planet. (d) One of the most notable discoveries was the Martian sand dunes, which displayed similar properties between those of North Africa.

30. (a) Traveling by air with children, especially during long-haul flights, can prove taxing for parents. (b) As children get bored easily when traveling, parents should devise a method for keeping them preoccupied. (c) Experts recommend to bring along items that provide distraction and amusement, like books, toys, and handheld games. (d) Although meals are provided during the flight, it is also advisable to come equipped with extra nourishment for between meals.

The Vocabulary and Grammar sections are complete. Do NOT start the Reading Comprehension section until instructed to do so. You are NOT allowed to open any of the other sections of the exam.

Reading Comprehension

DIRECTIONS

This part of the exam tests your ability to understand reading passages. There will be 35 questions in 40 minutes. Make sure to follow the proctor's instructions.

Part I Questions 1~10

Read the passage. Then choose the option that best completes the passage.

1. A museum featuring rare photographs and the favorite clothes of the late Princess Diana opened Thursday, _____. Her sons have criticized the museum for cashing in on the memory of their mother. The museum director refuted the accusation, saying that any proceeds not given to charity would go to the building's upkeep and employees' salaries. According to the director, half of the ticket sales will go towards Diana's favorite charities.

   (a) drawing the support of her estate
   (b) helping to educate people about the royal family
   (c) eliciting the protests of her children
   (d) enriching a museum at the expense of charities

2. When writing newspaper articles, you should _____. The lexicon at your disposal is constrained, because the text must be tailored to a diverse audience. This obliges a more imaginative and interesting approach because the use of jargon is not an option. By using precise, clear words that draw attention to the point you are making, you ensure that your readers understand what you have written. In this way, they will interpret your story how you want them to, and consequently you may convince them to read other articles you have written.

   (a) pursue storylines your editor approves
   (b) maintain a formal academic tone
   (c) use a suitable level of vocabulary
   (d) consider the views of a diverse readership

3.
   Dear Handyman Tools,

   I've been an avid user of your tools since my father presented me with a Handyman ratchet set for my 16th birthday. In my opinion, your company has a well-earned reputation for making durable, practical tools for the do-it-yourselfer, which is exactly why I was so distraught upon hearing that your production plant will move to Bangladesh. As a proud supporter of domestic manufacturing and American workers, I cannot in good conscience _____. I urge you to reconsider your decision.

   Respectfully yours,
   Elmer Boyle

   (a) continue patronizing your company
   (b) replace my most valuable tool
   (c) trust the longevity of your products
   (d) make purchases from a competitor

4. Drink Henan Fortified Water to _____. Henan Fortified Water is purified water infused with vitamins and dietary minerals such as calcium and potassium. The product is ideal for people who are not able to fulfill their recommended dietary allowances from the food they eat. The vitamins and minerals in Henan water improve the body's immune system, strengthening their defense against viruses and bacteria and lowering the risk of catching an infection.

(a) protect against waterborne diseases
(b) ensure you get your daily nutrients
(c) rid your body of harmful minerals
(d) keep yourself hydrated and fit

5. Documentaries, unlike feature films, generally do not fit the popular definition of "movies." Full-length films are often fictional and geared as much toward audience entertainment as they are toward the financial success of the producers. Documentaries, on the other hand, are the complete opposite of feature films, in the sense that these productions _____. Most documentaries present controversial political, historical, or social issues and are based on the directors' points of view. Despite their noncommercial approach, documentaries are starting to become financially viable.

(a) examine genuine circumstances and events
(b) always take profitability into consideration
(c) depend on critical acclaim to attract audiences
(d) are based on less fascinating characters

6. Before the advent of robots, carrying out scientific missions such as deep-sea explorations was unfeasible because of the likelihood of something going awry. However, with the aid of telerobots—specialized robots able to be controlled remotely via wireless networks or tethered connections—experts now have a dependable means of excavating underwater fossils, examining volcanic elements, and exploring outer space while remaining at a safe distance should anything go wrong. Scientists are ecstatic about their capability to _____.

(a) conduct intricate and risky operations
(b) develop innovative technology in their labs
(c) secure backing for deep-sea missions
(d) procure new robots from manufacturers

7. The Byzantine Empire preserved the last vestiges of the Roman Empire into the Middle Ages, _____. As a successor of the Roman Empire, the Byzantines retained much of the legal and cultural scaffolding of Ancient Roman society, but some of these elements were subverted by facets of Greek culture, which became so pervasive that Greek ultimately replaced Latin as the officially endorsed language of the empire. This amalgamation of influences contributed to the uniqueness of the Byzantine Empire.

(a) with primary influence from Latin cultures
(b) with no indication as to its ancient Roman heritage
(c) although it developed a distinct culture of its own
(d) although it took away the political authority of Rome

8. Politician Tom Blackford recently made an attempt to _____. His social media platforms were flooded with pictures of him cradling his newborn son, painting the picture of a dedicated family man. This is from a public official who has consistently voted for legislation that is anything but family friendly. The tactic didn't fly with the public, who pegged the photos as a media gambit and condemned Blackford as a schemer trying to resuscitate an ailing public image. Blackford disavowed any ulterior motives, claiming that any first-time father would have done likewise.

(a) bolster his reputation through his new status as a parent
(b) stop photos of his personal life from being published online
(c) clarify his stance on political issues that affect families
(d) deny that he has neglected his family in favor of his career

9.

Biographical Summary

Eva Perón's political aspirations were kindled during her tenure as president of a broadcast performers' union in Argentina. While presiding, she frequently praised the accomplishments of then labor secretary Juan Perón on a personal radio program, and she was popularly credited with coordinating the rally that emancipated Perón when political adversaries had him incarcerated. So popular was Eva's persona that her association with Juan's campaign led to his triumph in the 1946 election, soon after which the couple married. _____, Eva immersed herself in activities that reinforced the public's support for her husband's regime.

(a) Nonetheless
(b) Likewise
(c) Subsequently
(d) Despite this

10. Demographic data collected over the last several decades shows that Americans in their 20s tend to flock from their suburban family homes to more developed urban areas in search of better employment opportunities. By the time they reach their 30s, however, they display a general tendency to move back to the suburbs in order to settle down and raise their children. _____, long-term statistics of population movement reflect the established pattern of young adults moving from the suburbs to the city and back again.

(a) What's more
(b) That being said
(c) On the contrary
(d) In other words

Part II Questions 11~12
Read the passage. Then identify the option that does NOT belong.

11. The rise of the novel as a literary form coincided with the expansion of social opportunities to the masses. (a) In England, novelists Daniel Defoe and Charles Dickens discussed the benefits of living in a gradually opening society. (b) In India, novels blossomed during the British Raj, the period during which egalitarian influences from relatively liberal nations started to permeate Indian society. (c) Many novelists of the era were fascinated with the rise of industrialization. (d) Thus, the content of novels evolved to reflect the progressive social and cultural sensibilities of the times.

12. Attention to detail and openness to suggestions are two qualities that should be inherent in a good video editor. (a) Hence, be very thorough in evaluating what should be rejected or included in the finished product. (b) Interact with other people involved in the project and welcome advice from them while maintaining your independence. (c) Taking the time to review new techniques and learning to incorporate them into your own style will also help you improve. (d) In the end, the constructive criticism you provide will offer the benefit of a unique perspective.

Part III Questions 13~25

Read the passage and the question. Then choose the option that best answers the question.

13.
> **CashFlow Plus: Your Path to Financial Success**
>
> Would you like to secure the extra income necessary to fund a comfortable retirement? Property investment is the quickest path you can take to financial freedom, and our CashFlow Plus system will teach you how to get started.
>
> Earn thousands of dollars with only a few hours' work. All it takes is commitment, drive, and the CashFlow Plus DVD and book set. In no time, you'll be analyzing market trends and discovering the value to be found in properties facing bank liens or foreclosures.
>
> Let CashFlow Plus be your key to a prosperous future!

Q: What is the advertisement mainly about?

(a) Investing money in the stock market
(b) Learning how to become a broker
(c) Earning money purchasing real estate
(d) Getting a bank mortgage to buy property

14. Society for Responsible Pet Ownership (SRPO) President Amy Beck believes that all pets should be fixed to prevent reproduction once they reach six months of age. This is because sterilized animals do not have unwanted litters, are less aggressive and territorial, display more of the baby-like behaviors that most pet owners prefer, and have a lower chance of contracting cancers of the reproductive system. Beck and other members of the SRPO are on a crusade to educate pet owners and the general public about the benefits of reproductive operations.

Q: What is the passage mainly about?

(a) The debate surrounding animal overpopulation
(b) The animals operated upon by SRPO veterinarians
(c) Motivations for making pets infertile
(d) The ethical considerations of pet reproductive surgery

15. The atmosphere that envelops our planet today is very different from how it was billions of years ago. When the earth was still a growing mass of molten mantle and rock, it was wrapped in a toxic blanket of helium and hydrogen. As the earth's surface cooled, volcanic eruptions caused clouds of carbon dioxide, water vapor, and nitrogen to form in the atmosphere. Later, cyanobacteria appeared and began introducing oxygen into the atmosphere. The accumulation of oxygen in the atmosphere eventually produced the life-supporting mixture of air that we breathe today.

Q: What is the main topic of the passage?

(a) The significance of oxygen in earth's atmosphere
(b) The formation of earth's atmosphere
(c) The essential qualities of a life-supporting atmosphere
(d) The present composition of earth's atmosphere

16. Psychologists have long noted that toddlers are more captivated by toys that are placed beyond their reach than by those within their grasp. This observation in juvenile subjects is consistent with the results of a survey in which adult respondents rated challenging activities as more fulfilling than undemanding pursuits. These findings reveal the additional significance attaining a goal takes on when it is the result of a sustained effort.

Q: What is the passage mainly about?

(a) How people maintain their curiosity
(b) Ways of motivating people to overcome challenges
(c) The human basis for attributing worth
(d) Methods used to effectively get a child's attention

17.
> Dear colleagues,
>
> In a meeting with department managers this morning, it was decided that all employees should be required to wear uniforms, an illustration of which is attached. I know many of you will be surprised by this policy, because the company has never been strict with dress codes in the past, but the new CEO is insisting on it in the belief that a more consistent and professional appearance will improve our image. Employees will be given their uniforms in one month.
>
> Sincerely,
> Travis Howe

Q: Which of the following is correct according to the email?

(a) The old uniforms will be discarded by employees.
(b) The new uniform design has not been revealed.
(c) New uniforms will be given to workers this month.
(d) Uniforms regulations were enacted earlier today.

18. When a volcano erupts, liquefied rock called magma is ejected from within the earth through a hole at the volcano's summit. Sometimes, however, lava is trapped between layers of rock beneath the earth's surface and there's no place for it to go. This occurrence is called a laccolith, and it results in massive, breathtaking structures that jut hundreds of feet into the air, like Devil's Tower in the state of Wyoming. The laccoliths consist of the remaining lava after it has hardened, once the sediment that initially surrounded it has eroded away with the passage of time.

Q: Which of the following is correct according to the passage?

(a) Laccoliths are formed once enough sediment builds.
(b) Wyoming is renowned for its volcanic activity.
(c) Magma that surges upward cannot always escape.
(d) A laccolith is the scientific name for a volcanic eruption.

19.

> **Special Photography Exhibit**
>
> September 1 – November 30
> German National Peace Museum, Gallery 4
>
> Over 200 photos taken inside concentration camps by Nazi soldiers during World War II
>
> This exhibit explores the reality of German concentration camps, which were first established in 1933 as a means of detaining Jews and other individuals deemed undesirable by the Nazi party.
>
> Admission Fee
> Standard: $15
> Students/Seniors: $10
> Groups of 20 or more: $7 each
> Museum Members: Free

Q: Which of the following is correct according to the advertisement?

(a) The collection includes pictures shot inside containment areas.
(b) Groups of students can access the exhibition without a charge.
(c) The photos were taken in the years before the Second World War.
(d) Museum membership is available for seniors at a reduced price.

20. The Ancient Greeks thought that all matter comprised a mixture of earth, water, air, and fire. Humankind's comprehension of matter did not evolve beyond this until the 1600s, when the discovery of phosphorus prompted scientists to rigorously define the qualities of an element. Nowadays, it is accepted that an element is a substance that cannot be broken down further into simpler substances and is wholly composed of electrically charged particles. Since the 17th century, over 100 distinct elements have been encountered, 94 of which occur naturally on Earth and are not synthetic creations.

Q: Which of the following is correct according to the passage?

(a) There have been 94 elements identified.
(b) Phosphorus was the first indisputable element discovered.
(c) Electrically charged particles make up an element.
(d) The basic elements were detected by the Ancient Greeks.

21. The First Opium War was caused by an imbalance in trade between Britain and China. At the time, Chinese goods, such as tea, were hot commodities in Britain. The reverse, however, was not true. For £9 million of goods Britain exported, it bought £27 million from China. The British East India Company tilted things back in its favor by selling opium, grown on Indian plantations, to traders, who bought it with silver and transported it to China. Chinese officials, alarmed at this outflow of silver and the rise in opium addicts, seized a large opium shipment, sparking the war with Britain.

Q: Which of the following is correct according to the passage?

(a) The British had little interest in buying products from China.
(b) China's exports vastly outweighed those of Britain.
(c) Britain avoided exporting most of its Indian-grown opium.
(d) A lost opium shipment angered Chinese officials and started the war.

22.
Dear Robert Kilner,

We here at Magna Corporation are dedicated to our staff's professional development. Accordingly, we require all employees to complete no fewer than three accredited leadership courses annually. This is covered in full by management, provided receipts are submitted for reimbursement. As this calendar year draws to a close, it has come to our attention that you have yet to enroll in any courses. We urge you to remedy this promptly as opting not to enroll entails ending your employment with us when your current contract expires six months hence.

Sincerely,
Beverly Driscoll
Human Resources

Q: Which of the following is correct according to the passage?

(a) Ongoing training is required of employees with leadership roles.
(b) Employees are expected to pay for their own professional development.
(c) The employer is requesting that Robert Kilner take leadership training.
(d) Immediate termination will follow a refusal to enroll in courses.

23.

> **Economics**
>
> ## Yacht Maker Faces Upheaval
>
> Fantasy Yachts Inc. is in danger of closing down some of its manufacturing facilities after the company reported huge losses in the first quarter of the year. A company spokesperson revealed that Fantasy Yachts might take out a government loan to protect its plants from closure due to ballooning debts and shrinking sales.
>
> Company board members are also proposing an initial public offering to generate funds and streamlining personnel to avoid unnecessary expenses.

Q: What can be inferred from the passage?

(a) Company employees could possibly lose their jobs.
(b) New manufacturing plants will be built to boost production.
(c) A government takeover is needed to save the company.
(d) Mergers with competitors will solve the company's problems.

24. In a study conducted by Austrian researcher Friederike Range and his colleagues at the University of Vienna, it was concluded that dogs, like humans, have the ability to form abstract concepts. In the first phase of the study, the researchers rewarded a dog with a treat every time it chose pictures of canines over landscape photographs that were flashed on a touch screen. The dogs also learned to identify canines in a previously unseen set of photographs without being given a treat. Finally, the dogs chose pictures featuring both landscape and canines combined over those with landscapes alone.

Q: What can be inferred from the passage?

(a) Dogs can better categorize items when given a treat.
(b) Most dogs prefer pictures of landscapes to canines.
(c) Visual aids can help dogs become more intelligent.
(d) Dogs distinguish between elements in a complex photo.

25. The prospect of travel exceeding the speed of light is unfeasible given our current conception of physics. Namely, the theory of general relativity would be contravened; under routine circumstances, an object cannot exceed the speed of light, at least from the perspective of a proximal observer. If a sufficient quantity of gravitational force can be harnessed, however, the fabric of space-time can be bent so that an object can exceed the speed-of-light threshold. Such conditions are impossible to reproduce within a stable system, so the chance of a similar situation actually transpiring is remote.

Q: What can be inferred from the passage?

(a) The theory of general relativity only holds under ideal conditions.
(b) Observation of objects near the speed of light is impossible.
(c) The shape of space-time influences the velocity at which objects travel.
(d) A stable system is a prerequisite for surpassing the speed of light.

Part IV Questions 26~35

Read the passage and the questions. Then choose the option that best answers each question.

Questions 26-27

http://jobopening.sfchronicle.com/columnist

The San Fernando Chronicle
Job Opening: Columnist

The San Fernando Chronicle is looking for an experienced columnist who can offer a distinctive opinion on both local issues and national politics. The columnist will also be the public face of the newspaper, representing us at community gatherings and connecting with local readers.

Job Requirements:

- At least five years working in journalism is essential—those with a background in local news preferred.
- Must have a bachelor's degree in journalism or a related field.
- The capacity to produce columns expressing a unique voice and viewpoint at least twice a week.
- A strong ability to find and research news, particularly community-based stories.
- A firm understanding of the local area and its residents' multiethnic culture and socioeconomic differences is vital.
- Article editing and proofreading skills are necessary—experience with multimedia considered a plus.

Applicants must submit their résumé, the contact information of two recent references, three writing samples, and two proposals for columns. Please send your application to recruiting@sfchronicle.com no later than the 7th of May.

26. Q: Which of the following is correct according to the passage?

(a) The columnist will write exclusively about local political issues in San Fernando.
(b) The newspaper prefers to hire recent graduates of local journalism schools.
(c) The columnist will be expected to be present at neighborhood events.
(d) Applicants must submit two complete columns related to San Fernando.

27. Q: What quality must the newspaper's columnist possess?

(a) A high level of expertise in editing visual and auditory media
(b) Experience of being a reporter in a local newspaper or media outlet
(c) A grasp of the diversity in income and background of local people
(d) The ability to interview local residents for newspaper features

Questions 28-29

Kirkwall Ferry Company
29 Harbor Street, Brigantine,
New Jersey, United States, 07109

Expense Approval Request Form

Date of request: May 7
Requested by: Ross Shearer   Job title: Ferry Supervisor
Expense request details:

> On May 5, I was informed about our company's efforts to strengthen its safety standards. In compliance with the new policies, I had the deckhands conduct a full inspection of the WaveCharger ferryboat. Through this process, I reached the conclusion that we need some new life jackets.
>
> Of the 250 life jackets that we are required to have on board, 20 have been exposed to sunlight and ocean spray on the deck for a number of years. As a result, the fabric has faded and some of the straps have become worn out. I'm concerned that these flotation devices may not be dependable in the event of an emergency. On the other hand, the 230 life jackets that have been stored in our main passenger compartment are still in good condition, so I think we can keep them for a while. It would be best if we could buy the new life jackets before June 1, the start of our peak tourist season.

Estimated cost: $950

28. Q: Which of the following is correct according to the passage?

   (a) Kirkwall Ferry Company failed to meet some government standards.
   (b) A supervisor has placed an order for 250 life jackets.
   (c) Ferry deckhands will receive training regarding new safety procedures.
   (d) Some of the safety devices on the WaveCharger are kept outdoors.

29. Q: What can be inferred from the passage?

   (a) The number of ferry passengers will increase in June.
   (b) On-board personnel demonstrate emergency procedures before each sailing.
   (c) The WaveCharger is currently not able to operate at full capacity.
   (d) Ross Shearer performs an inspection on a monthly basis.

Questions 30-31

Salt and pepper are ubiquitous in Western cuisine, both as vital ingredients in cooking, and on tables in the form of shakers. This was not always the case, however, since salt and pepper have gone in and out of fashion over the course of culinary history. During the Middle Ages, the food eaten by Europe's aristocracy was highly seasoned, and salt and pepper were added to dishes while they were cooked. If salt was on the table, it was either in a salt cellar or was dispensed by the person carving the meat. However, because seasoning was expensive, most of the population ate much blander fare.

During the 16th and 17th centuries, European aristocratic cuisine gradually became less heavily seasoned. Culinary historians believe that this was because seasoning became widely available, meaning that it was no longer considered to be a luxury that only the wealthy could enjoy. The idea that spices had beneficial health properties also started to decline. In French cooking, meanwhile, the notion that the central ingredient of the meal should be allowed to shine led to less of an emphasis on seasoning. Nevertheless, salt and pepper never completely went away and were given a new lease on life when shakers became common in the early 20th century.

30. Q: What is the main topic of the passage?

   (a) The use of salt and pepper in the preservation of food
   (b) The trade in salt and pepper during the Middle Ages
   (c) A history of the use of seasoning in European cooking
   (d) An overview of the contemporary fashions in salt usage

31. Q: What can be inferred from the passage?

   (a) Most ordinary citizens in the Middle Ages could not afford salt and pepper.
   (b) Salt and pepper were the main commodities that were traded in the 16th and 17th centuries.
   (c) French cuisine was the leading culinary field in Europe during the Middle Ages.
   (d) Medical advances proved that the perceived health benefits of spices were unfounded.

Questions 32-33

Science Note

For centuries before the evolution of *Homo sapiens*, another humanoid species, the Neanderthals, lived throughout Europe and parts of Asia. Most early archaeologists concluded that these archaic humans were more primitive, without the mental capacity of modern humans. However, a more complex picture of Neanderthals has started to emerge, with evidence that they had a mixed diet, wore jewelry, and created art. This last discovery was made in Spain, where an international team of archaeologists found that many ancient cave paintings that were thought to be by early humans had been painted by Neanderthals.

Using carbon dating techniques, this team analyzed calcite crusts that had developed over ancient art works in several caves, revealing that they were painted at least 65,000 years ago. As humans only made their way to Europe 40,000 years ago, the works must have been by Neanderthals, who lived in Europe from around 120,000 years ago. The paintings, which include hand stencils and geometric shapes, display a degree of complexity that Neanderthals were not thought to be capable of, suggesting that our evolutionary cousins were much closer to humans in terms of cognition, perception, and creativity than previously imagined.

32. Q: What is the passage mainly about?

(a) New archaeological evidence of the complexity of Neanderthal behavior
(b) A refutation of an evolutionary link between Neanderthals and humans
(c) The recent application of carbon dating techniques in archaeology
(d) The development of Neanderthal communities across the Asian continent

33. Q: What can be inferred about Neanderthals from the passage?

(a) They first started living in Europe around 65,000 years before *Homo sapiens* evolved.
(b) They were driven to complete extinction by human activity around 120,000 years ago.
(c) They migrated to various locations in Europe from western Asia and northern Africa.
(d) They were present in some parts of the European continent 65,000 years ago.

Questions 34-35

Ogdan Ready to Get Greener
By Max Cooper

Disposing of any waste at the town landfill in Ogdan will cost more from April 1st. The council has decided to introduce the new landfill fees as a means of raising funds for improvements to the city's waste disposal system and discouraging overuse of the town's landfill.

At present, disposing of any items in the landfill incurs a flat rate charge of $10 per ton, which is intended to cover the cost of managing the landfill. Under the new tax, the price of each deposit will depend largely on the type of waste.

Active waste, including wood, ductwork, piping, and plastics, will be charged at $50 per ton. Inactive waste, on the other hand, such as earth, concrete, and glass will be charged at $2.50 per ton. This discrepancy reflects the difficulty in disposing of the former type of waste. Small deposits weighing a quarter ton or less will be charged the original flat rate.

The government asserted that most of the funds from the new fees will go towards a more comprehensive recycling system, which will fundamentally cut down on the amount of waste disposed and reduce Ogdan's reliance on the landfill. However, many residents have voiced objections to the fee increase, arguing that it will make waste disposal unaffordable for them.

34. Q: Which of the following will be charged at the most expensive rate?

   (a) A disposal of ten tons of concrete
   (b) A deposit of a quarter ton of glass
   (c) A third ton of earth
   (d) A ton of plastic waste products

35. Q: What is the main purpose of the news report?

   (a) To argue for the introduction of a better recycling system
   (b) To describe the problems of discarding waste in a landfill
   (c) To explain how a new charge on depositing waste will work
   (d) To suggest that landfill waste disposal should be taxed more

The Reading Comprehension section of the exam is complete. Please stay in your seat until the proctor tells you to leave. You are NOT allowed to open any of the other sections of the exam.

시험에 나올 문제를 미리 풀어보는
텝스 적중예상특강
해커스텝스 HackersTEPS.com

SELF-CHECK LIST

TEST 06은 잘 마치셨나요?
이제 다음의 SELF-CHECK LIST를 통해 자신의 테스트 진행 내용을 점검해 볼까요?

1. 나는 테스트를 마칠 때까지 완전히 테스트에 집중하였다.
   ☐ YES   ☐ NO

2. 나는 각 영역별 주어진 시간을 지켰다.
   ☐ LISTENING COMPREHENSION
   ☐ VOCABULARY & GRAMMAR   ☐ READING COMPREHENSION

3. 나는 시간 내에 모든 문제를 풀었다.
   ☐ LISTENING COMPREHENSION
   ☐ VOCABULARY & GRAMMAR   ☐ READING COMPREHENSION

4. 나는 특히 어렵게 느껴지는 영역이 있었다.
   ☐ LISTENING COMPREHENSION
   ☐ VOCABULARY & GRAMMAR   ☐ READING COMPREHENSION

5. 개선하고 싶은 사항
   _____
   _____
   _____
   _____
   _____

■ 개선해야 할 점은 반드시 다음 테스트에서 실천해야만 실력을 향상시킬 수 있습니다.
그리고 반드시 오답을 정리해서 같은 실수를 반복하지 않도록 유의하기 바랍니다.

해커스 텝스 최신기출유형 실전모의고사 문제집

해석·스크립트

TEST 01
TEST 02
TEST 03
TEST 04
TEST 05
TEST 06

TEST 01

LISTENING COMPREHENSION

Part I

1

M: Will you give us a ring from Maui?
W: _____

(a) Rest assured I'll keep in touch.
(b) You'll sure relish your stay there.
(c) Sure. My flight isn't until eleven.
(d) I'm nervous about proposing.

M: 마우이 섬에서 우리에게 전화해줄래요?
(a) 연락할 테니 안심하세요.
(b) 당신은 분명 거기서 머무르는 걸 즐기실 거예요.
(c) 물론이죠. 제 항공편은 11시나 되어야 있어요.
(d) 전 청혼하는 것 때문에 초조해요.

2

W: I haven't had time to cook.
M: _____

(a) Well, we can eat out.
(b) I don't care. I'm starving.
(c) Because I was out.
(d) That's so thoughtful.

W: 난 요리할 시간이 없었어.
(a) 뭐, 외식하면 되지.
(b) 상관없어. 배고파 죽겠어.
(c) 나는 외출했었거든.
(d) 정말 사려 깊구나.

3

M: Would you lend me an ear, Abby?
W: _____

(a) But you don't need to.
(b) Is everything all right?
(c) You should be upfront.
(d) Sure. I've figured it out.

M: 내 이야기 좀 들어줄래, Abby?
(a) 하지만 그러지 않아도 돼.
(b) 괜찮은 거야?
(c) 너는 솔직해져야 해.
(d) 물론이지. 나 그거 알아냈어.

4

W: We'll need an understudy for John's role, should he fall ill.
M: _____

(a) I thought the show went fine anyway.
(b) He's really not one to study, I'm afraid.
(c) Let's discuss it after the performance.
(d) I'll be happy to memorize his lines just in case.

W: John이 아프면, 우리는 그가 맡은 역할의 대역이 필요할 거야.
(a) 어쨌든 난 공연이 잘 진행되었다고 생각했어.
(b) 그는 정말 대사를 외우는 사람은 아닌 것 같아.
(c) 공연 후에 그것에 대해 논의해보자.
(d) 만약을 위해서 내가 그의 대사를 외워 둘게.

5

M: Good morning. Can I collect my laundry today?
W: _____

(a) Sure, we are taking drop-offs.
(b) Possibly. I'll have it delivered.
(c) We offer dry cleaning.
(d) Let me verify its status.

M: 안녕하세요. 오늘 세탁물을 찾으러 가도 될까요?
(a) 그럼요, 저희는 가져다주시는 것을 받아요.
(b) 아마도요. 제가 그걸 배달해 드릴게요.
(c) 저희는 드라이클리닝을 해 드려요.
(d) 제가 진행 상황을 확인해 볼게요.

6

W: His appearance makes me wonder if he's fallen on hard times.
M: _____

(a) I have few free moments.
(b) Ignore the rumors he's spread.
(c) You can't judge a book by its cover.
(d) Make an effort to look presentable.

W: 그의 모습을 보아하니 힘든 일이 많았었나 봐.
(a) 난 한가할 때가 거의 없어.
(b) 그가 퍼뜨린 소문은 무시해버려.
(c) 겉만 보고 속을 판단할 수는 없는 거야.
(d) 외모가 괜찮게 보이도록 노력 좀 해.

7

M: Anne, when do you plan to visit me?

W: _____

(a) I'll head home pretty soon.
(b) I have time off next week.
(c) Sorry. I had to leave early.
(d) Oh, thanks for inviting me.

M: Anne, 넌 언제 우리 집에 방문할 거니?
(a) 난 금방 집에 갈 거야.
(b) 난 다음 주에 일을 쉬어.
(c) 미안해. 나는 일찍 가봐야 했어.
(d) 아, 초대해줘서 고마워.

8

W: I hope you can suggest some high-end hotels for me.
M: _____

(a) I couldn't possibly intrude on your vacation.
(b) They'll make you feel welcome wherever you go.
(c) The price can't be that high, I'm sure.
(d) I only know of budget accommodations.

W: 나에게 고급 호텔들을 좀 추천해줬으면 해.
(a) 난 차마 네 휴가를 방해할 수가 없었어.
(b) 그것들은 네가 어디에 가든 환영받도록 느끼게 해 줄 거야.
(c) 내가 확신하는데, 가격이 그렇게 높을 리가 없어.
(d) 난 저렴한 숙박 시설만 알고 있어.

9

M: I'm studying for tomorrow's exam. I can't slack off.
W: _____

(a) Keep your nose to the grindstone.
(b) Provided it's part of the lecture notes.
(c) Ask a classmate to explain the material.
(d) You must be more motivated.

M: 난 내일 시험 공부를 하고 있어. 게으름을 부릴 수가 없어.
(a) 열심히 공부해.
(b) 그게 강의 노트의 일부라면 말이지.
(c) 내용을 설명해 달라고 반 친구한테 부탁해 봐.
(d) 넌 분명 더 자극받았겠다.

10

W: Is there a post office nearby?
M: _____

(a) I think they accept packages.
(b) Mail delivery occurs daily.
(c) Two blocks away at Second Street.
(d) You'll need to buy stamps.

W: 근처에 우체국이 있나요?
(a) 소포도 받는 것 같아요.
(b) 우편 배달은 매일 있어요.
(c) 두 블록 떨어진 2번가에 있어요.
(d) 우표를 사셔야 될 거예요.

Part II

11

M: At what age did your son start using full sentences?
W: Hmm... About two, I guess?
M: Wow! That's rather early, isn't it?
W: _____

(a) It's nothing out of the ordinary.
(b) He's much older than two now.
(c) No, it was only twice.
(d) Well, then let's wait and see.

M: 네 아들은 몇 살 때 완벽한 문장을 사용하기 시작했니?
W: 음… 아마도 두 살 때쯤인 것 같은데?
M: 와! 그건 꽤 이르네, 그렇지 않아?
(a) 그건 특이한 게 전혀 아냐.
(b) 그는 지금 두 살보다 훨씬 더 나이가 많아.
(c) 아니, 그것은 겨우 두 번이었어.
(d) 음, 그럼 기다려 보자.

12

W: You must be Bill. I'm your new lab partner.
M: Nice to meet you. Are you new?
W: I transferred from Clover College.
M: _____

(a) You'd better work diligently.
(b) I heard it's a good institution.
(c) Let me check the class roster.
(d) We should work together.

W: 네가 Bill이구나. 난 네 새로운 실험 파트너야.
M: 만나서 반가워. 신입생이니?
W: Clover 대학에서 편입했어.
(a) 부지런히 노력하는 게 좋을 거야.
(b) 거기 좋은 대학이라고 들었어.
(c) 내가 학급 명단을 확인해볼게.
(d) 우리는 함께 일해야 해.

13

M: I've never wanted a pet.
W: Why not? Many find them terrific companions.
M: They just don't seem worth the trouble.
W: _____

(a) I had a similar problem with mine.
(b) Perhaps I should reconsider it.
(c) The responsibility isn't for everyone.
(d) Actually, their care involves other costs.

M: 나는 애완동물을 키우고 싶다는 생각을 해본 적이 없어.
W: 왜? 많은 사람들이 애완동물을 아주 좋은 친구라고 생각하는데.
M: 그냥 그런 수고를 감당할 가치가 없는 것 같아.

(a) 내 애완동물에도 비슷한 문제가 있었어.
(b) 어쩌면 내가 그것을 다시 생각해봐야 할 것 같아.
(c) 모두가 감당할 수 있는 일은 아니지.
(d) 사실, 애완동물을 키우려면 다른 비용도 들어.

14

W: Hi, there. I'll have the pasta.
M: OK. Anything else you'd like to order?
W: Yeah. Do you still carry garden salads?
M: _____

(a) Sure, I'll have one too.
(b) They are too filling.
(c) Those are popular at lunch.
(d) I'll check if we have any.

W: 저기요. 전 파스타 주세요.
M: 알겠습니다. 더 주문하시겠습니까?
W: 네. 가든 샐러드를 아직도 파나요?

(a) 그럼요, 저도 하나 주세요.
(b) 그건 너무 배가 불러요.
(c) 그건 점심 때 인기가 있지요.
(d) 있는지 확인해 볼게요.

15

M: I missed you at the skating rink yesterday.
W: I had to rewrite a paper I accidentally deleted.
M: Really? That must have been annoying.
W: _____

(a) Yeah. I stayed there late.
(b) Well, I got a bad grade.
(c) I'd hate to be an annoyance.
(d) Annoyed is exactly how I felt.

M: 어제 스케이트장에서 네가 안 보이던데.
W: 실수로 지워버린 보고서를 다시 써야 했어.
M: 정말이야? 그거 분명 짜증났겠다.

(a) 맞아. 나는 늦게까지 그곳에 있었어.
(b) 음, 나는 안 좋은 성적을 받았어.
(c) 나라면 골칫거리는 되고 싶지 않을 거야.
(d) 짜증났다는 게 바로 내가 느낀 감정이야.

16

W: I grounded my daughter for skipping class last week.
M: Yikes! That's a little harsh, don't you think?
W: Maybe you're right, but parents need to be strict sometimes.
M: _____

(a) I feel a little bad about doing it now.
(b) She's only grounded for a few weeks.
(c) Not quite. Parenting is a difficult job.
(d) Fair enough. Children do need firm boundaries.

W: 우리 딸이 지난주에 수업을 빼먹어서 외출을 금지시켰어.
M: 이런! 그건 좀 심한 것 같은데, 그렇지 않니?
W: 네 말이 맞을지도 몰라, 하지만 부모는 때때로 엄격할 필요가 있어.

(a) 지금은 그렇게 한 것이 좀 속상해.
(b) 그녀는 겨우 몇 주 동안만 외출 금지였어.
(c) 별로 그렇지는 않아. 양육은 어려운 일이야.
(d) 그래. 아이들은 확고한 경계선이 필요하지.

17

M: Hi. Am I heading towards the orchard?
W: No, you should've made a left on Forest Road.
M: What do you suggest I do?
W: _____

(a) You'd better let me drive.
(b) Try to come back after the harvest.
(c) Stopping here is convenient.
(d) Turn around at the next intersection.

M: 안녕하세요. 제가 과수원으로 가고 있는 건가요?
W: 아뇨, Forest 로에서 좌회전을 하셨어야 해요.
M: 그럼 어떻게 해야 하죠?

(a) 제가 운전하는 게 낫겠네요.
(b) 수확기가 끝나고 다시 와보세요.
(c) 여기서 멈추는 게 편해요.
(d) 다음 교차로에서 유턴하세요.

18

W: Got any lunch plans?
M: I'll likely end up in the cafeteria, as usual.
W: Why don't we try the new Mexican place? My treat.
M: _____

(a) I'd love to, but there's none nearby.
(b) That's a really tempting offer.
(c) Really, you won't have to pay me back.
(d) It's OK, I thought you didn't like spicy food.

W: 점심 식사 약속이 있니?
M: 평소처럼 결국 구내 식당에 가게 될 것 같아.
W: 새로운 멕시코 식당에 가보는 게 어때? 내가 살게.

(a) 그러고 싶지만, 근처에 하나도 없어.
(b) 그것은 정말 솔깃한 제안이네.
(c) 정말로 내게 돈을 갚을 필요가 없어.
(d) 괜찮아, 난 네가 매운 음식을 좋아하지 않는다고 생각했어.

19

M: Pardon me, but you've been standing there a while.
W: Yes, I'm waiting for a bus.

M: Oh, they've stopped running tonight. Do you need a lift?
W: _____

(a) It's likely closed by now.
(b) If it's not out of your way.
(c) I live on Fifth Street.
(d) I'll wait for the next bus.

M: 실례합니다만, 거기에 한참 서 계시더군요.
W: 네, 버스를 기다리고 있어요.
M: 아, 오늘 밤에는 운행을 중단했어요. 제가 태워 드릴까요?

(a) 지금쯤이면 닫혀 있을 것 같아요.
(b) 가시는 길에서 벗어나는 게 아니라면요.
(c) 전 5번가에 살아요.
(d) 전 다음 버스를 기다릴게요.

20

W: I heard hackers got into the military's computer system.
M: They did. It's a complete disaster.
W: Just how much confidential information was stolen?
M: _____

(a) All it takes is a few computers and some code.
(b) The extent of the breach is still under investigation.
(c) This isn't confidential, so we can discuss it.
(d) It didn't take them long to crack the passwords.

W: 해커들이 군용 컴퓨터 시스템에 침입했다고 들었어.
M: 그랬지. 이건 완전한 참사야.
W: 정확히 얼마나 많은 기밀 정보가 도난당한 거야?

(a) 몇 대의 컴퓨터와 암호만 있으면 돼.
(b) 침해 규모는 아직 조사 중이야.
(c) 이것은 기밀이 아니라서, 우리가 그것을 논의할 수 있어.
(d) 그들이 비밀번호를 푸는 것은 오래 걸리지 않았어.

Part III

21

Listen to a conversation between two friends.

M: What's that on your knee?
W: Oh, it's a brace. I need it because I'm coming off an injury.
M: I've never worn one. Does it help?
W: Yeah. It gives support and additional protection to my knee.
M: It looks like it limits your mobility, though.
W: Well, yeah. But that's something I'm willing to compromise.

Q: What is the conversation mainly about?

(a) What caused the woman's injury
(b) How the woman's knee was affected
(c) Why the woman needs protective gear
(d) What compromise the woman made

두 친구 간의 대화를 들으시오.

M: 네 무릎에 그게 뭐니?
W: 아, 이건 보호대야. 내 부상이 나아가는 중이라 이게 필요해.
M: 난 한 번도 착용해본 적이 없어. 그게 도움이 되니?
W: 그럼. 무릎을 받쳐주고 추가적으로 보호도 해줘.
M: 그렇긴 한데, 네 움직임을 제한하는 것 같아.
W: 음, 그건 맞아. 하지만 그건 내가 기꺼이 타협할 수 있어.

Q: 주로 무엇에 관한 대화인가?

(a) 무엇이 여자에게 부상을 입혔는지
(b) 어떻게 여자의 무릎에 병이 나게 되었는지
(c) 왜 여자는 보호대가 필요한지
(d) 여자가 무엇을 타협하기로 했는지

22

Listen to a conversation at a university.

W: Hi. Do you know where the dean's office is?
M: On the second floor. It's the fourth room on your right coming from the stairs.
W: That's odd. I just went up there, but I didn't see it.
M: It's there, just past the cashier's window.
W: OK. I'll go and check again.
M: Here, let me go with you.

Q: What is the woman mainly doing in the conversation?

(a) Having a meeting with the dean
(b) Searching for the school cashier
(c) Checking whether the dean is in
(d) Seeking assistance finding a room

대학교에서의 대화를 들으시오.

W: 안녕하세요. 학장실이 어디 있는지 아세요?
M: 2층에 있어요. 계단을 올라가서 오른쪽으로 4번째 방이에요.
W: 이상하네요. 제가 방금 거기에 올라갔었는데, 못 찾았거든요.
M: 출납 창구 지나서 바로 거기에 있어요.
W: 알겠습니다. 다시 한번 가볼게요.
M: 이리 오세요, 제가 같이 가 드릴게요.

Q: 대화에서 여자는 주로 무엇을 하고 있는가?

(a) 학장과 회의를 하고 있다.
(b) 학교 출납원을 찾고 있다.
(c) 학장이 방에 있는지 확인하고 있다.
(d) 방을 찾는 데 도움을 구하고 있다.

23

Listen to a conversation between two acquaintances.

M: Wow. Take a look at that mountain bike on

display.
W: It's quite a specimen. What do you think it runs?
M: I'd guess somewhere around $300.
W: Probably more. I'd say over $400.
M: Are you willing to shell out that much for a bike?
W: Not really. But I know a few who would.

Q: What are the man and woman mainly discussing?

(a) The increasing cost of bicycles
(b) The possible price of a bicycle
(c) The money they must raise for a bike
(d) The features of a bicycle on display

두 지인 간의 대화를 들으시오.

M: 와. 진열되어 있는 저 산악자전거 좀 봐.
W: 대단한 제품이네. 값이 얼마나 나갈 것 같아?
M: 300달러 정도에서 왔다갔다할 것 같은데?
W: 아마 더 나갈 걸. 내 생각엔 400달러는 넘을 것 같아.
M: 너라면 자전거에 그렇게 많은 돈을 들이겠어?
W: 별로. 하지만 그럴 만한 사람들을 몇 알고 있지.

Q: 남자와 여자는 주로 무엇을 논의하고 있는가?

(a) 인상되는 자전거 가격
(b) 자전거의 예상 가격
(c) 자전거를 위해 모아야 할 금액
(d) 진열된 자전거의 사양

24

Listen to a conversation between a couple.

W: My ride is in the driveway. I'll catch you later.
M: Be sure to call when you arrive.
W: I'll do my best, but I'm not sure whether the ranch will have reception.
M: Oh, then could you call me along the way?
W: Sure. We'll probably stop somewhere for lunch.
M: Thanks. I just want to make sure that you're safe and sound.

Q: Which is correct according to the conversation?

(a) The woman forgot to bring her mobile phone.
(b) The man is planning to meet the woman for lunch.
(c) The woman is going to travel to a ranch.
(d) The man is expecting a phone call from a client.

커플 간의 대화를 들으시오.

W: 차가 진입로에 들어섰어. 나중에 이야기하자.
M: 도착하면 꼭 전화해.
W: 최선을 다해보겠지만, 목장에 수신이 잡힐지 잘 모르겠어.
M: 아, 그렇다면 가는 길에 전화해줄래?
W: 물론이지. 우리는 아마 점심을 먹기 위해 어딘가에 들를 거야.
M: 고마워. 나는 단지 네가 무사한지 확인하고 싶어.

Q: 대화에 따르면 맞는 것은 무엇인가?

(a) 여자는 자신의 휴대전화를 가져오는 것을 잊어버렸다.
(b) 남자는 점심을 먹기 위해 여자를 만날 계획이다.
(c) 여자는 목장으로 갈 것이다.
(d) 남자는 고객으로부터의 전화를 기다리고 있다.

25

Listen to a conversation between two friends.

M: Is that a new blouse you've got on?
W: It was an impulse purchase. What do you think?
M: It's gorgeous. It must have been expensive.
W: Actually, the price had been slashed.
M: Sounds like you got a steal.
W: Yeah, I'm very pleased.

Q: Which is correct about the woman according to the conversation?

(a) She bought an item she had always wanted.
(b) She received a discount on a purchase.
(c) She damaged an article of clothing.
(d) She recovered a blouse she had lost.

두 친구 간의 대화를 들으시오.

M: 네가 입은 블라우스는 새 옷이니?
W: 충동 구매였어. 어때?
M: 아주 멋져. 비쌌겠는걸.
W: 사실, 가격이 대폭 할인되어 있었어.
M: 너 횡재한 것 같다.
W: 맞아, 난 정말 기뻐.

Q: 대화에 따르면 여자에 대해 맞는 것은 무엇인가?

(a) 항상 원했던 물품을 샀다.
(b) 구매 시 할인을 받았다.
(c) 옷 한 벌을 훼손했다.
(d) 잃어버렸던 블라우스를 되찾았다.

26

Listen to a conversation between a couple.

W: The doctor is still worried about my cholesterol levels.
M: Didn't he prescribe you a cholesterol-lowering medication?
W: He did, but I'm going to use drugs as a last resort.
M: Then, how about lifestyle changes?
W: I'm trying a healthier diet, but it's hard.
M: I can relate. It took me a year and several tries to go vegetarian.
W: How did you make the change stick?
M: Eventually, my health concerns trumped my

craving for meat.

Q: Which is correct according to the conversation?

(a) Cholesterol medications have not worked for the woman.
(b) The woman refuses to try living a healthier lifestyle.
(c) The man attempted to stop eating meat more than once.
(d) Changing his diet eliminated the man's desire to eat meat.

커플 간의 대화를 들으시오.
W: 의사 선생님은 여전히 내 콜레스테롤 수치에 대해 걱정하셔.
M: 그분이 네게 콜레스테롤을 낮추는 약을 처방해주지 않으셨니?
W: 그렇기는 한데, 난 약을 최후의 수단으로 사용할 거야.
M: 그럼, 생활 방식에 변화를 주는 것은 어때?
W: 더 건강한 식사를 하려고 노력 중이긴 한데, 어려워.
M: 나도 공감해. 내가 채식주의자가 되는 데 일 년이 걸렸고 여러 번 시도했다.
W: 넌 어떻게 그 변화를 유지했니?
M: 결국, 건강에 대한 우려가 고기에 대한 욕구를 능가했어.

Q: 대화에 따르면 맞는 것은 무엇인가?
(a) 콜레스테롤 약은 여자에게 효과가 없었다.
(b) 여자는 더 건강한 생활 방식으로 살아보는 것을 거부한다.
(c) 남자는 고기를 그만 먹으려고 한 번 이상 시도했다.
(d) 식습관의 변화는 고기를 먹으려는 남자의 욕구를 없앴다.

27

Listen to a conversation about a blood drive.

M: Good morning. What can I do for you?
W: I'd like to be a part of the blood drive.
M: Certainly. Have you given blood before?
W: The last time was about a month and a half ago.
M: Sorry, but state regulations mandate a 60-day waiting period.
W: Oh, that's news to me. I'll hold off, then.

Q: Why is the woman unable to participate in the blood drive?

(a) She falls below a minimum age limit.
(b) She donated blood within the past 60 days.
(c) She is unable to provide some information.
(d) She was not on time for her appointment.

헌혈 캠페인에 관한 대화를 들으시오.
M: 안녕하세요. 무엇을 도와 드릴까요?
W: 헌혈 캠페인에 참여하고 싶어요.
M: 네, 전에 헌혈해본 적 있으세요?
W: 마지막으로 한 게 약 한 달 반 전이었어요.
M: 죄송하지만, 정부 규정상 60일간의 유예 기간이 필요해요.
W: 아, 그건 처음 듣네요. 그럼, 다음으로 미루죠.

Q: 여자는 왜 헌혈 캠페인에 참여할 수 없는가?

(a) 최저 연령 제한에 미치지 못한다.
(b) 지난 60일 이내에 헌혈을 했다.
(c) 일부 정보를 제공할 수 없다.
(d) 예약 시간을 지키지 않았다.

28

Listen to a conversation between a passenger and an airline representative.

W: I'd like to have this coach ticket upgraded to first-class.
M: I'm sorry, but your flight is already at capacity.
W: Are there any other options?
M: Well, there are unoccupied first-class seats on the next flight.
W: But the next flight has two stopovers.
M: My hands are tied. I'm sorry.

Q: Which is correct according to the conversation?

(a) The woman wants to amend her booking after the fact.
(b) The man suggested the woman take an earlier flight.
(c) The next flight does not fit the woman's schedule.
(d) The man refused to help the woman adjust her itinerary.

승객과 항공사 직원 간의 대화를 들으시오.
W: 이 일반석 표를 1등석으로 바꾸고 싶어요.
M: 죄송하지만, 손님이 타실 항공편은 이미 정원이 찼습니다.
W: 그럼 다른 방법은 없나요?
M: 음, 다음 항공편에는 비어 있는 1등석 자리가 있네요.
W: 하지만 다음 비행기는 두 군데나 경유해 가잖아요.
M: 그럼 어쩔 수가 없네요. 죄송합니다.

Q: 대화에 따르면 맞는 것은 무엇인가?
(a) 여자는 사후에 자신의 예약을 변경하고 싶어 한다.
(b) 남자는 여자에게 더 이른 비행기를 타라고 제안했다.
(c) 다음 비행기는 여자의 일정에 맞지 않는다.
(d) 남자는 여자의 여행 일정 조정을 도와주기를 거절했다.

29

Listen to a conversation between a couple.

M: Gretchen, there's a message on the answering machine for you.
W: Yeah. It was a representative from one of the universities I applied at.
M: What did it say? Did they tender an offer?
W: Just on a provisional basis. One of their professors filed for maternity leave.
M: I'd jump at the chance. A job's a job, after all.
W: I know, but I'm looking for a more permanent post.

Q: What can be inferred from the conversation?

(a) The man and woman are both out of work.
(b) The woman is an incoming college student.
(c) The man wants the woman to negotiate a better offer.
(d) The woman will pass on the job opportunity.

커플 간의 대화를 들으시오.
M: Gretchen, 자동 응답기에 네게 온 메시지가 있어.
W: 응. 내가 지원했던 대학들 중 한 곳의 대리인이었어.
M: 메시지에서 뭐래? 거기서 일자리를 주겠대?
W: 그냥 임시직이야. 거기 교수 중 한 명이 육아 휴직을 신청했대.
M: 나 같으면 일단 기회는 잡고 보겠어. 어쨌든, 일은 일이잖아.
W: 알아, 하지만 나는 더 영구적인 자리를 찾고 있어.
Q: 대화에서 추론할 수 있는 것은 무엇인가?
(a) 남자와 여자는 둘 다 직업이 없다.
(b) 여자는 대학 신입생이다.
(c) 남자는 여자가 더 나은 조건으로 협상하기를 바란다.
(d) 여자는 이번 일자리를 사양할 것이다.

30

Listen to two colleagues discuss office leave.

W: George, have you taken all your vacation days yet?
M: Yeah, a month ago. How about you?
W: I still have three. The manager just filled me in.
M: You know they don't carry over, right?
W: I know. I ought to use them up on an out-of-town trip with my family.
M: Well, just be sure to do it before the end of the year.

Q: What can be inferred from the conversation?

(a) The man is tired from a long flight.
(b) The woman aims to use all of her vacation days.
(c) The man needs advice on what to pack for a trip.
(d) The woman would like to change a reservation.

두 동료가 회사 휴가에 관해 이야기하는 것을 들으시오.
W: George, 휴가 이미 다 쓰셨어요?
M: 네, 한 달 전에요. 당신은요?
W: 전 아직 3일 남았어요. 부장님이 방금 저에게 알려주시더라고요.
M: 휴가가 이월되지 않는 거 아시죠?
W: 알아요. 가족과 도시 외곽으로 여행하는 데 그것들을 다 써야겠어요.
M: 어쨌든, 연말 전에 그렇게 하는 걸 잊지 마세요.
Q: 대화에서 추론할 수 있는 것은 무엇인가?
(a) 남자는 긴 비행으로 인해 지쳐있다.
(b) 여자는 휴가를 모두 사용하는 것을 목표로 한다.
(c) 남자는 여행을 위해 무엇을 챙길지에 대해 조언이 필요하다.
(d) 여자는 예약을 변경하고 싶어 한다.

Part IV

31

Looking to experience something breathtaking and electrifying? Go bungee jumping at the Zambezi Bridge, which overlooks southern Africa's Victoria Falls. You won't get this kind of exhilaration anywhere else. Be one of the few to feel the sensation of soaring through empty sky. Take a leap of faith at Zambezi Bridge and see Victoria Falls like you've never seen it before. Log on to jumpoffzambezi.com for more information.

Q: What is mainly being advertised?

(a) A thrilling outdoor activity in Africa
(b) A tourist spot near Victoria Falls
(c) A vacation resort near Victoria Falls
(d) An airborne tour of Africa

뭔가 숨 막히고 전율이 이는 경험을 원하십니까? 남아프리카의 빅토리아 폭포가 내려다 보이는 Zambezi 다리에서 번지 점프를 해보세요. 다른 어느 곳에서도 이런 종류의 쾌감은 느낄 수 없을 겁니다. 허공에 솟아오르는 기분을 만끽하는 몇 안 되는 사람 중 한 명이 되어 보세요. Zambezi 다리에서 자신을 갖고 도약해서, 전혀 색다른 빅토리아 폭포를 만나보세요. 더 많은 정보를 원하시면 jumpoffzambezi.com에 접속하세요.
Q: 주로 광고되고 있는 것은 무엇인가?
(a) 아프리카에서의 신나는 야외 활동
(b) 빅토리아 폭포 근처의 관광 명소
(c) 빅토리아 폭포 근처의 휴가 리조트
(d) 아프리카의 비행 투어

32

The country's lawmakers are being lauded for proposed legislation that purports to crack down on air pollution. I'm flabbergasted that no one in government realizes what a paper tiger these laws would be. They would establish air pollution quotas on the national level, meaning that pollution could reach dangerous levels in specific areas, but if the overall quota for the country is not exceeded, then no laws will have been broken. Up to five people a day are dying nationwide because of complications from air pollution, so baby steps like this won't cut it.

Q: What is the talk mainly about?

(a) Concern over legislation that is too lax on pollution
(b) Whether existing environmental laws are effective or not
(c) Disappointment with the government's refusal to support antipollution laws

(d) The personal impact of air pollution on individuals

국가의 입법자들은 대기 오염에 대해 단호한 조치를 취하려는 상정안으로 인해 칭찬받고 있습니다. 저는 정부의 어느 누구도 이 법안들이 종이호랑이에 불과할 것이라는 걸 깨닫지 못하는 것에 깜짝 놀랐습니다. 그것들은 전국적인 규모로 대기 오염 할당량을 규정할 것인데, 이는 오염이 특정 지역들에서 위험 수준에 다다를 수는 있지만, 국가 전체에 걸친 할당량이 초과되지 않는다면, 어떠한 법안도 위반되지 않을 것임을 의미합니다. 대기 오염으로 인한 합병증으로 인해, 전국적으로 하루에 최대 5명이 사망하고 있으므로, 이와 같은 걸음마 단계들은 오염을 줄일 수 없을 것입니다.

Q: 담화는 주로 무엇에 대한 것인가?
(a) 오염에 너무 관대한 법안에 대한 우려
(b) 기존의 환경 법안이 효과적인지 아닌지의 여부
(c) 정부가 오염 방지 법안의 지지를 거부하는 것에 대한 실망
(d) 대기 오염이 개인에 미치는 개별적인 영향

33

Here is our latest traffic advisory. Motorists should avoid the northbound lanes of Highway 91 if possible due to an overturned tractor trailer. Police and a tow truck have arrived at the scene, but it could take a while to clear the debris. Meanwhile, if you are traveling east toward the Bay Bridge, consider finding an alternate route as there is a huge pileup just west of the bridge. Finally, good news for those making their way to Interstate 12: Traffic in both directions is moving smoothly.

Q: What are drivers traveling toward the Bay Bridge advised to do?
(a) Turn west onto Interstate 12
(b) Follow detour signs on the highway
(c) Budget additional time due to bad traffic
(d) Find a way to bypass an accident

최신 교통 정보입니다. 운전자들은 전복된 대형 화물 트럭으로 인해 가능하면 91번 고속도로의 북쪽 방향 차선은 피하셔야겠습니다. 경찰과 견인차가 현장에 도착했지만, 잔해를 치우려면 시간이 좀 걸릴 수 있습니다. 한편, Bay 다리를 향해 동쪽으로 이동 중이시라면, 다리 바로 서쪽에 큰 연쇄 충돌 사고가 있으니 대체 도로를 찾으시기 바랍니다. 끝으로, 12번 고속도로로 가시는 분들께는 반가운 소식이 있습니다. 양방향 차선이 모두 소통이 원활합니다.

Q: Bay 다리를 향해 이동하는 운전자들은 무엇을 하기를 권고받는가?
(a) 12번 고속도로로 방향을 서쪽으로 바꾼다.
(b) 고속도로의 우회로 표지판을 따라간다.
(c) 교통 체증으로 인한 추가 시간을 할당한다.
(d) 사고를 우회할 길을 찾는다.

34

Humanity has yet to create an adhesive as efficient as that found on a gecko's feet. These amazing creatures can hold fast to most surfaces without the use of surface tension or liquid, although humidity does augment their adhesion ability. Bristle-like structures known as setae are what allow geckos to not only adhere strongly to surfaces, but also to peel back quickly, so they can skitter across ceilings as facilely as floors. The setae are also self-cleaning, which is paramount to geckos' survival, since accumulated debris interferes with adhesion, making them instant targets for predators.

Q: Which is correct according to the lecture?
(a) Geckos' setae are superior to any man-made adhesive.
(b) Liquid must be present for geckos' setae to function properly.
(c) Setae stick so strongly that they impede geckos' agility.
(d) Having debris to grasp facilitates the adhesion ability of geckos.

인류는 아직 도마뱀붙이의 발에서 발견되는 것만큼 효과적인 접착제를 만들어내지 못했습니다. 습기가 접착력을 증가시키기는 하지만, 이 놀라운 생명체는 표면 장력이나 액체의 이용 없이 대부분의 표면을 꽉 붙잡을 수 있습니다. 강모라고 알려진 털과 유사한 구조는 도마뱀붙이들이 표면에 강하게 붙어있도록 할 뿐만 아니라, 빠르게 다시 떨어지도록 하여 그들은 천장을 바닥만큼 쉽게 내달릴 수 있습니다. 또한 강모는 자동 세정식인데, 부스러기가 쌓이면 접착을 방해하여 도마뱀붙이가 포식자들의 즉각적인 표적이 되도록 하기 때문에 이는 도마뱀붙이의 생존에 가장 중요합니다.

Q: 강의에 따르면 맞는 것은 무엇인가?
(a) 도마뱀붙이의 강모는 어떤 인공 접착제보다 더 뛰어나다.
(b) 도마뱀붙이의 강모가 제대로 기능을 하기 위해서는 액체가 존재해야 한다.
(c) 강모는 너무 강하게 달라붙어서 도마뱀붙이의 민첩성을 방해한다.
(d) 움켜잡을 부스러기가 있는 것은 도마뱀붙이의 접착 능력을 촉진시킨다.

35

Radio RZ-FM is handing out backstage passes to see the band Desert Life in concert this Saturday at the Podium. Here's your chance to see, and even mingle with, members of the group behind the hit "Tomorrow I'll Tell" for free. The band will play all the old favorites you know by heart along with unreleased tracks from their upcoming album. Call within the next five minutes for a chance to meet the band, and we'll also throw in autographed photos of the band for the first 10 callers.

Q: Which is correct about Desert Life according to the advertisement?
(a) They will sell albums at the Podium.
(b) They will unveil fresh material.
(c) They will give away 10 free tickets.
(d) They will sign autographs at the concert.

RZ-FM 라디오가 이번 주 토요일 Podium에서 열리는 콘서트에서 Desert Life 밴드를 만나볼 수 있는 무대 뒤 출입증을 배포합니다. 히트곡 'Tomorrow I'll Tell'을 낸 그룹 멤버들을 무료로 만나고, 그들과 함께 어울릴 수 있는 기회까지 주어집니다. 밴드는 곧 발매될 음반에 수록된 미발표 곡과 함께 당신이 외우고 있는 모든 옛날 인기 곡을 연주할 것입니다. 이 밴드를 만날 기회를 잡으시려면 지금부터 5분 안에 전화주시고, 선착순 열 분께는 밴드의 사인이 담긴 사진도 덤으로 보내 드립니다.

Q: 광고에 따르면 Desert Life에 대해 맞는 것은 무엇인가?

(a) Podium에서 앨범을 판매할 것이다.
(b) 새로운 곡을 공개할 것이다.
(c) 10장의 무료 티켓을 배포할 것이다.
(d) 콘서트에서 사인을 할 것이다.

36

In the late 1800s, margarine manufacturers in the US started adding yellow food colorants to their oil-based white spread to make it more appealing to consumers. This was met with opposition from dairy farmers, as people began switching to the cheaper alternative to butter. Three states subsequently implemented new legislation dubbed the "pink laws," which stipulated that the makers of margarine had to dye their product an unsavory pink. Dairy farmers rejoiced, but their relief was short lived as the Supreme Court declared the policies unconstitutional and eventually reversed them.

Q: What can be inferred from the talk?

(a) Producers of butter were offended by the new "pink laws."
(b) Most people could not afford to buy real butter in the late 1800s.
(c) Dairy farmers were concerned about decreased profits.
(d) The Supreme Court was on the side of the butter producers.

1800년대 후반에, 미국의 마가린 제조업자들은 소비자들에게 더 매력적으로 보이도록 유성의 백색 스프레드에 노란색 식용 색소를 넣기 시작했습니다. 사람들이 버터의 더 저렴한 대체품으로 바꾸기 시작하자, 이는 낙농업자들의 반대에 부딪혔습니다. 그 후에 세 개의 주는 'pink laws'라고 불리는 새로운 법안을 시행했는데, 이 법안은 마가린 제조업자들이 그들의 제품을 맛이 없어 보이는 분홍색으로 착색시켜야 한다고 규정했습니다. 낙농업자들은 크게 기뻐했으나, 대법원에서 그 방침들이 헌법에 위배된다고 선고하고 결국 그것들을 뒤집었기 때문에 그들의 안도는 오래가지 못하였습니다.

Q: 담화에서 추론할 수 있는 것은 무엇인가?

(a) 버터 제조업자들은 새로운 'pink laws'로 인해 불쾌해 했다.
(b) 대부분의 사람들은 1800년대 후반에 진짜 버터를 살 형편이 안 됐다.
(c) 낙농업자들은 줄어든 수익을 걱정했다.
(d) 대법원은 버터 생산업자들의 편을 들어주었다.

Part V

37~38

Welcome, delegates, to our 20th Corporate Social Commitment Convention! Every two years, the convention provides a platform for America's socially responsible companies to discuss practical ways of giving back to the community. Since we last convened two years ago, corporate participants in the convention have provided direct assistance to dozens of underfunded schools, adding and improving spaces such as classrooms and computer labs. We've also helped independent farmers leverage technology to their advantage. These efforts have improved the lives of hundreds of assistance beneficiaries. The CSCC's executive director, Lena Dean, will be sharing a detailed report on this in a moment. But before I hand her the microphone, I'd like to reiterate that our mission here is to find ways to turn vision into action. Please keep this in mind as you network or attend one of our many workshops and seminars. We're here to find solutions to pressing problems and to effect positive change in society.

37. Q: What was accomplished in the past two years?

(a) The opening of a corporate headquarters
(b) The construction of school facilities
(c) The recruitment of new members
(d) The launch of a commemorative book

38. Q: Which is correct about the convention?

(a) It is an annual event for social workers.
(b) It encourages participants to actively support social causes.
(c) Its location changes every time it is held.
(d) It provides a venue for discussing investments.

대표 여러분, 제20회 기업 사회 공헌 대회에 오신 것을 환영합니다! 2년마다, 대회는 미국의 사회적으로 책임이 있는 회사들이 지역 사회에 환원할 유용한 방법들에 대해 논의할 토론장을 마련해 드립니다. 저희가 2년 전에 마지막으로 모인 이래로, 대회의 기업 참가자들은 교실과 컴퓨터실 같은 장소를 추가하고 개선하여, 수십 개의 예산이 부족한 학교에 직접적인 도움을 제공했습니다. 저희는 또한 자작농들이 그들에게 유리하게 기술을 활용하도록 도왔습니다. 이러한 노력은 수백 명의 지원 수혜자들의 삶을 개선시켰습니다. CSCC의 전무 Lena Dean이 곧 이에 대한 상세한 보고서를 공유할 것입니다. 그러나 그녀에게 마이크를 건네기 전에, 저는 여기에서 저희의 사명이 비전을 행동으로 옮길 방법을 찾는 것임을 다시 한번 말씀드리고 싶습니다. 여러분들이 인적 네트워크를 형성하거나 저희의 많은 워크숍과 세미나 중 하나에 참석하실 때 이를 명심해 주십시오. 저희는 시급한 문제들에 대한 해결책을 찾고 사회에 긍정적인 변화를 가져오기 위해 이 자리에 있습니다.

37. Q: 지난 2년 동안 무엇이 성취되었는가?

(a) 기업 본사 개업
(b) 학교 시설 공사
(c) 신규 회원 모집
(d) 기념 도서 출간

38. Q: 대회에 대해 맞는 것은 무엇인가?

(a) 사회복지사들을 위한 연례 행사이다.
(b) 참가자들이 사회적 대의명분을 적극적으로 지원하도록 장려한다.
(c) 개최될 때마다 장소가 달라진다.
(d) 투자에 대해 논의할 수 있는 장소를 제공한다.

39~40

The world's longest multihorse race, the Mongol Derby, was first held in 2009 and has taken place on an annual basis since then. The course spans 1,000 kilometers through Mongolia and replicates the ancient postal system, consisting of a series of horse stations, instituted by Genghis Khan in 1224. Injuries to participants are all but guaranteed as each one must grapple with 25 different half-wild horses from one station to the next. And, lacking luxuries such as bathrooms, the racecourse demands tremendous grit and endurance, with riders permitted only five kilograms' worth of survival gear for the entire 10-day ordeal. Indeed, the race is so tough that completing it, much less winning it, is considered a feat in itself. Less than half the contestants are expected to finish. Interestingly, just one of the race's past winners has been Mongolian. The rest, including two female riders, have come from as far away as Canada, Australia, and South Africa.

39. Q: Which is correct about the Mongol Derby according to the lecture?

(a) It has been held annually since 1224.
(b) It is based on a system of horse stations.
(c) Injuries are a rare occurrence during the event.
(d) Riders must use the same horse for all 10 days.

40. Q: What can be inferred about race contestants?

(a) They must have Mongol ancestry to participate.
(b) They have competed in other races of endurance.
(c) They are given a uniform set of rations to eat.
(d) They have a low likelihood of success.

세계에서 가장 긴 복마 경주인 몽골 경마 대회는 2009년에 처음 열렸으며 그 이후로 매년 개최되어왔습니다. 코스는 몽골 전역의 1,000킬로미터에 걸쳐 있고, 1224년에 칭기즈 칸에 의해 도입된, 일련의 역참으로 구성된 고대 우편 제도를 재현합니다. 각자 하나의 역에서 다음 역까지 25필의 다양한 반야생마들과 씨름해야 하기 때문에, 참가자들의 부상은 거의 확실합니다. 그리고, 화장실 같은 호사도 없고, 경주 코스는 엄청난 투지와 인내심을 요구하며, 경주자들에게는 전체 10일간의 시련 동안 5킬로그램의 생존 장비만이 허용됩니다. 사실, 경주는 너무 힘들어서, 우승하는 것은 말할 것도 없고, 완주하는 것은 그 자체로 위업이라고 여겨집니다. 참가자의 절반 이하가 완주한다고 예상됩니다. 흥미롭게도, 경주의 과거 우승자 중 단 한 명만이 몽골인이었습니다. 두 여성 경주자를 포함한 나머지는 캐나다, 호주, 그리고 남아프리카같이 멀리 떨어진 곳 출신입니다.

39. Q: 강의에 따르면 몽골 경마 대회에 대해 맞는 것은 무엇인가?

(a) 1224년부터 매년 개최되어왔다.
(b) 역참 제도에 기반을 두고 있다.
(c) 부상은 경기 중 드물게 발생한다.
(d) 경주자들은 10일 내내 같은 말을 이용해야 한다.

40. Q: 경주 참가자들에 대해 추론할 수 있는 것은 무엇인가?

(a) 참가하기 위해서는 몽골 혈통이어야 한다.
(b) 인내심이 필요한 다른 경주에서 경쟁했다.
(c) 동일한 식량 배급량을 받는다.
(d) 성공 가능성이 낮다.

VOCABULARY

Part I

1 A: 선생님, Mr. Beaumont께서 뵈러 오셨습니다.
   B: 그래요? 3시에나 올 거라고 기대했는데요.

2 A: 난 오늘 『전쟁과 평화』를 읽을 거야.
   B: 넌 현실적이지 않게 굴고 있어. 그 책은 1,400쪽이나 되잖아.

3 A: TV를 보느라 어젯밤에 과제물을 마치지 못했어.
   B: 넌 오늘 그것에 대해 벌충해야 할 거야.

4 A: 상점에 와인이 하나도 없었어.
   B: 정말? 지난번에 갔을 때는 선반이 병들로 가득 차 있던데.

5 A: John은 영리한 학생인 것 같아요.
   B: 저도 그렇게 생각해요. 실제로, 그는 아주 명석해요.

6 A: 동물원 사육사가 방금 사자들에게 커다란 고깃덩이들을 줬어.
   B: 와, 사자들은 정말 배가 고팠던 게 틀림없어. 먹이를 게걸스럽게 먹어 치우는 것을 봐.

7 A: Maurice는 내가 얘기해도 절대 자기 방을 청소하지 않아.
   B: 내 아들도 그래. 정말 불만스러워!

8 A: 아기가 피곤해서 우는 것 같아. 아기를 요람에 눕히고 교대로 흔들어주자.
   B: 오, 좋은 의견이야. 그렇게 하면 금세 아기를 달래서 잠들게 할 게 분명해.

9 A: 제가 세관 신고서를 작성하는 걸 도와주실 수 있나요?
   B: 물론이죠. 신상 정보를 기입한 다음 귀하께 해당되는 박스에 체크 표시를 하시면 됩니다.

10 A: 새로운 상사와는 어떻게 지내고 있나요?
   B: 별로 안 좋아요. 그녀는 좀 공격적이고 냉혹해요.

Part II

11 그 서점은 이미 모든 서적을 20% 할인하고 있고, 서점 회원들은 구매하는 서적에 대해 10% 추가 할인을 받을 수 있다.

12 비영리 법률 회사는 변호사를 선임할 경제적 여유가 없는 사람들에게 무료 법률 서비스를 제공한다.

13 Megan의 부모는 그녀가 그들이 허락하지 않은 사람과 결혼한 것에 대해 여전히 분개하고 있다.

14 외향적인 성격의 사람들은 말이 없는 사람들보다 다른 이들과 어울리는 것을 더 편하게 느낀다.

15 우기 동안에, 해안 지역에 있는 마을들은 범람하기 쉽다.

16 그 과학자는 약초 치료에 관한 그의 결론의 근거가 된 연구를 인용하도록 요청받았다.

17 세계 대전으로도 알려진 1차 대전은, 너무도 엄청난 규모였기 때문에 지구상의 모든 대륙에 영향을 미쳤다.

18 교수는 강의에서 밝힌 자신의 요지를 바이올린 현과 관련된 비유로 설명했다.

19 그 잡지는 성공하기 위해 극복하기 어려운 장애를 이겨내려고 노력한 사람들에 관한 기사에 돈을 지불한다.

20 아이작 뉴턴은 미적분학, 역학, 광학에서 그의 뛰어난 공헌으로 존경받는다.

21 Melanie와 그녀의 동료들은 몹시 바쁜 업무 일정으로 인해 더 이상 헬스장에 갈 시간이 없다.

22 여성의 안전을 증진하기 위해, 교통 당국은 특정 지하철 객차를 성별로 분리하는 것을 제안했다.

23 작가들은 이야기의 줄거리, 주제, 교훈에 적합하도록 등장인물들을 교묘히 다룬다.

24 이사진은 곤두박질 치는 주가가 회사의 재정 상태에 어떠한 영향을 미칠지에 대해 염려하고 있다.

25 병원들은 정부의 보건 및 안전 규정을 준수하는 지에 대한 연례 평가의 대상이다.

26 수면 부족은 어린이들에게 해로울 수 있는데, 그것이 호르몬 생성에 영향을 미쳐 결과적으로 성장을 저해할 수 있기 때문이다.

27 레오나르도 다빈치를 단지 예술가로만 여기는 것은 태만한 일일 것인데, 그가 다양한 분야에서 매우 재능이 있었기 때문이다.

28 알츠하이머병은 뚜렷한 증상 없이 모르는 사이에 진행되는 병이다.

29 그 정치인의 명성은 그가 CIA 첩보원들과 비밀리에 만나고 있었다는 사실이 드러나면서 훼손되었다.

30 Emma는 그녀의 아이가 세 살에 백과사전을 읽기 시작하자 그가 발달이 빠르다고 생각했다.

GRAMMAR

Part I

1 A: 상사가 당신이 요청했던 진급을 시켜주었나요?
  B: 네, 그리고 그는 제게 많은 보너스까지 주었어요.

2 A: 내가 어떻게 하면 딸이 잠자리에 들 때 얌전히 누워 있게 할 수 있을까요?
  B: 이야기를 읽어주세요. 끝날 때쯤이면, 그녀는 진정되어 있을 거예요.

3 A: 전에 태국 요리를 먹어본 적 있나요?
  B: 네. 전 특히 그런 종류의 요리를 좋아해요.

4 A: 5분 후에 출발하지 않으면, 나는 비행편을 놓칠지도 몰라.
  B: 알았어. 톨레도에 도착하면 꼭 전화해야 해.

5 A: 음식이 정말 맛있었어, 그렇지 않았니?
  B: 응, 하지만 야외 테이블을 이용할 수 있었더라면 더 좋았을 거야.

6 A: 국가 대표 수영팀이 엄격한 연습 일정을 갖고 있다고 들었어.
  B: 응, 그들의 코치가 매일 6시간씩 그들을 훈련시켜.

7 A: 축하해요. 당신 개가 강아지들을 막 낳았다고 들었어요.
  B: 맞아요, 그리고 모든 새로운 새끼들이 아주 연한색 털을 지녔어요.

8 A: 넌 왜 Alice가 여전히 공장에서 일하고 있는지 아니?
  B: 모르겠어. 그녀는 더 좋은 직장을 쉽게 구할 수 있을 텐데.

9 A: 와, 네 주방이 이렇게 깨끗한 걸 본 적이 없는 것 같아.
  B: 주방이 너무 더러워서, 몇 시간 동안 정리했어.

10 A: Webber 가족이 서비스업에 종사한다는 것이 사실인가요?
   B: 네. 그들의 사업은 여러 성공적인 호텔들로 이루어져 있어요.

Part II

11 열이 나는 기미가 없었기 때문에, 1일량의 항생제를 복용하는 것은 필요하지 않다.

12 개발팀의 팀원들은 효율적인 프로젝트 수행을 위해서 정기적으로 서로 의사소통해야 한다.

13 이 프로그램은 적절한 수준의 읽기에 큰 어려움을 겪는 4학년 학생들에게 도움을 준다.

14 음식 알레르기가 있는 사람들은 알레르기 반응을 겪지 않기 위해서 어떤 음식물들을 피해야 하는지를 염두에 두어야 한다.

15 그 수건들은 완전히 짜였기 때문에, 밖에 있는 줄에서 나머지 깨끗한 세탁물만큼 빨리 마를 것이다.

16 충동 구매를 막기 위해, 쇼핑하러 가기 전에 무엇을 사야 하는지에 대해 생각해야 한다.

17 조수는 그 프로젝트에 대한 정보가 기밀로 남아야 한다는 것을 오래전부터 알고 있었다.

18 다행히 온전하게 남겨진 그 병원을 제외하고는, 허리케인은 사실상 마을의 모든 것을 파괴시켰다.

19 그만의 벤처 사업을 시작해보라는 그의 아내의 제안이 아니었다면, Mr. Lee는 아마 빠듯한 수입으로 근근이 살았을 것이다.

20 청소년들 사이에서의 약물 남용은 보통 스트레스가 많은 일상 경험의 결과로 발생한다.

21 최근의 라디오 조사에 따르면, 조지 거슈윈의 작품들 중 가장 인기 있는 것들은 '랩소디 인 블루'와 '파리의 미국인'이다.

22 그 회사는 의사들이 암의 발병을 더 빨리 발견할 수 있게 하는 새로운 기술 개발을 전문으로 한다.

23 Amanda가 2시간짜리 강의를 위한 준비를 마치자마자 동료가 그 강의의 연기를 알려주기 위해 전화했다.

24 단단한 플라스틱 물질인 폴리카보네이트로 만들어진 물통들은 이제 다양한 색상과 크기로 이용이 가능하다.

25 은하수를 자세히 관찰하는 것은 과학자들이 우주의 본질에 대해 보다 잘 이해하도록 도울 것이다.

Part III

26 (a) A: 넌 어젯밤 Sarah Donnell 콘서트 표를 구할 수 있었니?
(b) B: 응. 내가 제일 좋았던 부분은 그녀가 그녀식으로 'Make Believe' 라는 곡을 공연할 때였어.
(c) A: 나도. 난 어느 누구도 그 노래를 그렇게 잘 부르는 것을 들어본 적이 없어.
(d) B: 맞아. 그 발라드 노래의 그녀의 버전은 정말로 원곡을 뛰어넘는 것이었어.

27 (a) A: 너 George가 테니스 칠 때 무엇을 하는지 알아챘어?
(b) B: 응. 경기하는 동안에 라켓을 잡은 손을 바꾸는 걸 보았어.
(c) A: 난 그가 양손잡이라는 걸 알고는 정말 깜짝 놀랐어.
(d) B: 이게 그가 왜 경기하는 모든 상대를 계속 이기는지 설명해주네.

28 (a) Baybridge 고등학교의 여러 학생들이 제대로 작동하지 않는 도서관 컴퓨터에 대한 문제점을 보고했다. (b) 그들은 구입한지도 얼마 안 된 컴퓨터 몇 대가 경고도 없이 갑자기 꺼진다고 주장했다. (c) 학교 측은 제조업체에 이 문제를 알렸고 기술진이 문제를 확인하기 위해 파견될 것이다. (d) 더 이상의 피해를 막기 위해서, 모든 문제가 해결될 때까지 영향을 받은 컴퓨터들은 사용되지 않을 것이다.

29 (a) 물질과 운동에 대한 연구라고 정의되는 물리학은 새로운 기술 개발에 이용된다. (b) 한때 허구적인 사색에 지나지 않았던 많은 개념들이 물리학 발전의 결과로 실현되고 있다. (c) 물리학에 대한 과학자들의 이해 덕분에, 텔레비전과 전자레인지 같은 현대적 기구들이 만들어질 수 있었다. (d) 더 나아가서, 물리학자들로 인한 발전이 없었더라면 우주 여행은 가능하지 않았을 것이다.

30 (a) 2012년 사우디아라비아에서 처음으로 발견된 중동 호흡기 증후군 코로나 바이러스(메르스)는 사람에게 상당한 위험을 끼친다. (b) 메르스는 주로 단봉낙타에서 퍼져왔지만, 바이러스에 걸린 동물들과의 접촉을 통해 사람도 감염될 수 있다. (c) 감염된 사람들은 고열과 근육통과 같은 다양한 증상과 합병증을 보일 수도 있지만, 바이러스에 감염된 일부는 전혀 증상을 보이지 않는다. (d) 메르스는 40%까지 사망에 이르게 하면서, 잠재적으로 치명적이기 때문에 적절한 개인 위생이 권고된다.

READING COMPREHENSION

Part I

1 수년간, 전문가들은 _____를 논의해왔다. 잠이 어린이의 성장을 조절하는 데 역할을 한다는 가능성에 대해 많은 관심이 쏟아져 왔다. 그러나 지난달 『소아과 학술지』에 실린 한 연구는 하루 중 절반을 자는 아기들이 밤에만 자는 아기들보다 평균적으로 키가 크지 않다고 밝힘으로써 이 가설을 반박한다. 의사들은 어린아이들이 모든 성장 잠재력을 달성하도록 돕는 데 유전자와 적절한 식사가 더 중요한 역할을 한다고 생각한다.

(a) 잠이 왜 중요한지
(b) 어린아이들에게 어떤 비타민이 필요한지
(c) 아기들이 왜 낮에 자는지
(d) 무엇이 유아의 신체 성장을 자극하는지

2 _____을/를 찾고 계십니까? Swift Tailors가 여러분을 도와 드리겠습니다. 기성복과 맞춤복의 모든 의류 제작에 대한 저희의 전문성이 귀하를 많은 사람들 속에서 확실히 돋보이게 해 드릴 것입니다. 또 사내 직원의 도움으로, 저희는 어떠한 공식적인 행사를 위한 정장과 드레스 주문도 처리할 수 있습니다. 실제로 귀하께서 시간이 촉박하시다면, 저희는 72시간 내에 귀하의 의복을 수선해서 배송하는 신속 수선 서비스를 제공합니다. Swift Tailors와 함께하시면 멋지게 보이기는 아주 쉽습니다.

(a) 구할 수 있는 가장 잘 팔리는 옷
(b) 유명 상표의 최신 정장
(c) 고급 제품을 위한 믿을만한 세탁소
(d) 화려한 옷을 사기에 적합한 상점

3 가톨릭 교회는 고등학생에게 성에 대해 가르치는 것이 청소년들 사이에서 그 주제에 대해 더욱 자유방임적인 태도를 갖게 할 것이라고 주장하지만, 이러한 주장을 뒷받침하는 증거는 거의 없다. 사실, 학교에서 성교육을 실시하는 나라들이 성에 대한 논의를 부모의 재량에 맡기는 나라들보다 10대 임신 및 강간 발생률이 30퍼센트 정도 더 낮다. 여기에서, _____고 유추할 수 있다.

(a) 10대에게 성교육을 하는 것은 유익하다
(b) 10대들은 타인에게서 성에 대해 배울 수 있다
(c) 교회가 국가 교육을 신뢰하지 않는다
(d) 부모들이 그 주제를 불편하게 여긴다

4 고대부터 배는 먼 땅을 탐험하는 데 사용되어 온 교통수단이었다. 국제 교역이 번성하면서, 외국 선원과 현지 선원이 배를 부두에 댈 때 효과적으로 메시지를 교환할 수 있는 방법이 모색되었다. 일련의 색색 깃발들이 정해졌고, 배들은 메시지에 따라 다양한 배열로 이 깃

발들을 올리고 내렸다. 미크로네시아, 크로아티아, 마다가스카르와 같이 멀리 떨어진 지역의 언어를 구사할 수 있어야 하는 대신, 선원들은 _____ 수 있었다.

(a) 해안에서 멀리 떨어져 있는 동안 의사소통할
(b) 보편적인 신호 체계에 의존할
(c) 공용어로 사업을 수행할
(d) 집에서 더 가까운 목적지에 집중할

5 피겨스케이팅 연기를 심사하려면 예술성 인식과 기술적 기량의 평가 사이에서 섬세한 균형 잡기가 필요하다. 단지 정해진 동작의 시각적 측면에만 관심을 두면 피겨스케이팅 선수가 보여주어야 하는 기술적 기량을 공정하게 평가하지 못한다. 마찬가지로, 점프는 꽉 짜인 전체 프로그램의 작은 일부에 불과하기 때문에 심사위원은 단순히 난이도만을 고려할 수도 없다. 연기를 효과적으로 평가하기 위해서는, 심사위원들이 _____.

(a) 동작을 만든 경험이 있어야 한다
(b) 선수들을 기술적 기량에 의해 평가할 수 있어야 한다
(c) 여러 관점에서 그것을 고려해야 한다
(d) 비평가가 예술 작품을 대하듯이 그것을 대해야 한다

6 _____이 아니었다면, 윌리엄 허셜 경은 천문학자가 되어서 1781년에 천왕성을 발견하지 못했을 것이다. 그가 결국 음악 교사이자 작곡가가 되기 전, 젊었을 때에는 밴드에서 연주를 했었다. 배움에 열심이었던 허셜은, 독학으로 학술 연구를 하다가 우연히 『완벽한 광학 시스템』이라는 제목의 책을 접하게 되었는데, 이 책 덕분에 구리, 주석, 안티몬으로 이루어진 거울들이 달린 자신만의 망원경을 만들게 되었다. 그는 그때까지 만들어진 것 중 가장 훌륭한 광학 기구로 여겨지던 그리니치 관측소에서 사용되던 망원경보다 훨씬 우수한, 대단한 품질의 망원경을 만들어냈다.

(a) 망원경 구조에 관한 책
(b) 천문학 문헌에의 접근
(c) 세계적 수준의 관측소에서의 경험
(d) 영국 과학 시설의 영향

7 대통령께,
저는 대통령께서 우리나라에서의 무제한적 토지 소유권을 외국인들에게 허용하는 법안을 승인하는 모습을 두려움 속에서 지켜보았습니다. 이는 위험한 전례를 만드는 것인데, 자금원이 더 풍부한 외국인에게 유리하도록 가난한 국민들이 토지에 대한 접근을 거부당할 수 있기 때문입니다. 그러한 사태는 분명히 경제적 불평등을 악화시킬 것입니다. 이러한 결정을 일방적으로 내리기보다, 국민 투표를 통해서 여론을 반영하는 것이 더 현명했을 것입니다. 우리 대다수는 _____를 원한다고 저는 확신합니다.

진심을 담아,
Scott Thompson

(a) 우리 영토가 국민들의 통제하에 있기
(b) 부자들이 가난한 자들에 대한 착취를 멈추기
(c) 우리 고유 문화에 대한 외국의 영향력이 줄기
(d) 토지 소유권 규정의 엄격함이 감소하기

8 과학자들이 _____에 대해 비관적이던 때가 있었지만, 연구가 그들에게 새로운 희망감을 제공하고 있다. 지구의 극한 환경에 대한 연구는 생명체가 거의 어떠한 환경에서도 살아남을 수 있다는 것을 밝혀냈다. 예를 들어, 섭씨 150도가 넘는 온도의 심해 분출구에서 생명체가 존재하는 것이 발견되면서, 지구상의 이러한

환경에서 생명체가 존재할 수 있다면 화성의 혹독한 환경에서도 살아남을 수 있을 것이라고 과학자들은 추측하게 되었다.

(a) 생명체가 살아가는 데 화성 대기의 적합성
(b) 지표면에서 극한 환경을 찾는 것
(c) 해저에서 생명체를 만나는 것
(d) 변동하는 환경에 대한 생물체의 적응력

9 산업 보고
Rainbow 롤러스케이트장은 기발한 마케팅 방법으로 경쟁에서 앞서고 있다. 물론, 그 롤러스케이트장은 18세에서 30세의 목표 고객을 겨냥한 효과적인 홍보 전략의 수립이라는 예상되었던 바를 했다. 하지만, 그 롤러스케이트장은 거기에서 멈추지 않았고, 전혀 다른 소비자층을 대상으로도 전용 광고 캠페인을 시행했다. _____, 주로 간과되는 노년 인구에게 다가가서, 그들이 젊은 시절에 했던 활동인 롤러스케이트에 대한 향수를 불러일으킴으로써 애용하도록 부추겼다.

(a) 그럼에도 불구하고
(b) 특히
(c) 그렇기는 하지만
(d) (둘째 대안을 소개하며) 그렇지 않으면

10 어제 오후 늦게 국가 법원에서의 폭발로 인해 판사 15명 중 7명이 사망한 후 Chango 공화국의 대법원은 혼란에 빠져있다. Chango 대통령은 정부가 이 사건을 신속히 조사할 것이고 사망자들을 대신하기 위해 곧 새로운 판사들이 임명될 것이라고 발표하여 국민들의 불안을 가라앉히고자 하였다. _____, 시민들은 추가 공격에 대한 공포로 집을 나서는 것을 두려워하여, 불안과 심한 불신의 분위기가 조성되고 있는 상황이다.

(a) 그렇기는 하지만
(b) 그러므로
(c) 그와는 반대로
(d) 사실은

Part II

11 아직도 후대까지 가족이 보유할 만한 꿈의 집을 찾고 계십니까? (a) 귀하의 꿈을 실현시켜 줄 Bradley Homes가 바로 여기에 있으니, 먼 곳에서 찾지 마세요. (b) 저희 일류 건축가와 기술자 인력들이 귀하가 아무런 사전 지식이 없어도 집을 설계하실 수 있도록 도와드립니다. (c) 이미 건축된 주택을 선호하신다면, 저희의 넓고 에너지 효율적인 주택 설계가 현대식 환경의 인상적인 분위기를 제공해 드립니다. (d) 귀하의 건축 디자인과 과거의 작업 모음을 제출하시려면 저희 웹 사이트를 방문하세요.

12 사람들은 중독을 치료할 수 있는 수단으로 영성을 오랫동안 연구해왔다. (a) 그들 중 한 명은 알코올 중독 방지회의 공동 설립자인 Bill Wilson으로, 그는 신의 도움이 없으면 알코올 중독을 극복할 수 없다고 믿었다. (b) 그는 알코올 중독자들이 격려하는 분위기 속에서 중독을 영구히 극복하도록 돕는 12단계 프로그램을 개발했다. (c) Wilson은 종교적인 신념에 의지하여 나쁜 습관을 버린 금주하는 알코올 중독자들이 힘겹게 노력 중인 중독자들에게 좋은 본보기가 될 것이라고 생각했다. (d) 그는 알코올 중독자들이 자기만의 정신적 귀의를 찾아내어 그것을 궁극적인 회복의 기반으로 삼기를 바랐다.

Part III

13
2015년 1월에서 3월까지의 경기 예측뿐만 아니라 지난 분기의 실적을 넘어서면서, 인도의 경제는 올해의 첫 세 달 동안 7.5% 성장했다. 그러한 수치에 의하면 경제 성장의 측면에서 인도가 중국을 앞서지만, 금융 전문가들은 그 통계 자료가 그렇게 정확하지는 않을 수도 있다고 경고한다. 인도는 성장을 측정하는 데 새로운 방법을 시행해 왔는데, 이 방법은 과장된 것이라고 일부 사람들에게 조롱을 받아왔다. 전문가들은 이 방법에 의해 제공된 수치가 공장 및 산업 생산량과 같은 경제 성장의 다른 지표들과 일치하지 않는다고 지적한다.

Q: 지문은 주로 무엇에 관한 내용인가?
(a) 보고된 인도의 경제 성장은 정확하지 않을 수도 있다.
(b) 성장을 측정하는 기존 방식은 시대에 뒤쳐졌으며 정확하지 않다.
(c) 공장과 산업 생산은 경제에 악영향을 주고 있다.
(d) 인도의 빠른 성장으로 인해 의도하지 않은 부작용이 있을 수도 있다.

14
북극곰에게는 두터운 털과 털 많은 발바닥은 물론, 피하 지방층이 있어 북극의 몹시 추운 온도를 견딜 수 있다. 그들은 육지에서뿐만 아니라 물속에서도 추위와 싸워야 하는데 얼룩큰점박이 바다표범과 같은 해양 포유류를 먹고 살기 위해서는 얼음을 파야 하기 때문이다. 그 결과, 북극곰은 헤엄치는 데 앞발을 사용하는 능력을 얻게 되었고, 얼음을 파기 위해 날카로운 발톱을 발달시켰다.

Q: 지문은 주로 무엇에 관한 내용인가?
(a) 북극곰이 취하는 공통적인 행동
(b) 북극곰이 겪는 신체 발달
(c) 북극곰이 가진 식습관
(d) 북극곰이 살아남는 데 도움이 되는 특징들

15
새로운 연구 덕분에, 시내 고등학교의 수학 교사들은 왜 그렇게 많은 학생들이 이 과목에 흥미를 느끼지 못하는지에 대한 통찰력을 얻고 있다. 연구에 따르면, 학생들은 교실에서 논의되는 수학 개념들이 그들의 일상생활에 조금도 적용된다고 생각하지 않는다. 게다가, 연구자들은 대수학이나 미적분학 같이 고등학교 수학에서 다뤄지는 많은 주제들이 매우 추상적이라는 것을 발견했다. 학생들은 일상에서 마주치는 구체적인 상황에 적용할 수 있는 과목들을 선호한다.

Q: 지문의 주제는 무엇인가?
(a) 교사들이 수학을 배우는 학생들에게 자극을 줘야 하는 이유
(b) 수학 교육이 중요한 이유
(c) 수학이 이론적인 방식으로 교육되는 이유
(d) 학생들이 수학을 매력 없다고 생각하는 이유

16
20세기 이전에, 시인들은 운이 맞고 운율 형식을 따르는 시를 쓰도록 기대되었다. 하지만, 많은 사람들이 사용하는 전통적인 구조를 무시하고, 대신 자유시나 무운시를 쓰기로 택한 이들이 있었다. 무운시가 운율은 유지하지만 운이 맞지 않는 반면, 자유시는 눈에 띄는 어떠한 형식도 없다. 이렇게 정형화된 체계가 없는 형식을 사용하고 대중화함으로써, 그들은 다른 시인들이 작품을 쓸 때 더 큰 자유를 행사하도록 영감을 주었고 그전까지 엄격한 형식에 겁을 먹었던 이들에게 자유롭게 쓰도록 동기를 부여했다.

Q: 지문은 주로 무엇에 관한 내용인가?
(a) 무운시보다 자유시를 선호했던 작가들
(b) 운율이 있는 시와 운이 맞는 시의 차이점
(c) 작업에 새로운 접근 방법을 도입했던 시인들
(d) 일정한 체계가 없는 시의 독특한 요소

17
휴버트 부스는 영국 해군이 그에게 설계하도록 의뢰한 선박보다, 그 이후에 카펫을 청소하는 방법을 혁신한 것으로 더 기억된다. 그의 흡입 방식 진공청소기는 기다란 플라스틱 관과 개조된 운반대에 고정된 공기 펌프가 달려 있었다. 그의 발명품은 매우 인기를 끌어 고객들은 투명한 관을 장착하여 기계가 카펫에서 먼지를 빨아들이는 것을 볼 수 있게 해달라고 요청할 정도였다. 부스의 진공청소기는 1950년대에 후버 진공청소기에 자리를 내줄 때까지 20세기 전반기 동안 시장을 지배했다.

Q: 지문에 따르면 휴버트 부스에 대한 내용과 일치하는 것은?
(a) 과거에 영국 군대와 일했다.
(b) 진공청소기를 휴대할 수 있게 하는 운반대를 발명했다.
(c) 시야에서 먼지를 가리기 위해 투명한 진공관의 덮개를 만들었다.
(d) 1950년대에 흡입 방식 진공청소기를 개발했다.

18
Alfred에게,

네 상태가 나아져서 더 이상 물리 치료를 받지 않는다는 소식을 들으니 기뻐. 네 회복에 비추어 볼 때, 이제 우리가 계획해 왔던 휴가를 추진할 수 있을 것 같아. 내가 염두에 두고 있는 휴가지와 할인 요금을 제공하는 항공사 목록을 네게 이메일로 보내줄게. 내가 여행사와 일을 시작할 수 있도록 여행 가능한 장소에 대한 네 의견을 알려주면 고맙겠어.

잘 지내,
Cristina

Q: 다음 중 편지의 내용과 일치하는 것은?
(a) Alfred는 Cristina의 부상에 대해 방금 알았다.
(b) Alfred는 여행사에 티켓을 예약해야 한다.
(c) Cristina는 공동으로 결정하기를 바란다.
(d) Cristina는 가장 저렴한 여행을 택하고 싶어한다.

19
Oryx상 시상식에서 단거리 선수 Archie Barnes가 다른 후보들을 제치고 2년 연속 올해의 선수로 영예를 안은 최초의 인물이 되었다. Barnes는 Oryx상 추천 위원회 회원들로부터 과반수의 표를 얻었는데, 이 위원회에는 여러 과거 수상자들도 포함되어 있었다. 이러한 최근의 성공은 그를 전설적인 올림픽 수영 선수 Mark Smythe와 같은 2회 수상자들과 대등한 위치에 올려놓았고, Jesse Jones 이래 가장 많은 상을 받은 단거리 주자로 만들었다. 이 행사는 체육계에 가장 크게 기여한 운동선수들을 표창하기 위해 매년 개최된다.

Q: 지문에 따르면 다음 중 Barnes에 대한 내용과 일치하는 것은?
(a) 그전까지 이뤄진 적이 없는 위업을 달성했다.
(b) 2년 전에 트로피를 받았다.
(c) 선정 위원회로부터 만장일치로 선출되었다.
(d) Mark Smythe보다 더 유능한 운동선수로 여겨진다.

20
EZ-Iron과 함께 항상 멋지게 보이세요!

EZ-Iron은 기능성과 편리성을 염두에 두고 고안된 혁신적인 다리미입니다.

· 방해되는 전기 코드와 작별을 고하세요! EZ-Iron의 전기 코드 없는 디자인은 어디서나, 언제나 그것을 사용하는 것을 쉽게 만들어 줍니다.
· 다림질할 것이 많으신가요? EZ-Iron의 건전지는 완충 기준으로 1시간까지 지속됩니다.
· 다시는 옷을 손상하지 마세요! EZ-Iron의 특별하게 코팅된 밑바닥은 옷감에 달라붙지 않아서, 여러분이 옷을 태울 가능성을 낮게 만들어 줍니다.

다림질할 때마다 전문적인 결과를 얻으시려면, EZ-Iron을 선택하세요.
더 알아보시려면 www.eziron.com을 방문하세요.

Q: EZ-Iron이 그것의 특징들을 통해 방지해주는 문제는 무엇인가?
(a) 정기적으로 교체되어야 하는 코팅
(b) 금속 온도의 변동
(c) 기기의 밑바닥에 의해 손상되는 옷감
(d) 건전지의 지나치게 긴 충전 시간

21
머리 부상, 뇌졸중, 또는 뇌종양으로 뇌세포가 손상되면 치매에 걸릴 수 있다. 의사소통 장애와 기억 상실은 이 질환의 두 가지 전형적인 징후이고, 우울증 또한 치매의 시작을 나타낼 수 있다. 치매는 보통 75세 이상인 사람에게서 발병하지만, 젊은 사람들에게서도 발병할 수 있다. 치매는 관리는 할 수 있어도 일반적으로 치료는 불가능한데, 드문 경우 호전되는 것으로 알려져 있다.

Q: 지문에 따르면 다음 중 치매에 대한 내용과 일치하는 것은?
(a) 뇌세포를 손상시켜 뇌졸중에 빠뜨릴 수 있다.
(b) 나이가 많은 사람들에게만 발병한다.
(c) 사람의 언어 능력에 영향을 미친다.
(d) 희귀 질병이지만 치료 가능한 퇴행성 질환이다.

22
고객님께,

신형 IN1933 휴대 전화를 구입해 주셔서 감사합니다. 전화기를 사용하시기 전에, 긁힌 자국이나 눈에 보이는 결함이 없는지 기기 표면을 점검하시기 바랍니다. 손상된 기기는 포장 상자 안에 들어 있는 선불 주소 라벨을 이용하여 저희에게 반송해 주십시오. IN1933 전화기 전부는 교체와 수리를 모두 포함하여 1년간 품질 보증이 되오니 안심하셔도 좋습니다. 만약 구입 후 1년 내 전화기에 결함이 있을 경우, 완전한 새 제품으로 무상 교체해 드립니다. 귀하의 새 전화기를 마음껏 즐기세요!

IN1933 영업팀 일동

Q: 편지에 따르면 다음 중 IN1933에 대한 내용과 일치하는 것은?
(a) 수리를 했다면 품질 보증 대상에 포함되지 않는다.
(b) 주요 부품과 서비스에 평생 품질 보증이 적용된다.
(c) 1년 후에 자동으로 교체될 것이다.
(d) 결함이 있을 경우 무료로 반송될 수 있다.

23
논평 > 정치
정부 정실 인사 발동

자유당의 주요 후원자를 국립 문화 위원회의 위원장으로 임명한 것은 정치적인 은혜가 얼마나 우리 정부 구석구석에 스며들어 있는지를 입증한다. 명백하게도, 작은 사례금이나 선거 운동 지지는 더 이상 핵심 세력에게 충분한 보상이 되지 않는다. 존경받는 예술가들과 지식인들이 역사상 맡아온 직책을 정치적 측근에게 내주는 것은, 이 행정부가 국정을 운영하기보다 자신이 소유한 권력에 대한 지배력을 굳히는 데 더 열중하고 있다는 것을 보여준다.

Q: 글쓴이가 가장 동의할 것 같은 진술을 무엇인가?
(a) 자유당은 정치적 경쟁자들에게 다가가기 위해 노력해야 한다.
(b) 협력자들에게 권력직을 제공하는 것은 정부를 더욱 효율적으로 만든다.
(c) 현 국립 문화 위원회 위원장은 그 업무를 할 자격이 없다.
(d) 정치적 협력자들은 정부로부터 금전적 특혜를 받는 편이 더 낫다.

24
암흑 물질은 현대 천문학과 우주론에서 가장 획기적인 개념 중 하나이다. 1970년대에 Vera Rubin이 그 존재를 입증한 이래, 암흑 물질은 우주에서 관측되는 이상 현상들에 대해 가장 널리 받아들여지는 원인이 되었다. 암흑 물질 이론은 빅뱅 이후 우주의 팽창 속도가 줄어들고 있다는 추측이 틀렸음을 입증했다. 오히려, 암흑 물질은 우주의 물체들을 끊임없이 더 멀리 흩어지게 해서, 우주의 팽창 속도를 더 빠르게 하는 것으로 보인다.

Q: 지문에서 추론할 수 있는 것은 무엇인가?
(a) 천문학자들과 우주론자들은 암흑 물질의 기능을 다르게 해석한다.
(b) 암흑 물질은 우주의 확장에 대한 인식을 바꾸었다.
(c) 우주의 팽창은 암흑 물질에 의해 지연되고 있다.
(d) 우주의 팽창 속도는 결국 정체될 것이다.

25
주목: 서비스직원들 노조 회의

서비스 직원 노조원들은 퇴직자 관련 사안을 포함하는, 조직 내규 변경안에 대한 의견 수렴 회의에 참석하시기 바랍니다.

노조 간부들은 노조원들의 책무를 관리하는 규정에 대한 실질적인 개정과 더불어 조합비와 복리 후생 정책의 개정안을 논의할 예정입니다.

논의 후에 공개 토론회가 열릴 것이고, 참석자들은 질문하실 수 있습니다. 조직은 내년 간부 선거 때 내규 변경안이 도입 될 것이라 예상하므로, 지금 여러분의 제안이 우리가 앞으로의 활동에 집중하는 데 도움이 될 것입니다.

Q: 지문에서 추론할 수 있는 것은 무엇인가?
(a) 참석자들은 기부금을 내도록 요청받을 것이다.
(b) 새로운 간부를 임명하고 난 후 내규가 개정될 것이다.
(c) 조합의 복리 후생이 유일한 논점이다.
(d) 정책 개정은 회의에서 시행되지 않을 것이다.

Part IV

26~27
공사 검사관 구인

Hansen & Lin 주식회사는 인디애나폴리스 지역 내 지하 상수도 기반 시설의 정기 점검을 위해 자격을 갖춘 공사 검사관을 모집합니다. 합격자는 도급업체에 의해 수행된 모든 공사가 안전 요건과 고객 요구에 부합하는지 확실히 하기 위해 공사를 점검할 것입니다. 그 사람은 모든 문제를 도급업체에 알리고 고객들이 공사의 상황에 대해 계속 가장 최근의 정보를 알 수 있도록 할 것입니다.

약 80년 동안, Hansen & Lin 주식회사는 도시 수질 관리와 관련된 여러 공사에 착수해왔습니다. 우리는 공학적 우수성과 관련하여 다수의 업계 상을 받았고 고용하는 모든 사람에게 매우 높은 기대를 가집니다. 따라서, 지원자들은 아래 사항을 반드시 갖춰야 합니다:

· 도시 공학 학사 학위
· 최소 5년의 관련 경력
· 공공 기반 시설 검사 자격증

지원자들은 일주일에 5시간에서 10시간 정도 지역 내에서 이동해야 할 것이기 때문에, 차량과 운전 면허증을 보유해야 합니다. 또한, 직무를 시작하고 나서 30일 이내에 12시간짜리 업무 현장 안전 강의가 수강 되어야 합니다. 더 많은 정보를 위해서는 555-8824로 전화하십시오.

26.Q: 다음 중 지문의 내용과 일치하는 것은?
(a) 직무는 공사의 진척에 대해 고객들과 소통하는 것을 포함할 것이다.
(b) 공학상을 받은 지원자들이 선호된다.

(c) Hansen & Lin 주식회사는 다수의 산업군에서 공사를 해왔다.
(d) Hansen & Lin의 본사는 80년 동안 인디애나폴리스에 있었다.

27. Q: 지원자가 고용된 후에 곧 무슨 일이 일어날 것인가?
(a) 회사 정보를 기밀로 유지하는 동의서에 서명을 받을 것이다.
(b) 상수도 기반 시설 검사에 관한 자격증 시험이 주어질 것이다.
(c) 업무 환경의 안전에 관한 강좌가 이수 될 것이다.
(d) 회사의 보유 차량 중 한 차량이 배정될 것이다.

28~29

Lisa Groves [오전 11:40]
안녕하세요, Trevor.
오늘 판매 안내서를 수령하기 위해 이따 당신의 사무실에 들를 것이라고 당신에게 말하는 것을 잊었네요. 내일 아침 무역 박람회에서 그것들을 배부하기로 되어 있기 때문에 정말 가능한 한 빨리 안내서를 받아야 해요. 괜찮으시면 오후 3시까지 거기로 갈게요. 오늘 아침에 잠시 들르기를 바라고 있었지만, 산 마테오의 고객에게서 전화를 받았어요. 운이 좋지 않게도, 그것이 제가 예상한 것보다 길게 이어졌어요.

Trevor Drake [오후 12:15]
안녕하세요, Lisa.
안내서는 이미 모두 포장되어 수령 준비가 되었어요. 저는 점심시간 이후에 공항으로 동료를 태우러 가야 해서, 대략 오후 3시 30분까지는 사무실에 돌아와 있지 않을 거예요. 다른 어떤 약속도 없기 때문에 그 이후로는 어느 시간이든 완전히 괜찮아요. 사실, 오시면 커피도 한 잔 할 수 있어요. 저희가 가볼 수 있고 사무실과 정말 가까운 괜찮은 카페가 있어요.

28. Q: Lisa는 왜 메시지를 썼는가?
(a) 소책자 몇 권의 레이아웃을 바꾸기를 원한다.
(b) 잠재 고객을 다루는 것에 관해 약간의 조언을 원한다.
(c) 가까운 도시로 출장을 가기를 원한다.
(d) 다가오는 행사를 위한 인쇄물 몇 권을 받기를 원한다.

29. Q: 다음 중 대화의 내용과 일치하는 것은?
(a) Lisa는 오늘 오후에 Trevor의 사무실 근처에서 고객을 만날 것이다.
(b) Trevor는 오후 3시에 사무실 외부에 있을 것이다.
(c) Lisa는 오늘의 무역 박람회를 위한 문서 몇 장을 인쇄하려고 계획한다.
(d) Trevor는 동료를 위한 항공편을 예약해야 한다.

30~31

인도 독립 지도자 마하트마 간디는 영국의 인도 식민지화에 대한 그의 비폭력 저항의 철학을 표현하기 위해 샤탸그라하의 개념을 개발했다. 다른 시민 불복종의 형태들과는 달리, 샤탸그라하의 개념에는 형이상학적인 의미가 주입되어 있었다. 샤탸그라하라는 용어는 직역하면 산스크리트어로 '진리를 견고하게 파악함'을 뜻하고, 간디는 그것을 '진리로부터 탄생한 힘'으로 정의했다. 그는 진리는 세계의 필수적인 본질을 나타내고, 독립운동은 기만자들, 즉 영국 식민지 개척자들을 필연적으로 이기게 할, 진리의 힘을 상징한다고 믿었다.

샤탸그라하는 인도에서 영적 인사이자 정치적 지도자로서 간디의 이중적 지위를 반영하는데, 이것이 그가 인도 대중 사이에서 종교적 열정을 불러일으키도록 도왔다. 샤탸그라하를 수행할 때, 간디는 독립운동가들이 적들에 대한 화를 품지 않고, 어떤 형태의 보복이든 피하고, 또한 자발적으로 체포에 복종하도록 교육했다. 실제로, 이것이 영국 지배에 대항하는 거대한 규모의 평화적 저항을 불러왔고, 식민지 경제를 교착 상태로 만들었다. 영국이 이러한 전략에 보통 폭력으로 대응했기 때문에, 현상 유지의 이점에 관한 그들의 주장은 쉽게 반박되었다.

30. Q: 지문의 주제는 무엇인가?

(a) 정치적 사상가로서와 독립 지도자로서의 간디의 역할 갈등
(b) 저항 운동의 성공에 있어 지도력의 중요성
(c) 영국 사회에서 간디의 가르침의 영적 중요성
(d) 식민 지배에 대한 간디의 평화적 저항의 철학적 개념

31. Q: 지문에서 추론할 수 있는 것은 무엇인가?
(a) 영국은 영국의 인도 지배가 토착민들에게 이롭다고 정당화했다.
(b) 인도 독립 운동가들이 항상 간디의 비폭력 저항의 교훈에 충실한 것은 아니었다.
(c) 간디의 샤탸그라하의 개념은 주로 인도의 헌신적인 힌두교도들을 겨냥했다.
(d) 샤탸그라하는 인도 독립 이후 여러 국가에서 정치적 전략으로 채택되었다.

32~33

지구의 자기 역전

지구의 자기장은 행성의 중심부로부터 아주 멀리 떨어진 공간까지 뻗어 있다. 행성의 용해된 핵에서 나오는 전류에 의해 발생되는 이 자기장은, 태양으로부터 오는 태양풍을 굴절시키고 따라서 오존층을 보존하여, 지구에 생명이 존재하게 해준다. 그것은 또한 인간들에게 항해의 중요한 수단이 되어왔는데, 그들은, 서기 12세기 이래로, 정확하게 자기 위치를 알기 위해 나침반을 사용하면서 자기장을 활용해왔다. 하지만, 대부분의 사람들이 알아차리지 못하는 것은 이 자기장이 가끔 뒤집히고, 따라서 남쪽과 북쪽이 서로 교체된다는 것이다.

지질학 기록을 연구함으로써, 연구자들은, 비록 완료되려면 수천 년이 걸리지만, 이 반전이 20만 년에서 30만 년마다 일어난다는 것을 발견했다. 이 과정 중에, 자극은 점진적으로 이동하고, 이는 자극이 여러 차례 이상의 위치에 나타나게 한다. 현재, 자북극은 매년 북쪽으로 40마일가량 이동하고 있고, 이는 반전이 진행 중인 것이 아니라면, 임박했음을 암시한다. 무엇이 이것을 야기하는지는 불명확하지만, 몇몇 이론가들은 지질구조판이 요인이라고 생각한다. 그것들의 이동이 지구 핵 내부의 철의 흐름을 바꾸고 반전을 유발할 수 있다. 원인이 무엇이든지 간에, 이러한 역전은 지구상의 동식물 군에 어떤 중대한 영향도 미치지 않았던 것으로 보인다.

32. Q: 지구의 자기장에 대한 글쓴이의 요지는 무엇인가?
(a) 태양열에 의해 발생하는 현상이다.
(b) 남극과 북극의 연례적인 역전을 야기했다.
(c) 수 세기에 걸쳐 힘이 감소하고 있다.
(d) 반전이 가능함이 밝혀졌다.

33. Q: 지문에서 추론할 수 있는 것은 무엇인가?
(a) 자기 역전은 우주의 모든 행성에서 일어난다.
(b) 지구의 철 흐름은 자기장의 방향에 영향을 미친다.
(c) 자극들의 이동은 그것들이 역전하면서 속도가 빨라진다.
(d) 가장 최근의 자기장 반전은 지난 세기에 일어났다.

34~35

월간 신문

칼럼: 국내 전자 기기 산업
Hugh Chang 씀

많은 경제학자들이 말할 것처럼, 무역 적자가 지속되는 것은 국가의 경제 성장에 부정적인 영향을 끼칠 수 있다. 지난 10년 동안, 우리가 수출한 20억 달러의 두 배가 넘는, 평균 50억 달러의 전자 제품을 매년 수입하면서, 우리는 전자 기기 관련 적자를 발생시켰다. 다행히도, 최첨단 수입품과 수출품의 양이 균형 잡히기 시작하면서, 이러한 경향이 작년에 갑작스럽게 변화했다. 수입량은 22억 달러까지 폭락한 반면에 수출량은 25억 달러까지 증가했다.

이 변화에는 두 가지 주요 원인이 있는데, 첫 번째는 외국 상품에

대한 관세를 올리는 정부의 적극적인 결정으로, 이는 국내 전자 기기 산업의 호황을 일으켰고, 그것을 더욱 경쟁력 있게 해주었다. 두 번째로, 지난 몇 년 간 여러 국가 사이에 체결된 무역 협정이 전자 기기 수출량을 증가시켰다. 이 분야의 성장이 우리 경제에 다양한 이익을 가져다줄 수 있기 때문에 전문가들은 이 호황이 계속되기를 바란다. 따라서 국가의 전자 기기 수출량이 수입량을 확실히 추월하게 하고, 무역 적자가 없어지게 하기 위해 지속적인 정부 행동이 요구된다.

34. Q: 다음 중 기사의 내용과 일치하는 것은?

(a) 제조업자들은 여러 다른 국가들에서 설비를 운영하기 시작했다.
(b) 전자 기기 수출품의 양에 증가가 있었다.
(c) 지난 10년간의 수출량은 총 50억 달러였다.
(d) 대부분의 구매자들은 국내에서 제작된 제품보다 수입된 전자 기기를 선호한다.

35. Q: 글쓴이가 가장 동의할 것 같은 진술은 무엇인가?

(a) 수입된 전자 기기에 대한 세금을 인상하는 것은 시장을 덜 경쟁적이게 만들 것이다.
(b) 정부는 국내 제품의 판매 증진에 영향력이 컸다.
(c) 무역 적자는 종종 경제 성장을 위해 필수적이다.
(d) 대부분의 국가는 다른 국가들과의 무역 협정에 충실하려고 노력한다.

TEST 02

LISTENING COMPREHENSION

Part I

1
W: Can I see the project results now?
M: _____

(a) Too many to mention.
(b) Yeah, we're in the planning stage.
(c) I'm just about done.
(d) No, I thought it was easy.

W: 프로젝트 결과물을 지금 볼 수 있을까요?
(a) 거론하자면 너무 많아요.
(b) 네, 저희는 기획 단계에 있어요.
(c) 거의 다 끝냈어요.
(d) 아뇨, 전 그게 쉬웠다고 생각했어요.

2
M: Let your niece know she's in my thoughts.
W: _____

(a) She'll tell you her answer.
(b) She's doing great.
(c) Thanks for asking.
(d) I'll pass that along.

M: 네 조카딸에게 내가 그녀 생각을 하고 있다고 알려 줘.
(a) 그녀가 네게 대답해줄 거야.
(b) 그녀는 잘 지내고 있어.
(c) 물어봐 줘서 고마워.
(d) 그 이야기를 전달할게.

3
W: I can't tell you how thrilled I am you came to the party.
M: _____

(a) I'll make sure not to invite many people.
(b) I wouldn't have missed it for anything.
(c) I'll be there for sure tonight.
(d) You shouldn't say such things.

W: 네가 파티에 와서 내가 얼마나 기쁜지 말로 다 할 수 없어.
(a) 사람들을 많이 초대하지는 않도록 할게.
(b) 난 무슨 일이 있어도 이 파티를 놓치지 않았을 거야.
(c) 오늘 밤에 꼭 거기에 갈게.
(d) 넌 그런 것들을 말해선 안 돼.

4
M: It annoys me that you never say what's on your mind.
W: _____

(a) I would if you weren't so judgmental.
(b) I'm glad that matter's resolved.
(c) That's what annoys me about it too.
(d) Please let me speak my mind.

M: 난 네가 무슨 생각을 하는지 절대 말해 주지 않는 게 짜증나.
(a) 네가 그렇게 비판적이지 않다면 말할 거야.
(b) 그 문제가 해결되어서 다행이야.
(c) 그것에 대해 날 짜증나게 하는 것도 그거야.
(d) 내 생각을 말하게 해줘.

5
W: You are an integral member of this company.
M: _____

(a) My patience is waning.
(b) It's an impressive accomplishment.
(c) In that case, I'll keep you company.
(d) I appreciate the vote of confidence.

W: 당신은 이 회사에서 없어서는 안 될 직원이에요.
(a) 저의 인내심이 줄어들고 있어요.
(b) 인상적인 성과네요.
(c) 그렇다면, 제가 당신과 동행할게요.
(d) 그 지지에 감사해요.

6
M: I can't decide what movie to watch.
W: _____

(a) I already saw one last week.
(b) I heard it's showing soon.
(c) Let's read the critics' reviews.
(d) I'd choose a nearby theater.

M: 무슨 영화를 봐야 할지 결정을 못하겠어.
(a) 난 이미 지난주에 하나 봤어.
(b) 그게 곧 상영할 거라고 들었어.
(c) 평론가들의 영화평을 읽어보자.
(d) 난 가까운 극장을 선택할래.

7
W: I could use an escape to the tropics.
M: _____

(a) I'll save some for later.
(b) You'll have such a great time.
(c) A getaway would do you wonders.
(d) I'll consider your proposal.

W: 난 열대 지방으로 떠나버리고 싶어.
(a) 난 나중을 위해 좀 아껴둘래.
(b) 넌 정말 즐거운 시간을 보낼 거야.
(c) 휴가를 갔다 오면 훨씬 좋아질 거야.
(d) 네 제안을 고려해볼게.

8

M: The company has offered me a raise.
W: _____

(a) I can rise to the challenge.
(b) I'm afraid I'll have to decline.
(c) I'm thinking about calling it quits.
(d) I guess your efforts have paid off.

M: 회사에서 내게 급여 인상을 해줬어.
(a) 난 시련을 잘 극복할 수 있어.
(b) 난 거절해야 될 것 같아.
(c) 일을 그만둘까 생각 중이야.
(d) 네 노력이 성과가 있는 것 같네.

9

W: The new science teacher is very demanding.
M: _____

(a) I didn't know she was being replaced.
(b) No. I'm taking a different class.
(c) Right, a lot was demanded of her.
(d) I'll say. She's a real slave driver.

W: 새로 오신 과학 선생님은 너무 요구하시는 게 많아.
(a) 난 그분이 대체되었다는 것을 몰랐어.
(b) 아니. 나는 다른 수업을 듣고 있어.
(c) 맞아, 많은 것이 그분에게 요구되었지.
(d) 맞아. 그분은 정말 엄한 선생님이야.

10

M: There's a good chance that Lisa will get the promotion.
W: _____

(a) She should submit her résumé.
(b) She's certainly earned it.
(c) She takes a lot of chances.
(d) It's great that she got promoted.

M: Lisa가 승진할 가능성이 높아요.
(a) 그녀는 이력서를 제출해야 해요.
(b) 그녀는 분명 그만한 자격이 있어요.
(c) 그녀는 모험을 많이 해요.
(d) 그녀가 승진했다니 잘됐네요.

Part II

11

W: I met Melissa's boyfriend recently, and he was really something else!
M: Let me guess. You felt he was condescending?
W: How did you know?
M: _____

(a) That's his way. He talks down to everyone.
(b) He knows Melissa through mutual friends.
(c) I can't say. I have yet to meet him.
(d) He was too polite to say so himself.

W: 최근에 Melissa의 남자 친구를 만났는데, 그는 정말 대단한 사람이더라!
M: 내가 맞춰볼게. 그가 잘난 체한다고 느꼈지?
W: 어떻게 알았어?
(a) 그게 그의 방식이야. 그는 모두를 깔보는 투로 말하지.
(b) 그는 서로 아는 친구를 통해 Melissa를 알고 있어.
(c) 글쎄. 난 아직 그와 만난 적이 없어.
(d) 그는 매우 예의가 발라서 스스로 그렇게 말할 수는 없었어.

12

M: Good luck in the dance competition this weekend.
W: Thanks. I hope I don't forget the steps.
M: You'll manage. Just rehearse as often as you can.
W: _____

(a) You should show me how.
(b) Ours is strictly a ballroom dancing contest.
(c) That's what I don't remember.
(d) I've been doing that every day.

M: 이번 주말에 있을 댄스 경연대회에서 행운을 빌어.
W: 고마워. 스텝을 잊지 않아야 할 텐데.
M: 넌 잘할 거야. 그냥 연습을 최대한 자주 해.
(a) 어떻게 하는지 나한테 보여줘.
(b) 우리 것은 엄밀히 말하면 사교 댄스 경연대회야.
(c) 내가 기억 못하는 게 바로 그거야.
(d) 난 매일 그걸 하고 있어.

13

W: Excuse me. Are you enrolled here?
M: I am. Do you need assistance?
W: Yeah. Can you direct me to the dean's office?
M: _____

(a) The class is usually at Grimsley Hall.
(b) I'm sure he's approachable.
(c) Probably on campus.
(d) I'm headed there. Follow me.

W: 실례합니다. 여기 재학생이신가요?

M: 네. 도움이 필요하신가요?
W: 네. 학장실이 어딘지 알려주실 수 있으세요?

(a) 그 수업은 주로 Grimsley 홀에서 있어요.
(b) 그는 분명 다가가기 쉬울 거예요.
(c) 아마 캠퍼스에 있을 거예요.
(d) 저도 거기로 가는 길이에요. 저를 따라오세요.

14

M: Hey, could you move your car? I need to pull out.
W: Sure thing. I know how chaotic parking here can be.
M: By the way, didn't you live in Holmes Hall sophomore year?
W: _____

(a) I knew your face rang a bell.
(b) Yes, but there's no parking lot.
(c) Classes are tougher these days.
(d) I can give you directions there.

M: 저기요, 차 좀 옮겨 주시겠어요? 제가 빠져나가야 해서요.
W: 물론이죠. 이곳에 주차하는 게 얼마나 혼란스러울지 알아요.
M: 그런데, 2학년 때 Holmes Hall에서 살지 않으셨어요?

(a) 낯이 익다 했어요.
(b) 그렇긴 한데, 거긴 주차장이 없어요.
(c) 요즘 수업들은 더 어려워요.
(d) 거기 가는 길을 알려 드릴 수 있어요.

15

W: Mike, when are our projects due?
M: Wednesday. We have to turn them in before twelve.
W: Is there a chance the deadline will be extended?
M: _____

(a) The due date was postponed.
(b) We should submit one.
(c) It's worth taking a chance.
(d) I wouldn't count on it.

W: Mike, 우리 과제가 언제까지야?
M: 수요일. 12시 전에 제출해야 해.
W: 마감 기한이 연장될 가능성이 있을까?

(a) 마감일이 미뤄졌었어.
(b) 우리는 하나 제출해야 해.
(c) 시도해볼 가치는 있어.
(d) 나라면 기대하지 않을 거야.

16

M: Why did you buy a new Internet modem?
W: Because my home connection is slow as molasses.
M: Are you sure it's not because of your provider?
W: _____

(a) I've been told installation is free.
(b) I hope that they speed it up.
(c) That hadn't crossed my mind.
(d) It happens to be the reason.

M: 왜 새로운 인터넷 모뎀을 구입했니?
W: 집의 인터넷 연결은 너무 느려서 말이야.
M: 제공 업체 때문에 그런 건 아니고?

(a) 난 설치가 무료라고 들었어.
(b) 그들이 속도를 높여 주었으면 좋겠어.
(c) 그건 미처 생각을 못했네.
(d) 그게 바로 그 이유야.

17

W: I hate people who stick their noses into my business.
M: I concur, but why are you bringing it up?
W: A co-worker keeps asking personal questions.
M: _____

(a) It goes beyond personality.
(b) Try not to be so nosy.
(c) Employee input is crucial.
(d) It's best to brush off busybodies.

W: 나는 내 일에 쓸데없이 참견하는 사람들이 싫어.
M: 동의는 한다만, 왜 그런 이야기를 꺼내는데?
W: 한 직장 동료가 자꾸 사적인 질문을 하잖아.

(a) 그건 성격 문제를 넘어선 거야.
(b) 참견하지 않으려고 노력해 봐.
(c) 직원의 조언은 중요해.
(d) 참견하기 좋아하는 사람은 무시하는 게 최고야.

18

M: Your son is due to be born any day now, isn't he?
W: Yes, my husband and I can't wait!
M: Have you guys settled on a name yet?
W: _____

(a) We still aren't sure when the baby is due.
(b) We're waiting to see if it's a boy or a girl.
(c) We're still narrowing down our options.
(d) We both like that name a lot.

M: 네 아들이 곧 태어날 예정이지, 그렇지 않니?
W: 응, 남편과 나는 너무 기다려져!
M: 너희 부부는 이미 이름을 정했니?

(a) 언제 아기가 나올지 아직 잘 모르겠어.
(b) 아들인지 딸인지 알아보려고 기다리고 있어.
(c) 아직 선택의 범위를 좁히고 있는 중이야.
(d) 우리 둘 다 그 이름이 정말 마음에 들어.

19

W: Is your old email account still active?
M: It's the only one I have.
W: Then how come you didn't respond to my message?
M: _____

(a) I didn't have one back then.
(b) I closed that account.
(c) Don't worry. I'll make a copy.
(d) I wanted to speak with you in person.

W: 네 예전 이메일 계정이 아직도 유효하니?
M: 내 계정은 그거 하나뿐이야.
W: 그럼 왜 내 메일에 답장을 보내지 않았어?

(a) 당시에는 계정이 없었어.
(b) 난 그 계정을 닫았어.
(c) 걱정하지 마. 내가 복사할게.
(d) 너와 직접 이야기하고 싶었어.

20

M: I had no idea you disliked fast food.
W: Really? I thought that was clear.
M: I don't recall you explicitly stating that.
W: _____

(a) I'll be sure to remind you later.
(b) Then you weren't paying attention.
(c) It's one of my favorite restaurants.
(d) Let's come back another time.

M: 난 네가 패스트푸드를 싫어하는 줄 전혀 몰랐어.
W: 정말? 그 점은 명확하다고 생각했는데.
M: 네가 그걸 분명히 말한 기억이 안 나는데.

(a) 나중에 네게 꼭 상기시켜 줄게.
(b) 그렇다면 네가 관심을 기울이고 있지 않았던 거야.
(c) 그곳은 내가 가장 좋아하는 식당들 중 하나야.
(d) 다음번에 다시 오자.

Part III

21

Listen to a conversation between a customer and a restaurant employee.

M: Good afternoon. I'd like a table for five at 7:30, please.
W: Certainly. What name will the booking be under?
M: Kurt Morrison. We'll also need a booster seat.
W: OK, that can be arranged. Five guests total, correct?
M: Indeed. And that's for the nonsmoking section.
W: OK, you're all set. Check in with the hostess when you arrive.

Q: What is the man mainly doing in the conversation?

(a) Making plans for a dinner show
(b) Amending an earlier reservation
(c) Ensuring a table is nonsmoking
(d) Booking a table for dinner

고객과 식당 직원 간의 대화를 들으시오.

M: 안녕하세요. 7시 30분에 다섯 명 예약하고 싶습니다.
W: 물론이죠. 예약은 누구 이름으로 해 드릴까요?
M: Kurt Morrison이요. 저희는 어린이용 보조 의자도 하나 필요합니다.
W: 네, 그것도 마련할 수 있습니다. 총 다섯 분, 맞으시죠?
M: 그렇습니다. 그리고 금연 구역으로 해주세요.
W: 네, 모두 준비가 되었습니다. 도착하시면 여지배인에게 말씀해 주세요.

Q: 대화에서 남자는 주로 무엇을 하고 있는가?

(a) 디너쇼 계획을 세우고 있다.
(b) 이전의 예약을 수정하고 있다.
(c) 금연 좌석인지 확인하고 있다.
(d) 저녁 식사를 위해 자리를 예약하고 있다.

22

Listen to a conversation between two friends.

W: This theme park is top-notch.
M: I told you. Aren't you glad I brought you?
W: Sure. What should we do first?
M: How about the horror train? It's really scary.
W: I'm up for it. How about the roller coaster after?
M: I'm game if you are.

Q: What are the man and woman mainly discussing?

(a) What rides they would like to try
(b) Which ride is the most frightening
(c) How they feel about the theme park
(d) Why the theme park is entertaining

두 친구 간의 대화를 들으시오.

W: 이 놀이공원은 최고야.
M: 내가 말했잖아. 내가 데리고 와서 기쁘지 않아?
W: 물론이지. 우리 뭐부터 할까?
M: 공포 열차 어때? 그건 정말 무서워.
W: 찬성이야. 그 다음에는 롤러코스터 어때?
M: 너만 좋다면 난 좋아.

Q: 남자와 여자는 주로 무엇을 논의하고 있는가?

(a) 두 사람이 타려고 하는 놀이기구가 무엇인지
(b) 가장 무서운 놀이기구가 어느 것인지
(c) 그 놀이공원에 대해 어떻게 느끼는지
(d) 그 놀이공원이 재미있는 이유가 무엇인지

23

Listen to a conversation between two acquaintances.

M: Have you made up your mind about leasing the apartment?
W: Well, I'm still up in the air.
M: It's the cheapest you can find in the area.
W: I know. It's quite far from my office, though.
M: But there's a subway station around the corner.
W: I'll need a few more days before I can decide.

Q: What is mainly happening in the conversation?

(a) The man is pointing out local amenities.
(b) The woman is expressing ambivalence over a rental.
(c) The woman is reconsidering a lease.
(d) The man is finding the woman a new unit.

두 지인 간의 대화를 들으시오.

M: 그 아파트를 임대하기로 결정하셨나요?
W: 글쎄요, 아직은 미정이에요.
M: 그 아파트는 이 지역에서 찾을 수 있는 가장 저렴한 거예요.
W: 알아요. 그렇지만, 아파트가 제 사무실에서 꽤 멀어요.
M: 하지만 길 모퉁이만 돌면 지하철 역이 있어요.
W: 결정하려면 며칠이 더 필요해요.

Q: 대화에서 주로 무엇이 일어나고 있는가?

(a) 남자가 지역의 편의 시설을 알려주고 있다.
(b) 여자가 임대에 대해 주저함을 표현하고 있다.
(c) 여자가 임대하는 것을 재고하고 있다.
(d) 남자가 여자에게 새로운 아파트를 찾아주고 있다.

24

Listen to two friends discussing college tuition.

W: I think I made a terrible choice.
M: What decision are you talking about?
W: My uncle wanted to support my university studies.
M: And you refused his help?
W: Yeah. Now, I have to work part-time just to afford tuition.
M: I would have never declined such an opportunity.

Q: Which is correct about the woman according to the conversation?

(a) She is being sponsored by her uncle.
(b) She will ask her uncle for money.
(c) She accepted a scholarship to pursue her studies.
(d) She regrets not accepting assistance.

두 친구가 대학 등록금에 관해 이야기하는 것을 들으시오.

W: 내가 형편없는 선택을 한 것 같아.
M: 무슨 결정을 이야기하는 거야?
W: 삼촌은 나의 대학 공부를 지원해주시길 원하셨어.
M: 그런데 너는 그 도움을 거절했고?
W: 맞아. 이제는, 단지 등록금을 마련하기 위해서 파트타임으로 일을 해야 해.
M: 나라면 그런 기회를 절대 거절하지 않았을 거야.

Q: 대화에 따르면 여자에 대해 맞는 것은 무엇인가?

(a) 삼촌에게서 후원을 받고 있다.
(b) 삼촌에게 돈을 요구할 것이다.
(c) 공부를 계속하기 위해서 장학금을 받았다.
(d) 도움을 받지 않은 것을 후회한다.

25

Listen to a conversation between two friends.

M: Let's congratulate Tom — he nabbed a role in an action film.
W: Wow! That's surprising, though.
M: What, that he finally landed an acting job?
W: No. I just can't imagine him as an action hero. He's not exactly the heroic type.
M: Oh, he's not the lead. He plays the bookish sidekick.
W: Well, that suits him perfectly!

Q: Which is correct according to the conversation?

(a) Tom is auditioning for the main role in an action movie.
(b) The woman doubts Tom has any ability as an actor.
(c) The woman thinks Tom lacks the demeanor of an action hero.
(d) The man is unsure what role Tom will play in the movie.

두 친구 간의 대화를 들으시오.

M: Tom을 축하해주자, 그가 액션 영화에서 배역을 따냈어.
W: 와! 그런데 놀라운걸.
M: 뭐가, 그가 드디어 연기를 하게 된 것이 말이야?
W: 아니. 난 그냥 그가 액션 영웅으로 나오는 것이 상상이 안 돼. 그가 엄밀히 영웅다운 타입은 아니잖아.
M: 아, 그가 주인공은 아니야. 책 읽기 좋아하는 조수 역을 한대.
W: 음, 그것은 그에게 딱 어울리네!

Q: 대화에 따르면 맞는 것은 무엇인가?

(a) Tom은 액션 영화의 주인공 역을 위해 오디션을 보고 있다.
(b) 여자는 Tom이 배우로서 조금의 재능이라도 있는지 의심한다.
(c) 여자는 Tom이 액션 영웅의 품행이 부족하다고 생각한다.
(d) 남자는 영화에서 Tom이 어떤 배역을 맡을지 잘 모른다.

26

Listen to a conversation about tickets to a play.

W: Excuse me. When will the new play premiere?

M: It debuts on February 9 and runs until March 12.
W: Great. Two tickets for opening night, please.
M: I'm sorry, but those tickets have already been snapped up.
W: Really? When's the earliest available showing?
M: Well, there are a few available seats the third night.
W: OK. I'll take two seats for that.

Q: Which is correct according to the conversation?

(a) The play's run has been prolonged a month.
(b) The new play will premiere on March 12.
(c) The woman did not receive her first preference.
(d) The woman will buy tickets at the door.

연극 표에 관한 대화를 들으시오.
W: 실례합니다. 새 연극이 언제 초연하나요?
M: 2월 9일에 시작해서 3월 12일까지 공연합니다.
W: 좋네요. 개막일 밤 표를 두 장 주세요.
M: 죄송하지만, 그날 밤 표는 벌써 팔렸습니다.
W: 정말이요? 가장 빨리 관람할 수 있는 공연은 언제인가요?
M: 음, 셋째 날 밤에 빈 좌석이 몇 개 있습니다.
W: 좋아요. 그걸로 두 자리 예매할게요.

Q: 대화에 따르면 맞는 것은 무엇인가?
(a) 그 연극 공연은 한 달 연장되었다.
(b) 새 연극은 3월 12일에 초연할 예정이다.
(c) 여자는 처음에 선호했던 것을 얻지 못했다.
(d) 여자는 입구에서 표를 살 것이다.

27

Listen to two friends discussing housing.

M: Apartment complexes have been popping up everywhere lately.
W: Word on the street is that it's due to the government offering developers tax breaks.
M: Well, that would explain it.
W: Yeah. All this new construction is bound to put downward pressure on prices.
M: Great! It should also give home buyers more options for housing.
W: That's an outcome we can all live with.

Q: What outcome does the man expect from recent events?

(a) Citizens will pay lower taxes.
(b) People will have more housing choices.
(c) Investors will buy up more real estate.
(d) Homes will become more expensive.

두 친구가 주택 공급에 관해 이야기하는 것을 들으시오.
M: 아파트 단지들이 최근에 사방에서 갑자기 생겨나고 있어.
W: 소문에 의하면 정부가 개발업자들에게 세금 우대를 제공하는 것 때문이래.
M: 음, 그걸로 설명이 되겠네.
W: 응. 이 모든 신규 건축은 가격이 떨어지게끔 압력을 가하게 될거야.
M: 굉장해! 그건 주택 구매자들에게 주택에 대한 더 많은 선택권도 주겠네.
W: 그건 우리 모두가 받아들일 수 있는 결과지.

Q: 남자는 최근에 일어난 일로부터 어떤 결과를 기대하는가?
(a) 시민들이 더 낮은 세금을 지불할 것이다.
(b) 사람들이 더 많은 주택 선택권을 가질 것이다.
(c) 투자자들이 더 많은 부동산을 매수할 것이다.
(d) 주택이 더 비싸질 것이다.

28

Listen to a conversation between two colleagues.

W: I really dread this afternoon's meeting.
M: Yeah, I expect we'll be under the gun.
W: What if they say I'm responsible for blowing the sales contract?
M: Just rest assured that I've got your back.
W: I knew you would cover for me.
M: Well, what goes around comes around.

Q: Which is correct according to the conversation?

(a) The woman messed up a business deal.
(b) The woman's annoyed by the man's comments.
(c) The man plans to stick up for the woman.
(d) The man intends to wash his hands of responsibility.

두 동료 간의 대화를 들으시오.
W: 전 오늘 오후 회의가 정말 두려워요.
M: 맞아요, 우리는 스트레스를 많이 받을 거예요.
W: 만약 그들이 판매 계약을 날려버린 것에 대해서 책임이 나에게 있다고 말하면 어쩌죠?
M: 제가 도와줄 테니 안심해요.
W: 당신이 나를 감싸줄 것을 알고 있었어요.
M: 뭐, 가는 게 있으면 오는 것도 있는 법이니까요.

Q: 대화에 따르면 맞는 것은 무엇인가?
(a) 여자가 사업 거래를 망쳤다.
(b) 여자는 남자의 말에 짜증이 나 있다.
(c) 남자는 여자를 옹호할 계획이다.
(d) 남자는 책임을 맡지 않으려고 하고 있다.

29

Listen to a conversation between a customer and a coffee shop employee.

M: Pardon me. Is this the only Broward Coffee House nearby?
W: No way. A handful are within a stone's throw of here.

M: Oh, no. I'm supposed to meet a friend at a Broward Coffee House in the vicinity, but I don't know which one.
W: Well, you may want to check the Bay Street one.
M: Is there a particular reason?
W: It's the most popular one in the area.

Q: What can be inferred from the conversation?

(a) The man's friend works at Broward Coffee House.
(b) The man is having trouble finding Bay Street.
(c) Broward Coffee House is a large chain.
(d) Bay Street has several coffee shops.

고객과 커피숍 직원 간의 대화를 들으시오.
M: 실례합니다. 이곳이 근처에서 유일한 Broward Coffee House인가요?
W: 그럴 리가요. 여기서 가까운 곳에 몇 개가 더 있어요.
M: 아, 이런. 근처에 있는 Broward Coffee House에서 친구를 만나기로 했는데, 어느 곳인지 모르겠어요.
W: 그렇다면, Bay 가에 있는 지점을 확인해보세요.
M: 특별한 이유가 있나요?
W: 그곳이 이 지역에서는 가장 인기 있는 곳이거든요.

Q: 대화에서 추론할 수 있는 것은 무엇인가?
(a) 남자의 친구는 Broward Coffee House에서 일한다.
(b) 남자는 Bay 가를 찾는 데 어려움을 겪고 있다.
(c) Broward Coffee House는 대규모 체인점이다.
(d) Bay 가에는 여러 개의 커피숍이 있다.

30

Listen to a conversation at a bookstore.
W: I need to pick up a book for my literature class, but I can't recall its title or author.
M: Do you recollect what genre it's in?
W: I think it's a mystery novel.
M: Can you tell me when it came out?
W: Oh, it's a new one. The professor said it hit shelves last month.
M: OK. I'll narrow my search using those categories.

Q: What can be inferred from the conversation?

(a) The man works in the literature department.
(b) The man located a book the woman wanted.
(c) The woman misplaced a book she was reading.
(d) The woman was assigned a book to read.

서점에서의 대화를 들으시오.
W: 문학 수업에 책을 가져가야 하는데, 책 제목이나 저자가 기억이 안 나네요.
M: 책이 어떤 장르에 속하는지는 기억하세요?
W: 추리 소설인 것 같아요.
M: 언제 출간되었는지 말해주실 수 있어요?
W: 아, 신간이에요. 교수님께서 지난달에 출간되었다고 말하셨어요.
M: 좋아요. 그 범주들을 이용해서 검색을 좁혀볼게요.

Q: 대화에서 추론할 수 있는 것은 무엇인가?
(a) 남자는 문학부에서 일하고 있다.
(b) 남자는 여자가 원했던 책을 찾아냈다.
(c) 여자는 읽고 있었던 책을 둔 곳을 잊어버렸다.
(d) 여자는 읽을 책을 지정받았다.

Part IV

31

Set aside money automatically with Universal Bank's PaySaver account. This service is open to Universal Bank checking account holders enrolled in our direct deposit program. Every payday, a preset amount is automatically transferred to your separate PaySaver account. Not only is the service hassle-free, but it also offers a high interest rate and a low minimum balance. Please contact 1-800-UB-SAVES for more information.

Q: What is mainly being advertised?

(a) A checking account at a bank
(b) A method of automating savings
(c) A bank offering high interest rates
(d) A service to manage employee payroll

Universal 은행의 PaySaver 계좌에 자동으로 돈을 저축하세요. 이 서비스는 저희 자동이체 프로그램에 등록한 Universal 은행 당좌 예금 계좌 소지자에게 제공됩니다. 월급날마다, 약정된 금액이 자동으로 귀하의 별도 PaySaver 계좌로 이체됩니다. 이 서비스는 번거로운 절차가 없을 뿐만 아니라, 높은 이자율과 낮은 최소 예치금도 제공합니다. 보다 많은 정보를 원하시면, 1-800-UB-SAVES로 연락 바랍니다.

Q: 주로 광고되고 있는 것은 무엇인가?
(a) 은행의 당좌 예금 계좌
(b) 저축을 자동으로 하는 방법
(c) 고금리를 제공하는 은행
(d) 직원 급여를 관리하는 서비스

32

We've talked about how fish species that are scavengers feed on carrion and waste products. Because of this trait, they are considered the janitors of the marine world and are used to keep aquariums clean. This commercial popularity poses a problem, though, since taking them from their habitat keeps them from carrying out their role in the ecosystem. In one city, for instance, the government had to buy scavengers from aquarium wholesalers and dump them in a contaminated lake to purify the water. Given the polluted state of many of our oceans and waterways, the absence of these scavenger fish represents a serious ecological risk.

Q: What is the main topic of the lecture?

(a) Scavengers typically found in lakes
(b) Laws regulating scavenger sales
(c) A consequence of a fish's attribute
(d) The protection of the nation's environment

우리는 청소물고기라는 어종이 어떻게 썩은 고기와 쓰레기를 먹고 사는지에 대해 이야기해왔습니다. 이러한 특성 때문에, 그것들은 해양 세계의 청소부로 인식되고 수족관을 깨끗하게 유지하는 데 이용되고 있습니다. 하지만 이러한 상업적인 인기가 문제를 일으키는데, 청소물고기들을 서식지로부터 데려오는 것은 그들이 생태계에서 자신의 역할을 수행하지 못하도록 하기 때문입니다. 한 도시를 예로 들면, 정부는 물을 정화하기 위해 수족관 도매업자로부터 청소물고기를 사서 오염된 호수에 쏟아부어야만 했습니다. 우리의 바다와 수로의 다수가 오염된 상태임을 고려해볼 때, 이 청소물고기들의 부재는 심각한 생태학적 위험을 나타냅니다.

Q: 강의의 주제는 무엇인가?

(a) 호수에서 일반적으로 발견되는 청소물고기
(b) 청소물고기 판매를 규제하는 법령
(c) 한 물고기의 특성으로 인한 결과
(d) 국가 환경의 보호

33

Hi. You've reached Sue Carter. Please be informed that I'll be extending my holiday leave for two more weeks. If you are a client calling about pending storyboards, please rest assured that I will have them completed upon my return. However, if the matter is urgent, feel free to contact the main office to speak to another artist. If you have questions regarding any work completed before I left, you may contact me through the mobile number listed on our Web site. Thank you, and have a good day.

Q: What should a caller do to inquire about finished work?

(a) Speak to an employee at the main office
(b) Call a phone number posted online
(c) Send Ms. Carter an email
(d) Visit a Web site to leave a comment

안녕하세요. Sue Carter입니다. 제가 휴가를 2주 더 연장할 것임을 알려드립니다. 미결 스토리보드 때문에 전화하신 고객이라면, 제가 돌아오자마자 그것들을 완료할 것이니 안심하시기 바랍니다. 하지만, 만약 급한 건이라면, 언제든지 본사에 연락하여 다른 아티스트에게 문의하시기 바랍니다. 제가 떠나기 전에 끝냈던 작품에 대해서 질문이 있으시면, 저희 웹 사이트에 기재된 휴대폰 번호로 제게 연락하실 수 있습니다. 감사합니다, 좋은 하루 보내세요.

Q: 완성된 작품에 대해 문의하려면 전화 건 사람은 무엇을 해야 하는가?

(a) 본사 직원과 이야기한다.
(b) 온라인에 게시된 전화번호로 전화한다.
(c) Ms. Carter에게 이메일을 보낸다.
(d) 의견을 작성하기 위해 웹 사이트를 방문한다.

34

Today, I'm going to talk about minimalists, artists who reject the conviction that art is a medium for self-expression and instead concentrate on fabricating unpretentious and objective works. They are convinced that aesthetics is central to art, and pieces should be free of underlying messages or reflections of the artist's character. In a nutshell, they think that paintings and sculptures should provide viewers with an uncluttered visual experience that is easy to appreciate. This is why their works are impersonal and absent of extraneous elements.

Q: Which is correct about minimalists according to the lecture?

(a) They want art to facilitate communication.
(b) They produce work devoid of any personal meaning.
(c) They embed ideas within pleasing images.
(d) They strive for visually complex compositions.

오늘, 예술이 자기 표현을 위한 매체라는 신념을 거부하고 대신 꾸밈 없고 객관적인 작품을 제작하는 것에 집중하는 예술가들인 미니멀리스트에 대해서 이야기하려고 합니다. 그들은 미학이 예술의 중심이고, 작품은 숨어 있는 메시지나 예술가의 개성을 반영하는 것에서 자유로워야 한다는 신념을 갖고 있습니다. 간단히 말해서, 그들은 그림과 조각이 관람객들에게 감상하기 쉬운 정돈된 시각적 경험을 제공해야 한다고 생각합니다. 이것이 그들의 작품이 비개인적이고 이질적인 요소들이 없는 이유입니다.

Q: 강의에 따르면 미니멀리스트들에 대해 맞는 것은 무엇인가?

(a) 예술이 의사소통을 촉진하기를 원한다.
(b) 어떠한 개인적인 의미도 없는 작품을 만든다.
(c) 보기 좋은 이미지들 안에 생각을 끼워 넣는다.
(d) 시각적으로 복잡한 작품들을 만들려고 노력한다.

35

In response to recent kidnappings, the Samboan County Police Department urges parents to exercise caution. Since most of these heinous acts have been perpetrated near campuses, parents should ensure that children are safe when walking to and from school and should instruct them to stay in well-lit areas, walk in groups, and avoid strangers. Although patrols have been stepped up in school neighborhoods, the police request continued public vigilance. Anyone with knowledge of a possible threat should contact the authorities immediately.

Q: Which is correct according to the instructions?

(a) Kidnappings are unheard of in Samboan County.

(b) Parents should accompany children at all times.
(c) Students should steer clear of unfamiliar people.
(d) Policemen will be patrolling campuses.

최근의 유괴 사건들에 대한 대응으로, Samboan 주립 경찰서는 부모님들이 주의를 기울여줄 것을 당부 드립니다. 이러한 흉악 행위의 대부분이 학교 근처에서 일어나기 때문에, 부모님들은 등하굣길에 아이들이 안전한지 확인하고, 자녀가 밝은 곳에 머물고, 무리를 지어 걸으며, 낯선 사람은 피하도록 지도해야 합니다. 학교 인근에서 순찰이 강화되었지만, 경찰은 시민들의 지속적인 경계를 요청 드립니다. 위협 가능성을 인지한 분은 누구든지 지체 없이 관계 당국에 연락하여 주시기 바랍니다.

Q: 안내에 따르면 맞는 것은 무엇인가?

(a) 유괴는 Samboan 주에서는 전례가 없다.
(b) 부모들은 항상 아이들과 동행해야 한다.
(c) 학생들은 모르는 사람들을 피해야 한다.
(d) 경찰관이 교내를 순찰할 것이다.

36

I want to talk about the misuse of Internet access among our staff, an issue that has gone on because of its seeming triviality. This problem is severely affecting our company's productivity. Some of our employees devote a disconcerting amount of time at the office visiting social networking sites, blogging, and on personal email. Others download music and even view obscene content at their workstations. It is a form of theft, because these people are taking the company's money while producing nothing of value in return.

Q: What can be inferred from the talk?

(a) Internet abuse has been overlooked.
(b) The company lacks a policy for Internet use.
(c) Workers are not completing assigned tasks.
(d) The company will block some external Web sites.

저는 사소해 보이기 때문에 계속되어온 문제인, 우리 직원들의 인터넷 접속 남용에 대해 이야기하고 싶습니다. 이 문제는 우리 기업의 생산성에 심각한 영향을 끼치고 있습니다. 우리 직원 중 일부는 사무실에서 당혹스러울 정도의 시간을 소셜 네트워킹 사이트 방문, 블로그, 그리고 개인 이메일에 할애합니다. 다른 이들은 업무용 컴퓨터에서 음악을 다운로드 받거나 심지어 외설적인 콘텐츠를 보기도 합니다. 이는 일종의 절도죄인 데, 이런 사람들은 회사의 돈을 받으면서 그 대가로 아무런 가치도 생산하지 않기 때문입니다.

Q: 담화에서 추론할 수 있는 것은 무엇인가?

(a) 인터넷 오용은 간과되어왔다.
(b) 회사에는 인터넷 사용에 대한 정책이 부족하다.
(c) 직원들은 맡은 일을 완료하지 않고 있다.
(d) 회사는 일부 외부 웹 사이트를 차단할 것이다.

Part V

37~38

Thank you all for attending today's tour of Yamato's facilities. Let me begin by giving you a brief glimpse into the company's background and liquor-making practices. Yamato Winery began producing sake, Japanese rice wine, over 200 years ago and actually traces its basic methodology to traditions of remote antiquity. In the 1980s, we began exporting our rice wine to the West and, sell nearly three million liters every year in the US alone. Our sake is a perfect blend of the finest ingredients and well-honed techniques. We still use only fresh water that comes from a mountain spring on Kyushu Island, and it is combined with a premium rice variety grown at our company-owned farms in Japan's Saga region. Then, our products are bottled and stored according to age-old practices. Later, you will get a chance to sample our wide range of rice wines and perhaps even pick up a bottle or two from our gift shop.

37. Q: What is the speaker mainly talking about?

(a) Yamato Winery's improvement of the wine-making process
(b) Yamato Winery's rapid growth since the 1900s
(c) The features of Yamato's rice wine production
(d) The popularity of Yamato sake in the West

38. Q: Where does Yamato Winery get its rice from?

(a) A farm in the United States
(b) A company-owned island
(c) A mountain area
(d) A region in Japan

오늘 Yamato 시설 견학에 참석해 주셔서 모두 감사드립니다. 이 회사의 배경과 주류 제조 기법을 간략하게 살펴보는 것으로 시작하겠습니다. Yamato Winery는 약 2백 년 전에 일본식 청주인 정종을 생산하기 시작했으며 기본적인 방법은 사실 먼 고대의 전통까지 거슬러 올라갑니다. 1980년대에, 저희는 서양으로 저희 청주를 수출하기 시작했으며, 미국에서만 매년 3백만 리터 가까이 판매합니다. 저희 정종은 가장 좋은 재료와 잘 연마된 기술의 완벽한 조합입니다. 저희는 여전히 규슈 섬의 산속 샘에서 나오는 깨끗한 물만을 사용하며, 그것은 일본 사가 지역 내의 회사 소유 농장에서 재배되는 고급 쌀 품종과 결합됩니다. 그리고 나서, 저희 제품은 옛날부터 전해오는 기법들에 따라 병에 담기고 보관됩니다. 이따가 여러분은 다양한 종류의 청주를 시음할 기회가 있을 것이며, 아마도 저희 기념품점에서 한두 병을 구매하실 수도 있을 것입니다.

37. Q: 화자는 주로 무엇을 이야기하고 있는가?

(a) Yamato Winery의 주류 제조 과정의 발전

(b) 1900년대 이후 Yamato Winery의 급속한 성장
(c) Yamato의 청주 생산의 특징
(d) 서양에서의 Yamato 정종의 인기

38. Q: Yamato Winery는 어디에서 쌀을 가져오는가?
(a) 미국의 한 농장
(b) 회사 소유의 섬
(c) 산간 지역
(d) 일본의 한 지역

39~40

Let's continue our discussion of the brain. As I was saying, the corpus callosum is the bundle of nerve fibers that links the brain's hemispheres, acting as a kind of bridge that spans the two symmetrical halves. It facilitates the transmission of signals between our left brain and right brain. It is also crucial to eyesight, balance, and touch. In recent years, it has been associated with memory capacity and handedness, or whether a person favors the right or left hand. It is this emerging area of research that I'd like to focus on today. While experts viewed handedness as an oddity in the past, studies are revealing that it accounts for a number of physical and mental differences between left-handed and right-handed people. In general, left-handed individuals possess a larger abundance of neurons in the corpus callosum than right-handed people, which translates into a capacity to recall certain information. So, while right-handed folks can memorize reams of details about a subject like the Civil War, lefties can more proficiently recollect contextual details, like where and when they encountered the information.

39. Q: What is the speaker mainly doing in the talk?
(a) Explaining how recall is linked to handedness
(b) Speculating about the memorization skills of righties
(c) Underlining the corpus callosum's importance
(d) Describing how the brain encodes information

40. Q: According to the talk, how do left-handed people differ from right-handed people?
(a) They encounter difficulties recalling dates and places.
(b) Their left brains exhibit a genetic abnormality.
(c) They require contextual clues to properly interpret facts.
(d) Their corpus callosum has a greater number of neurons.

뇌에 대한 논의를 계속합시다. 이야기했듯이, 뇌량은 뇌의 반구들을 잇는 신경 섬유들의 다발이며, 대칭적인 두 개의 절반을 연결하는 일종의 교량 역할을 합니다. 그것은 우리의 좌뇌와 우뇌 간의 신호 전달을 용이하게 합니다. 시력, 균형, 촉각에 있어도 매우 중요합니다. 최근 몇 년 동안, 그것은 기억력과 잘 쓰는 손, 혹은 사람이 오른손이나 왼손을 선호하는지의 여부와 연관되어 왔습니다. 오늘 제가 중점을 두고자 하는 것은 바로 이 부상하는 연구 분야입니다. 과거에는 전문가들이 어느 한쪽 손을 잘 쓰는 것을 특이한 것으로 보았지만, 연구는 이것이 왼손잡이와 오른손잡이 사람들 사이의 여러 신체 및 정신적 차이를 설명해 준다고 밝히고 있습니다. 일반적으로, 왼손잡이인 사람들은 오른손잡이인 사람들보다 뇌량에 더 많은 양의 뉴런을 가지고 있는데, 이는 특정 정보를 기억할 수 있는 능력으로 해석됩니다. 따라서, 오른손잡이인 사람들은 남북 전쟁과 같은 주제에 대한 많은 세부 정보를 기억할 수 있는 반면, 왼손잡이들은 그 정보를 접했던 장소나 시기와 같은 문맥상의 세부 정보를 더 능숙하게 기억할 수 있습니다.

39. Q: 담화에서 화자가 주로 하고 있는 일은 무엇인가?
(a) 기억력이 잘 쓰는 손과 어떻게 연관되는지 설명하고 있다.
(b) 오른손잡이의 기억 능력에 대해 추측하고 있다.
(c) 뇌량의 중요성을 강조하고 있다.
(d) 뇌가 정보를 어떻게 암호화하는지 설명하고 있다.

40. Q: 담화에 따르면, 왼손잡이인 사람들은 오른손잡이인 사람들과 어떻게 다른가?
(a) 날짜와 장소를 기억할 때 어려움을 겪는다.
(b) 좌뇌가 유전적 기형을 보인다.
(c) 사실을 제대로 이해하기 위해 문맥상의 단서가 필요하다.
(d) 뇌량이 더 많은 뉴런을 가지고 있다.

VOCABULARY

Part I

1 A: 관리자가 그 제안을 승인했나요?
   B: 아뇨, 거절했어요. 그는 그 프로젝트를 위한 예산이 비현실적이라고 생각해요.

2 A: 교수님, 교수님의 수업을 청강해도 될까요?
   B: 미안하지만, 학부생들은 법학 수업의 참관이 허락되지 않아요.

3 A: 네가 감자튀김을 좋아하지 않다니 의외야.
   B: 음, 난 기름진 음식을 먹으면 메스꺼워져.

4 A: 우리가 여권을 들고 다녀야 한다고 생각하니?
   B: 아니, 안전하게 호텔 객실에 두고 가자. 여권을 잃어버리지 않도록 주의해야 해.

5 A: Crystal에게 오늘 밤에 영화 보러 가자고 했어?
   B: 그러려고 했는데, 용기를 낼 수가 없었어.

6 A: 저 상자에 와인 잔들을 넣지 말았어야 했어.
   B: 짐꾼들이 거칠게 다루지 않을 거야. 내가 깨지기 쉽다고 적어놨어.

7 A: 내 컴퓨터는 부팅이 잘 안 돼.
   B: 결함이 있는 하드 드라이브 때문일지도 몰라.

8 A: Erin은 그녀의 아버지 차를 허락 없이 몰다가 후진하면서 나무를 들이 받았어.
   B: 오, 곤란하게 되었네. 그녀의 아버지는 화가 머리끝까지 치밀 거야.

9 A: 와, Cindy는 어젯밤에 정말 너무 오래 머물러서 눈총을 샀어.
   B: 정말 그래. 그녀는 내 취침 시간이 한참 넘어서까지 남아 있었어.

10 A: 오늘 아침에 사장님이 내 캐비닛을 뒤지고 있었어.
   B: 정말? 그는 도대체 뭘 찾고 있었을까?

Part II

11 방호복은, 유황 산과 같이, 부식성의 반응을 보이는 물질의 유출에 따른 부상을 막기 위해 고안되었다.

12 독일의 독재자 아돌프 히틀러는 그의 연설을 통해 민족주의자들의 신뢰를 얻은 후 국가 권력을 획득했다.

13 성급하게 말을 하는 사람들은 말하기 전에 신중하게 생각하지 않은 것에 대해 종종 후회한다.

14 강력한 연안 지진이 일어난 직후 바닷물이 빠져나갔고, 이는 쓰나미가 임박했다는 것을 의미했다.

15 파티에 초대받은 소녀들 중 한 명은 입을 만한 괜찮은 옷이 없어서 파티에 가지 않기로 결심했다.

16 새로 고용된 영업부장은 그 지역에서 기업의 마케팅 사업을 감독할 것이다.

17 아이를 기르는 일은 많은 부모들에게 일생의 노고일 수 있다.

18 독자들은 편집자에게 편지를 써서 잡지의 내용에 대한 그들의 의견을 표현하도록 권장된다.

19 Mr. Baker는 시장 조사와 전략에 대한 예리한 통찰력 때문에 그 직위에 고용되었다.

20 그 영화는 백만장자가 되기를 열망했지만 결국 타인의 자선에 의지해서 살게 된 한 남자에 관한 것이었다.

21 와인 상점의 고객들은 대개 화이트 와인 특유의 단맛보다 레드 와인의 풍부한 맛을 선호한다.

22 태국을 강타했던 거대한 파도는 특히 파괴적이었는데 그것이 많은 해안 주민들을 쓸어버렸기 때문이다.

23 가격은 수요가 증가하면 올라가고, 감소하면 내려가는 식으로 자주 오르내린다고 알려져 있다.

24 농구에서의 경쟁 관계에도 불구하고, Alexander와 Christian은 계속 서로 마음이 맞았다.

25 주춤거리는 시청률 때문에, LNB Network의 Harry Acton 토크쇼는 아마도 폐지될 것이다.

26 대학들은 캠퍼스에서의 음주 규정을 적절하게 시행하는 데 도움을 주는 방편에 대한 개요서를 받았다.

27 연설가는 일부 청중이 화가 났을 때 문제를 부추겼다는 비난을 받았지만, 그는 고의가 아니었다고 주장했다.

28 대통령은 텔레비전 생중계로 의료 보험 제도의 세부 사항들을 발표할 것이다.

29 세계 통합을 이루기 위해서, 전 세계의 국가들은 편협한 행위를 규탄해야 한다.

30 마을을 덮었던 짙은 아침 안개는 떠오르는 해에 의해 흩어졌다.

GRAMMAR

Part I

1 A: Dave, 네가 설거지할 차례야.
   B: 하지만 지난번과 그 전에도 내가 설거지를 했어.

2 A: 축구팀에서 George보다 더 뛰어난 선수는 없어.
   B: 맞아. 난 그의 속도와 재주에 놀라.

3 A: 이 광고지를 붙이려면 무엇을 사용할 수 있을까요?
   B: 압정이나 테이프 중 하나가 필요해요.

4 A: Hal 제과점이 어디에 있는지 아세요?
   B: 기차역 입구 바로 옆에 있어요.

5 A: 제 소포가 언제 발송될 예정인지 어떻게 알 수 있을까요?
   B: 그것이 발송된 후에 통지를 받으실 거예요.

6 A: 넌 토요일 밤 Ada의 파티에 참석할 수 있을 것 같니?
   B: 아니, 이번 주말에 회사에서 심야 회의가 있어서.

7 A: 너희 부모님께서 네가 약혼해서 기뻐하셨니?
   B: 응. 그들은 제일 먼저 날 축하해주신 분들이었어.

8 A: 어젯밤에 대통령이 했던 연설을 보셨나요?
   B: 네, 봤어요. 그는 국내에서 가장 논쟁이 되는 쟁점들 중 하나에 대해 연설했어요.

9 A: 난 네가 탄 비행기가 8시에 도착하기로 되어 있다고 생각했어.
   B: 눈보라만 아니었어도, 비행기가 이렇게 늦게 도착하지는 않았을 거야.

10 A: 당신은 Bob이 범인이라고 어떻게 확신하는 건가요?
   B: 의심의 여지가 없어요. 그가 돈을 횡령했다고 자백했어요.

Part II

11 사람들이 거의 모든 세미나에 참석하지 않아서, 주최자들은 협의회의 성과에 대해 점점 더 걱정이 되었다.

12 철도 시스템을 처음 이용하는 외국인 방문객들은 종종 혼란스러워 한다.

13 한 연구는 공격적인 마케팅을 사용하는 회사들이 그렇지 않은 회사들보다 더 빠른 재정적 성장을 경험한다는 것을 발견했다.

14 한 인터뷰에서, 그 배우는 자신의 발언이 농담이었음을 설명하며, 공개적으로 사과했다.

15 쓰레기 처리장으로 지정되지 않은 구역에서 쓰레기를 버리다가 잡히는 사람들은 벌금을 내야 한다.

16 새로운 휴대용 게임기가 전 세계적으로 크게 인기를 얻은 것은 게임 업계의 모두에게 놀라운 일이었다.

17 현재 Kroogle은 보다 강력한 보안 조치들을 실시하고 있기 때문에, Kroogle 이메일 계정을 사용하시는 분들은 더 이상 개인정보에 대해 걱정하지 않으셔도 됩니다.

18 매머드의 뼈대가 수백만 년 동안 보존되어 있었기 때문에, 고생물학자들에게 그 종에 관한 새로운 증거를 제공했다.

19 모든 기업들이 퇴직자를 위한 의료 혜택을 없앤 것은 아니다.

20 그 회사는 작년에 생산 부족으로 손실을 겪었음에도 불구하고, 올해에는 어느 정도 입지를 회복할 수 있었다.

21 투표가 합산되고, 뉴스 앵커는 대통령 선거의 최종 결과를 보도했다.

22 최근의 인플루엔자 발생에 대한 원인이 아직 밝혀지지 않았기 때문에, 공무원들은 사람들에게 예방 접종을 받도록 권고한다.

23 3층에 있는 TV 스튜디오는 다큐멘터리 수상작들을 제작한 폭넓은 이력으로 유명하다.

24 체중을 감량하기 위해서 식사를 거르는 것은 결코 권장할만한 방법이 아닌데, 이는 건강에 좋지 않은 만큼이나 효과적이지도 않다.

25 실망스럽게도, Jill과 그녀의 남편이 극장에 도착하기 전에 연극은 시작했다.

Part III

26 (a) A: 당신이 이번 주말에 있는 워크샵의 계획과 진행을 담당한다고 들었어요.
(b) B: 네, 전 많은 압박을 받고 있어요. 처리해야 할 일들이 아주 많이 남아 있어요.
(c) A: 음, 그것들이 해결되면 제게 알려주세요. 다른 직원들에게 일정표를 보내야 하거든요.
(d) B: 물론이죠. 상황이 확정되면, 당신에게 제일 먼저 알려드릴게요.

27 (a) A: 일주일 내내 고생하며 썼던 보고서를 제출할 준비가 됐니?
(b) B: 아쉽게도, 처음부터 다시 시작해야 돼.
(c) A: 지난번에 나랑 이야기했을 때 넌 제출할 준비가 거의 다 됐었잖아.
(d) B: 초안을 읽는 도중에, 내 손가락이 미끄러져서 뜻하지 않게 모두 다 지워버렸어.

28 (a) 지난 3월, 싱가포르는 잇따른 수많은 어류의 죽음을 목격했는데, 무수한 사체가 부두로 밀려 올라왔다. (b) 플랑크톤이 갑자기 그리고 급격하게 증식하는 것인 플랑크톤 대발생이 그 원인으로 밝혀졌다. (c) 바닷물의 위생 상태를 점검한 후, 당국은 실제로 플랑크톤의 대발생을 예측하여 어부들에게 보호 구역으로 그들의 어류를 옮기도록 경고했다. (d) 그러나, 그들은 플랑크톤 대발생의 속도와 강도를 과소평가했기 때문에, 대부분은 이 경고에 따라 충분히 빠르게 행동하지 않았다.

29 (a) 미국 스키팀의 가장 유명한 멤버들 중 한 명은 4종목 스키 경주 선수인 Lindsey Vonn이다. (b) Vonn은 불과 24살에 2회 연속으로 월드컵 종합 타이틀을 석권한 최초의 미국인 여성이다. (c) 월드컵 우승뿐만 아니라, 그녀는 네 번의 세계 선수권 대회 메달과 여러 올림픽 메달을 땄다. (d) 이러한 위업들은 그녀가 미국 스키 경주 역사상 가장 성공한 여성이 되도록 하였다.

30 (a) 코끼리는 기다란 코와 상아로 특징지어지는 육지에 사는 대형 포유류이다. (b) 한때 존재했던 수백 종의 코끼리 가운데 세 가지 종, 즉 사바나, 포레스트, 아시안 코끼리만이 현재 남아 있다. (c) 이 살아남은 종들이 발견되는 곳은 아프리카와 아시아, 두 대륙뿐이다. (d) 기후 변화, 서식지 상실, 인간의 침범은 코끼리의 상태가 멸종 위기에 처한 동물이 되도록 하였다.

READING COMPREHENSION

Part I

1 저축 예금은 당신이 재정적인 자유를 얻도록 도와줄 수 있습니다. 처음에는, 플러스 통장 잔고를 유지하기 위해 자제하는 것이 매우 힘들 수도 있습니다. 잊지 말아야 할 가장 중요한 점은 물질적인 욕구에 굴복하지 않고 가능한 한 많이 저축하는 것입니다. 처음 몇 달 동안은, 총수입의 10퍼센트를 저축에 할당하도록 노력하고, 매달 저축을 하는 것이 본능적인 행동이 되어 점차 노력이 적게 들게 되면 이 비율을 늘려가십시오. 몇 년 후면, 저축 예금을 보유하는 것이 _____ _____ 임을 깨달을 겁니다.

(a) 생활 방식의 필수적 변화
(b) 관리하기 쉬운 일
(c) 구매를 위한 필수 도구
(d) 많은 예금을 보관하는 장소

2 상리 공생, 즉 다른 두 종 간의 이로운 연대는 아카시아 개미와 쇠뿔 아카시아 나무에서 나타난다. 개미가 나뭇잎을 먹는 동물들을 막아주는 동안, 아카시아 나무는 개미에게 먹이와 서식지를 제공한다. 이러한 상호 간의 이로운 관계는 개미와 인간 사이에도 분명히 존재하지만, 이 작은 생물이 인간과 맺는 관계는 쉽사리 눈에 띄지 않기 때문에 대부분의 사람들은 이러한 관계에 대해 알지 못한다. 대신, 인간은 개미를 해충으로 여긴다. 이로 인하여 _____.

(a) 개미와 인간 사이에 상리 공생 관계가 생긴다
(b) 사람들은 개미로부터 나무를 보호한다
(c) 더 많은 사람들이 개미를 연구한다
(d) 개미는 사람들에 의해 박멸된다

3 나는 중국의 시골을 여행하면서, 어떻게 _____를 깨닫게 되었다. 내가 방문했던 모든 마을에서, 고대 석조 건축물이 늘어선 아름다운 경관이 패스트푸드 식당과 편의점이 들어선, 콘크리트와 유리로 만들어진 크고 흉물스러운 건물들로 망쳐져 있었다. 이러한 조용한 시골 마을들이 현대성을 향해 진보하는 조짐을 보이는 것은 좋지만, 나는 이 시골 마을들이 단지 삭막한 도시들의 복제판이 되기 위해 자신들의 유산을 말살하고 있다는 것이 걱정된다.

(a) 진보가 사람들의 생활 방식을 변화시키는지
(b) 풍경이 점차 변해 왔는지
(c) 도시화가 한 지역의 정체성을 파괴할 수 있는지
(d) 도시와 시골 건축물이 다른지

4 한 민간 단체가 _____ 도전을 하고 있다. 이 프로젝트에 매진하는 증거로, 이 단체는 12에이커의 토지를 취득했는데, 이곳에 여러 다세대 주택이 건설되어 어림잡아 노숙자 천 가구로 하여금 거리에서 지내면서 직면하는 일상의 고통에서 벗어나도록 해줄 것이다. 뿐만 아니라, 이 단체는 몇몇 기업체에 이 주택에 들여놓을 가전제품을 기부해줄 것을 설득했다. 끝으로, 이 단체는 입주 후에도 주택을 유지하는 데 드는 재정적 부담을 감당하겠다고 서약했다.

(a) 노숙자에게 가전제품을 배포하는
(b) 사고 피해자의 집을 재건하는
(c) 불우한 사람들에게 영구적인 거주지를 제공하는
(d) 고용 전망과 관련하여 가난한 사람들을 도와주는

5 여기 InfoTech Managed Solutions에서, 우리 고객들은 대체로 자사의 기술 지원과 데이터 관리 서비스에 대해 긍정적인 반응을 보였지만, 몇몇 고객 서비스 직원들의 태도에 대해서는 우려감을 나타냈습니다. 이 문제를 처리하기 위해, 인사부는 모든 직원들을 대상으로 고객 서비스 재교육 과정을 시작했습니다. 아울러, 경영진은 직원 개발 프로그램의 일부로 최신 고객 서비스 기술에 대한 워크숍을 제도화할 계획입니다. 이러한 조치들은 _____ 것으로 기대됩니다.

(a) 우리가 고객들과 소통하는 방식을 개선할
(b) 우리 고객 서비스 직원들로부터의 관심이 쏠리지 않게 할
(c) 신입 사원의 채용 기준 개선으로 이어질
(d) 고객 서비스 재교육 과정의 중요성을 강조할

6 1977년부터 2006년까지 쿠웨이트의 왕 Sheikh Sabah의 통치 기간은 _____. 그가 국정을 이끈 첫날부터 Sheikh의 정책은 국회의원들의 반대에 부딪혔다. 그는 국회의 간섭에 대응하여 1986년에 국회를 해산시켰고 반대 의견을 진압하기 위해 언론 검열을 시행했다. 국내가 혼란한 가운데, 1990년에 이라크가 쿠웨이트를 침공했고, 이 때문에 Sheikh는 사우디아라비아로 망명해야 했다. 그는 다국적 군사 작전으로 이라크가 패배하자 쿠웨이트로 돌아왔으나, 그의 통치에 대한 반발로 그의 정치적 영향력은 제한되었다.

(a) 정치 불안과 무력 충돌로 특징지어졌다
(b) 군사적 승리의 결과로 확립되었다
(c) 국회가 해산되었을 때 확고해졌다
(d) 사우디아라비아의 침공으로 간섭을 받았다

7 Mr. Peeves께,

본 학과는 귀하의 통신사 근무에 대한 학점 인정 요청을 검토했습니다. 아시다시피, 학점으로 인정하는 학부생 인턴 과정은 매 학기 시작 전에 공지됩니다. 이 방침은 학생들이 전공 분야와 관련된 근무 기회를 발견했을 때 사안별로 변경될 수 있지만, 인턴 과정이 시작되기 전에 승인되어야 합니다. 귀하가 요청하신 경우처럼, 그러한 승인이 소급적으로 인정되는 것은 불가능합니다. 상황이 이러하므로, _____.

진심을 담아,
Mr. Roy Culler
신문방송학과장

(a) 취업을 위한 휴학은 인정됩니다
(b) 귀하의 경력은 학업 성적에 반영되지 않을 것입니다
(c) 학생 인턴십은 다음 학기까지 기다려야 합니다
(d) 귀하는 이번 학기에 대체 과목을 선택해야 합니다

8 여성의 달을 기념하여, 국가 여성 위원회는 장래가 유망한 가수들의 재능을 소개하는 축제를 후원하고 있습니다. 모든 수익금은 가정 폭력 피해자를 돕는 사회 프로그램을 지원하는 데 쓰일 것입니다. 사회에서 남성 우월주의의 잔재를 청산하는 일에 진전이 있었지만, 여성들은 여전히 남성 가족 구성원과 동거인으로부터 신체적인 피해를 당하고 있습니다. 이 문제는 함께 조치를 취해야만 해결될 수 있습니다. 당신이 _____는 것을 보여주려면 이 콘서트에 참여하십시오.

(a) 여성에 대한 폭력의 종식을 지지한다
(b) 여성 인권 운동가를 격려한다
(c) 가정 폭력이 양성에게 영향을 준다는 것을 안다
(d) 성차별이 더 이상 존재하지 않는다는 것을 안다

9 덴마크의 Carl 왕자는 자국이 스웨덴으로부터 독립을 되찾은 후 노르웨이의 왕위에 올랐다. 그는 통치권을 갖자마자, 고대 스칸디나비아식 이름인 Haakon을 사용하여 Haakon 7세가 되었다. 이것으로 그는 스칸디나비아인의 생활에서 전통이 차지하는 중요성에 대한 존경을 보여주어 국민의 사랑을 받았고, 제2차 세계 대전 중에는 아돌프 히틀러와 같은 막강한 지도자들로부터 퇴위하라는 압력을 받았음에도 불구하고 Haakon 7세는 그런 요구에 저항함으로써 국민의 존경을 더 받았다. _____, 1957년 그가 서거했을 때 수십만 명이 자신의 국민을 진심으로 이해했던 국왕을 잃은 것을 애도했던 것은 그리 놀랍지 않다.

(a) 그러므로
(b) 대조적으로
(c) 그렇기는 하지만
(d) 게다가

10 민주주의와 자유에 대한 경의가 표현된, 베토벤의 교향곡 제3번은 원래 나폴레옹에 대한 찬사여서, '보나파르트'라고 제목이 붙여졌는데, 이는 작곡가가 프랑스의 통치자를 이러한 이상의 상징으로 여겼기 때문이었다. 그래서, 나폴레옹이 스스로를 황제로 선포했을 때, 베토벤은 경악했는데, 이는 개인의 권리를 제한하고 독재로 이어질 것이라고 그가 우려했던 행동이었다. _____, 작곡가는 나폴레옹의 어떤 흔적도 작품의 의도를 손상시키지 않도록 하기 위해 교향곡의 이름을 바꿨고, 그 곡을 자신의 후원자인 로브코비츠에게 바쳤다.

(a) 반면에
(b) 즉
(c) 확실히
(d) 따라서

Part II

11 알렉산더 그레이엄 벨의 배경은 그의 전화기 발명이 결실을 맺는데 대단히 중요했다. (a) 그의 아버지와 형제들은 음성 의사소통의 뛰어난 대가들이었는데, 이는 벨에게 어렸을 때부터 발성 훈련을 시켜주었다. (b) 전기를 통해 소리를 전달하고자 했던 그의 꿈은 어머니와 부인을 괴롭히던 청각 장애로 인해 자극을 받았다. (c) 벨은 보스턴 대학에 있는 발성 생리학과에서 일하게 되었으며, 수익성 높은 청각학 개인 진료도 했다. (d) 벨의 친지들은 지속적인 지원을 해주었으며 그가 장치의 특허를 받도록 격려해주었다.

12
과거에는, 어부 개개인이 바다에 나가 간소한 도구를 사용하여 물고기를 잡곤 했다. (a) 일반적으로 어망을 사용하였으며, 어획량은 남은 면 몇 마리 내다팔 수 있는 것을 제외하고 보통 가족의 필요를 채우기에 딱 충분했다. (b) 그러나, 요즈음 대부분의 해산물은 복잡한 대규모 상업용 낚시 기법을 사용하여 잡는다. (c) 현대적 방법은 전통적인 어부가 이용하던 것과는 현저히 다른, 성능 좋은 원양 어선과 정교한 기계 장비를 이용한다. (d) 오늘날, 대부분의 구역이 제철에 이르기 무섭게 상업적 어부들에게 약탈당하고 있기 때문에 많은 소규모 어부들은 어획량의 감소에 대해 불평하고 있다.

Part III

13
Ms. Pan께,

제가 이전에 견적에 대해 문의했을 때 요청하신 대로, 저희 주방 사진 몇 장을 동봉했습니다. 1980년대에 지어진 곳이라, 자연적인 마모로 인한 피해가 큽니다. 스타일도 물론 최신으로 해주시기 바랍니다. 주방의 허름한 상태를 보시고, 개조할 경우 제가 지불하게 될 비용 견적을 내주시기 바랍니다. 신속한 답변 기대합니다.

진심을 담아,
Sharon Gorman

Q: 이메일은 주로 무엇에 관한 내용인가?
(a) 주방 개조에 대한 동의
(b) 주방의 좋지 못한 상태에 대한 비난
(c) 주방을 개조하는 데 드는 비용에 대한 요청
(d) 집주인과의 부동산 거래

14
과학 평론

새로운 뇌 연구는 수면의 기능을 밝혔다. 과학자들은 수면 중에 뇌에 있는 작은 틈이 확장된다는 것을 발견했는데, 이는 독소가 배출될 수 있는 통로를 넓히는 것이다. 이러한 공간은 글림프 시스템이라고 알려진 일종의 배관 시스템을 형성하는데, 이 시스템은 뇌 구석구석까지 뇌척수액이 흐를 수 있게 하는 것이다. 수면은 통로와 작은 틈으로 이루어진 이 망을 효과적으로 열어서, 깨어있을 동안보다 뇌척수액이 독성 물질을 훨씬 더 빠르게 내보내도록 한다. 이것이 수면이 손상과 악화에 대항하는 보호 수단의 일종으로 기능한다는 것을 나타낸다.

Q: 글쓴이의 요지는 무엇인가?
(a) 수면은 독소가 손상을 유발하지 못하도록 뇌를 닫는다.
(b) 뇌 시스템은 수면 중에 뇌의 유해한 물질을 내보낸다.
(c) 글림프 시스템은 뇌가 잠을 잘 때에만 활성화된다.
(d) 수면은 뇌세포 간의 공간을 넓히는 액체로 뇌를 잠기게 한다.

15
고대 로마에서, 입법 의회에 참여하기 열망하는 사람들은 로마 시민권을 보유해야 했다. 일반적으로 이것은 로마 시민의 적법한 자녀에게 출생 시에 부여되었지만, 다른 경우에는, 로마인으로 태어나지는 않았지만 로마에 충성하는 사람들이 귀화 시민권을 받았다. 해방된 노예들이 시민권을 취득하는 것도 가능했다. 그러나 의회가 오로지 수도에서만 개최되었기 때문에, 정치적 발언권을 얻고자 하지만 로마 밖에 살고 있는 사람들에게 로마 시민권은 쓸모가 없었다.

Q: 지문은 주로 무엇에 관한 내용인가?
(a) 로마 시민들의 자녀에 대한 적법성 부여
(b) 통치의 중심지로서 로마의 선정
(c) 로마 시민권을 얻는 방법
(d) 로마 의회의 선거 방식

16
지방 정책 입안자들은 대중 매체가 사설에서 비판받은 사람들로부터 답변을 받아 공개할 것을 요구하는 법안이 정확한 보도를 보장할 것이라고 생각하기 때문에, 그 법안을 통과시키고 싶어한다. 하지만 이 법안이 언론에 어떤 영향을 미치겠는가? 언론사들은 자사가 발행하거나 방송하는 내용에 대한 전적인 편집권을 잃고, 부정적인 반응을 이끌어내는 것을 피하기 위해 자체 검열하게 될 것이다. 나는 이 법안이 언론의 자유를 억압하고 언론이 대중에게 정보를 공개하지 않도록 만들 것이라고 생각한다.

Q: 지문의 요지는 무엇인가?
(a) 입법자들은 매체 보도가 진실하다는 것을 보장해야 한다.
(b) 언론은 편향된 보도에 대한 혐의를 다뤄야 한다.
(c) 대중 매체는 외부의 개입으로부터 자유로워야 한다.
(d) 대중 매체 종사자들은 공인을 비판하지 않도록 권고된다.

17
Mr. Kowalski께,

취임을 환영합니다! 노동 조합의 위원장으로서, 귀하께서 회사 대표로 임명되셔서 저는 매우 기쁩니다. 저는 귀하와 만족스러운 관계를 정립하기를 고대하며, 회사의 성장을 위해 협조할 것을 약속 드립니다. 뿐만 아니라, 노조는 더 화목한 근무 환경을 조성하는 데 전력을 다하고 있습니다. 그런 만큼, 직원들은 귀하가 새로운 최고 경영자로서 이전 경영진이 해결하지 못하고 남겨둔 문제들을 해결하겠다는 약속을 이행하실 것을 기대합니다.

존경을 담아,
Stanley Malkovich

Q: 다음 중 편지의 내용과 일치하는 것은?
(a) Mr. Kowalski는 Mr. Malkovich가 회사를 운영하는 것을 돕겠다고 약속했다.
(b) Stanley Malkovich는 회사의 새로운 대표를 임명하는 것을 도왔다.
(c) 조합원들은 더 나은 보상 제도를 요구하고 있다.
(d) Mr. Malkovich는 최고 경영자가 해결되지 않은 문제들을 처리하기를 기대한다.

18
발달하는 인간 배아에서, 최초로 형성되기 시작하는 기관은 심장이다. 수정 후 3주 만에 희미한 심관이 발달한다. 이 징후는 곧 태아기의 심장 박동의 시작으로 이어지는데, 대체로 수정된 지 1개월 후이다. 혈관은 바로 그 직후 나타나기 시작하는데, 이는 배아의 다른 기관계 발육을 촉진시킨다. 심장이 박동하기 시작할 때, 배아는 1센티미터도 채 안 되지만, 순환계의 성장에 따라 그 후 몇 주 안에 배아의 길이가 두 배로, 또 다시 두 배로 늘어나게 된다.

Q: 다음 중 지문의 내용과 일치하는 것은?
(a) 심장은 태어나기 전에 완전히 형성되는 유일한 기관이다.
(b) 배아는 처음 한 달 동안 길이가 두 배가 된다.
(c) 심관 발달이 심장 박동보다 먼저 일어난다.
(d) 심관은 혈관으로 바뀔 것이다.

19
Green Bin으로 쓰레기 양을 줄이세요

Green Bay EcoTechnologies는 Green Bin을 선보이게 되어 자랑스럽게 생각합니다. 단돈 300달러로, 이 고급 퇴비통은 여러분의 주방과 정원에서 나오는 자연 분해성 쓰레기를 모두 처리하여, 배출하던 쓰레기 양을 70퍼센트로 줄여줄 것입니다.

게다가, Green Bin을 통해, 여러분은 정원에서 쓸 수 있는 가정에서 만든 무료 비료를 얻으실 수 있습니다! 이 기기는 퇴비를 만드는 공정을 가속화해서, 여러분 정원의 수확량을 단 21일 만에 늘려줍니다. 더 효과적인 원예와 더 풍부한 수확량은 식료품비 절감을 의미합니다.

Green Bin과 함께라면 이 모든 것이 여러분의 것이 될 수 있습니다.

Q: 다음 중 지문의 내용과 일치하는 것은?

(a) 퇴비를 만드는 것은 원예를 더욱 생산적이게 한다.
(b) Green Bay는 농장용으로 고안된 제품을 생산한다.
(c) Green Bin은 음식물 쓰레기를 재활용할 필요를 없앤다.
(d) Green Bin은 대형 주방이 있는 가정을 위한 것이다.

20. 인도네시아의 한 동물원에서, 독이 있는 도마뱀 종인 커다란 암컷 코모도왕도마뱀이 수컷 상대와의 아무런 접촉이 없었음에도 불구하고 20개의 알을 낳으면서 강렬한 호기심의 대상이 되었다. 보도에 따르면 이 파충류 Audrey가 수컷과의 교제를 통하지 않고 새끼를 낳은 최초의 암컷 코모도왕도마뱀이 될 수 있을 것이라고 한다. 한 기민한 동물원 직원이 우리 안에서 Audrey에게 먹이를 주다가 우연히 알을 발견했다. 또 다른 암컷 코모도왕도마뱀이 5년 전에 무성 생식을 한 것으로 보고되었지만, 알은 하나도 부화되지 않았었다.

Q: 지문에 따르면 다음 중 코모도왕도마뱀 Audrey에 대한 내용과 일치하는 것은?

(a) 인도네시아 동물원에서 그것의 인기는 오랜 시간에 걸쳐 공고해져 왔다.
(b) 처음으로 무성 생식을 한 동물이 아니어서 관심을 거의 받지 못했다.
(c) 그것의 알은 예기치 않게 우연히 발견되었다.
(d) 무성으로 알을 낳은 최초의 코모도왕도마뱀이다.

21. 물이 전기의 좋은 전도체라고 흔히 오해되지만, 완벽한 상태에서 물은 효과적인 절연체로 기능할 것이다. 물 분자는 산소와 수소에 불과하며, 둘 다 유리된 이온의 형태로 전하를 만들지 못한다. 그러나, 자연에서 발견되는 물이나 심지어 병에 든 생수조차 결코 완전히 순수하지 않고 용질의 형태로 오염 물질을 포함한다. 용질은—일반적으로 소금—전하를 가지고 있고 물에 잘 녹는다. 그 때문에 물은 전도성이 생겨서 물과 전기 사이의 어떠한 접촉이라도 사람들에게 감전사의 위험 요인이 된다.

Q: 다음 중 지문의 내용과 일치하는 것은?

(a) 용질을 더하면 물에서 이온이 없어진다.
(b) 병에 든 생수에는 용질이 덜 포함되어 있다.
(c) 물은 안에 들어 있는 불순물 때문에 전도성이 있다.
(d) 자연에서 발견되는 물은 좋은 절연체로 작용한다.

22. 윌리엄 포크너의 많은 동시대 사람들이 복잡한 이야기를 쓰는 그의 능력을 칭찬했으나, 다른 사람들은 그의 불필요하게 복잡한 단어 사용에 대해 비판했다. 어니스트 헤밍웨이는 그러한 비판자 중 한 명이었다. 포크너가 1949년에 노벨상을 받자, 헤밍웨이는 수상 후에 확실한 걸작을 쓴 사람이 아무도 없었으므로 포크너의 다음 소설이 실패할 것이라고 냉소적으로 말했다. 저격은 계속해서 심해졌고, 포크너가 헤밍웨이의 단음절어 취향을 비판하자, 알려진 바로는 헤밍웨이가 "가엾은 포크너, 그는 정말 긴 단어에서 큰 감동이 나온다고 생각하는 것인가?"라고 반문했다고 한다.

Q: 헤밍웨이는 왜 포크너를 비난했는가?

(a) 포크너가 불필요하게 어려운 단어를 사용한다고 생각했다.
(b) 포크너의 책이 너무 길다고 생각했다.
(c) 포크너의 문학적 성공에 겨룰 수 없었다.
(d) 포크너의 이야기 속 주제가 너무 냉소적이라고 여겼다.

23. 작가들을 만나세요

여러분은 농구 전설인 David Bronson과 Lyle Hart의 『경기가 우리의 것이었을 때』의 독점 책 사인회에 초대받았습니다.
장소는 아래와 같습니다:

Powell's 서점
Fairview로 2373번지
Long Beach, CA 90803

11월 13일, 토요일, 오후 1시 — 4시

두 과거 거물을 만날 기회를 놓치지 마세요! 그들이 1980년대 주 선수권 대회에서 서로에 대항하여 경기했을 때 싹튼 치열한 경쟁에 대해 이야기하는 것을 듣고, 그들이 어떻게 은퇴 후 20년이 다 지나서 원한을 극복하고 마침내 그것에 대한 회고록을 공동 집필하게 되었는지 알아보세요.

표를 구매하시려면 www.powellsbooks.com에 방문하세요. 구매된 표 한 장당 『경기가 우리들의 것이었을 때』 한 부가 딸려 있습니다.

Q: 지문에서 Bronson과 Hart에 대해 추론할 수 있는 것은 무엇인가?

(a) 유년기 때 서로에 대항하여 경기하기 시작했다.
(b) 같은 농구 팀의 일원이었다.
(c) 선수 경력이 끝난 뒤 친해졌다.
(d) Long Beach에서 자서전 작업을 했다.

24. 기업 부문에는, 황금 낙하산이라고 알려진 일종의 계약이 존재한다. 주요 경영진에게 주어지는 황금 낙하산은 회사 합병의 결과로 경영진이 해고당하게 되면 상당한 혜택을 주는 것인데, 후한 현금 보너스와 스톡 옵션은 흔하다. 이 관행을 지지하는 여러 주장들 중에서, 가장 설득력 있는 것은 황금 낙하산이 CEO가 회사에는 이익이 되지만 그들의 지위를 위태롭게 할지 모르는 합병들을 막지 않도록 한다는 것이다.

Q: 글쓴이가 황금 낙하산에 대해 가장 동의할 것 같은 진술은 무엇인가?

(a) 수용자가 더 객관적인 사업 결정을 내리게 한다.
(b) 합병 직후에 제공될 때 가장 효과가 있다.
(c) 곧 닥쳐올 경영진의 해고에 대해 초기 징조를 나타낸다.
(d) 의도치 않게 경영진들이 빨리 사임하도록 부추길 수 있다.

25. 당첨될 기회를 잡으러 Derm 미용실에 방문하세요!

올 4월 Derm 미용실의 10주년을 기념하여, 축하하기 위한 추첨 행사를 가질 예정입니다!

참가는 간단합니다. 4월 1일과 4월 30일 사이에 저희의 모든 미용 서비스와 제품에 지불하는 5달러마다, 여러분은 추첨권을 한 장씩 받으실 것입니다. 상품은 저희 가게에 딸린 부티크에서 주어집니다!

1등 상품: Strength Vita 샴푸 1년 치
2등 상품: Wave Goodbye 모발 염색약 6개월 치
3등 상품: Ultra-Shine 컨디셔너 한 통

당첨자는 5월 1일에 전화로 공지될 것입니다.
상품은 현금으로 교환될 수 없습니다.

Q: 광고에서 추론할 수 있는 것은 무엇인가?

(a) 미용실은 그것의 상점에서 모발 제품을 판매한다.
(b) 미용실은 4월에 가게에 딸린 부티크를 연다.
(c) 홍보 기간에는 관리 가격이 인하될 것이다.
(d) 가장 추첨권이 많은 고객이 1등 상품을 탈 것이다.

Part IV

26~27

취업 기회

Franklin 교외에 위치한 고급 숙박 시설인 Grand Wilmington 호텔이, 호텔 관리자의 소임을 다할 숙련되고, 활발하고, 근면한 사람을 찾고 있습니다.

당신의 직무들은 무엇입니까?

호텔 관리자로서, 당신은 일상 업무 처리를 맡을 것입니다. 직무들은 일정을 수립하는 것, 예산을 짜는 것, 업무를 위임하는 것, 그리고 고객 문의에 응대하는 것을 포함합니다. 당신은 또한 직원들을 채용하고, 면접보고, 그들의 직무에 필수적인 기술을 교육할 것입니다.

우리가 찾는 것은 무엇입니까?

Grand Wilmington의 높은 기준에 맞춰 이러한 직무들을 수행하기 위해서는, 200개 이상의 객실이 있는 5성급 호텔을 관리한 최소 3년의 경력이 필수적입니다. 당신은 또한 완전히 공인된 관광 학교의 학위를 보유해야 하며, 직원들로 이루어진 다수의 팀들을 감독할 수 있어야 하고, 영어와 스페인어 모두에 능통해야 합니다.

자격을 갖춘 지원자들은 이력서를 두 명의 이전 고용주의 연락처 정보와 함께 jobs@grandwilmington.com으로 늦어도 8월 5일까지 보내도록 장려됩니다.

26. Q: 호텔 관리자의 직무 중 하나는 무엇인가?
(a) 호텔 구석구석의 정기 안전 점검 수행
(b) 호텔 홍보를 위한 마케팅 일정의 수립
(c) 직무에 요구되는 능력에 대한 신입 직원들 교육
(d) 숙박 기간 중 호텔에 대한 투숙객의 의견 수집

27. Q: 다음 중 광고의 내용과 일치하는 것은?
(a) 지원자들은 과거 고용주들의 추천서 두 부를 제출해야 한다.
(b) 여러 언어에서의 능숙함은 이 직무의 필요조건이다.
(c) 지원자들은 8월 5일 이후 완성된 지원서를 제출해야 한다.
(d) 관리자는 Grand Wilmington의 여러 지점을 맡는다.

28~29

프랜시스 스콧 피츠제럴드와 같은 수준으로 자신의 세대를 축약적으로 보여준 미국 작가들은 거의 없었는데, 그의 소설과 단편들은, 젊은 미국인들이 전통적인 사회적 풍습을 혼란시켰던 시대인 재즈 시대의 정신을 정확히 담아냈다. 피츠제럴드의 첫 소설 『낙원의 이쪽』은, 그 시대의 청년에 대한 그것의 묘사로 즉각적인 돌풍을 일으켰다. 14년 후에 출판된, 그의 마지막 완성작 『밤은 부드러워』는, 프랑스 리비에라 지역에 거주했던 미국계 이주민들의 현실 도피와 타락을 묘사했다. 처음에 이 책은 저조하게 판매되었고 시대의 흐름을 따라잡는 데 실패했다고 비난받았지만, 현대 비평가들은 이제 『밤은 부드러워』를 피츠제럴드의 걸작이라고 여긴다.

하지만, 그의 가장 많이 읽힌 책은 『낙원의 이쪽』이나 『밤은 부드러워』가 아니라 『위대한 개츠비』이다. 이 소설에서, 피츠제럴드는 등장인물들을 통해 미국 사회의 양면을 탐구한다. 주인공인 제이 개츠비는, 평범한 배경에서 아메리칸 드림을 이룸으로써 지위가 상승했지만, 도덕적으로 더럽혀졌다. 반면에, 서술자인 닉 캐러웨이는, 올바른 가치관이라는 사치를 누릴 여유가 있는, 특권 상류층의 삶을 살았다. 『위대한 개츠비』는 재즈 시대의 흥분과 방탕의 표현, 그리고 또한 그것이 미국 문화에 대해 폭로하는 것으로 인해 오늘날 독자들에게 울림을 준다.

28. Q: 다음 중 프랜시스 스콧 피츠제럴드에 대한 내용과 일치하는 것은?
(a) 그의 마지막 완성 소설은 대중의 찬사를 받지 않았다.
(b) 그는 재즈 시대의 선도적인 구성원들에 의해 만들어진 유행에 반대했다.
(c) 그의 책 『낙원의 이쪽』은 해외로 이주한 사람들에 관한 이야기이다.
(d) 그는 젊은 미국인들의 낙관주의를 묘사하는 경향이 있었다.

29. Q: 두 번째 단락에서 글쓴이가 주로 말하는 것은 무엇인가?
(a) 『위대한 개츠비』는 그 이야기가 벌어지는 시대를 성공적으로 묘사하지 않는다.
(b) 『위대한 개츠비』는 미국의 사회적 현실에 대한 통찰력을 제공한다.
(c) 『위대한 개츠비』는 자전 소설로 읽힐 수 있다.
(d) 『위대한 개츠비』는 그것의 자극적인 장면들 때문에 논란을 불러일으켰다.

30~31

아메리카앨리게이터들은 그들의 긴 수명으로 잘 알려져 있는데, 다수가 인간만큼 오래 산다. 거대한 크기를 고려했을 때, 그들은 일생에 걸쳐 성장을 계속한다고 생각되었지만, 새로운 연구가 이것이 사실이 아닐지도 모른다는 것을 밝혔다. 사우스캐롤라이나, 조지타운의 야생 동물 센터에서 진행된 연구는, 앨리게이터들에 대한 35년 치의 정보를 수집하여 분석했고 이 생물들의 대부분이 25살에서 35살 사이에 최대 크기에 도달했다는 것을 밝혔다. 이는 민물 크로커다일과 같은, 비슷한 종의 성장 양상과 아주 닮아 있다.

아마 더 놀랍게도, 이 팀은 암컷 앨리게이터들이 성장을 멈춘 뒤에도 수 해 동안 번식을 계속할 수 있다는 것을 밝혔다. 연구의 한 표본은 심지어 68살의 나이에 건강한 알 한 무더기를 낳았다. 이는 앨리게이터들은 중년쯤에 가장 번식력이 높다는, 과학자들이 이전에 믿어왔던 그들에 관한 오래된 관념 또한 뒤집었다. 이 발견들은 그것들이 사우스캐롤라이나의 앨리게이터 사냥이 금지된 지역에서 나왔기 때문에 유의미하다. 이 보호받는 앨리게이터들로부터 나온 정보는 따라서 성장과 노화의 자연적 양상을 밝힌다. 게다가, 주의 나머지 지역의 보호받지 않는 생물들의 정보와 이 정보를 비교함으로써, 연구자들은 일반적으로 이 종에 미치는 사냥의 영향에 대한 더 깊은 이해를 얻을 수 있다.

30. Q: 지문의 주제는 무엇인가?
(a) 다양한 종의 앨리게이터와 민물 크로커다일 간의 유사성
(b) 아메리카앨리게이터의 생애 주기에 관한 한 연구의 결과들
(c) 앨리게이터들이 만년에 성장을 계속한다는 발견
(d) 사우스캐롤라이나의 앨리게이터 개체 수를 보존하려는 시도

31. Q: 지문에서 추론할 수 있는 것은 무엇인가?
(a) 사우스캐롤라이나의 몇몇 지역에서는 앨리게이터를 사냥하는 것이 허용된다.
(b) 많은 앨리게이터 종은 멸종 위기의 생물 목록에 올라가 있다.
(c) 앨리게이터 종은 최소 일 년에 한 번 알을 낳는다.
(d) 앨리게이터들은 그들의 크기 때문에 연구하기 어렵다.

32~33

교육 신문

대학 등록금 급등
독자의 코멘트
Joey185 | 3시간 전

당신은 대학 등록금 급등 관련 문제를 제대로 인지하고 있지 않은 것 같군요. 이 문제에 대한 당신의 분석은 등록금은 대폭 인상되는 반면, 교육의 질은 그렇지 않다는 것을 거론하지 않습니다. 많은 대학은 정부의 예산 삭감 때문이라고 말하며, 수업료를 인상했습니다. 하지만 임직원들에게 그렇게 터무니없게 높은 급여를 지급하면서 동시에 그렇게 해서는 안 됩니다. 보도에 따르면 수업료 급등을 발표했던 대학의 일부 총장들은 일 년에 도합 100만 달러가 넘는 급여와 상여금을 받는데, 이는 정말 지나치다고 생각합니다. 대학의 자원은 직원들뿐만 아니라 학생들에게도 유용해야 합니다.

더욱이, 학생들의 재정적 부담은 증가하는 와중에, 많은 대학은 돈

을 아껴 그것을 다른 용도로 사용하기 위해 그들이 제공하는 강의의 수를 줄였습니다. 이는 학생들에게 가능한 학문적 선택권의 수를 제한하고 그들에게서 필수적인 학습 기회들을 빼앗습니다. 기관들이 전반적인 학습 경험을 강화하지 않고 등록금을 인상하는 것은 불합리합니다. 전국의 대학들은 수준 이하의 강의에 시달릴 뿐만 아니라, 그들은, 최악의 시설들은 말할 것도 없이, 형편없는 정보통신 체계와 한정적인 도서관 자료들로도 고통받습니다. 더 높은 등록금으로 얻는 늘어난 소득은, 임직원들의 주머니를 채워줄 게 아니라, 이러한 잘못들을 바로잡는 데 사용되어야 합니다.

32. Q: 글쓴이가 주로 하고자 하는 것은 무엇인가?
(a) 수업료 인상이 대학 직원들에게만 유용하다는 것을 지적하기
(b) 대부분의 대학 과정들이 겪는 예산 삭감을 정당화하기
(c) 교수들과 학생들의 필요를 충족시키기 위한 타협안을 제안하기
(d) 대학 입학처에 의해 이행된 불공정한 업무에 주의를 집중시키기

33. Q: 대학은 왜 더 적은 강의들을 제공하기 시작했는가?
(a) 특정 학문 분야에서 교육받은 강사를 찾을 수 없다.
(b) 강의실에 전자 장비를 갖추어 주기에 한정된 예산을 보유한다.
(c) 학생들에게 직업을 찾는 데 실용적인 기술들을 제공하기를 원한다.
(d) 수업 외의 다른 것들에 돈을 지출하기를 원한다.

34
~
35

수 해에 걸친 평등을 향한 투쟁

유럽 계몽주의 시대동안 자유주의 사상의 인기에 자극받아, 1800년대 중반에서 후반까지 페미니스트 운동의 구성원들은 여성들에게 남성들에게 주어지는 것과 동등한 정치적, 사회적, 그리고 경제적 기회들을 부여할 개혁을 촉구했다. 그들의 노력은 두드러지게 가부장적인 사회에 의해 그들의 성에 가해지는 불평등에 주의를 환기시켰다. 그들은 여성들이 투표하고, 공부하고, 일하고, 재산을 소유하도록 허가될 것을 요구했다. 그들은 남성의 보호를 필요로 하는 더 약한 성별의 구성원 대신에 박탈할 수 없는 확실한 권리를 지닌 지적인 존재로서 대우받기를 원했다.

이러한 초기의 페미니스트들은 많은 측면에서 성공했지만, 1950년대쯤에 페미니즘은 거의 완전히 사라졌었는데, 이때 여성들은 주부로서 그들의 남편과 가족을 돌보도록 장려되었다. 그러다가 1960년대에, 페미니스트 활동의 부활이 있었고, 이는 종종 제2의 페미니즘 물결이라고 불린다. 그것은 작가 베티 프리단에 의해 엄청나게 영향을 받았는데, 그녀는 여성들이 집에 머무름으로써 그들의 가능성을 한정시키고 있다고 말했다. 당대의 또 한 명의 저명한 인물은 언론인 글로리아 스타이넘으로, 그녀는 남성 착취자들에 대항하는 여성들의 혁명을 요구했다. 그녀는 여성이 자신이 선택하기만 하면 경력을 추구하도록 허용하는 성 역할 없는 사회의 지지자였다.

34. Q: 다음 중 1800년대 페미니스트 운동에 대한 내용과 일치하는 것은?
(a) 남성 폭력에 저항하는 수단으로서 시작했다.
(b) 여성들이 공직을 얻는 것이 허용되고 나서 등장했다.
(c) 여성들에게 결혼 생활에서 동등한 발언권을 주도록 의도되었다.
(d) 지지자들은 여성들이 완전한 사회적 권리를 지닌 개인으로 대접받기를 원했다.

35. Q: 글로리아 스타이넘에 대해 추론할 수 있는 것은?
(a) 종종 성 역할이 대중 매체의 영향을 받는다고 말했다.
(b) 남성들이 여성들의 능력을 바라보는 관점을 상당히 크게 바꿨다.
(c) 착취에 저항하기 위해 폭력을 사용하는 것의 지지자였다.
(d) 여성들이 직장에서 성취를 추구해야 한다고 생각했다.

TEST 03

LISTENING COMPREHENSION

Part I

1

M: Is there anything else I can get you?
W: _____

(a) A little more than that.
(b) Nothing at the moment.
(c) Sure, you can have it.
(d) Yeah, thanks for your help.

M: 뭐 좀 더 갖다 드릴까요?
(a) 그것보단 좀 더요.
(b) 지금으로선 괜찮아요.
(c) 물론이죠, 가져가세요.
(d) 네, 도와줘서 고마워요.

2

W: Tim, this is Rae Hill. I can't recall if you've met.
M: _____

(a) Pleased to meet you.
(b) That depends on her.
(c) I'm familiar with that.
(d) I believe we have.

W: Tim, 이분은 Rae Hill이에요. 두 분이 만난 적이 있는지 기억이 안 나네요.
(a) 만나서 반가워요.
(b) 그건 그녀에게 달려 있어요.
(c) 전 그걸 잘 알아요.
(d) 저희 만난 적이 있는 것 같은데요.

3

M: How long before the test results come out?
W: _____

(a) I'll take the test soon.
(b) Expect them by Monday.
(c) Any time you decide.
(d) It took me an hour.

M: 시험 결과가 나올 때까지 얼마나 더 있어야 할까?
(a) 나 곧 시험 봐.
(b) 월요일까지는 나올 거라 예상하고 있어.
(c) 네가 결정하면 언제든지.
(d) 난 한 시간이 걸렸어.

4

W: I don't really need to get my driver's license.
M: _____

(a) I'm sure it'd come in handy later.
(b) Yeah, it's going to expire in a few weeks.
(c) It's my first time behind the wheel.
(d) My father let me drive his before.

W: 난 정말 운전 면허증을 딸 필요가 없어.
(a) 나중에 그것이 쓸모가 있을 거라고 확신해.
(b) 맞아, 그것은 몇 주 후에 만료될 거야.
(c) 내가 차를 운전하는 것은 이번이 처음이야.
(d) 아버지는 전에 내가 아버지 차를 운전하도록 허락하셨어.

5

M: Which Desert Rats album do you think is the best one?
W: _____

(a) That one is available in stores.
(b) They wrote rock ballads.
(c) You should listen to them.
(d) Hard to say. They're all great.

M: 어느 Desert Rats 앨범이 최고라고 생각하니?
(a) 그건 상점에서 구할 수 있어.
(b) 그들은 록 발라드 곡을 썼어.
(c) 넌 그것들을 들어봐야 해.
(d) 말하기가 어렵네. 모두 다 훌륭해.

6

W: Losing your job must have been devastating.
M: _____

(a) Winning isn't everything.
(b) I've been on the lookout for one.
(c) Well, let me extend my sympathy.
(d) It was certainly a letdown.

W: 일자리를 잃어서 엄청나게 충격받았겠다.
(a) 이기는 게 다가 아냐.
(b) 난 일자리를 찾고 있었어.
(c) 그래, 동정을 베풀게 해줘.
(d) 확실히 허탈하더라.

7

M: Aren't you blowing the issue way out of proportion?
W: _____

(a) Yes, I'm glad we sorted out the issue.
(b) I appreciate that you see things my way.
(c) It's affected me more than you think.
(d) But I measured the proportions.

M: 너 그 문제를 지나치게 확대 해석하는 건 아니니?
(a) 응, 우리가 그 문제를 해결했다니 기뻐.
(b) 네가 내 입장에서 상황을 봐줘서 고마워.
(c) 그건 네가 생각하는 것보다 나에게 영향을 더 많이 미쳤어.
(d) 하지만 난 그 비율을 재어 보았어.

8

W: Are the roads safe for driving?
M: _____

(a) I have my driver's license.
(b) The snow has already melted.
(c) Merge into the other lane.
(d) Traffic is flowing now.

W: 도로가 운전하기에 안전한가요?
(a) 전 운전 면허증이 있어요.
(b) 눈이 이미 녹았어요.
(c) 다른 차선으로 서서히 바꿔봐요.
(d) 지금은 교통이 원활해요.

9

M: I'd like to go out, but I've got to hit the books.
W: _____

(a) Come back before curfew.
(b) You should return them to the library.
(c) Studies should take priority.
(d) I'd love to accompany you.

M: 나가고 싶은데, 공부를 해야 돼.
(a) 통금 시간 전에는 돌아와.
(b) 넌 그것들을 도서관에 반납해야 해.
(c) 공부가 우선이 되어야지.
(d) 기꺼이 같이 갈게.

10

W: The photocopier is jammed. Can you lend me a hand?
M: _____

(a) It's a predicament.
(b) I'm not very tech savvy.
(c) I can estimate the damage.
(d) No one can help me out of this jam.

W: 복사기에 종이가 걸렸어. 나 좀 도와줄 수 있어?
(a) 이건 곤경이네.
(b) 난 기계에 대해서는 잘 몰라.
(c) 난 그 손해를 추정할 수 있어.
(d) 누구도 이 곤경에서 나를 도와줄 수 없어.

Part II

11

M: Excuse me. Are you Kelly McCool?
W: Yes, I am. What can I do for you?
M: My friend over there wants you to have this bouquet.
W: _____

(a) But I didn't order one.
(b) I already have that bouquet.
(c) Sorry, I'm short on cash.
(d) Oh, how sweet of him.

M: 실례합니다. 당신이 Kelly McCool이신가요?
W: 네, 접니다. 무슨 일이시죠?
M: 저기에 있는 제 친구가 당신이 이 꽃다발을 가지길 원해요.
(a) 하지만 전 그걸 주문하지 않았는데요.
(b) 전 이미 그 꽃다발이 있어요.
(c) 죄송한데, 현금이 모자라요.
(d) 아, 그분은 정말 상냥하시네요.

12

W: How could you forget my birthday?
M: I've been really busy these days.
W: I know. But a simple telephone call would have sufficed.
M: _____

(a) You could return it.
(b) Please let me make it up to you.
(c) That's no excuse.
(d) Sorry I missed your call.

W: 어떻게 내 생일을 잊을 수가 있어?
M: 나 요즘 너무 바빴어.
W: 알아. 하지만 전화 한 통이면 충분했을 거야.
(a) 네가 다시 전화를 했어도 되잖아.
(b) 내게 만회할 기회를 줘.
(c) 그건 변명이 안 돼.
(d) 네 전화를 못 받아서 미안해.

13

M: It's been about a year since you left the city to live in the country, right?
W: Yes, and I couldn't be happier with how things turned out.
M: So, you're not bored with the lifestyle?
W: _____

(a) I wish there was a bit more to do, too.
(b) Not at all. It's a nice change of pace.
(c) I really expected to be happier out here, but I'm not.
(d) It's my fault. I shouldn't have moved so far away.

M: 네가 도시를 떠나 시골에 산 지 일 년 정도 되었네, 그렇지?
W: 응, 그리고 난 모든 일이 돌아가는 것에 대해 더 행복할 수는 없어.
M: 그럼, 그 생활 방식이 지루하지 않다는 거지?
(a) 나도 할 일이 조금 더 많길 바라.
(b) 전혀 지루하지 않아. 좋은 기분 전환이야.
(c) 난 여기에서 더 행복할 거라고 정말 기대했는데, 그렇지 않아.
(d) 내 잘못이야. 그렇게 멀리 이사를 가지 말았어야 해.

14

W: Do you want a hand with that project?
M: Actually, yes. The deadline's this Friday.
W: What do I need to do?
M: _____

(a) That's OK. I can meet deadlines.
(b) I need you to give me a hand.
(c) Here, let me go over the details.
(d) Thanks, that's so kind of you.

W: 그 프로젝트에 도움이 필요한가요?
M: 사실, 그래요. 마감일이 이번 금요일이에요.
W: 내가 뭘 하면 되죠?
(a) 괜찮아요. 마감일을 지킬 수 있어요.
(b) 당신의 도움이 필요해요.
(c) 여기, 자세한 사항을 알려 줄게요.
(d) 고마워요, 정말 친절하시네요.

15

M: Why'd you choose this apartment?
W: The location. It's a stone's throw from the office.
M: That must make commuting easy.
W: _____

(a) It's more spacious than my old apartment.
(b) I may move closer to work.
(c) You bet. It's a breeze.
(d) Yeah, but I spend more on gas.

M: 왜 이 아파트를 선택했어요?
W: 위치 때문에요. 사무실에서 매우 가깝거든요.
M: 통근하기가 쉽겠어요.
(a) 여긴 저의 저번 집보다 더 넓어요.
(b) 직장에 더 가까이 이사할지도 몰라요.
(c) 물론이죠. 식은 죽 먹기예요.
(d) 네, 그런데 기름 값이 더 들어요.

16

W: I'm so upset. I left my favorite umbrella on the subway.
M: Let's check with the Lost and Found department.
W: I think it's a bit of a long shot, don't you?
M: _____

(a) What a relief that someone turned it in.
(b) Well, you still don't know if it's lost or not.
(c) That's true, but it can't hurt to ask.
(d) Keep it in a safe place where you won't lose it.

W: 너무 속상해. 지하철에 내가 좋아하는 우산을 두고 내렸어.
M: 분실물 센터에 확인해보자.
W: 거의 승산이 없는 것 같은데, 그렇지 않니?
(a) 누군가가 그것을 돌려줘서 다행이야.
(b) 글쎄, 아직 그것을 잃어버렸는지 아닌지 모르잖아.
(c) 그건 그렇지만, 물어본다고 손해 볼 건 없잖아.
(d) 잃어버리지 않을 안전한 장소에 그것을 보관해.

17

M: I don't think your father approves of me.
W: Give him time. He'll warm up to you eventually.
M: Is there anything I can do to get on his good side?
W: _____

(a) He won't think highly of that.
(b) That won't help your case any.
(c) Patience is the best approach.
(d) I wouldn't recommend it.

M: 너희 아버지께서 나를 괜찮다고 생각하시지 않는 것 같아.
W: 아버지께 시간을 드리자. 결국엔 너를 좋아하게 되실 거야.
M: 그분께 호감을 얻기 위해 내가 할 수 있는 것이 있을까?
(a) 그는 그걸 높게 평가하지 않으실 거야.
(b) 그건 네 경우에는 도움이 전혀 안 될 거야.
(c) 인내가 최고의 방법이야.
(d) 그건 추천하지 않을래.

18

W: I'm elated over the new express train.
M: Me too. It's got blazing speed.
W: If only it were connected to the suburbs.
M: _____

(a) My stop is beyond that.
(b) I heard it will be in the near future.
(c) It depends on where you're going.
(d) It's more affordable that way.

W: 나 새로운 급행 열차 때문에 너무 신나.
M: 나도야. 대단한 속도로 가더라.
W: 교외 지역에도 연결되기만 하면 좋을 텐데.
(a) 내 정류장은 거기를 지나서 있어.
(b) 조만간 그렇게 될 거라고 들었어.
(c) 네가 어디를 가느냐에 따라 달라.
(d) 그런 식이 더 저렴해.

19

M: Good morning. Is there anything I can help you with?
W: Yeah. I'm looking for a hooded sweatshirt.
M: Well, our thick winter ones are on clearance.

W: _____

(a) I'm looking for something less bulky.
(b) But it has to be a thick sweatshirt.
(c) Take a look at the clearance rack.
(d) I'll wait until they're on sale.

M: 안녕하세요. 도움이 필요하신가요?
W: 네. 저는 모자 달린 운동복을 찾고 있어요.
M: 음, 모자 달린 두꺼운 겨울용 운동복들은 재고 정리 판매 중이에요.

(a) 전 좀 덜 두꺼운 옷을 찾고 있어요.
(b) 하지만 그건 두꺼운 운동복이어야 해요.
(c) 재고 정리 상품 진열대를 둘러보세요.
(d) 그것들이 세일할 때까지 기다릴 거예요.

20

W: Have you kept in touch with Jamie since she moved away?
M: Absolutely. She emails me frequently from Spain.
W: How is she adjusting to life overseas?
M: _____

(a) You must've heard wrong—she's not working at the moment.
(b) She rarely contacts me these days, so I'm not sure.
(c) If you want, I can find some opportunities abroad for you.
(d) She says she can't imagine living anywhere else now.

W: Jamie가 이사 간 후로 연락해본 적이 있어?
M: 물론이지. 그녀는 스페인에서 내게 자주 이메일을 보내.
W: 그녀는 해외 생활에 어떻게 적응하고 있어?

(a) 네가 잘못 들은 게 틀림없어. 그녀는 지금 일을 하고 있지 않아.
(b) 요즘 그녀가 내게 연락을 거의 안 해서, 잘 모르겠어.
(c) 네가 원하면, 외국에 있는 기회를 알아봐 줄 수 있어.
(d) 그녀는 이제 다른 곳에서 사는 건 상상할 수도 없대.

Part III

21

Listen to a conversation between two roommates.

M: Can we talk about you inviting your friends over?
W: Sure. Was there an issue?
M: I just wish you had filled me in about their visit ahead of time.
W: Oh, I'm sorry. I didn't think you'd mind.
M: I also live here, so I'd like to have a say in what goes on.
W: OK. I'll be sure to run it by you next time.

Q: What is the man mainly doing in the conversation?

(a) Getting to know a roommate's friends
(b) Reminding a roommate to be quieter
(c) Telling a roommate not to invite friends over
(d) Asking a roommate to give advance notice

두 룸메이트 간의 대화를 들으시오.

M: 네 친구들을 초대하는 것에 대해 우리 이야기를 좀 할 수 있을까?
W: 물론이지. 무슨 문제 있었어?
M: 난 단지 그들의 방문에 대해 네가 미리 알려줬으면 해.
W: 아, 미안해. 네가 싫어할 줄 몰랐어.
M: 나도 여기 사니까, 일어나는 일에 대해 말할 권리가 있어.
W: 알았어. 다음번엔 너한테 꼭 말해줄게.

Q: 대화에서 남자는 주로 무엇을 하고 있는가?

(a) 룸메이트의 친구들을 알아가고 있다.
(b) 룸메이트에게 더 조용할 것을 상기시키고 있다.
(c) 룸메이트에게 친구들을 초대하지 말라고 말하고 있다.
(d) 룸메이트에게 미리 기별을 달라고 요청하고 있다.

22

Listen to a conversation between two co-workers.

W: You still have 16 deliveries to make?
M: It's ridiculous. Two drivers are far from adequate.
W: The warehouse is bottlenecked with orders as well.
M: The company is always understaffed during the holidays.
W: Yeah, that's because the company won't hire any extra hands.
M: I know. All they care about is saving money.

Q: What is the conversation mainly about?

(a) The shortage of the employees
(b) The warehouse backlog slowing down deliveries
(c) The inaction of the company's administration
(d) The effect the holiday season has on orders

두 동료 간의 대화를 들으시오.

W: 넌 아직 배달할 게 16개 남았지?
M: 이건 터무니없어. 운전사 두 명은 결코 충분하지 않아.
W: 창고도 주문들로 인해 병목 상태야.
M: 이 회사는 연휴 동안 항상 일손이 모자라.
W: 맞아, 그건 회사가 더 많은 일손을 고용하지 않을 것이기 때문이지.
M: 그러게. 그들이 관심 있는 건 돈을 아끼는 게 전부야.

Q: 주로 무엇에 관한 대화인가?

(a) 직원의 부족
(b) 배송을 지연시키는 창고의 밀린 일
(c) 회사 경영진의 태만
(d) 연휴 기간이 주문에 미치는 영향

23

Listen to a conversation at a hotel.

M: Good morning. What can I do for you?
W: I'd like to be transferred to another room, please.
M: Is there an inconvenience of some sort? What is your concern?
W: There's an odor of cigarette smoke.
M: But your room is nonsmoking, correct?
W: Purportedly, but someone took the liberty of disregarding the rules.

Q: What is the woman mainly doing in the conversation?

(a) Requesting to be moved to a smoking room
(b) Expressing dissatisfaction with a room
(c) Checking out from an inhospitable hotel
(d) Criticizing a guest who smoked in her room

호텔에서의 대화를 들으시오.

M: 안녕하세요. 무엇을 도와 드릴까요?
W: 다른 방으로 옮기고 싶어요.
M: 어떤 불편한 점이 있으십니까? 무슨 문제죠?
W: 담배 연기 냄새가 납니다.
M: 하지만 손님 방은 비흡연실인데, 맞나요?
W: 저도 그렇게 알고 있었는데, 누군가 마음대로 규칙을 무시했네요.

Q: 대화에서 여자는 주로 무엇을 하고 있는가?

(a) 흡연실로 옮겨달라고 요청하고 있다.
(b) 방에 대한 불만을 나타내고 있다.
(c) 불친절한 호텔에서 체크아웃하고 있다.
(d) 그녀의 방에서 담배를 피운 손님을 비난하고 있다.

24

Listen to a conversation about a credit card.

W: Hello, fraud protection hotline. This is Carol.
M: Yes, my credit card is missing, and I need to rescind any recent transactions that may appear.
W: Can you recall when the card was last in your possession?
M: I was pickpocketed while heading home from work.
W: Well, I'm not seeing any unauthorized charges on my end.
M: Thank goodness. I can breathe easy.

Q: Which is correct about the man according to the conversation?

(a) He is awaiting a replacement card.
(b) He utilized the card to pay for transportation.
(c) He was victimized while commuting.
(d) He noticed suspicious credit transactions.

신용 카드에 관한 대화를 들으시오.

W: 안녕하세요, 사기 방지 상담 전화입니다. 저는 Carol입니다.
M: 네, 제가 신용 카드를 잃어버려서, 최근에 발생했을지 모를 모든 거래를 취소하려고 합니다.
W: 언제 마지막으로 카드를 소지하고 계셨는지 기억하시나요?
M: 직장에서 집으로 가는 도중 소매치기를 당했습니다.
W: 음, 제 쪽에는 어떠한 미승인 결제 내역도 보이지 않습니다.
M: 다행이네요. 이제야 한숨 놓겠어요.

Q: 대화에 따르면 남자에 대해 맞는 것은 무엇인가?

(a) 교체할 카드를 기다리고 있다.
(b) 대중교통 비용을 지불하기 위해 카드를 사용했다.
(c) 통근길에 피해를 입었다.
(d) 의심스러운 신용 카드 거래를 알아챘다.

25

Listen to two friends discuss an exam.

M: I'm panicking about the calculus exam tomorrow morning.
W: How come? You've been cramming for weeks.
M: I'm not retaining anything, though. The textbook is too overwhelming.
W: Just review the essential points.
M: To be honest, I've struggled with the material all term.
W: I bet you know more than you think you do.
M: Thanks for the pep talk. I should go study more.

Q: Which is correct about the man according to the conversation?

(a) He started studying for the exam at the very last minute.
(b) He has a weak grasp of the lecture content this semester.
(c) He has a chemistry exam scheduled for the next morning.
(d) He feels confident in his ability to ace the upcoming exam.

두 친구가 시험에 관해 이야기하는 것을 들으시오.

M: 난 내일 아침의 미적분학 시험이 너무 두려워.
W: 왜? 넌 몇 주 동안 시험 공부를 해왔잖아.
M: 그래도 난 아무것도 기억이 안 나. 교과서는 너무 버거워.
W: 그냥 중요한 요점을 복습해봐.
M: 솔직히 말하면, 난 학기 내내 내용에 대해 어려움을 겪어 왔어.
W: 난 네가 생각하는 것보다 더 많이 알고 있을 거라고 장담해.
M: 격려의 말 고마워. 가서 좀 더 공부해야겠어.

Q: 대화에 따르면 남자에 대해 맞는 것은 무엇인가?

(a) 막판에 가서 시험 공부를 시작했다.
(b) 이번 학기의 강의 내용을 잘 이해하지 못하고 있다.
(c) 다음 날 아침에 화학 시험이 있다.
(d) 다가오는 시험에서 A를 받을 자신의 능력을 확신한다.

26

Listen to a conversation between a salesperson and a customer.

W: Welcome to SmartTalk Wireless. How can I assist you?
M: I'm looking for a new smartphone, preferably one with a good camera.
W: Then, I suggest this model. It also has a massive six-inch display.
M: I see. What about the battery life and storage space?
W: After a full charge, the battery lasts 12 hours. And there's 16 gigabytes of storage.
M: That's it for storage? I take lots of photos, so that won't be enough.

Q: What feature is the man dissatisfied with?

(a) The battery life
(b) The display size
(c) The storage space
(d) The image enhancement tool

판매원과 고객 간의 대화를 들으시오.

W: SmartTalk Wireless에 오신 것을 환영합니다. 무엇을 도와드릴까요?
M: 저는 되도록이면 좋은 카메라가 있는 새 스마트폰을 찾고 있어요.
W: 그럼, 이 모델을 추천해드려요. 이것은 6인치의 넓은 화면도 가지고 있어요.
M: 그렇군요. 배터리 수명과 저장 공간은 어떤가요?
W: 완전히 충전하면 12시간 지속됩니다. 그리고 16기가바이트의 저장 공간이 있습니다.
M: 저장 공간은 그게 다인가요? 저는 사진을 많이 찍기 때문에, 그걸로는 충분하지 않을 거예요.

Q: 남자는 어떤 기능에 만족하지 않는가?

(a) 배터리 수명
(b) 화면 크기
(c) 저장 공간
(d) 화질 개선 도구

27

Listen to a conversation between two friends.

M: You won't believe what happened last night.
W: Don't tell me you and Gina broke up.
M: No. I popped the question to her, and she said yes.
W: I'm surprised it took you so long to ask her.
M: The engagement band cost me $3,000, which took months to accumulate.
W: That's a small price to pay for a lifetime of partnership.

Q: Why did it take the man so long to propose?

(a) He had a serious argument with his girlfriend.
(b) He has known his fiancée for only a few months.
(c) He was saving money for a ring.
(d) He did not feel financially secure.

두 친구 간의 대화를 들으시오.

M: 어젯밤 무슨 일이 있었는지 넌 믿지 못할 거야.
W: 너랑 Gina가 헤어진 건 아니겠지.
M: 아니. 그녀에게 청혼했는데, 승낙했어.
W: 네가 그녀에게 청혼하는 데 그렇게 오래 걸렸다니 놀라워.
M: 약혼 반지에 3천 달러가 들었는데, 그걸 모으느라 몇 달 걸렸거든.
W: 평생의 반려자를 얻는 비용치고는 적은 편이지.

Q: 남자는 청혼하는 데 왜 그렇게 오래 걸렸는가?

(a) 여자 친구와 심각한 말다툼을 했다.
(b) 그의 약혼녀를 안 지 몇 달밖에 되지 않았다.
(c) 반지를 위해 돈을 모았다.
(d) 재정적으로 안정됐다고 느끼지 않았다.

28

Listen to a conversation between two acquaintances.

W: Mr. Wheeler, could you please autograph a copy of your memoir?
M: Sure. You look familiar. Do we have the same alma mater?
W: We took screenwriting together. I'm surprised you still recognize me.
M: Your face rang a bell. Have you kept up with writing?
W: Yes. I'm on the lookout for a publisher, in fact.
M: Fantastic. I can go over your manuscript, if you'd like.

Q: Why does the woman approach the man?

(a) She recognizes him from a class.
(b) She wants him to sign a book.
(c) She has some feedback on his manuscript.
(d) She would like him to recommend a publisher.

두 지인 간의 대화를 들으시오.

W: Mr. Wheeler, 당신 회고록에 사인 좀 해주실래요?
M: 물론이죠. 낯이 익네요. 우리 같은 학교를 나왔나요?
W: 우리 극작 수업을 같이 들었어요. 아직도 절 알아보신다니 놀랍네요.
M: 당신 얼굴이 낯이 익었어요. 계속 글을 쓰셨어요?
W: 네. 실은, 출판사를 찾고 있어요.
M: 훌륭하네요. 원하신다면, 제가 당신 원고를 검토해 드릴 수 있어요.

Q: 여자는 왜 남자에게 말을 거는가?

(a) 같은 반이었던 남자를 알아보았다.
(b) 남자가 책에 서명해 주기를 원한다.
(c) 남자의 원고에 대한 약간의 의견이 있다.
(d) 남자가 출판사를 추천해 주길 바란다.

29

Listen to a conversation at an educational institute.

M: Do you have any experience teaching one-on-one?
W: I don't, but I used to be a substitute teacher at a community college.
M: That's good to know. Can you describe your role in further detail?
W: I taught sophomore composition.
M: I think your background would certainly suffice.
W: That's encouraging to hear.

Q: What can be inferred from the conversation?

(a) The man is offering the woman a permanent post.
(b) The woman is seeking a tutoring position.
(c) The man is incapable of giving instruction.
(d) The woman will teach college-level English.

교육 기관에서의 대화를 들으시오.

M: 일대일로 가르쳐본 경험이 있으십니까?
W: 아니요, 하지만 지역 전문 대학에서 임시 교수를 했었습니다.
M: 그거 좋군요. 당신의 역할에 대해 좀 더 자세히 설명해주실 수 있습니까?
W: 2학년 작문을 가르쳤습니다.
M: 제 생각에 당신의 배경이면 분명히 충분할 것 같습니다.
W: 그렇게 말씀해주시니 용기가 나네요.

Q: 대화에서 추론할 수 있는 것은 무엇인가?
(a) 남자는 여자에게 평생 직장을 제공하고 있다.
(b) 여자는 개인 교습 일자리를 구하고 있다.
(c) 남자는 강의할 능력이 없다.
(d) 여자는 대학 수준의 영어를 가르칠 것이다.

30

Listen to a conversation between two friends.

W: You haven't heard a single word that I've said.
M: That's not true. I'm trying to be attentive.
W: I asked you a question, but you didn't respond.
M: I'm sorry. Actually, my mind has been drifting.
W: I can sense that. What's wrong?
M: My nephew is in the hospital.

Q: What can be inferred about the man from the conversation?

(a) He is concerned about a relative.
(b) He got bored with the conversation.
(c) He just returned from the hospital.
(d) He has an introverted personality.

두 친구 간의 대화를 들으시오.

W: 넌 내가 한 얘기를 한 마디도 안 들었구나.
M: 그렇지 않아. 난 경청하려고 노력하고 있어.
W: 내가 너한테 질문했는데, 넌 대답이 없었잖아.
M: 미안해. 사실, 내 정신이 딴 데 가 있었어.
W: 그런 것 같았어. 뭐가 문제야?
M: 내 조카가 병원에 있거든.

Q: 대화에서 남자에 대해 추론할 수 있는 것은 무엇인가?
(a) 친척을 걱정하고 있다.
(b) 대화에 지루해 하고 있다.
(c) 막 병원에서 돌아왔다.
(d) 내성적인 성격을 지니고 있다.

Part IV

31

Tourism in India had previously been booming, but analysts are not expecting a rebound anytime soon. The country's tourism sector continues to experience its worst slump in decades, months after terror attacks paralyzed India. During peak tourism season, inbound arrivals were down over 32 percent from the prior year. Travelers remain reluctant about their personal safety in spite of the additional police patrols and safety precautions that have been instigated.

Q: What is the news report mainly about?

(a) The peak in Indian tourists traveling abroad
(b) The ongoing tourism crisis harming India
(c) India's approach to combating terror attacks
(d) Safety issues with India's infrastructure

인도 관광은 한때 호황을 누렸으나, 분석가들은 곧 회복될 것으로는 전망하지 않고 있습니다. 테러 공격이 인도를 마비시킨 지 몇 달 뒤, 국가의 관광 산업 부문은 수십 년 만에 최악의 불황을 계속해서 겪고 있습니다. 관광 성수기 동안, 입국자들이 전년 대비 32퍼센트 이상 감소했습니다. 순찰대 증원과 안전 예방 조치가 실시되었음에도 불구하고 관광객들은 신변의 안전을 확신하지 못하고 있습니다.

Q: 뉴스 보도는 주로 무엇에 대한 것인가?
(a) 해외여행을 가는 인도 관광객들 수의 정점
(b) 인도에 피해를 주는 계속되는 관광 위기
(c) 테러 공격에 맞서는 인도의 접근법
(d) 인도의 기반 시설에 대한 안전성 문제

32

Once you enter the medical field, effectively treating cancer patients will be a foremost concern. Current treatment methods need improvement because they disrupt activity not just in cancerous cells, but throughout the body. This may soon change, however, as Tel Aviv University researchers have developed a drug-delivery technique. It uses microscopic bubbles to make sure drugs intravenously injected into patients' bodies only target cancer cells, thereby avoiding unintentional damage to healthy cells.

Q: What is the main idea of the talk?

(a) The effect of cancer medication is unpredictable.
(b) Identifying cancer cells no longer requires surgery.
(c) A novel cancer treatment method has few side effects.
(d) A new pharmaceutical keeps cells cancer-free.

일단 의학 분야에 처음 발을 디디면, 암 환자들을 효과적으로 치료하는 것이 최우선의 관심사가 될 것입니다. 현 치료법은 암세포의 활동뿐만 아니라, 모든 신체의 활동을 억제하기 때문에 개선이 필요합니다. 그러나 텔아비브 대학 연구진이 약물 전달 기술을 개발함에 따라 이는 곧 바뀔 수도 있습니다. 이 방법은 미세한 기포를 이용하여 환자 체내에 정맥 주사로 주입된 약물이 암세포만 겨냥하도록 하여, 건강한 세포에 의치 않은 손상을 입히는 것을 막습니다.

Q: 담화의 요지는 무엇인가?

(a) 암 치료제의 효능을 예측하는 것은 불가능하다.
(b) 암세포 확인은 더 이상 수술을 요하지 않는다.
(c) 새로운 암 치료법은 부작용이 적다.
(d) 새로운 약은 세포가 암에 걸리는 것을 막아준다.

33

People think that hard work is the unequivocal determinant of financial success. They insist that as long as employees exert themselves to their fullest and take their professions seriously, they will be rewarded. Well, giving your all in anything that you do is indeed one of the fundamental prerequisites to success. But I would have to say that if you do not become a "smart worker", diligence and hard work may not be enough. You also have to learn to make sound judgments career-wise, and to be resourceful when performing tasks.

Q: What is the main idea of the talk?

(a) Financial gain is the sole determinant of success.
(b) Mental discernment is a crucial aspect of success.
(c) Companies value substantial effort over discipline.
(d) Diligent workers typically fail in their careers.

사람들은 열심히 일하는 것이 금전적 성공을 위한 확실한 결정 요인이라고 생각합니다. 그들은 직원들이 최선을 다해 일하고 자신의 직업을 진지하게 여기는 한, 보상받을 것이라고 주장합니다. 물론, 자신이 하는 일이 무엇이든 전력을 다하는 것은 실제로 성공을 위한 근본적인 전제 조건 중 하나입니다. 하지만 저는 만약 '똑똑한 직원'이 되지 않으면, 근면과 노력만으로는 충분하지 않을 수 있다는 점을 밝혀두고 싶습니다. 직업적인 면에서 현명하게 판단하고, 업무를 수행할 때 수완을 발휘하는 법도 배워야 합니다.

Q: 담화의 요지는 무엇인가?

(a) 금전적 이익이 성공의 유일한 결정 요인이다.
(b) 지적 통찰력이 성공의 결정적인 측면이다.
(c) 기업들은 자제력보다 상당한 노력을 더 높이 평가한다.
(d) 성실한 근로자는 일반적으로 자신의 직업에서 실패한다.

34

In response to the grim mood the recession has engendered, a group of designers has decided that the reappearance of vividly colored retro clothing is long overdue. There's nothing solemn or modest about their collection, which embraces the flamboyant. Those uncomfortable wearing loud prints may opt for the group's vintage accessories, like oversized sunglasses and beaded necklaces. So far, the designers' collection has been greeted with open arms by the public.

Q: What motivated the designers to come up with their clothing collection?

(a) A prevailing sense of negativity
(b) A growing nostalgia for better times
(c) A demand for celebrity-inspired outerwear
(d) A need for less expensive clothing

불황이 낳은 우울한 분위기에 대응하여, 한 무리의 디자이너들이 강렬한 색상의 복고풍 의류의 재등장이 한참 전에 일어났어야 했다고 판단했습니다. 화려함을 아우르는 그들의 컬렉션에는 엄숙하거나 수수한 면이 전혀 없습니다. 요란한 무늬를 입는 것이 불편한 이들은 커다란 선글라스와 구슬 목걸이 같은 빈티지 액세서리를 선택할 수 있습니다. 지금까지, 그 디자이너들의 컬렉션은 대중들에게 열렬한 환영을 받아왔습니다.

Q: 디자이너들이 의류 컬렉션을 내놓도록 동기 부여한 것은 무엇인가?

(a) 만연한 부정적 느낌
(b) 더 나은 시대에 대한 고조되는 그리움
(c) 유명 인사에게 영감받은 겉옷에 대한 수요
(d) 덜 비싼 의류에 대한 수요

35

Escriptor caters to writers interested in freelance employment. We afford our writers with the freedom to work from home by electronically linking them with corporate patrons offering assignments that range from technical writing to press releases. We are also currently soliciting résumés for full-time database manager positions at our administrative headquarters in Portland. If you seek to rapidly cultivate new clientele, visit www.escriptor.com now.

Q: Which is correct about Escriptor according to the advertisement?

(a) They train writers to perform research.
(b) They publish all genres of written material.
(c) They seek new employees at the main office.
(d) They have openings for writers in Portland.

Escriptor는 프리랜서 직에 관심이 있는 작가들을 만족시켜 드립니다. 저희는 작가들을 전문 저술에서부터 보도 자료에 이르는 업무를 제공하는 기업 고객들과 컴퓨터상으로 연결시켜 작가들에게 재택 근무의 자유를 제공합니다. 저희는 또한 현재 포틀랜드에 있는 저희 행정 본부에서 정규 데이터베이스 관리직의 이력서를 받고 있습니다. 새로운 고객층을 빠르게 구축하고자 하신다면, 지금 www.escriptor.com에 방문하십시오.

Q: 광고에 따르면 Escriptor에 대해 맞는 것은 무엇인가?

(a) 조사를 하도록 작가들을 훈련시킨다.
(b) 모든 종류의 기록물을 출판한다.
(c) 본사에 새 직원을 고용하고자 한다.
(d) 포틀랜드에서 작가를 구한다.

36

Immigration issues are again being heavily debated in the US. Convinced that immigrants are detrimental to the country's economy and security, several groups are pressuring the government to tighten immigration laws. Honestly, I don't think legislative grandstanding will solve anything. National chauvinism will not wither the market for illegal labor or stop the smuggling of migrants across the border. The government can better confront immigration problems by focusing resources on human traffickers.

Q: Which is correct according to the talk?

(a) Economic problems have reduced immigration concerns.
(b) Immigration reform has been enacted in the US.
(c) Nationalism motivates those wanting harsher immigration laws.
(d) Punishing illegal immigrants is a shrewd policy.

이민 문제가 미국에서 다시 심각하게 논쟁이 되고 있습니다. 이민자들이 국가 경제와 안보에 유해하다는 확신을 갖고, 몇몇 단체들은 정부가 이민법을 엄격하게 적용하도록 압력을 가하고 있습니다. 솔직히 말해서, 저는 입법상의 과시 행위로는 아무것도 해결하지 못할 것이라고 생각합니다. 맹목적 애국심은 불법적인 노동 시장을 위축시키거나 국경을 넘어오는 이민자들의 밀입국을 멈추게 하지 못할 것입니다. 정부는 인신매매범들에 자원을 집중함으로써 이민 문제에 보다 잘 대응할 수 있을 것입니다.

Q: 담화에 따르면 맞는 것은 무엇인가?

(a) 경제 문제가 이민 문제를 감소시켜 왔다.
(b) 미국에서 이민 개혁안이 제정되었다.
(c) 국수주의가 더 엄격한 이민법을 요구하는 사람들에게 동기를 부여하고 있다.
(d) 불법 이민자를 처벌하는 것은 현명한 정책이다.

Part V

37~38

Could I have everyone's attention, please? At 3:30 p.m. tomorrow, our fire alarms will go off since we will be carrying out an evacuation drill. The objective of the exercise is to substantiate that students are aware of evacuation procedures in the event of an actual emergency. There will be no interruptions to your schedule prior to the sounding of the alarm. However, you don't need to prepare a lesson for the final class period of the day. The drill is expected to take about 50 minutes. And if it ends before that, you may let your students go home early. Please note that, unlike other drills that are held throughout the course of the year, no officials from the fire department will attend this one. Instead, it will be up to you to guide students toward the exits. If you have any questions, please let me know. Thank you.

37. Q: Who would this talk likely be targeting?

(a) Security officers
(b) Educators
(c) Course enrollees
(d) Firefighters

38. Q: Which is correct according to the talk?

(a) Emergency procedures will be determined tomorrow.
(b) An alarm will go off after the last class of the day.
(c) Students will be informed that an emergency drill is planned.
(d) A school normally conducts emergency drills with assistance.

여러분 모두 주목해 주시겠습니까? 내일 오후 3시 30분에, 대피 훈련을 실시할 것이기 때문에 화재 경보가 울릴 예정입니다. 훈련의 목적은 학생들이 실제 비상사태 시 대피 절차에 대해 알고 있다는 것을 입증하기 위함입니다. 경보가 울리기 전에는 여러분들의 일정에 대한 방해는 없을 것입니다. 그러나, 당일 마지막 수업 시간을 위해서는 수업을 준비하실 필요가 없습니다. 훈련은 약 50분이 소요될 것으로 예상됩니다. 그리고 만일 그 전에 종료된다면, 여러분은 여러분의 학생들을 집에 일찍 보내셔도 됩니다. 연중 개최되는 다른 훈련과 달리, 소방서 공무원들이 이번 훈련에는 참석하지 않는다는 점을 유의하시기 바랍니다. 그 대신에, 학생들을 출구로 안내하는 것은 여러분의 책임입니다. 만약 질문이 있으시다면, 저에게 알려주십시오. 감사합니다.

37. Q: 이 담화는 누구를 대상으로 할 것 같은가?

(a) 경비원
(b) 교사
(c) 수업 등록자
(d) 소방관

38. Q: 담화에 따르면 맞는 것은 무엇인가?

(a) 비상사태 절차는 내일 결정될 것이다.
(b) 경보는 당일 마지막 수업 이후에 울릴 것이다.
(c) 학생들은 비상 대피 훈련이 계획되어 있다는 통지를 받을 것이다.
(d) 학교는 보통 도움을 받아 비상 대피 훈련을 실시한다.

39~40

Among the Renaissance artists, Leonardo da Vinci was probably the most versatile. He was the prototypical well-versed "Renaissance man." Aside from painting the *Mona Lisa* and *The Last Supper*, da Vinci was an accomplished sculptor, architect, and engineer. His notebooks are filled with all manner of sketches and studies for artistic and scientific projects, including technical contraptions that were centuries ahead of their time. Beyond demonstrating his magnificent draftsmanship, da Vinci's notebooks reveal a highly inquisitive mind and keen powers of observation. It's here you will find the *Vitruvian Man*, his famous analysis of the aesthetically ideal human proportions. Depicting a figure superimposed onto another figure, this beautiful drawing is the result of painstaking measurements of the human body. The *Vitruvian Man* is a perfect example of da Vinci's advanced understanding of math, science, and art, fields that take inspiration from da Vinci's unique genius to this day.

39. Q: What is the speaker's main point about Leonardo da Vinci?

(a) His work realistically depicted the human body.
(b) He was accomplished in numerous realms.
(c) His creations combined elements of art and science.
(d) He was first and foremost a fine arts painter.

40. Q: What can be inferred about Leonardo da Vinci?

(a) His most famous piece of art is the *Vitruvian Man*.
(b) He was the first artist to achieve fame during the Renaissance.
(c) He left examples of exploratory work in his personal documents.
(d) His projects led to a revival of interest in science and technology.

르네상스 예술가들 중, 레오나르도 다빈치가 가장 다재다능한 인물이었을 것입니다. 그는 조예가 깊은 '르네상스적 교양인'의 원형이었습니다. 『모나리자』와 『최후의 만찬』을 그린 것 외에도, 다빈치는 뛰어난 조각가이자 건축가이며, 기술자였습니다. 그의 노트는 그 시대보다 수 세기 앞선 과학 기술 장치들을 포함하여, 예술 및 과학적 프로젝트들을 위한 온갖 종류의 스케치와 연구들로 가득 차 있습니다. 그의 훌륭한 제도 실력을 보여주는 것을 넘어, 다빈치의 노트는 매우 탐구적인 정신과 예리한 관찰력을 드러내 줍니다. 이 노트에서 여러분은 미학적으로 이상적인 인체 비율에 대한 그의 유명한 분석인 『Vitruvian Man』을 볼 수 있습니다. 다른 인물 위에 포개진 인물을 묘사한 이 아름다운 그림은 인체에 대해 고심한 측정의 결과물입니다. 『Vitruvian Man』은 오늘날까지 다빈치의 유일무이한 천재성에서 영감을 받는 분야인 수학, 과학, 미술에 대한 다빈치의 앞선 이해의 완벽한 예시입니다.

39. Q: 레오나르도 다빈치에 대한 화자의 요지는 무엇인가?

(a) 그의 작품은 인체를 현실적으로 묘사했다.
(b) 그는 많은 분야에서 기량이 뛰어났다.
(c) 그의 창작품은 미술과 과학 요소를 결합했다.
(d) 그는 맨 처음에 순수 예술 화가였다.

40. Q: 레오나르도 다빈치에 대해 추론할 수 있는 것은 무엇인가?

(a) 그의 가장 유명한 예술 작품은 『Vitruvian Man』이다.
(b) 그는 르네상스 시대에 명성을 얻은 첫 예술가였다.
(c) 그는 개인 기록물에 탐구적인 작업의 예시들을 남겼다.
(d) 그의 프로젝트들은 과학과 기술에 대한 관심의 부흥으로 이어졌다.

VOCABULARY

Part I

1 A: 전기 요금을 냈니?
   B: 미안, 깜빡 잊었어. 내일 다시 한 번 알려 줘.

2 A: 호텔 직원들이 따뜻하고 호의적이어서 좋네요.
   B: 네, 그들은 정말 친절하네요.

3 A: 당신의 보석 판매로 얼마를 받기를 예상하시나요?
   B: 전혀 모르겠어요. 아직 감정을 받지 않았거든요.

4 A: Nikki는 약속 시간에 맞게 도착하는 법이 없어.
   B: 응, 그녀는 항상 늦어.

5 A: 벌써 3일째 야근이야. 지긋지긋해.
   B: 대목이잖아. 불평해봐야 소용없어.

6 A: 감독님이 항상 우리 경기 내용에 대해 흠을 잡아서 맥이 빠져.
   B: 맞아. 그는 우리에게 너무 비판적이야.

7 A: Helen은 우리 일에 간섭하기를 좋아하는데 난 그게 정말 싫어!
   B: 맞아. 가끔 그녀는 정말 참견하기 좋아해.

8 A: 이 길이 주립 도서관으로 가는 길인가요?
   B: 맞아요, 하지만 길이 갈라지는 곳에서 우회전하셔야 해요.

9 A: 우리 반에는 정말 말이 없는 학생이 있어요.
   B: 음, 그 아이를 말하게 하는 방법이 있을 거예요.

10 A: 의사 선생님이 필요한 정보를 알려주셨나요?
    B: 네, 선생님께서 제가 복용했으면 하는 약의 잠재적인 부작용을 열거해주셨어요.

Part II

11 수사의 세부 사항들은 경찰에 의해 기자 회견에서 공개되었다.

12 비평가들은, 차별적 언어와 시각적 폭력으로 가득 찬 게시물들이 널린 인터넷이, 일탈적인 행동을 정상화한다고 경고한다.

13 말라리아는 감염된 말라리아 모기를 통해 한 사람에게서 다른 사람에게로 전염된다.

14 졸업생 대표의 졸업 연설은 진리와 정의가 군림하는 그녀의 이상적인 사회에 대해 묘사했다.

15 현재의 경기 침체는 특히 제조업과 무역업에서 수천 개의 일자리 손실을 낳았다.

16 Greg은 Lydia가 전에 취했던 것을 본 이후로, 그녀가 통제불능이 될 수도 있기 때문에 음주를 자제하라고 경고했다.

17 Leah는 아들을 낳고 난 후 어머니가 되는 것에 시간을 쏟기 위해 일을 그만두었다.

18 중국에는 13억 명 이상의 주민이 있어서, 중국을 세계에서 가장 인구가 많은 나라로 만든다.

19 스카이다이빙은 적절한 훈련을 받지 않으면 당신을 큰 위험에 처하게 할 수 있는 과격한 스포츠이다.

20 고양이는 한때 이집트인들에게 신성한 동물로 여겨져서, 신으로 숭배되었다.

21 많은 공상 과학 소설들은 지구의 생명체를 관찰하기 위해 지구를 찾아오는 외계인들을 등장시킨다.

22 아침 햇살에 비치는 아름다운 하얀 집은 언덕 비탈 높은 곳에 자리잡고 있었다.

23 어떤 페인트는 접촉 시 피부에 염증을 일으키는 화학 물질을 포함한다.

24 과학자들은 토착이 아닌 식물들이 급속히 퍼지는 근본적인 이유가 생태계 내의 구조와 관련이 있다는 이론을 제시한다.

25 캘리포니아의 한 회사는 퍼시피카를 방문하는 관광객들에게 전기로 작동하는 이륜 자동차 Segway의 신나는 탑승을 제공한다.

26 화산의 불길한 우렛소리조차 인근에 있는 주민들을 대피하도록 설득하지 못했다.

27 양측은 계약서에 규정된 모든 요점에서 의견의 일치를 이루었다.

28 그 업무가 막판에 주어졌을 수도 있지만, 책임자는 그것이 그렇게 소홀히 처리될 것이라고는 예상하지 못했다.

29 Hurst 상원 의원은 자신이 정치 스캔들에 연루되었다는 소문에 당황했다.

30 Michael은 종종 너무 믿기 어려운 경험들을 이야기해서 모두들 그가 그것들을 꾸며냈다고 생각한다.

GRAMMAR

Part I

1 A: 언제 잠자리에 들든 상관없이, 나는 밤에 잠들 수가 없어.
   B: 아마도 너는 카페인이 덜 들어간 음료수를 마셔야 할 거야.

2 A: 새로운 연극이 너무 슬프고 감동적이라고 들었어.
   B: 나 그거 봤는데, 극장 안에 있던 아이들과 어른들 모두가 울었어.

3 A: Carrie도 새로 회사에 들어왔나요?
   B: 아니요. 12월이 되면, 그녀가 이곳에서 일한 지 일 년이 될 겁니다.

4 A: 독서 모임의 회원들은 내가 우리 집에서 모임을 열길 원해.
   B: 내가 너라면, 그러기를 꺼릴 것 같아.

5 A: 회사 직원 모두가 주말에 있는 야유회에 오나요?
   B: 회계부의 Marcia를 제외하고는 모두 참석하기로 했어요. 그녀는 오지 못한대요.

6 A: 네 노트북 컴퓨터가 서재에 없는 것 같아.
   B: 내 여동생이 부엌에서 쓰고 있는 게 틀림없어.

7 A: 오늘 Madeline은 왜 점심시간 후에 출근했나요?
   B: 그녀는 오늘 아침에 병원에 간다고 했어요.

8 A: 우리의 확장 계획에 대해 어떻게 생각하십니까?
   B: 꽤 어려운 프로젝트가 될 것 같습니다.

9 A: Natalie가 지난주에 일을 그만두었나요?
   B: 네. 왜냐하면 두 달치가 넘는 월급이 밀렸는데 하나도 못 받았거든요.

10 A: Althea가 자신의 약혼에 대해 너에게 얘기했니?
    B: 응. 그 소식에 흥분해서, 나에게 바로 전화했더라.

Part II

11 그녀는 빨간불을 알아차리지 못했다. 만약 그렇지 않았다면 그녀는 더 빨리 멈췄을 것이다.

12 모든 임대 계약은 예비 거주자가 그들의 아파트를 사용하기 전에 승인되어야 한다.

13 그 영화가 최근에 막을 내린 영화제에서 아무런 상도 받지 못한 것은 놀라운 일이었다.

14 실험실에서 사용되는 화학 물질들은, 많은 물질들이 고휘발성이므로, 적절한 용기에 보관되어야 한다.

15 다른 출판사가 Jay Bard의 초기 소설들을 출간했기 때문에, 전체 시리즈를 출간하는 것은 고려되지 않고 있다.

16 심리학과는 아동 행동에 관해 연구한 다섯 명의 학생들에게 장학금을 수여했다.

17 TV를 배달한 후에, 기술자는 그것을 무료로 설치해주었다.

18 컴퓨터의 전체 데이터베이스를 검사하면서, 바이러스 프로그램은 작업을

마칠 때까지 검사 결과를 보여주지 않았다.

19 고대의 가장 큰 제국은 기원전 550년에 현재의 이란에 세워졌다.

20 앤 설리번의 지도가 없었다면 헬렌 켈러는 그녀를 둘러싼 세상으로부터 계속 고립된 채로 남겨졌을 것이다.

21 그 재정 지원이 동물 실험과 관련된 연구를 지지한다는 의미는 결코 아니었다.

22 전기 팀은 그 조명이 제대로 작동하지 않고 있었던 이유를 알지 못했다.

23 빵은 빵에 들어 있는 당과 단백질 분자가 화학적으로 상호 작용하는 메일라드 반응 때문에 구워지면 갈색으로 변한다.

24 다른 지역보다 집세가 더 비싸다고 알려진 도시의 아파트에서 집을 구하는 부부들이 줄고 있다.

25 계약업체들은 한때 레크리에이션 센터였던 건물을 개조하기 위한 심의 기관을 통한 허가를 받을 수 있었다.

Part III

26 (a) A: 우리 시민학 시험에 어느 과들이 나올 거 같아?
   (b) B: 선생님께서 3과와 4과가 나올 거라고 알려주셨을 때 넌 결석했었구나.
   (c) A: 안 돼! 그 과들을 복습하지 않는다면 나는 시험에서 낙제하고 말 거야.
   (d) B: 네가 그것들을 철저하게 읽기만 하면, 잘 볼 거야.

27 (a) A: 그렇게 얇은 재킷을 입기에는 오늘 좀 춥지 않니?
   (b) B: 내가 이 재킷을 더 이상 입지 않겠다는 게 낫겠다는 말이야?
   (c) A: 내 말 오해하지 마, 재킷은 멋져. 난 그저 네 건강이 걱정될 뿐이야.
   (d) B: 걱정은 고맙지만, 사실, 이 재킷은 보기보다 따뜻해.

28 (a) 아시아 잉어는 북미 영해의 외래종으로, 그것들은 많은 환경학자들이 우려하도록 만들었다. (b) 증가하는 그들의 수는 수중 생태계에 상당한 위협을 가한다. (c) 잉어는 플랑크톤과 같은 방대한 양의 미생물을 잡아먹어서, 토착종이 먹을 것을 전혀 남겨두지 않는 것으로 알려져 있다. (d) 그 지역의 토착종이 존속하려면, 그 잉어의 개체수는 지속적으로 억제되어야 한다.

29 (a) 아메리카 대륙을 식민지로 만들려고 출발하기 전에, 크리스토퍼 콜럼버스는 그의 탐험에 자금을 댈 방법들을 찾는 데 많은 시간을 보냈다. (b) 콜럼버스는 2년 동안 로비를 하고 협상한 끝에 결국 스페인의 왕과 왕비를 접견하는 것을 허락받았다. (c) 그는 자신의 여정이 성공하기 위해서 그들이 무엇을 그에게 제공해줘야 하는지를 설명했다. (d) 그의 요구들은 대부분 수용되었지만, 아무도 그가 탐험에서 돌아올 거라고 기대하지는 않았다.

30 (a) 22살의 Aktarer Zaman은 자신이 지난 11월에 유나이티드 항공과의 소송에 휘말렸다는 것을 알게 되었다. (b) 그 항공사는 Zaman이 웹 사이트를 만들어서 항공기 승객들이 '비밀스러운' 저렴한 항공료를 찾을 수 있게 한 것에 대해 그를 고소했다. (c) 그의 사이트의 인기가 폭발한 후에야 그는 곤경에 빠졌고, 법정으로 소환되었다. (d) 그는 항공사가 그를 상대로 소송을 계속할 것이라고 예상하지만, 판사가 결국 그 사건을 기각했을 때 그는 안도했다.

READING COMPREHENSION

Part I

1 오늘날 사람들은 더 이상 단순히 제품을 구매하는 것에 만족하지 않는다. 그들은 그들의 구매가 대의를 지지할 것처럼 느끼고 싶어한다. 대부분의 다국적 기업들은 이를 인지하여, 요즘 소비자들의 인정 많은 측면에 호소하기 위해 '책임' 마케팅 전략을 채택하고 있다. '책임 마케팅'이란 판촉 활동과 자선 사업의 접목을 의미한다. 예를 들어, 몇몇 주요 생수 회사들이 그들의 제품을 홍보하는 유명 인사들의 대의명분에 대해 재정 지원을 한다. 기업들은 특정 비정부 조직들과 자선 재단에게 _____.

(a) 홍보에 대한 조언을 한다
(b) 사회적인 책임을 느낀다
(c) 마찬가지로 재정 지원을 한다
(d) 이용 가능한 수익금을 활용한다

2 Olive에게,

이번 등반이 즐거웠긴 하지만, 나는 내 계획에서 심각한 실수를 저질렀다는 것을 깨달았어. 여행을 떠나기 몇 주 전에, 등산 용품점에 들러 새 부츠를 포함해서 필요한 모든 장비를 구입했어. 그런데, 등산 첫날이 지나자, 발에 물집이 잡혀서 고통스러웠고 발이 너무 심하게 부어올라서 일어서기도 힘들었던 바람에 나머지 등산 일정을 연기해야 했어. 난 여전히 즐겁게 지내고 있지만, 등산했다면 느꼈을 즐거움에는 비할 수 없어. 난 _____ 했어.

건강 조심해,
Brooke으로부터

(a) 좀 더 편한 휴가를 갔어야
(b) 먼저 새로운 장비에 발을 적응시켰어야
(c) 불필요한 장비에 돈을 덜 낭비했어야
(d) 여행에 필요한 체력을 준비했어야

3 나는 내가 살아온 시간보다 더 오랫동안 자영업자이셨던 아버지가 전산화된 스프레드시트에 거래 기록 입력을 시작하시도록 마침내 설득했다. 아버지는 볼펜과 종이에서 멀어지는 변화를 꺼려하셨지만, 컴퓨터에 데이터를 입력하는 것이 곧 자연스러워지셨다. 바로 지난달 아버지의 가게에 화재가 나서 그곳에 보관되던 거의 모든 서류들이 파손되자, 이 결정이 중요했음이 입증되었다. 다행히, 회계 자료는 다른 장소에 안전하게 보관되어 있었지만, 이러한 위기일발의 상황은 아버지가 _____ 것을 분명히 했다.

(a) 또 다른 재앙에 대비하셔야 한다는
(b) 경영에 대한 가족의 조언을 구하셔야 한다는
(c) 거래 내역을 계속해서 종이에 적으실 것이라는
(d) 적시에 회계 방식을 바꾸셨다는

4 성별에 관계없이, 많은 사람들은 _____.
손톱이 손가락 끝의 연약한 조직을 보호하기 때문에, 그들은 심미적인 목적뿐만 아니라 위생상의 이유로도 이 일에 시간과 관심을 쏟는다. 손톱 밑에는 때가 끼기 쉽기 때문에, 손을 입이나 코 주변에 가져갈 때 세균의 확산을 예방하기 위해 적절한 관리가 중요하다. 게다가, 큐티클을 잘 정리하면 손거스러미나 다른 보기 흉한 각질이 잘 생기지 않는다.

(a) 때때로 손거스러미 문제에 직면한다
(b) 하나의 패션으로 손톱을 기른다
(c) 다양한 이유로 손을 씻는다
(d) 세심하게 손톱을 관리한다

5 오늘날, 사람들은 1889년에서부터 1929년까지 _____ 이었던 것에 대해 여전히 감탄한다. 에펠탑은 파리의 거리 위로 300미터 솟아 있고 서로 맞겹쳐진 연철 기둥들로 이루어져 있다. 1929년 이전에는, 이 건물의 규모에 조금이라도 필적하는 건축물이 없었다. 에펠탑은 로마 성 베드로 대성당의 둥근 지붕이나 기자 대피라미드보다 두 배 높았다. 이 탑은 2년 만에 세워졌는데, 이는 에펠탑의 거대한 높이보다 사람들을 훨씬 더 놀라게 했다.

(a) 현존하는 최대의 둥근 지붕 구조 건물
(b) 역대 최고로 빠르게 건설된 탑
(c) 세계에서 사람이 세운 가장 높은 건물
(d) 에펠을 기리기 위해 지정된 가장 웅장한 기념물

6 스물세 살이었을 때, 나는 평화 봉사단에 가입했고 아프리카에 있는 나라 말라위로 파견되었다. 우리의 목표는 지역 수로를 오염시키기 시작했던 오수를 적절히 처리할 도시 하수 처리 시설을 건설하는 일이었다. 우리는 지역 주민들의 협동과 지원에 기뻤으며, 나는 개발 도상국의 국민들에게 지역 사회를 물질적으로 개선하고자 하는 갈망은 있지만 재원이 없다고 확신했다. 이러한 깨달음에 이끌려, 나는 내 일생을 이 사람들을 위해 그리고 _____을 찾아내는 데 바치기로 결심했다.

(a) 그들이 수질 오염을 통제할 수 있는 최선의 방법
(b) 하수 문제를 다루는 최선의 방법
(c) 그들이 극심한 빈곤에서 벗어날 방법
(d) 필요한 물질적 지원을 제공할 방법

7 낙오 학생 방지법과 같은 결과 중심의 계획이 미국 교육을 변화시켰다. 아이들이 얼마나 잘 학습했는지를 측정하는 데 적용되는 높아진 엄격함은 또한 교사가 얼마나 잘 가르쳤는지에 관심을 돌렸다. 실제로, 학생의 시험 점수는 교사의 효율성을 측정하는 척도가 되었다. 그러한 방법은 교사의 성과를 깔끔하게 수량화하지만, 그것의 정확성은 여전히 의심스럽다. 왜냐하면, 단 하나의 점수는 결코 교사의 능력에 대한 종합적인 관점을 제공할 수 없기 때문이다. 가르치는 일이 얼마나 복잡하고 변화가 많은 직업인지를 고려해볼 때, _____는 것은 명백히 잘못 판단한 것으로 보인다.

(a) 그 기준들이 지지되는 것을 보장할 방법이 없다
(b) 우리가 그러한 엄격한 제도 아래에서 모든 학생들이 성공하길 기대한다
(c) 교사들은 학생들을 시험 성적으로 선발한다
(d) 교사의 성과가 전적으로 학생들의 성적에만 근거해야 한다

8 No Sweat Center의 수상 경력이 있는 피트니스 프로그램이 마침내 이곳에 오게 되었으며, 체인의 지역 확장의 일환으로, 집에서 하는 훈련 프로그램에 등록하시는 선착순 100분께 월 수강료를 25퍼센트 할인해 드립니다. No Sweat은 가정과 직장에서 할 수 있는 개인 트레이닝을 합리적인 가격으로 제공하기 때문에, No Sweat의 특별 관리만 있으면 바쁜 스케줄 때문에 뱃살을 뺄 수 없다거나, 근육질 상체를 만들 수 없다거나, 이두근과 삼두근을 만들 수 없다는 핑계는 더 이상 댈 수 없습니다. 만일 여러분이 _____을/를 바라신다면, 702-NO-SWEAT으로 전화하세요.

(a) 가장 종합적인 헬스 클럽
(b) 일정 조정이 가능한 운동 프로그램
(c) 가정에서 사용할 수 있는 운동 기구
(d) 비싸지 않은 헬스장 회원권

9 항생제 내성에 대한 역사적 통찰
항생제의 남용으로 인해, 많은 박테리아들이 약에 내성을 지니게 되었다. 일례로 결핵균은 1980년대 이후로 일반적인 항생제로는 치료할 수 없게 되었다. 포도상구균과 같은 다른 균들도 이미 1940년대 후반부터 항생제에 대한 내성을 갖기 시작했다. 1950년대경, 그 균에 감염된 환자들 중 40퍼센트가 일반적인 치료법이었던 페니실린에 반응하지 않았다. _____, 내성을 지닌 장구균의 발생이 미국 전역으로 확산되었고, 이는 수천 명의 감염자들이 치명적인 심장병 및 방광염에 걸리게 했다.

(a) 그러는 동안에
(b) 특히
(c) 사실상
(d) 예를 들어

10 수천 년 전에 만들어진 이래로, 호머의 고전 서사시 『오디세이』는 전 세계 독자들에게 철저히 조사되고 상세히 분석되어왔다. 그 고대 시의 각 장은 다양한 주제와 실험적인 요소들을 포함하는데, 이는 작품의 난해한 내용에 대한 여러 다른 해석과 복잡한 논쟁의 원인이 되어 왔다. _____, 평범한 사람뿐만 아니라 문학에 정통한 학자들도 어쩔 수 없이 종종 이 명작과 관련된 많은 주제들을 노력을 들여 찾아내고 공부한다.

(a) 게다가
(b) 그 대신에
(c) 그렇지 않으면
(d) 그러므로

Part II

11 중국 문화에서, 커다란 자루를 들고 있는 풍채 좋은 부처의 모습은 부와 성공을 상징한다고 알려져 있다. (a) 부처의 거대한 자루는 보화, 더 명확히 말하면 승리의 전리품을 뜻한다. (b) 한편, 부처의 웃는 얼굴은 우리가 살면서 마주치는 시련에 승리한 기쁨을 나타낸다. (c) 아시아 전역의 많은 문화권에서 숭배되는 부처는 때때로 마르고 금욕적인 사람으로 묘사되기도 한다. (d) 그러한 묘사는 성공이 고난을 이겨낸 사람에게만 주어진다는 부처의 말을 반영하는 것이다.

12 미술 평론가들은 얀 반 에이크의 대표작인 『아르놀피니 부부의 초상』에서 정확히 무엇이 묘사되었는지에 대해 다른 의견을 가진다. (a) 이 초상화는 상인 계층의 부부를 묘사하는데, 일부 사람들에게는 결혼과 다산을 상징하는 것으로 여겨진다. (b) 그 초상화의 여성이 임신 중이라는 것을 나타내며, 그녀의 몸통 부분에서 눈에 띄게 불룩한 부분을 과시하고 있다는 것은 이 관점을 뒷받침한다. (c) 하지만, 그러한 관점은 그 화가가 여성의 형태를 정확히 묘사하기 위해 얼마나 노력했는지를 고려하지 않는다. (d) 그러나 일부 평론가들은 그 여성이 아이를 가진 것이 아니라 그 당시의 유행하는 스타일로, 스커트를 몸통 쪽으로 올리고 있는 것일 뿐이라고 주장하면서, 이러한 해석을 거부한다.

Part III

13 디젤과 가솔린 중에서 어느 엔진이 우수한지에 대한 논쟁이 수십 년간 엔지니어들 사이에서 맹렬히 계속되어왔다. 그러나, 사실은 분명하다. 가솔린 엔진은 연료로부터 30%라는 꽤 많은 에너지를 실제 동력으로 전환한다. 디젤은 그것을 20% 정도 능가한다. 그들의 신뢰성 또한 적수가 없다. 점화 플러그가 고장 날 때 가솔린 엔진을 따라 다니는 털털거리는 소리는 디젤 엔진에는 별 문제가 되지 않는데, 후자(디젤 엔진)가 연료를 점화하기 위해 점화 장치 대신에 압축을 사용하기 때문이다. 마지막으로, 디젤은 가솔린보다 더 낮은 온도에서 더 깨끗하게 작동되어서, 효율성에서 우세하다.

Q: 디젤 엔진에 대한 글쓴이의 요점은 무엇인가?

(a) 20%의 연료 전환율은 그들이 뒤쳐지는 한 부분이다.
(b) 여러 측면에서 가솔린 엔진을 능가한다.
(c) 가솔린 엔진보다 덜 강력하지만 더 믿을만하다.
(d) 점화 플러그에 대한 의존이 디젤 엔진에게 상당히 유리하게 작용한다.

14 Middleton 어린이 도서관

Middleton 어린이 도서관은 Middleton 침례 교회가 운영하는 사업입니다. 미취학 아동과 ESL 학생들을 위한 독서 교실도 운영하고 있는 이 도서관은 전적으로 이 교회의 주일 미사 헌금에서 재정 지원을 받습니다. 그러나, 최근 증가하는 비용으로, 도서관은 운영비 조달이 어려운 상황에 직면하게 되었습니다. Middleton 교회는 이 도서관을 계속해서 개방하고 잘 유지할 수 있도록 교구민들이 더 많은 지원을 해줄 것이라 믿고 있습니다.

Q: 광고의 요지는 무엇인가?

(a) 이 도서관은 더 많은 ESL 교실을 열 것이다.
(b) 이 도서관은 재정 지원이 더 많이 필요하다.
(c) 이 도서관은 운영비를 삭감하려 해왔다.
(d) 이 도서관은 앞으로 유료 강의를 제공할 것이다.

15 비만 연구

비만의 위험 요인과 원인을 밝혀내는 것은 과학에서 상당한 화제가 되어왔고, 미국 심리학회에 의해 발표된 새로운 연구는 한 원인으로 성격을 정확히 지적한다.

연구에 의하면, 갑자기 신경질적으로 변하고 성실성과는 거리가 먼 성격을 가진 사람들은 과체중으로 고심할 가능성이 크다. 특히, 충동성은 어려워질 조짐이 보이면 바로, 유혹에 넘어가고 체중 감량의 노력을 그만두게 하는 주요 특징들 중 하나로 밝혀졌다.

Q: 글쓴이의 요점은 무엇인가?

(a) 과체중은 개인의 성격에 악영향을 줄 수 있다.
(b) 신경과민이면서 성실한 사람들은 과식하는 경향이 있다.
(c) 증거는 다이어트가 기존의 생각보다 훨씬 더 어렵다는 것을 보여준다.
(d) 연구는 성격적 특성이 비만의 주요 결정 요인이라고 제시한다.

16 지점은 일 년에 두 번 일어나는 현상으로, 계절에 따라 천구 상에서의 태양의 위치가 지평선과 비교하여 가장 높은 곳에 있거나 가장 낮은 곳에 있을 때이다. 지축의 기울기에 따라, 극점에서 가까운 지역은 낮과 밤이 극도로 길어지거나 짧아지기도 한다. 극점이 태양 쪽으로 기울면, 태양이 지평선 위에 24시간 동안 머문다. 한편, 태양의 반대쪽으로 기울어진 극점에서는 정반대 현상이 일어난다. 그곳에서는 하루 종일 지평선 위에 태양이 뜨지 않는다.

Q: 지문에서 주로 논의하는 것은 무엇인가?

(a) 지점이 계절 변화에 미치는 영향
(b) 지점일 때 태양과 지구의 관계
(c) 어떻게 지점이 지축의 위치를 바꾸는지
(d) 태양이 낮의 길이를 결정하는 데 어떤 역할을 하는지

17 당신의 개인용 컴퓨터를 PMC-300 태블릿으로 바꾸세요!

10.5인치 LCD 액정이 달린 가벼운 태블릿인 PMC-300은, 영화를 감상하거나, 인터넷에서 검색을 하거나, 밀린 업무를 따라잡는 데 가장 알맞습니다.

특징:
- 128기가바이트의 내부 저장소
  (PMC-G256 메모리 카드의 포함으로 256기가바이트까지 확장 가능)
- 빠르게 충전되는 대용량 배터리
  (18시간까지 지속 가능)
- 고화질 전면과 후면 카메라
- 사진 편집 프로그램 Blue Oceans가 딸려 있음

PMC-300은 전국의 전자 제품 매장에서 구할 수 있고 단돈 489.99달러에 판매됩니다. 물건이 남아있는 동안 구입하세요!

Q: 지문에 따르면 다음 중 PMC-300에 대한 내용과 일치하는 것은?

(a) 사무실에서 사용되도록 의도되었다.
(b) 파일을 저장하기 위한 외부 장치를 필요로 한다.
(c) 두 가지 다른 버전으로 나온다.
(d) 한 이미지 취급 소프트웨어를 포함한다.

18 구스타브 플로베르는 1857년에 『보바리 부인』을 출간한 후 부도덕하다는 이유로 재판에 회부되었다. 이 책은 사랑과 부, 그리고 사회적 신분에 대한 욕구로 인해 부적절한 관계를 맺는 중산층 여인 엠마 보바리에 대한 이야기이다. 플로베르는 그 소설이 실은 부도덕성의 위험성을 경고한다는 변호사 Marie-Antoine-Jules Senard의 변론 덕분에 무죄 선고를 받았다. Senard는 이 소설이 완벽한 삶에 대한 스스로의 환상에 사로잡힌 엠마와 같은 계층 여성들이 직면했던 곤경을 드러냈을 뿐이라고 덧붙였다. 이 작품은 사회 문제에 대한 비판적인 저술로 여겨졌다.

Q: 다음 중 플로베르의 『보바리 부인』에 대한 내용과 일치하는 것은?

(a) 출간하자마자 노동자 계층의 환호를 받았다.
(b) 통제할 수 없는 야망의 위험성을 묘사한다.
(c) Senard는 부도덕성을 이유로 그것을 금지시켰다.
(d) 플로베르는 엠마라는 여인의 사후에 그것을 썼다.

19 오늘날 목욕은 매일의 청결 유지를 위해 중요한 부분을 차지하지만, 중세 후기에는 결코 일상적인 습관이 아니었다. 16세기 유럽인들은 물이 질병을 옮긴다고 믿었다. 수인성 오염 물질로 인해 발생한다고 여겨졌던 선페스트가 빈번히 창궐하여 수많은 사람들이 사망하자, 그 믿음은 강화되었다. 사람들은 건강에 악영향을 미칠까 두려워서 목욕하기를 꺼렸다. 19세기에 의사들이 비누와 물로 몸을 씻으면 질병을 일으키는 세균이 무력해진다고 소개하고 나서야 목욕은 청결을 위한 습관으로 자리잡았다.

Q: 다음 중 지문의 내용과 일치하는 것은?

(a) 정수는 선페스트 치료법으로 사용되었다.
(b) 19세기 의사들은 목욕을 건강한 습관이라고 홍보하였다.
(c) 16세기 유럽에서는 정기적인 목욕이 행해졌다.
(d) 선페스트는 오염된 물에 의해 발생하는 질병이다.

20

엽산은 건강한 임신을 위해 필수적이지만, 안타깝게도 많은 여성들은 이 비타민을 충분히 섭취하는 것을 등한시합니다. 이분척추와 무뇌증과 같이, 신경관에 영향을 미치는 심각한 선천적 결함들은 식품이나 보충제를 통해 얻어지는 충분한 양의 엽산으로 예방될 수 있다. 척추와 뇌는 신경관으로부터 발달하는데, 이 신경관은 임신한 첫 달 이내에 형성되기 때문에, 임신한 이후에 보충제를 섭취하기 시작한 여성들은 엽산의 이점을 얻지 못할 수도 있다. 이는 의사들이 여성들에게 임신을 하려고 하기 전에 엽산을 먹기 시작하라고 권고하는 이유이다.

Q: 지문에 따르면 다음 중 맞는 것은 무엇인가?
(a) 충분한 엽산 섭취는 성공적인 임신에 있어 부수적이다.
(b) 보충제를 섭취하는 것은 엽산을 얻는 데 좋지 않은 방법으로 여겨진다.
(c) 신경관 결함은 임신의 마지막 단계에서만 나타난다.
(d) 적절한 엽산 수치는 가장 큰 효과를 위해 임신 전에 달성되어야 한다.

21

Watkins 교장 선생님께,

제3회 연례 아마추어 예술 경연대회 수상자는 3월 28일에 선정될 예정입니다. 시상식 3일 전에 출품된 모든 그림을 전시할 예정입니다. 최종 선정 과정에서 출품작으로 인정되려면, 3월 25일 전에 작품을 제출해야 한다고 학생들에게 부디 당부해 주시기 바랍니다. 수상자 발표일은 아직 확정되지 않았으나, 분명히 3월 29일이나 30일 중 하루가 될 것입니다.

진심을 담아,
청소년 예술 후원회
Claire Fuentes 드림

Q: 다음 중 편지의 내용과 일치하는 것은?
(a) 학생들은 작품을 3월 28일에 제출해야 한다.
(b) 수상자는 늦어도 3월 30일까지는 발표될 것이다.
(c) 전시회는 시상식과 같은 날에 열린다.
(d) 수상작은 3월 25일 이전에 결정될 것이다.

22

위험하다는 악평을 종종 받아온 압력솥은 사실은 가장 안전하고 유용한 요리 기구 중 하나이다. 부당한 평판은 초기 세대의 기능 장애에서 기인했으나, 요즘에는 방출 밸브와 같은 안전 혁신 장치들이 사고가 나는 것을 방지해주고 소비자로 하여금 압력솥이 매일의 식사를 빨리 요리할 수 있다는 신속성을 안전하게 즐길 수 있도록 하고 있다. 장치는 밀폐되어 있으므로 압력솥 내부의 압력 증가가 가스레인지 위의 프라이팬보다 높은 온도를 만들어내는데, 압력과 온도는 직접적으로 관련되어 있기 때문이다.

Q: 다음 중 압력솥에 대한 내용과 일치하는 것은?
(a) 처음 출시되었을 당시 밸브에 결함이 있었다.
(b) 음식 준비를 신속하게 하는 데 유용하다.
(c) 온도를 최대한 높이기 위해 전열선을 사용한다.
(d) 약간의 부상 위험이 있지만 여전히 인기가 있다.

23

시장님께,

저는 우리 도시의 많은 사업장에서 현금 거래 시 공식 영수증을 발행하지 않는다는 점이 염려됩니다. 저는 영수증을 요구할 때마다, 신기하다는 듯이 저를 바라보는 시선을 느낍니다. 저는 법에 규정된 공식 영수증을 요구함으로써 소비자로서의 권리를 행사하고 싶지만, 점원들은 다른 소비자들이 요구하지 않는다는 이유로 제 요구를 귀찮아 하는 것 같습니다. 영수증을 발행하지 않음으로써, 사업장은 마땅히 내야 할 판매세를 적게 신고할 수 있습니다. 집행되지 않을 것이라면 정부는 왜 법을 제정하는지요?

존경을 담아,
Ernest Daz 올림

Q: 편지에서 추론할 수 있는 것은 무엇인가?
(a) 상점 주인들은 소비자들을 속이는 죄를 범한다.
(b) 이 도시의 사업주들은 현금 거래를 불편해 한다.
(c) 대부분의 점원들은 영수증을 제공해야 한다는 것을 모르고 있다.
(d) 구매 영수증을 주지 않으면 사업장은 더 많은 돈을 벌지도 모른다.

24

뉴스 > 정치

곤경에 처한 Brookes Island 시장

Brookes Island 시장은 어제 다양한 비영리 단체들에 의해 탄핵 소원을 받고 충격에 빠졌다. 고소인들은 시장이 대중의 신뢰를 저버리고 이 섬 도시의 몇 가지 법률을 위반했다고 말했다. 그를 비난하는 사람들은 시장이 섬의 평화와 질서를 보호해야 하는 그의 의무를 이행하지 않는다고 주장한다.

고소를 조사할 책임이 있는 Brookes Island 시의회는 정부에 대한 대중의 신뢰가 위태로우므로, 시장이 실제로 그의 직무를 소홀히 했는지 즉시 밝혀내야 한다.

Q: 글쓴이가 가장 동의할 것 같은 진술은 무엇인가?
(a) 즉각적인 수사가 이 도시를 위한 최선이다.
(b) 시장은 권력을 장악하면서 타락의 길을 걸었다.
(c) 시의회는 탄핵 소원을 거부해야 한다.
(d) 시의회에 의해 새로운 시장이 선임되어야 한다.

25

다른 마을이나 도시로 이사할 때, 차이점들이 나타날 수 있다는 사실을 염두에 두어야 합니다. 한 지역 사회에 존재하는 규범에 둔감한 것은 많은 사회적 문제를 야기할 수 있습니다. 도시에서, 젊은 커플이 데이트를 즐기는 것은 흔한 일이지만, 유레카처럼 보수적인 도시에서, 특히 밤에 단둘이 있는 젊은 남녀를 어르신들이 본다면 공개적으로 나무랄 것입니다. 게다가, '비행을 저지르는' 10대들의 부모들은 자녀의 행실을 바로잡지 않으면 그 지역 사회에서 쫓겨날 위기에 처할지도 모릅니다.

Q: 지문에서 추론할 수 있는 것은 무엇인가?
(a) 사람들은 엄격한 사회적 규범 때문에 유레카를 피한다.
(b) 모든 지역 사회에는 각각의 도덕적 잣대가 있다.
(c) 새로운 곳으로 이사하는 사람들은 사회적 규범을 따를 필요가 없다.
(d) 문화적 규범은 장소마다 반드시 비슷한 행태가 나타나게 해준다.

Part IV

26~27

모든 새 애호가들 모집

만약 여러분이 새 관찰을 취미로 삼는 데 관심이 있다면, 펜실베이니아 야생 동물 협회에 의해 제공되는 특별한 입문 강좌인, '비행'을 고려해보세요.

이 세 시간짜리 수업은 우리 지역 토종 조류에 대한 개관으로 시작합니다. 그다음에, 여러분은 저희 시설의 울타리 내에서 토종 조류들이 지은 몇몇 실제 둥지들을 관찰할 기회를 가질 것입니다. 그런 다음, 여러분은 몇몇 녹음된 새 소리를 듣고 그것을 스스로 해보는 연습을 할 것입니다. 마지막으로, 반 전체가 교외에서 오후 동안 조류 관찰을 하러 떠날 것입니다. 저희의 전문 가이드가 여러분과 다른 참가자들을 많은 수의 새가 있는 지역으로 안내할 것입니다. 그는 여러분이 보는 것들을 식별하도록 돕기 위해, 여러분에게 지역 새들의 사진을 제공할 것입니다. 당신에게 필요한 모든 것은 우리의 깃털이 난 친구들을 가까이서 살펴보고 친해지기 위한 쌍안경 한 쌍뿐입니다.

강좌의 비용은 인당 35달러입니다. 등록하기 위해서, www.pwi.com 으로 방문하여 등록 링크를 클릭하세요.

26. Q: 지문은 주로 무엇에 관한 내용인가?
(a) 새들의 사회적 행동에 대한 교육 영상
(b) 초보 새 관찰자들에게 필요한 지식을 제공하는 프로그램
(c) 펜실베이니아의 토종 조류의 정확한 위치를 찾아내는 최고의 기법
(d) 몇몇 멸종 위기의 야생 동물을 보호하기 위해 취해지는 조치들

27. Q: 가이드가 참가자들에게 무엇을 줄 것인가?
(a) 한 쌍의 쌍안경
(b) 교본
(c) 지역 야생 동물의 사진
(d) 몇몇 음성 파일

28~29

수신: kowalski19@greymail.com
발신: donation@mercianimal.com
제목: 당신의 기부에 감사드립니다 – Mercy Animal Farm

Mr. Kowalski씨께,

Mercy Animal Farm의 선행에 투자해주신 것에 대해 감사드립니다. 당신의 기부금 1,000달러는 자선 기금 수익이 감소하고 있는 시기에 특히 귀중한 도움을 제공합니다. 당신의 것과 같은 기부금은 필수적인 먹이 주기와 재활 프로그램을 유지하도록 돕고 더 많은 쓸모없어진 동물들을 구조할 수 있게 합니다. 아시다시피, 우리는 동물들이 구입되지 않으면 도살될 운명에 처했을 때 종종 그들을 즉각 구입하도록 요구받습니다. 우리는 근처 보호소에 맡겨진 버림받은 애완동물들을 구조하기 위해서도 노력합니다.

감사의 표시로, 당신은 택배로 무료 티셔츠를 받을 것입니다. 그 셔츠는 지역 예술가인 Elizabeth Mason에 의해 디자인되었습니다. 저는 이 기회를 이용하여 당신이 도울 수 있는 다른 방법들이 있다는 것을 상기시켜드리고 싶습니다. 저희는 몇 시간에서 수일까지 이어질 수 있는 봉사 활동 기회를 제공합니다. 봉사자들은 우리 건물이나 근처 호텔에서 머물러도 좋습니다. 우리는 또한 당신이 당신의 친구들을 농장의 사진들과 여러 정보를 나누는 소셜 미디어 페이지로 안내해준다면 감사하겠습니다.

진심을 담아,
Misha Campbell
사업부 부장

28. Q: Mr. Kowalski의 기부의 일부는 무엇에 사용될 것인가?
(a) 도살할 예정인 동물들의 인수
(b) 버림받은 애완동물들을 위한 두 번째 보호소 설립
(c) 축산물을 생산하는 농장의 재건
(d) 시설을 방문하는 관광객들을 위한 프로그램의 유지

29. Q: 다음 중 Mr. Kowalski에 대한 내용과 일치하는 것은?
(a) 그는 동물 복지를 목표로 하는 자선 단체를 대표한다.
(b) 그의 친구들은 자선 단체에 그의 자선 기금과 대등한 기부금을 낼 것이다.
(c) 그는 특별히 디자인된 의류 한 점을 받을 것이다.
(d) 그의 기부는 그에게 호텔에 무료로 머물 자격을 준다.

30~31

봉건적 패권을 위한 전쟁

1590년에, 일본 봉건 영주인 도요토미 히데요시는, 그가 그의 권력에 대한 거대한 위협으로 여겼던 호조 일족에 대한 포위 공격을 주도했다. 그러나, 히데요시의 군이 오다와라에 있는 호조 성을 둘러싸고 진영을 설치했을 때 실제로 싸움은 거의 일어나지 않았다. 그들은 단지 모든 물건과 사람이 성에 들어가거나 성으로부터 나가는 것을 차단했다. 3개월 후, 호조는 그들의 식량을 다 소진했고, 또한, 히데요시의 군인들과 사무라이 병사들에게 수로 현저하게 압도당한다는 것을 깨닫고, 항복했다.

뒤이어, 호조의 소유지는 히데요시의 대장군에게 넘어간 한편, 호조 일족의 수장인 우지나오와 그의 아내는 코야산으로 추방당했다. 호조 일족이 완벽하게 약화되었음을 확실하게 하기 위해, 히데요시는 우지나오의 아버지와 삼촌의 자결을 강요했다. 우지나오는 그다음 해에 병으로 죽었고, 그것은, 가문 내 최연장자 남성들의 죽음과 함께, 히데요시가 호조 일족이 다시 권력을 얻는 것을 효과적으로 방지하게 해주었다. 따라서, 히데요시의 지배에 있어 가장 큰 잠재적인 장애물은 영구적으로 제거되었고 그는 일본 대부분에 대한 그의 지배를 더욱 공고히 할 수 있었다.

30. Q: 다음 중 히데요시의 군대에 대한 내용과 일치하는 것은?
(a) 오다와라에서 호조에 대항해 수많은 전투에서 싸웠다.
(b) 호조 일족이 항복하게 하기 위해 굶주림을 이용했다.
(c) 군인보다 더 많은 수의 사무라이를 포함했다.
(d) 성 포위 공격 이후 정복한 땅을 분할했다.

31. Q: 지문에서 추론할 수 있는 것은 무엇인가?
(a) 우지나오는 아버지와 삼촌을 배신했기 때문에 죽음에서 벗어났다.
(b) 포위 공격 이전의 가문 분쟁이 호조 일족의 몰락에 기여했다.
(c) 우지나오의 친척들은 권력을 가질 수 있도록 히데요시를 타도할 계획을 가지고 있었다.
(d) 강제 자결은 호조 일족에 대한 히데요시의 지배를 보장하기 위한 수단으로 사용되었다.

32~33

아마존 열대 우림이 완전히 파괴될 위험에 처해 있다. 브라질에서만, 추가적인 농지에 대한 수요가 지난 6년 동안 열대 우림의 거의 15만 제곱킬로미터를 완전히 파괴되게 했다. 가축 목장 경영과 작물 생산 같은 농업 벤처 사업이 이 국가의 수출 산업을 활성화했는지는 몰라도, 그것들은 열대 우림의 파괴에도 상당히 기여했다. 토지 소유주들과 농부들은 가축, 콩, 그리고 옥수수에 대한 해외의 요구를 충족시키기 위해 삼림 지대를 개간했다.

식물의 손실뿐만 아니라, 삼림 파괴는, 동물들의 주거지가 파괴되면서, 그 지역의 동물 개체 수에 압박을 가하고 있다. 수가 감소함에 따라, 그 어느 때보다 더 많은 아마존 동식물종이 멸종 위기의 생물 목록에 올라 있다. 더 많은 농지에 대한 수요는 인간에게도 부정적인 영향을 끼치고 있다. 원주민들은 거대 기업, 때로는, 정부 관리들에 의해 그들의 원래의 고향에서 몰아내어 지고 있다. 토착 사회가 분열되고 주류 문화에 동화되면서 그들의 언어와 문화가 상실되기 때문에, 이 분산은 원주민 문화를 위험에 처하게 한다. 아마존 지역의 모든 곳에서 삼림 파괴의 영향이 목도되고 있음에도 불구하고, 더 큰 손실을 억제하기 위한 노력은 상대적으로 거의 행해지지 않고 있다.

32. Q: 지문의 제목으로 가장 적절한 것은 무엇인가?
(a) 열대 우림 손실로 인한 동물 개체 수의 증가
(b) 삼림 파괴가 아마존 열대 우림의 생명에 미치는 영향
(c) 브라질의 농업에 미치는 아마존의 이점
(d) 희귀한 아마존 식물 종의 빠른 소멸

33. Q: 다음 중 아마존 열대 우림에 대한 내용과 일치하는 것은?
(a) 다른 어떤 삼림보다 더 많은 멸종 위기에 처한 동식물종의 고향이다.
(b) 15만 제곱킬로미터 가까이가 작년에 파괴되었다.
(c) 세계적인 농업 수요가 아마존 열대 우림의 삼림 파괴의 한 원인이다.
(d) 농장으로 이주하는 사람들을 위한 주택을 건설하기 위해 파괴되고 있다.

34~35

현대 노숙자 위기

Tara Jones 씀

저는 주요 도시 지역의 노숙자들이 긴급하게 처리되어야 한다고 생각합니다. 주거 비용이 계속해서 급등함에 따라, 점점 더 많은 사람이 뉴욕, 로스앤젤레스, 그리고 시카고를 포함하는, 우리나라의 여러 대도시에서 터무니없는 가격이 매겨진 주거 시설에 배척당하고 있습니다.

샌프란시스코를 예로 들면, 그곳은 임대료 중앙값이 평균 월 소득의 약 50퍼센트입니다. 당연히, 대부분의 사람은 그만큼을 지급할 여유가 없습니다. 놀랄 것도 없이, 도시의 많은 노숙자들은 사실 직업을 가지고 있지만, 아파트에 지불할 충분한 돈을 벌지 않습니다.

주거 공급을 늘리고 가격을 낮추기 위해서, 도시들은 새로운 주택이나 아파트의 건설을 제한하는 건축 규제를 완화해야 합니다. 더 나아가, 일하는 사람들이 주택을 매입하기 위해 대출을 요청할 때 더 많은 보조가 제공되어야 합니다.

그러나, 정부가 취할 수 있는 가장 유의미한 조치는, 더 낮은 소득의 사람들을 위해 더 저렴한 주거지를 짓는 것입니다. 이 문제를 영속화하기만 하는 더 많은 임시 노숙자 쉼터를 건설하기보다는, 가격이 알맞은 주택을 짓는 것이 많은 노숙자들에게 길에서 벗어나는 방법을 제공할 것입니다. 노숙자 문제가 절망적으로 보일지라도, 정치인들이 해결하려는 의지만 갖춘다면 이 문제는 해결될 수 있습니다.

34. Q: 왜 샌프란시스코의 일부 사람들은 노숙자인가?
(a) 도심 내에서 직업을 구할 수 없다.
(b) 그들의 소득이 도시에서의 생계비를 충당하기에 불충분하다.
(c) 정부에 의해 일부 지역에 거주하는 것이 제한되었다.
(d) 최근 경기 침체 동안 그들의 주택을 잃었다.

35. Q: Tara Jones에 의해 주장된 것이 아닌 것은?
(a) 정부는 건축 규제의 정도를 완화해야 한다.
(b) 적은 소득을 버는 사람들이 감당할 수 있는 더 많은 주거 시설이 지어져야 한다.
(c) 돈을 빌리기를 원하는 사람들에게 지원이 제공되어야 한다.
(d) 당국은 노숙자들을 위해 더 많은 쉼터를 건설해야 한다.

TEST 04

LISTENING COMPREHENSION

Part I

1

M: How have things been going lately?
W: _____

(a) I'll be all right.
(b) I'm still considering it.
(c) I can't complain.
(d) I appreciate your concern.

M: 요즘 어떻게 지냈니?
(a) 난 괜찮아질 거야.
(b) 난 아직 그걸 고려 중이야.
(c) 그럭저럭 잘 지내.
(d) 신경 써줘서 고마워.

2

W: Is this bus ever going to come? It's been thirty minutes!
M: _____

(a) We're only halfway there, though.
(b) Could be that it's stuck in traffic.
(c) I checked. They come every ten minutes.
(d) You're right. We boarded the wrong bus!

W: 이 버스가 오기는 하는 거야? 30분이나 됐어!
(a) 그렇지만 우리는 겨우 절반밖에 오지 못 했는걸.
(b) 버스가 교통 체증으로 꼼짝 못하고 있나 봐.
(c) 내가 확인했어. 버스는 10분마다 와.
(d) 네 말이 맞아. 우리는 엉뚱한 버스를 탔어!

3

M: Buying textbooks is going to cost me a fortune.
W: _____

(a) Don't worry. The bookstore won't run out.
(b) It's faster to order them online.
(c) Not if you get them secondhand.
(d) I wonder how I'm going to do all that reading.

M: 교과서를 사는 데 큰돈이 들 거야.
(a) 걱정 마. 서점의 물품이 다 떨어지지는 않을 거야.
(b) 그것들을 온라인으로 주문하는 것이 더 빨라.
(c) 그것들을 중고로 산다면 그렇지 않을 거야.
(d) 내가 어떻게 그 모든 것을 읽어야 할지 모르겠어.

4

W: It's been a while since we've spoken, hasn't it?
M: _____

(a) Let's wait for it.
(b) Thanks for asking.
(c) You've got that right.
(d) I think so. Take care.

W: 우리가 이야기를 나눈지도 한참 됐네요, 그렇지 않나요?
(a) 그것을 기다려 봐요.
(b) 물어봐 줘서 고마워요.
(c) 당신 말이 맞아요.
(d) 저도 그렇게 생각해요. 잘 지내요.

5

M: We should wait here until Harry shows up.
W: _____

(a) We ought to invite him.
(b) He might be a while, though.
(c) I'd be shocked if he arrives.
(d) He won't agree to that.

M: 우리는 Harry가 올 때까지 여기서 기다려야 해.
(a) 우리는 그를 초대해야 해.
(b) 하지만, 그는 좀 걸릴지도 몰라.
(c) 난 그가 오면 놀랄 거야.
(d) 그는 그것에 동의하지 않을 거야.

6

W: Weren't you blown away by Jenny's review?
M: _____

(a) True. She tried too hard.
(b) She told you to review it.
(c) It exceeded my expectations.
(d) Yes, I felt like she blew it.

W: Jenny의 논평에 감명받지 않았니?
(a) 맞아. 그녀는 너무 무리했어.
(b) 그녀가 네게 그걸 검토하라고 했어.
(c) 그건 내 기대 이상이었어.
(d) 응, 그녀가 다 망쳐버린 것 같았어.

7

M: Your new apartment is quite small.
W: _____

(a) Less to clean, if you ask me.
(b) I'd get something spacious.
(c) I put down the minimum deposit.
(d) I can always renovate it.

M: 네 새 아파트는 꽤 작구나.
(a) 내가 볼 때는, 청소할 게 줄어든 거야.
(b) 나라면 넓은 걸로 구할 거야.
(c) 난 최소한의 보증금을 지불했어.
(d) 내가 언제든지 그걸 수리할 수 있어.

8

W: Which volunteer organization are you affiliated with?
M: _____

(a) I put in time at a homeless shelter.
(b) We recently underwent a merger.
(c) I send monetary contributions.
(d) I must make a decision.

W: 당신은 어느 자원봉사 단체와 관계가 있나요?
(a) 전 노숙자 쉼터에 시간을 쏟고 있어요.
(b) 우리는 최근에 합병을 겪었어요.
(c) 전 기부금을 보내요.
(d) 전 결정을 내려야 해요.

9

M: How about heading out once the rain lets up?
W: _____

(a) No way. We'll catch a cold.
(b) When it rains, it pours.
(c) Sure. I'm in no hurry to leave.
(d) I suggest waiting a bit.

M: 빗발이 약해지면 출발하는 게 어때?
(a) 안 돼. 우린 감기에 걸릴 거야.
(b) 엎친 데 덮친 격이네.
(c) 그러자. 난 급하게 떠날 거 없어.
(d) 좀 기다려 보자.

10

W: I get the idea you're not fond of Roger.
M: _____

(a) Yeah, I admire what he's done.
(b) I see him as deceitful.
(c) He can say what he wants.
(d) We should ask him to be certain.

W: 넌 Roger를 별로 좋아하지 않는 것 같아.
(a) 맞아, 난 그가 해낸 일을 존경해.
(b) 난 그가 부정직하다고 생각해.
(c) 그는 하고 싶은 말을 할 수 있어.
(d) 확실히 하려면 그에게 물어봐야 해.

Part II

11

W: I'm going to take a Pilates class. Interested?
M: Maybe, but my evenings are booked solid.
W: How about weekday mornings, then?
M: _____

(a) It might be too intensive.
(b) Time is of the essence.
(c) That suits me just fine.
(d) I'm going to attend regularly.

W: 난 필라테스 강습을 들을 거야. 관심 있어?
M: 어쩌면, 하지만 내가 저녁에는 너무 바빠서.
W: 그럼, 평일 아침은 어때?
(a) 그건 너무 격렬할지도 몰라.
(b) 시간이 제일 중요하지.
(c) 그 시간이 나에게는 딱 괜찮아.
(d) 난 규칙적으로 출석할 거야.

12

M: Do you think Cindy will be OK in school?
W: Of course. Why? Are you worried?
M: Well, she's younger than most of her classmates.
W: _____

(a) Her grades will improve.
(b) She said it wasn't true.
(c) We'd better call the school.
(d) I'm not concerned in the least.

M: Cindy가 학교 생활을 잘 할까요?
W: 당연하죠. 왜요? 걱정이 되세요?
M: 음, 그 애가 대부분의 반 친구들보다 어려서요.
(a) 그녀의 성적은 향상될 거예요.
(b) 그녀가 그건 사실이 아니라고 했어요.
(c) 우리가 학교에 전화해 보는 게 좋겠어요.
(d) 난 조금도 걱정이 안 돼요.

13

W: When do we need to be at the airport?
M: By 5. Departure is at 6.
W: Is there time to grab a bite on the way?
M: _____

(a) Arriving early is prudent.
(b) Let's ask when we get there.
(c) It'd be better if we just ate there.
(d) Don't worry. We're on time.

W: 우리가 언제까지 공항에 도착해야 하지?
M: 5시까지. 출발이 6시야.
W: 가는 길에 간단히 요기할 시간이 있을까?
(a) 일찍 도착하는 게 현명하지.

(b) 그곳에 도착하면 물어보자.
(c) 거기서 먹는 게 나을 거야.
(d) 걱정하지 마. 우린 시간에 맞게 왔어.

14

M: Good morning. You called for a plumber?
W: Yes. There's something wrong with my tub.
M: Can you be more specific?
W: _____

(a) It was installed last week.
(b) It won't drain properly.
(c) It's in the bathroom.
(d) I don't know how to fix it.

M: 안녕하세요. 배관공 부르셨지요?
W: 네. 욕조에 문제가 있어서요.
M: 더 구체적으로 말씀해 주실래요?
W: _____

(a) 그건 지난주에 설치되었어요.
(b) 물이 잘 안 빠져요.
(c) 그건 욕실에 있어요.
(d) 전 그걸 어떻게 고치는지 모르겠어요.

15

W: I thought we were going to the park.
M: We will, but I'm engrossed in this show right now.
W: But the sun's going down.
M: _____

(a) It'll be closed at dusk.
(b) I know. I need to rise and shine.
(c) I don't mind taking walks after dark.
(d) It won't hold you up.

W: 난 우리가 공원에 가는 줄 알았는데.
M: 갈 거야, 근데 난 지금은 이 쇼에 빠져 있어서.
W: 하지만 해가 지고 있어.
M: _____

(a) 그곳은 해 질 무렵에 문을 닫을 거야.
(b) 알아. 나는 정신차리고 일어나야 해.
(c) 난 어두워진 후에 산책하는 것도 괜찮아.
(d) 그것은 널 지체시키지 않을 거야.

16

M: Why isn't the Internet working in the office?
W: Not sure. It's been down for about 10 minutes now.
M: You didn't think to contact IT?
W: _____

(a) Not usually, since I don't go online much.
(b) It's fine. We don't expect it to go down.
(c) I was waiting to see if it's just temporary.
(d) No, I'd rather ask the IT department what to do.

M: 왜 사무실의 인터넷이 안 되고 있죠?
W: 모르겠어요. 한 10분 전부터 작동이 안 되고 있어요.

M: IT 부서에 연락할 생각을 안 해본 건가요?
(a) 전 온라인에 자주 접속하지 않아서, 보통 그렇지 않아요.
(b) 괜찮아요. 우리는 그것이 내려갈 것이라고 예상하지 않아요.
(c) 그저 일시적인 것인지 알아보려고 기다리고 있었죠.
(d) 아뇨, 전 차라리 무엇을 해야 할지 IT 부서에 물어보겠어요.

17

W: Have you ever held an office job?
M: No. I don't like working for anyone.
W: How do you support yourself, then?
M: _____

(a) You can depend on me.
(b) You have a point there.
(c) I now hold two jobs.
(d) I run my own business.

W: 사무직 일을 해보신 적 있으세요?
M: 아니요. 전 누군가를 위해 일하는 걸 좋아하지 않아서요.
W: 그럼, 어떻게 생계를 꾸리시나요?
(a) 저를 믿도록 해요.
(b) 당신 말도 일리가 있네요.
(c) 전 지금 두 가지 일을 해요.
(d) 전 제 사업을 운영해요.

18

M: I wish I had a different biology teacher.
W: Why do you say that?
M: She goes over the lectures in too much detail.
W: _____

(a) I like when my teachers clarify things.
(b) I prefer experiments to lectures.
(c) You shouldn't rely on notes alone.
(d) Tell her to explain it better.

M: 난 생물 선생님이 다른 분이라면 좋겠어.
W: 왜 그렇게 말하는 거야?
M: 그분은 수업 시간에 지나치게 자세히 설명하셔.
(a) 난 선생님들께서 분명히 설명해주시면 좋던데.
(b) 난 강의보다는 실험이 더 좋아.
(c) 노트 필기에만 의존하면 안 돼.
(d) 더 잘 설명해달라고 말씀드려.

19

W: Our office needs some sprucing up.
M: A few plants would change the whole atmosphere.
W: Do you think the company would cover the expense?
M: _____

(a) I never thought plants could make such a difference.
(b) We're just waiting on your approval.

(c) I had no idea it was so expensive.
(d) I bet it can be worked into the budget.

W: 우리 사무실은 좀 단장될 필요가 있어요.
M: 화초 몇 개가 전체적인 분위기를 바꿔줄 거예요.
W: 회사가 그 비용을 부담해줄 거라고 생각해요?

(a) 화초가 그렇게 차이를 만들 거라곤 전혀 생각 못 했어요.
(b) 우리는 그저 당신의 승인을 기다리는 중이에요.
(c) 그것이 그렇게 비싼 줄 몰랐어요.
(d) 그것을 우리의 예산에 포함시킬 수 있다고 장담해요.

20

M: You should submit your essay for publication.
W: Actually, I've been tossing around the idea.
M: I wouldn't hesitate. It's full of promise.
W: _____

(a) In that case, I'd better get on it.
(b) It was the top submission.
(c) I'm awaiting the publisher's response.
(d) But if you snooze, you lose.

M: 당신의 수필이 출판되도록 제출해봐요.
W: 실은, 그 계획에 대해 생각해보고 있었어요.
M: 저라면 망설이지 않겠어요. 그건 아주 유망하다고요.

(a) 그렇다면, 그것을 진행해봐야겠네요.
(b) 그건 최고의 제출서였어요.
(c) 전 출판사의 응답을 기다리고 있어요.
(d) 하지만 미적거린다면, 기회를 놓칠 거예요.

Part III

21

Listen to a conversation between two friends.

M: I've made up my mind. I'm relocating overseas.
W: Good for you. You've been ruminating on that for ages.
M: It's time that I broadened my horizons.
W: Have you decided yet where you'll go?
M: Probably Switzerland. I have distant relatives there.
W: I'm sure you'll enjoy living in such a beautiful place.

Q: What is the conversation mainly about?

(a) The man's relatives who live overseas
(b) The man's love of international travel
(c) The man's job prospect in Switzerland
(d) The man's resolution to move abroad

두 친구 간의 대화를 들으시오.

M: 난 결심했어. 난 외국으로 이사할 거야.
W: 잘됐다. 네가 정말 오랫동안 숙고해왔던 일이잖아.
M: 내 지평을 넓힐 때가 됐지.
W: 어디로 갈지는 벌써 정했어?
M: 아마 스위스로 갈 것 같아. 그곳에 먼 친척이 있거든.
W: 네가 그런 아름다운 곳에서의 삶을 즐기게 될 거라고 확신해.

Q: 주로 무엇에 관한 대화인가?

(a) 남자의 외국에 사는 친척들
(b) 해외여행에 대한 남자의 애호
(c) 남자가 스위스에서 직업을 구할 가능성
(d) 외국으로 이사하려는 남자의 결심

22

Listen to a conversation between two friends.

W: Ben, I'd like to buy you dinner later.
M: Dinner? Why on earth?
W: I want to make amends for our fallout the other day.
M: Oh, I've let bygones be bygones.
W: But I still feel guilty for saying mean things to you.
M: I've already forgiven you.

Q: What is the woman mainly doing in the conversation?

(a) Thanking the man for forgiving her
(b) Soliciting a companion to share dinner
(c) Attempting to express her feelings of regret
(d) Begging the man to accept her apology

두 친구 간의 대화를 들으시오.

W: Ben, 내가 나중에 저녁을 사고 싶어.
M: 저녁이라고? 도대체 왜?
W: 며칠 전에 다툰 것에 대해 보상하고 싶어서.
M: 아, 난 지난 일은 잊어버리기로 했어.
W: 하지만 난 네게 못되게 이야기했던 것에 대해 아직도 죄책감을 느껴.
M: 난 벌써 널 용서했는걸.

Q: 대화에서 여자는 주로 무엇을 하고 있는가?

(a) 자신을 용서해준 것에 대해 남자에게 고마워하고 있다.
(b) 저녁을 같이 먹을 동반자를 구하고 있다.
(c) 후회의 감정을 표현하려고 하고 있다.
(d) 자신의 사과를 받아달라고 남자에게 애원하고 있다.

23

Listen to a conversation at a supermarket.

M: Do you think these are non-GMO vegetables?
W: I'm not sure. Do you want to go to the organic section instead?
M: No. I'm on a budget, and organic produce is so expensive.
W: I have an idea. Why don't you start growing some at home?
M: I wouldn't know where to begin. I'm not exactly a green thumb.
W: My friend grows lettuce and tomatoes in

containers. She said it's easy.

M: Well, I wouldn't have anywhere to put them since my apartment is tiny.

W: She grows them on her balcony. I think it's worth a try.

Q: What is the woman mainly trying to do in the conversation?

(a) Explain why genetic modification is bad
(b) Attempt to convince the man to buy organic food
(c) Encourage the man to create a vegetable garden
(d) Suggest the man needs to move to a bigger apartment

슈퍼마켓에서의 대화를 들으시오.

M: 이것들이 유전자를 변형하지 않은 채소라고 생각해?
W: 잘 모르겠어. 대신 유기농 코너에 가볼래?
M: 아니. 예산은 한정되어 있고, 유기농 농산물은 너무 비싸.
W: 나한테 좋은 생각이 있어. 집에서 좀 재배하기 시작하면 어때?
M: 난 어디부터 시작해야 할지 몰라. 엄밀히 말하자면 난 식물 재배에 재능이 없어.
W: 내 친구는 통 안에 양상추와 토마토를 키워. 그녀는 그것이 쉽다고 말했어.
M: 글쎄, 내 아파트는 작아서 그것들을 둘 곳이 없을 거야.
W: 그녀는 발코니에서 재배해. 내 생각엔 시도해볼 만한 것 같아.

Q: 대화에서 여자는 주로 무엇을 하려고 하는가?

(a) 유전자 변형이 왜 나쁜지 설명하기
(b) 남자에게 유기농 식품을 사도록 설득해보기
(c) 남자에게 텃밭을 만들라고 권하기
(d) 남자가 더 큰 아파트로 이사가야 한다고 제안하기

24

Listen to a conversation between a teacher and a student.

W: George, I expected more from you on the last exam.
M: I understand, Ms. Hill. I'm having a hard time focusing lately.
W: Is something bothering you?
M: Well, I'm overwhelmed from the stress I encounter outside of school.
W: Sorry to hear that, but your academic performance is suffering.
M: I know. I have to keep up with my studies better.

Q: Which is correct about the man according to the conversation?

(a) He is struggling to keep up with his classmates.
(b) He used to be the top student in class.
(c) His personal life hampers his scholastic achievement.
(d) His lack of preparation made him fail.

선생님과 학생 간의 대화를 들으시오.

W: George, 난 지난 시험에서 네가 더 잘할 거라고 기대했단다.
M: 알아요, Ms. Hill. 제가 요즘 집중하는 데 어려움을 겪고 있어서요.
W: 무슨 괴로운 일이라도 있니?
M: 음, 학교 밖에서 받는 스트레스 때문에 어쩔 줄 모르겠어요.
W: 그 말을 들으니 안됐구나, 하지만 학업 성적이 나빠지고 있잖니.
M: 알아요. 제 학업에 뒤쳐지지 않도록 더 노력해야겠죠.

Q: 대화에 따르면 남자에 대해 맞는 것은 무엇인가?

(a) 급우들에게 뒤쳐지지 않으려고 애쓰고 있다.
(b) 학급에서 최우등생이었다.
(c) 사생활이 학업 성적을 방해한다.
(d) 준비 부족으로 인해 시험에서 낙제했다.

25

Listen to two colleagues discussing a protest.

M: Can you believe Friday's protest was rescheduled?
W: The city government was completely justified in calling for its postponement.
M: But so many civic groups were eager with anticipation.
W: I know. I heard there were substantiated reports of a security breach, though.
M: I doubt that. The government just overreacted to news reports.
W: Maybe they know something we don't.

Q: Which is correct according to the conversation?

(a) The man learned of the cancellation from the news.
(b) The woman questions the government's response.
(c) The man considers the delay within reason.
(d) The woman concurs with the protest's postponement.

두 동료가 시위에 관해 이야기하는 것을 들으시오.

M: 금요일 시위 일정이 바뀌었다는 게 믿겨져요?
W: 시 정부가 그것의 연기를 요구한 것은 전적으로 당연했어요.
M: 하지만 정말 많은 시민 단체들이 몹시 기대에 차 있다구요.
W: 알아요. 하지만 치안상의 허점에 대한 확실한 보도들이 있었다고 들었어요.
M: 글쎄요. 그냥 정부가 뉴스 보도에 과도하게 반응했던 거예요.
W: 어쩌면 그들은 우리가 모르는 뭔가를 알고 있나 보죠.

Q: 대화에 따르면 맞는 것은 무엇인가?

(a) 남자는 뉴스에서 취소에 대해 들었다.
(b) 여자는 정부의 반응에 이의를 제기하고 있다.
(c) 남자는 연기가 합당하다고 생각하고 있다.
(d) 여자는 시위의 연기에 찬성한다.

26

Listen to a conversation about ceramics lessons.

W: I'm mulling over taking ceramics lessons this month.
M: There's this place offering them downtown called Fire It Up.
W: That doesn't ring a bell.
M: It just opened, but I hear the instructors are great.
W: Are you familiar with their rates or lesson schedule?
M: I'll give you their street address so you can stop by and ask.

Q: Which is correct according to the conversation?

(a) The woman has enrolled in ceramics classes.
(b) The woman is familiar with the new institute.
(c) The man has worked with the ceramics instructors.
(d) The man suggests inquiring in person.

도자기 강좌에 관한 대화를 들으시오.
W: 이번 달에 도자기 강좌를 들을까 생각 중이야.
M: 시내에 그런 강좌를 제공하는 Fire It Up이라는 곳이 있어.
W: 들어본 적이 없는 것 같은데.
M: 얼마 전에 연 곳인데, 강사들이 대단하다고 들었어.
W: 그들의 강습료나 강습 시간에 대해서도 잘 알고 있니?
M: 네가 한번 들러서 물어볼 수 있게 주소를 알려줄게.

Q: 대화에 따르면 맞는 것은 무엇인가?
(a) 여자는 도자기 강좌에 등록했다.
(b) 여자는 새로운 학원을 잘 알고 있다.
(c) 남자는 도자기 강사들과 일해본 적 있다.
(d) 남자는 직접 문의할 것을 제안하고 있다.

27

Listen to a conversation between two acquaintances.

M: The portion sizes and the presentation of the entrées were splendid, don't you think?
W: Yes, everything was fantastic.
M: How about heading out for an after-dinner drink?
W: That sounds nice, but I'm afraid it's getting quite late.
M: Is it all right if I escort you home, then?
W: I'd be grateful if you did.

Q: Which is correct about the man and woman according to the conversation?

(a) They were satisfied with the cuisine.
(b) They decided to order some beverages.
(c) They are both obliged to return home soon.
(d) They will return to their shared home.

두 지인 간의 대화를 들으시오.
M: 메인 요리의 1인분 양과 상차림이 굉장했어, 그렇게 생각하지 않아?
W: 응, 모든 것이 환상적이었어.
M: 후식으로 한잔하러 가는 건 어때?
W: 좋긴 한데, 시간이 꽤 늦어지고 있어서 말이야.
M: 그럼, 내가 집까지 바래다주면 괜찮지?
W: 그래주면 고맙지.

Q: 대화에 따르면 남자와 여자에 대해 맞는 것은 무엇인가?
(a) 요리에 만족했다.
(b) 음료수를 시키기로 했다.
(c) 둘 다 곧 집으로 돌아가야 한다.
(d) 그들이 함께 사는 집으로 돌아갈 것이다.

28

Listen to a conversation between two friends.

W: What was your take on the comedian?
M: I actually had to prevent myself from dozing off.
W: Really? I thought his jokes were hilarious.
M: I feel like he just coasted through his performance.
W: That's true of most entertainers. At least he had flair.
M: There are far more compelling comedy shows on TV.

Q: Which is correct according to the conversation?

(a) The man nodded off during the performance.
(b) The man considered the show tedious.
(c) The woman thinks the jokes were off-color.
(d) The woman knows entertainers with more talent.

두 친구 간의 대화를 들으시오.
W: 그 코미디언에 대한 네 느낌은 어땠어?
M: 실은 졸린 걸 참아야 했어.
W: 정말? 나는 그의 농담이 엄청 재미있다고 생각했는데.
M: 난 그가 공연을 그냥 설렁설렁 하는 것처럼 느꼈어.
W: 그건 대부분의 연예인들도 마찬가지야. 적어도 그는 타고난 재능은 있었어.
M: TV에는 훨씬 더 흡인력 있는 코미디 쇼들도 있어.

Q: 대화에 따르면 맞는 것은 무엇인가?
(a) 남자는 공연 중에 깜빡 졸았다.
(b) 남자는 쇼가 따분하다고 생각했다.
(c) 여자는 쇼의 농담이 상스럽다고 생각한다.
(d) 여자는 더 많은 재능이 있는 연예인들을 알고 있다.

29

Listen to a conversation at a tutoring lesson.

M: Thanks for tutoring me! I got an A minus on my chemistry test.
W: No problem. That's why you hired me.

M: You know, I've also been struggling in physics and math.
W: I could lend you a hand if you need it.
M: Really? I'd pay you more.
W: Sure. I'll pencil in some additional hours.

Q: What can be inferred about the woman from the conversation?

(a) She works part-time as a tutor.
(b) She teaches several subjects.
(c) She graded some of the man's tests.
(d) She needs to buy some supplies.

과외 수업에서의 대화를 들으시오.
M: 저를 개인 교습해주셔서 감사합니다! 화학 시험에서 A 마이너스를 받았어요.
W: 천만에. 그게 바로 네가 나를 고용한 이유인걸.
M: 저기, 제가 물리학과 수학에서도 어려움을 겪고 있어요.
W: 만약 네가 필요하다면 도움을 줄 수 있어.
M: 진짜요? 더 지불할게요.
W: 그래. 일단 추가적인 시간을 예정에 넣어 둘게.

Q: 대화에서 여자에 대해 추론할 수 있는 것은 무엇인가?
(a) 개인 지도 교사로서 파트타임으로 일한다.
(b) 여러 과목을 가르친다.
(c) 남자의 시험 일부의 성적을 매겼다.
(d) 몇몇 물품을 사야 한다.

30

Listen to a conversation between a police officer and a driver.

W: License and registration, please.
M: What seems to be the problem, officer?
W: Not to worry. This is a routine check.
M: I thought maybe I had broken a traffic rule.
W: No, no moving violation. Just making sure drivers are registered and in compliance.
M: OK, I'm just not accustomed to being pulled over.

Q: What can be inferred about the man from the conversation?

(a) He does not often receive traffic citations.
(b) He unintentionally violated a traffic rule.
(c) He is not used to seeing police on patrol.
(d) He has never been arrested before.

경찰관과 운전자 간의 대화를 들으시오.
W: 운전 면허증과 자동차 등록증 좀 보여주십시오.
M: 무엇이 문제이죠, 경찰관님?
W: 걱정 안 하셔도 됩니다. 이건 정기 검문입니다.
M: 제가 교통 법규를 어긴 줄 알았어요.
W: 아뇨, 주행 중 교통 위반은 아닙니다. 단지 운전자들이 등록되어 있는지와 법규를 준수하고 있는지 알아보는 것입니다.
M: 알겠습니다, 저는 그저 불러 세워지는 것에 익숙하지 않아서요.

Q: 대화에서 남자에 대해 추론할 수 있는 것은 무엇인가?
(a) 교통 위반 딱지를 자주 떼이지 않는다.
(b) 자기도 모르는 사이에 교통 법규를 어겼다.
(c) 순찰 중인 경찰을 보는 것에 익숙하지 않다.
(d) 전에 한 번도 체포된 적이 없다.

Part IV

31

What I'd like to discuss next is the Voynich manuscript. This enigmatic 16th-century illuminated text contains ciphers written in an unidentified script. Linguists and cryptographers are split on whether its contents have esoteric meaning, but many of the included diagrams appear to portray the formulation of medicinal compounds and principles of alchemy. An aura of secrecy continues to surround this work, since it has yet to be deciphered and its real author remains anonymous.

Q: What is the main topic of the lecture?

(a) The implications of the Voynich manuscript
(b) The mystique associated with a document
(c) The vain attempts to decode an archaic text
(d) The linguistic connotations of the Voynich manuscript

다음으로 논의하고 싶은 것은 Voynich 필사본입니다. 이 수수께끼 같은 16세기 채색 필사본은 확인되지 않은 문자로 쓰여진 암호들을 포함하고 있습니다. 언어학자들과 암호 사용자들은 그 내용에 선택된 소수만이 아는 의미가 있는지에 대해 의견이 갈리지만, 포함된 많은 그림들은 약용 혼합물들의 공식과 연금술의 원리를 묘사하고 있는 것으로 보입니다. 아직 판독되지 못했으며 실제 작가도 미상으로 남아 있어, 비밀스러운 기운이 계속 이 작품을 감싸고 있습니다.

Q: 강의의 주제는 무엇인가?
(a) Voynich 필사본이 암시하는 내용
(b) 한 문서에 관련된 불가사의
(c) 고대 원고를 해석하려는 헛된 노력
(d) Voynich 필사본의 언어적 함축

32

Do you want to learn the rules of the road but don't want to sacrifice a month's worth of nights or weekends? Then enroll at SmartDrive. We use an accelerated instructional method approved by the National Drivers' Alliance, or NDA, that will allow you to gain confidence behind the wheel in less than two weeks. Sign up now and take advantage of the promotions we've lined up on discounted insurance premiums.

Q: What is the main point of the advertisement?

(a) SmartDrive trains drivers with prior experience.
(b) The NDA considers SmartDrive the top academy.
(c) SmartDrive is meant for busy people.
(d) SmartDrive offers students low-cost insurance.

교통 규칙에 대해 배우고는 싶지만 한 달이나 되는 밤이나 주말을 희생하시고 싶지는 않으십니까? 그렇다면 SmartDrive에 등록하십시오. 저희는 전국 운전자 연합, 즉 NDA로부터 인가받은 속성 교습법을 사용하여 2주 내에 자신 있게 운전할 수 있도록 가르쳐 드립니다. 지금 등록하시고 판촉으로 제공해 드리는 할인된 보험료 혜택을 누리십시오.

Q: 광고의 요지는 무엇인가?

(a) SmartDrive는 운전 경험이 있는 운전자들을 교육시킨다.
(b) NDA는 SmartDrive를 최고의 교육 기관이라고 여긴다.
(c) SmartDrive는 바쁜 사람들을 위한 것이다.
(d) SmartDrive는 수강생들에게 저렴한 보험을 제공한다.

33

The scientific community postulates that the known universe is composed predominantly of dark matter. But the more controversial question is what exactly constitutes dark matter. While we've yet to fully fathom it, we are cognizant of what it is not. It doesn't resemble prototypical matter, which emits radiation or responds to electromagnetic forces. The lack of these attributes makes it difficult to spot dark matter, but we know it exists because of the enormous gravitational pull it exerts on everything else. It's really peculiar.

Q: Which is correct about dark matter according to the talk?

(a) Scientists are on the verge of fully understanding it.
(b) Its presence cannot be confirmed absolutely.
(c) It is resistant to the effects of electromagnetism.
(d) The gravity it produces causes the universe to contract.

과학계는 알려진 우주가 대부분 암흑 물질로 이루어져 있다고 가정합니다. 그러나 더 논란을 불러일으키는 질문은 정확히 무엇이 암흑 물질을 구성하는가입니다. 아직 완전히 이해하지는 못했지만, 우리는 그것이 무엇이 아닌지는 인지하고 있습니다. 그것은 방사선을 방출하거나 전자기력에 반응하는 원형 물질과는 비슷하지 않습니다. 이러한 특성들의 부재는 암흑 물질을 알아내는 것을 어렵게 하지만, 우리는 그것이 다른 모든 것에 가하는 거대한 중력 때문에 이 암흑 물질이 존재한다는 것을 압니다. 그것은 매우 독특합니다.

Q: 강의에 따르면 암흑 물질에 대해 맞는 것은 무엇인가?

(a) 과학자들은 그것을 완전히 이해하기 직전에 있다.
(b) 그것의 존재는 확실하게 확인될 수 없다.
(c) 그것은 전자기의 영향에 저항력이 있다.
(d) 그것이 만들어내는 중력은 우주의 수축을 야기한다.

34

My lecture is about attaining naturalized citizenship abroad. Foreign nationals can become eligible for Japanese citizenship after five years if they renounce their original nationality. Ireland requires the same length of stay but without demanding renunciation. Meanwhile, the Dominican Republic offers dual citizenship to foreign investors in as little as two years. Denmark, on the other hand, doesn't allow dual citizenship and only naturalizes foreign residents who stay a minimum of nine years. Canada isn't as strict, as citizenship can be acquired after a three-year stay.

Q: When can a foreign resident become a citizen of Ireland?

(a) After two years
(b) After three years
(c) After five years
(d) After nine years

제 강의는 해외에서 귀화 시민권을 취득하는 것에 관한 내용입니다. 외국 국적자들은 그들의 본래 국적을 포기하면 5년 후에 일본 시민권에 대한 자격을 얻을 수 있습니다. 아일랜드 역시 동일한 체류 기간을 요하지만 국적 포기를 요구하지는 않습니다. 한편, 도미니카 공화국은 외국인 투자자들에게 2년 만에 이중 국적을 제공합니다. 반면, 덴마크는 이중 국적을 허용하지 않고 최소 9년 동안 체류한 외국인 거주자들만 귀화시켜줍니다. 캐나다는 그만큼 엄격하지 않은데, 3년의 체류 이후에 시민권이 취득될 수 있습니다.

Q: 외국인 거주자는 언제 아일랜드의 시민이 될 수 있는가?

(a) 2년 후에
(b) 3년 후에
(c) 5년 후에
(d) 9년 후에

35

In local business news, restaurateur Katherine Ross announced that preparations are in motion to increase the reach of her famous smoked ribs franchise from coast to coast. After opening her 10th restaurant in Oklahoma, Ross decided to collaborate with private financier Jake Goldberg to open outlets in other regions of the country. Given Goldberg's track record of setting up successful restaurant chains, the chance to work together was one Ross couldn't resist.

Q: Why did Katherine Ross choose to work with Jake Goldberg?

(a) He owns a popular smoked rib franchise.
(b) His restaurant operations are on a national scale.
(c) His business has been successful in

Oklahoma.
(d) He has launched profitable dining establishments.

지역 비즈니스 뉴스에서, 식당 경영자 Katherine Ross는 그녀의 유명한 훈제 갈비 체인점을 전국적으로 늘릴 준비가 진행 중이라고 발표했습니다. 오클라호마 주에 그녀의 열 번째 식당을 개업한 뒤, Ross는 개인 자본가 Jake Goldberg와 제휴하여 국내 다른 지역에 직판점을 열기로 결정했습니다. 성공적인 레스토랑 체인점들을 개설한 Goldberg의 실적을 감안하면, 함께 일할 이 기회는 Ross가 반대할 수 없는 것이었습니다.

Q: Katherine Ross는 왜 Jake Goldberg와 함께 일하기로 결정했는가?
(a) 그는 한 인기 있는 훈제 갈비 체인점을 소유하고 있다.
(b) 그의 레스토랑 사업은 전국적인 규모이다.
(c) 그의 사업은 오클라호마 주에서 성공적이었다.
(d) 그는 수익성이 좋은 식당들을 열어왔다.

36

Fellow residents, don't you find it odd that a dysentery outbreak has coincided with the ongoing construction projects in our municipality? This development has produced jobs for us, yes, but it's also behind the infections. Surely, our children's well-being comes first, and so we must act on their behalf. My proposal is to file a petition with the mayor to put a temporary halt on development. If our elected leader will not take heed of our plight, then we will bring the matter to the judiciary.

Q: Which statement would the speaker most likely agree with?
(a) Construction companies violated municipal laws.
(b) A ban on development is unlikely to be issued.
(c) Dysentery was uncommon prior to the building projects.
(d) The mayor should be blamed for the health problems.

주민 여러분, 우리 지방 자치체에서 이질 발생이 진행 중인 건설 프로젝트와 동시에 일어나고 있는 것이 이상하다고 생각하지 않으십니까? 이 개발은 우리에게 일자리를 창출해 주었습니다, 맞습니다, 하지만 그것은 전염병의 배후에 있기도 합니다. 분명, 우리 아이들의 건강이 최우선이기 때문에, 우리는 그들을 위해서 행동을 취해야 합니다. 저의 제안은 개발을 일시적으로 중단시켜 달라는 진정서를 시장에게 제출하자는 것입니다. 우리가 선출한 대표가 우리의 어려움에 귀를 기울이지 않는다면, 우리는 그 문제를 사법부로 가져갈 것입니다.

Q: 화자는 어느 진술에 가장 동의할 것 같은가?
(a) 건설 회사들은 지방 자치법을 위반했다.
(b) 개발 사업에 대한 금지는 내려질 것 같지 않다.
(c) 건축 프로젝트 전에는 이질이 드물었다.
(d) 시장이 보건 문제에 대한 책임을 져야 한다.

Part V

37~38

Hello, Ms. Sanborn. I am calling from Metrowide Realty to let you know that I've found an office space you may be interested in. It's located on the 15th floor of Spectrum Tower, a mixed-use building containing both residences and commercial units on the corner of Davis and Main. The unit in question has only recently been vacated. I checked it out just now, and everything is in working order. It's in fairly decent condition, and all it really needs is a fresh coat of paint and new furnishings. More importantly, the property is in a highly desirable area. That means it's probably going to go quickly. I therefore urge you to act fast. Call me as soon as you can so I can schedule a visit for us right away. The keys are always available since a manager is on-site 24 hours a day. In the meantime, I'll e-mail you details about the property.

37. Q: Which is correct about the speaker?
(a) He is interested in applying for a job offered by Ms. Sanborn.
(b) He wants to meet on the corner of Davis and Main.
(c) He visited an office space before making the call.
(d) He has already obtained the keys to an apartment.

38. Q: Why is Ms. Sanborn urged to return the call immediately?
(a) A space will need extensive renovations.
(b) A property may not be available for long.
(c) A contract must be signed before a deadline.
(d) A building manager is waiting for a response.

안녕하세요, Ms. Sanborn. 당신이 관심 있으실 만한 사무실 공간을 찾았음을 알려 드리고자 Metrowide 부동산에서 전화 드립니다. 그곳은 Spectrum Tower의 15층에 위치하고 있으며, Davis와 Main 가의 모퉁이에 있는 주거 및 상업 공간을 모두 갖춘 복합 용도 건물입니다. 논의되고 있는 이 공간은 최근에 막 비워졌습니다. 저는 방금 전에 그곳을 점검했으며, 모든 것이 정상적으로 작동하고 있습니다. 이곳은 상당히 괜찮은 상태이고, 필요한 것은 새로운 페인트칠과 새로운 가구 설치 정도입니다. 더 중요한 것은, 이 건물이 매우 탐나는 지역에 있다는 것입니다. 이는 이곳이 아마도 금방 팔릴 것임을 의미합니다. 따라서 서두르시기를 강력히 권합니다. 바로 저희의 방문 일정을 잡을 수 있도록 가능한 한 빨리 제게 전화해주시기 바랍니다. 열쇠는 관리인이 매일 24시간 현장에 있으므로 항상 사용 가능합니다. 그 사이에, 건물에 대한 세부 사항을 이메일로 보내드리겠습니다.

37. Q: 화자에 대해 맞는 것은 무엇인가?
(a) Ms. Sanborn이 제안한 일자리에 지원하는 데 관심이 있다.

(b) Davis와 Main 가의 모퉁이에서 만나기를 원한다.
(c) 전화를 하기 전에 사무실 공간을 방문했다.
(d) 이미 아파트 열쇠를 구했다.

38. Q: 왜 Ms. Sanborn은 즉시 전화 회신하도록 권고받는가?
(a) 장소가 대규모의 수리를 필요로 할 것이다.
(b) 건물이 구매 가능하도록 오래 남아 있지 않을 것이다.
(c) 계약서가 마감 기한 이전에 서명되어야 한다.
(d) 건물 관리인이 답변을 기다리고 있다.

39~40

A lot of astronomers would like to send astronauts on interplanetary and interstellar missions to learn more about the nature of the universe. However, there are many hurdles preventing such voyages from being carried out. The most significant of these is the lack of a suitable fuel to power vessels to the furthest reaches of the solar system and beyond. Currently, liquid hydrogen is used in most rockets as it burns with efficiency. However, this fuel must be kept at the intensely low temperature of minus 423 degrees Fahrenheit in order to prevent it from expanding, which could cause the fuel tank to explode. Meanwhile, the coldness of liquid hydrogen poses other issues. Metal exposed to it, for instance, can become brittle and result in the fuel leaking out. Therefore, while NASA considers the application of liquid hydrogen to be one of its most important technical accomplishments, the risks associated with it are too great to use in space exploration. Instead, long-range flights will require a much more stable fuel source that can handle extreme environments.

39. Q: What is the speaker mainly talking about?
(a) The rapid development of fuel storage technology
(b) The consequences of continuing to use traditional fuels
(c) The types of vessels needed for deep space travel
(d) The primary obstacle standing in the way of space travel

40. Q: What can be inferred from the talk?
(a) The stability of liquid hydrogen is affected by temperature changes.
(b) Fuel tanks used in rockets are in need of improvement.
(c) NASA is concealing the drawbacks of using liquid hydrogen.
(d) Scientists are working on developing cheaper fuels.

많은 천문학자들은 우주의 본질에 대해 더 많이 알기 위해 우주 비행사들을 행성 간, 항성 간 우주 비행에 보내고 싶어 합니다. 그러나, 이러한 탐험이 이행되는 것을 막는 많은 장애물들이 있습니다. 이 중 가장 중대한 것은 우주선을 태양계의 가장 먼 구간과 그 이상으로 나아가게 하기에 적합한 연료의 부재입니다. 현재는, 액체 수소가 효율적으로 소비되므로 대부분의 로켓에 사용됩니다. 그러나, 이 연료는 팽창하는 것을 방지하기 위해 화씨 영하 423도의 극히 낮은 온도로 유지되어야 하는데, 연료의 팽창은 연료 탱크가 폭발하게 할 수도 있습니다. 한편, 액체 수소의 냉기는 또 다른 문제를 야기합니다. 예를 들어, 그것에 노출된 금속은 부서지기 쉬워질 수 있으며 연료가 유출되는 결과를 낳을 수 있습니다. 따라서, NASA는 액체 수소의 활용을 자사의 가장 중요한 기술적 업적 중 하나로 여기지만, 이와 관련된 위험성은 우주 탐험에 이용하기에는 너무 큽니다. 대신에, 장거리 비행은 극심한 환경을 견딜 수 있는 훨씬 더 안정적인 연료원을 필요로 할 것입니다.

39. Q: 화자가 주로 무엇을 이야기하고 있는가?
(a) 연료 보관 기술의 급속한 발전
(b) 전통적인 연료를 계속 사용하는 것의 결과
(c) 먼 우주 여행에 필요한 우주선의 종류
(d) 우주 여행에 방해가 되는 주요 장애물

40. Q: 담화에서 추론할 수 있는 것은 무엇인가?
(a) 액체 수소의 안정성은 온도 변화에 영향받는다.
(b) 로켓에 사용되는 연료 탱크는 개선이 필요하다.
(c) NASA는 액체 수소를 사용하는 것의 단점을 감추고 있다.
(d) 과학자들은 더 저렴한 연료를 개발하는 중이다.

VOCABULARY

Part I

1 A: 조심해요! 제 드레스에 와인을 쏟을 뻔했잖아요!
   B: 죄송합니다. 제가 중심을 잃었어요.

2 A: 난 Brandon만큼 다재다능한 연기자를 본 적이 없어.
   B: 맞아, 그는 배우, 코미디언, 가수가 모두 하나로 합쳐진 사람이야.

3 A: 제가 주간 회의를 매주 금요일로 옮겼어요.
   B: 괜찮아요. 그 시간이 제게도 좋습니다.

4 A: 요즘 스팸 메일들을 정말 많이 받아.
   B: 짜증 나겠구나. 그냥 무시해 버려.

5 A: 따님이 좋은 성적을 받고 있다고 들었어요.
   B: 네. 과외 선생님을 고용한 것이 성과를 거뒀어요.

6 A: Pam이 더위에 지쳐서 의식을 잃었다고 들었어.
   B: 응, 그녀는 잠깐 의식을 잃었었어.

7 A: 왜 제가 독감 예방 주사를 맞아야 하죠?
   B: 바이러스에 면역이 되도록 해주거든요.

8 A: 이사회가 프로젝트에 대한 우리의 재정 지원 요청을 승인하면 좋겠어요.
   B: 좋은 소식이 있어요. 이사회가 벌써 그 요청을 승인하는 데 동의했어요.

9 A: 난 Sally의 옷에 대해 Helen이 했던 말이 상당히 무례했다고 생각해.
   B: 아마 말이 잘못 나온 걸 거야. 난 그녀가 악의는 없었다고 확신해.

10 A: 마일리지 카드의 문제점은 한 항공사만 이용하도록 한다는 거야.
   B: 사실, 항공사의 제휴사 항공편을 이용할 때도 마일리지를 쌓을 수 있어.

Part II

11 파산 신청을 피하기 위해 회사가 검토하고 있는 대안들이 회의에서 논의될 것이다.

12 그 호텔은 이용률을 높이기 위한 노력으로 새로운 홍보 활동을 시작했다.

13 본사의 경영진은 신규 지사의 잠재적인 문제점들을 정확히 찾아내기 위해 컨설턴트를 고용했다.

14 Dr. Richland는 여러 민간 단체들로부터 그의 의료 연구를 위한 지원금을 받았다.

15 수은 온도계는 부적절하게 처리되면 수원을 오염시키기 때문에 금지되어야 한다.

16 대통령은 사회, 정치, 경제 이슈들의 최근 정황을 잘 알아두기 위해 주요 신문과 잡지들을 읽는다.

17 회원들은 그 단체에서 진행 중인 프로젝트를 지원하기 위해 재정적으로 기여하도록 요청된다.

18 이 회사는 다양성을 수용하여 개인의 민족성, 성별, 또는 성 정체성에 상관없이 사람을 고용한다.

19 사회가 점점 더 편견이 없어지고 있기 때문에, 한때 소수자들을 일컫기 위해 사용되었던 많은 단어들이 이제는 경멸적인 의미로 여겨진다.

20 타인과 관계를 맺는 데 어려움을 겪고 사회로부터 소외된 사람들은 대체로 사회적인 접촉에서 움츠리는 경향이 있다.

21 용의자는 그가 차량을 훔쳤음을 인정하도록 경찰로부터 강요를 당했다고 주장한다.

22 출산할 준비가 되면, 임산부는 고통을 덜기 위해 국부 마취제를 요구할 수 있다.

23 몇 세기 동안, 천문학자들은 다른 행성에 생명체가 존재하는 것에 대해 숙고해왔다.

24 노르웨이의 전설에서, 발키리들은 죽은 전사들 중 가장 용감한 전사들을 선택하기 위해 오딘 신이 보낸 처녀들이었다.

25 2013년 스페셜 올림픽 동안 7만 명 이상의 사람들이 한국의 평창 올림픽 경기장에 모였다.

26 부모는 자녀가 투정을 부릴 때 지나친 관심을 보여서는 안 되는데 이는 부정적인 행동을 강화시킬 뿐이기 때문이다.

27 그 외교관은 관료들을 교묘히 다뤄 국경을 넘은 배낭여행객들을 석방시키게끔 하기 위해 협상 기술을 사용했다.

28 소설 끝 부분에서의 마지막 대립 이후, 등장인물들의 운명은 대단원에서 밝혀졌다.

29 그 권투 선수의 우승은 그가 시합 전에 금지된 약물을 복용하였다는 혐의가 확인되자 취소되었다.

30 많은 무고한 민간인들이 전쟁 기간 동안 체포되고 감금당했다.

GRAMMAR

Part I

1 A: 너 Todd Farmer의 신간 추리 소설 읽었어?
   B: 응, 그런데 내 기대에 훨씬 못 미쳤어.

2 A: Jennifer는 어디에 있어요? 그녀가 오늘 집회를 이끌기로 되어 있는데요.
   B: 그럼 안되는데요. 참석자 대부분이 그녀에게 정말 의존하고 있어요.

3 A: 당신의 보고서는 어떻게 되고 있나요?
   B: 이 속도로는 마감 기한을 맞출 수 없을 것 같아서, 당신의 도움이 필요할 거예요.

4 A: 오늘 아침에 Mandy의 발표 봤어요?
   B: 아뇨, 회의가 있었어요. 놓쳐서 정말 유감이에요.

5 A: Joe가 그의 그 오랜 친구와 함께 사업을 운영하지 않던가?
   B: 맞아. 그와 Mark가 레스토랑을 공동 소유하고 있어.

6 A: 면접은 어땠던 것 같아?
   B: 괜찮았어, 그런데 내 미래의 전망에 대한 질문을 받았을 때 뭐라고 말해야 할지 모르겠더라.

7 A: 새 가구를 사는 건 너무 돈이 많이 들어.
   B: 내가 상태가 괜찮아 보이는데 버려진 소파 몇 개를 길에서 봤어.

8 A: 응급 처치 수업을 위해서 우리가 준비해야 할 것이 있니?
   B: 아니, 우리에게 필요한 모든 장비를 강사가 제공하기로 되어 있어.

9 A: 넌 댄스팀에 어떻게 들어갔어?
   B: 듣자하니, 그들이 지역 대회에서 내가 브레이크 댄싱을 하고 있던 걸 발견했나 보더라고.

10 A: 학생들이 이 과제에 열심히 임했어요.
   B: 맞아요, 그들이 그것에 최선을 다했다는 것을 분명히 알 수 있어요.

Part II

11 Jeremy는 새 일을 시작하기 전에, 특정 정보를 비밀로 유지할 것을 규정하는 비밀유지계약에 서명했다.

12 분석가들은 소비자들이 두 주스 중에서, 어느 쪽이든 더 건강에 좋은 것을 선호할 거라고 예측한다.

13 Mike Sullivan은 동쪽 해안에 휘몰아치는 허리케인을 생중계로 보도하고 있으며 지난 몇 시간 동안 그렇게 해왔다.

14 더 많은 양의 탄수화물이 포함된 식단은 건강에 부정적인 영향을 초래할지도 모른다.

15 챔피언 결정전에서 그들이 이기지 못했기 때문에, 그 팀은 분명히 오늘 우울한 분위기일 것이다.

16 마케팅팀은 할인 판매로 고객을 유치하려는 그들의 시도가 좋지 않은 생각이었다는 것을 깨달았다.

17 더욱 기민한 정신을 유지하기 위해, 컴퓨터 화면 앞에서 하루를 보내는 사람들은 하룻밤에 최소 7시간의 수면을 취해야 한다.

18 꾸준한 추세로 높아지는 해양 산성도는 그 분야의 수많은 전문가들에게 주목을 받아왔다.

19 그 작가들은 마감 시간 5분 전이 되어서야 기사를 완성했다.

20 CTG 전기 회사는 국가 안전 규정에 따라 월례 공장 시찰을 실시할 것이다.

21 엄밀히 따지면 회사의 동업자는 아니지만, Roger Habbs는 그의 후한 기부 덕분에 동업자로 오랫동안 인정받아왔다.

22 인도 주차가 불법일지라도, 사람들은 급할 때는 여전히 그렇게 한다.

23 세인트루이스 경찰대의 신임 경찰로서, Henry는 그의 업무 분야에서 예상된 것보다 조금 더 많은 위험에 부딪히게 되었다.

24 점점 더 경쟁이 치열해지는 시장에서 성공하려면, 오늘날의 선두 기업들은 효과적인 광고를 통해 경쟁사와의 차별화를 꾀해야 한다.

25 뉴질랜드의 동물학자 4명은 몇 달 전에 그 곤충을 처음 본 이래로 그들이 찾아다녔던 희귀종 곤충의 보금자리 위치를 찾아냈다.

Part III

26 (a) A: 우리 주문이 어떻게 처리되었는지 알아보게 상점에 전화줄래요?
(b) B: 벌써 했어요. 거기서 물품을 금방 배송해 주겠다고 약속했어요.
(c) A: 무엇 때문에 이렇게 오래 걸리는 거죠? 물품은 몇 시간 전에 도착했어야 했어요.
(d) B: 음, 거기서는 배송이 사실 내일로 예정되어 있다고 알고 있더군요.

27 (a) A: 이봐, Jackson. 우리 대학교에서 이번 여름에 제공하는 봉사 활동 프로그램에 대해서 들었니?
(b) B: 응, 캄보디아에서 하는 거라고 들었어. 안정상의 문제 때문에, 예상했던 것보다 지원자들이 많이 없대.
(c) A: 휴가를 포기하려는 지원자들을 찾는 것도 쉽지 않다고 생각해.
(d) B: 맞아. 사실 그게 내가 신청을 망설이는 한 가지 이유야.

28 (a) 영양은 가느다란 사지, 작고 갈라진 발굽, 뾰족한 통각을 가진 초식 포유동물이다. (b) 이 우아한 동물은 90종으로 이루어져 있으며, 그 중 다수는 아프리카에서 볼 수 있다. (c) 영양이 사슴처럼 생겼기 때문에, 많은 사람들은 그 둘이 매우 밀접하게 관련되어 있다고 생각할지 모른다. (d) 그러나, 영양은 솟과에 속하는 것으로 사슴이 속한 사슴과에 속하지 않는다.

29 (a) 천문학자들은 유럽의 우주 탐사 로켓인 '필레 착륙선'이 지구로 다시 정보를 전송해오기 시작해서 기뻐하고 있다. (b) 그 탐사선은 혜성에 착륙했으나 2014년 11월에 동력이 바닥났다. (c) 혜성의 환경 조건이 변화되자 그 탐사선은 다시 작동하여, 2015년 6월 13일에 데이터 패킷을 보내기 시작했다. (d) 과학자들은 탐사선에 축적되어온 모든 저장된 데이터를 복구할 수 있기를 바라고 있다.

30 (a) 최근에, 3차원 형태의 입체 과학 기술이 전자 회사, 특히 오락 산업을 중심으로 한 회사들 사이에서 부활하고 있다. (b) 영화, TV, 그리고 그외 분야의 전문가들은 시각 매체를 경험하는 새롭고 획기적인 수단을 제공하기 위해 그 과학 기술을 활용하고 있다. (c) 사람들은 오락이 미래에 어떤 특성을 제공하기를 기대하는지 설문 조사를 받았을 때, 대부분이 보다 높은 몰입도를 선택했다. (d) 그 결과, 기업들은 더 많은 자극을 제공하기 위해 3차원 형태의 입체 과학 기술을 이용하여 이용자들을 그러한 미래로 데려가고자 힘쓰고 있다.

READING COMPREHENSION

Part I

1 연구자들은 돌묵상어가 계절마다 서식하는 깊이를 바꾼다는 것을 항상 알고 있었다. 그러나, 전문가들을 어리둥절하게 했던 점은 겨울 동안 일부 돌묵상어들이 완전히 자취를 감춰버리는 것이었다. 좀 더 자세히 알기 위해 해양 생물학자들은 최첨단 추적 장치를 사용하여 몇몇 상어들을 감시했다. 이 연구를 통해 대부분의 상어들이 남미 부근의 열대 바다로 이동했다는 사실이 밝혀졌다. 연구자들은 이 발견 덕분에 돌묵상어가 _____ 이유를 찾는 데 도움이 될 수 있을 것이라고 생각한다.

(a) 주기적으로 이동하려고 하는
(b) 따뜻한 열대 바다를 피하는
(c) 추적 장치로 탐지되지 않는
(d) 해수면 근처에 머무르는

2 극한 날씨에 운전을 할 때, 교통 법규를 따르는 것은 매우 중요하다. 날씨가 궂으면 편법을 사용하여 목적지에 도달하고 싶어질 법하지만, 특히 길이 미끄럽거나 안개 때문에 앞이 잘 보이지 않을 때, 지나치게 서두르다 보면 사고 가능성이 높아진다. 책임 의식 있는 운전자라면 궂은 날씨에도 침착해야 하고 불필요한 위험을 무릅쓰는 것을 삼가야 한다. 그러므로, _____ 노력하라.

(a) 험한 날씨에는 운전을 피하도록
(b) 제한 속도를 준수하여 주의하도록
(c) 미끄럽지 않은 길을 찾도록
(d) 승객의 안전을 보장하도록

3 대표적인 미국 가구 디자이너인 Charles와 Ray Eames의 재산 상속녀가 그들의 작품 경매에 제동을 걸었다. 이 분쟁은 Eames 부부가 생전에 그들 작품의 대다수를 위탁했던 Marilyn과 John Neuhart와의 관계에서 기인한 것이다. Eames 부부의 손녀이자 유산 집행인인 Lucia Eames는 Neuhart 부부에게 그 재산에 대한 영구적 소유권이 없으며, 그들이 그 디자이너들과의 관계를 악용하고 있다고 생각한다. Neuhart 부부는 _____ 는 암시에 동의하지 않으며, 그 예술품들을 박물관에 기증하겠다는 의지를 표명했다.

(a) 그들이 Eames 부부에게서 부당하게 이득을 보려 한다
(b) Charles와 Ray Eames가 그들의 결정을 승인하지 않았다
(c) Lucia Eames가 논란에 싸인 그 재산을 원래 소유했다
(d) 그들이 Eames 부부의 가족에게 그들의 소장품을 팔아야 한다

4 수십 년간, 의료 전문가들은 흡연자들이 담배의 해로운 영향 때문에 젊은 나이에 사망할 가능성이 더 높다고 주장해왔다. 이탈리아

도시 밀라노의 사례는 이 도시가 _____는 점에서 놀랍다. 사실, 밀라노 시민 2백만 명 가운데 13만 명은 75세 이상이다. 밀라노 시민의 상당 비율이 흡연자라는 점을 고려하면, 이 도시의 노령 인구가 많다는 사실은 특히 놀랍다.

(a) 비흡연 젊은이들의 수가 지나치게 많다
(b) 노년층에게 금연을 장려한다
(c) 이러한 가정과 상반되는 것으로 보인다
(d) 흡연 인구가 꽤 많다

5.
Diego에게,
나는 _____에 대한 찬사를 멈출 수 없어. 나와 나의 고문인 Anand 박사님이 하고 있는 최첨단 실험들은 분자 생물학에 상당한 영향을 미칠 거야. 비록 나는 주 60시간 근무하는 실습생에 불과하고 급여도 얼마 못 받지만, 우리 연구에 대한 열정은 이것을 보람 있게 해. 난 지금 주요 학술지에 우리 둘의 이름으로 제출할 학술 기사를 수정하고 있어. 사실, 난 그만 꾸물거리고 다시 타자를 쳐야 해. 건강히 잘 지내!
사랑을 담아,
Dora로부터

(a) 내 학술 연구 인턴십
(b) 대학 생물학 교수로서의 생활
(c) 내 연구팀의 실습생들
(d) 내가 지금 쓰고 있는 과학 학술지

6. 중견 광고 회사의 인사 책임자로서, 나는 대학에서 인문학이 죽었음을 개탄한다. 철학, 역사학, 논리학 같은 과목들은 내가 예비 직원들에게서 기대하는 기량들을 계발하는 데 정말 필수적이다. 이 과목들을 공부하는 학생들이 자신의 생각을 글로 제시할 때 필요로 하는 명료성과 정확성은 말할 것도 없고, 비판적 추론 능력은 어떤 사무 환경에서건 가장 중요하다. 요즘에는, 학생들이 _____ 4년의 학부 과정을 쉽게 넘길 수 있다.

(a) 상업에 필요한 과목들을 공부하면서
(b) 협력할 준비가 되지 않은 채
(c) 인문학 수업들에 허덕이며
(d) 지성을 충분히 계발하지 않고도

7. 전반적인 순이익이 감소했지만, Perfect Palette는 _____. 투자 무역부에서 표로 나타낸 판매 통계에 따르면 Perfect Palette는 지난해 구입된 전체 가정용 페인트 중 45퍼센트를 차지하여, 경쟁사를 앞질렀다. 업계 내부에서는 Perfect Palette의 탄탄한 매출액의 이유로 회사의 능수능란한 마케팅 기술과 제품의 향상된 내구성을 들었다. 이전 판매율 1위였던 Pigments 주식회사는 시장 점유율의 25퍼센트만을 차지하여, 올해 2위로 물러났다.

(a) 총 생산량을 두 배로 늘렸다
(b) 주주들을 위해 최대 매출액을 달성했다
(c) 시장 점유율 1위를 달성했다
(d) 친환경 페인트를 출시했다

8. 『은하수를 여행하는 히치하이커를 위한 안내서』 TV 시리즈는 최초의 인터넷 서비스 제공업체, 즉 ISP가 출현하기 3년 전인 1981년에 처음 방영되었다. 이 방송이 시작되었을 때, 인터넷은 _____. 이 히치하이커 쇼에서는 모든 주제에 대한 정보를 알려주는 '전자책'이 등장했는데, 오늘날 어디서나 접속 가능한 무선 인터넷 노트북 컴퓨터의 전조라고 볼 수 있다. 1990년대 초 웹 브라우저가 개발되면서 가정용 컴퓨터로 멀리 떨어진 서버에 있는 멀티미디어 콘텐츠에 접속하는 일이 마침내 실현 가능하게 되었지만, 소비자들의 인터넷 도입률이 상업적으로 중요해진 것은 10년이 지나서였다.

(a) 시장 점유율을 빼앗기 시작했다
(b) 처음에는 오락 매체로 떠올랐다
(c) 아직 대중의 인식에 침투하지 못했었다
(d) 컴퓨터 사용 능력을 지닌 이들이 자유롭게 이용할 수 있었다

9. 주 의회 의원 Yuri Yusuf는 뇌물 수수 건으로 부패 척결 대책 위원회에 의해 공식적으로 기소되었는데, 만일 유죄 판결을 받을 경우, 15년에서 20년 형을 받을 수 있습니다. 전해진 바에 의하면 그가 사업가 Gerry Reno에게 9만 달러를 받은 거래 행위가 자금 세탁 수사 중이던 감시팀의 테이프에 포착되었다고 합니다. 검사는 증거가 확보된 지 정확히 일주일 후에 기소했습니다. _____, 한 목격자는 Yusuf가 몇몇 다른 사건에서도 '돈다발 선물'을 받았다는 진술서를 제출했습니다.

(a) 그렇기는 하지만
(b) 결국
(c) 그럼에도 불구하고
(d) 게다가

10. 감각적인 요소들을 대비시키면 영화 장면에 극적인 인상을 보완할 수 있다. 예를 들어, 『대부』에서는 주인공이 자기 딸의 죽음에 괴로움으로 절규하는 순간에 소리가 갑자기 사라진다. 소리의 부재는 등장인물의 슬픔을 극대화하고 그의 고독을 상징적으로 보여주며, 이 심란한 인물을 가슴 아프게 표현한다. _____, 이 장면은 관객들에 미치는 영향을 증대시키는 깊이를 얻는다.

(a) 따라서
(b) 예를 들어
(c) 이와는 반대로
(d) 대신에

Part II

11. 미국 영화 산업의 '황금기'는 1927년부터 1950년대 말까지 지속되었으며, 이 기간 동안 영화에 관한 몇 가지 획기적인 사건들이 일어났다. (a) 최초의 '말하는' 영화 『재즈 싱어』는 1927년 개봉되어, 무성 영화 시대의 막을 내렸다. (b) 영화사들은 1927년 이후에 몇 편의 무성 영화를 제작했지만, 이 장르의 영화는 결국 점차적으로 사라졌다. (c) 『백설 공주와 일곱 난쟁이』는 1937년에 제작되어 첫 번째 만화 영화가 되었다. (d) 2년 후, 수익이 물가 상승률로 조정되었을 때 역대 가장 높은 수익을 거둔 영화인 『바람과 함께 사라지다』가 개봉되었다.

12. '성공담'이라는 개념은 보통 순전히 투지로만 금전적 성공을 이루는 가난한 이들에게 적용된다. (a) 하지만, 성공에 관해서라면 우리는 행운의 역할을 축소해서 말할 수 없다. (b) 역사는 행운이 부족해서, 그들의 투지에도 불구하고 가난에서 벗어나지 못한 사람들의 사례로 가득 차 있다. (c) 가난한 이들에게는 밝은 미래에 대한 신념이 부족한데, 그들은 다른 이들에 비해 그들의 사회적 지위를 높일 수 있는 기회를 훨씬 덜 인지한다. (d) 그러므로, 대부분의 일당 소득자들이 증명하듯이, 신의 섭리와 투지의 결합은 성공하는 데 필수적이다.

Part III

13
쇼핑할 시간이 없으신가요? Robertson의 VIP 서비스를 이용해 보세요!
Robertson의 VIP 서비스는 당신의 삶을 더 편안하게 하고 당신의 시간을 확보해드릴 것입니다.

간단히:
1. Pinehill Mall에 있는 저희 지점에 방문하세요.
2. 고객 서비스 카운터에 당신의 식료품 목록을 맡기세요.
3. 당신의 식료품이 픽업되고 결제될 준비가 되었다는 것을 알려주는 문자 메시지를 기다리세요.

모든 것이 당신을 위해 준비되게 할 수 있는데 왜 물품을 찾고 계산대에서 기다리느라 시간을 낭비하시나요? 이 서비스에 대해 자세히 알아보시려면, 오늘 Robertson을 방문하세요!

Q: 주로 광고되고 있는 것은 무엇인가?
(a) 상점의 자동화된 계산대
(b) VIP 고객들을 위한 특별 할인
(c) 쇼핑몰의 포장 배달 서비스
(d) 상점의 쇼핑 대행 시스템

14
다음 달 Comenius 대학 도서관에서 인기 소설들이 경매될 것입니다. 본 행사는 국립 독서 클럽의 현직 회장인 이 대학 졸업생 Ivan Tomka의 지휘하에 진행되고 있습니다. 이 기금 모금 활동의 수익금은 진행 중인 도서관 재단장에 쓰여질 것입니다. 경매 참가 방법에 대한 더 많은 정보를 원하시면, Moritz Hall에 있는 대학 정보 센터를 방문하거나 www.nbclub.com.sk에 접속하십시오.

Q: 다음 중 공고의 내용과 일치하는 것은?
(a) Ivan Tomka는 Comenius 대학의 회장 대행이다.
(b) 경매는 국립 독서 클럽의 후원을 받는다.
(c) 경매의 수익은 도서관을 보수하는 데 쓰일 것이다.
(d) 사람들은 웹 사이트를 통해 경매에 등록할 수 있다.

15
100미터 달리기 같은 경주에서는, 몇 가지 중요한 요소들이 도착 시간에 영향을 미친다. 가장 효율적으로 달리기 위해서는, 이상적인 보폭 길이가 확보되어야 하는데, 주자의 체격 분석을 통해 코치가 이를 결정할 수 있다. 덧붙여, 최대 속도를 유지하기 위해서, 주자들은 상체를 트랙과 수직이 되게 유지해야 하며 보폭과 리듬이 맞게 양팔을 앞뒤로 움직여야 한다. 마지막으로, 출발 신호에 대한 재빠른 반응은 다른 경쟁자들보다 앞서서 스타팅 블록에서 뛰쳐나가는 데 매우 중요하다.

Q: 지문의 주제는 무엇인가?
(a) 달리기에 가장 적합한 신체 유형
(b) 빨리 출발하기 위해 주자들이 사용하는 기술
(c) 단거리 선수들이 최고 성적을 내는 방법
(d) 코치들이 주자들의 보폭을 분석하는 방법

16
별의 경이로움
저희 시립 천문관의 주요 목표는 천문학의 경이로움을 대중에게 알리는 것입니다. 천문관의 둥근 반구형 천장은 별들과 행성들, 다른 천체들의 영상이 비춰지는 스크린으로 사용됩니다. 천문관은 어안 렌즈와 레이저 영사 설비가 장착된 최신형 최고급 디지털 영사기 시스템을 사용하여, 영상이 매우 선명합니다. 매일 열리는 스카이 쇼는 오후 1시에 시작해서 4시에 끝납니다. 스카이 쇼는 어린이와 어른 모두를 틀림없이 사로잡을 것입니다.

스카이 쇼에 대해 더 자세한 정보를 원하신다면, 저희 웹사이트인 www.cityplanetarium.org를 방문해주시기 바랍니다.

Q: 지문은 주로 무엇에 관한 내용인가?
(a) 다가오는 행사에 대한 시립 천문관의 일정
(b) 시립 천문관의 장비에 대한 예정된 업그레이드
(c) 시립 천문관에서 아이들을 위한 다양한 교육 활동
(d) 시립 천문관에서 이용 가능한 시설과 서비스

17
Mr. Gordon께,

Smock 패션 디자인 학교는 학생들의 혁신적인 창작품들을 전시하기 위한 패션쇼를 개최할 예정입니다. 행사는 7월 23일 목요일 오후 5시에 학교 강당에서 개최될 것입니다. 올해, 저희는 전시 중인 디자인을 비평해줄 학교 졸업생 몇 분을 초대하는 것이 도움이 되리라고 생각했으며, 위원회는 귀하를 비평가 중 한 분으로 모시고자 합니다. 저희 학생들이 기술을 연마할 수 있도록 도움을 베풀어 주시기 바랍니다.

진심을 담아,
Robin Jackson

Q: 초대장에 따르면 다음 중 패션쇼에 대한 내용과 일치하는 것은?
(a) 학교 졸업생들의 작품을 전시할 것이다.
(b) 졸업생들과 학생들이 만나도록 시도하고 있다.
(c) Mr. Gordon의 뛰어난 창작품들을 전시할 것이다.
(d) 주된 목표는 학생들에게 진로 기회를 연결해주는 것이다.

18
1970년대부터 1990년대까지, 대부분의 컴퓨터 데이터는 플로피 디스크에 저장되었다. 플로피 디스크는 1967년에 IBM에 의해 발명되었으며 1971년에 일반 대중이 사용할 수 있게 되었다. 그것은 1980년대에 광디스크가 도입될 때까지 가장 선진화된 휴대용 저장 매체로 남아 있었다. 레이저 기술은 광디스크 상에 정보를 부호화하기 위해 활용되므로, 그것은 플로피 디스크가 할 수 있는 것보다 수백 배 혹은 수천 배 더 많은 데이터를 저장할 수 있다. 광디스크 기술은 CD와 기록용 DVD와 같은 발명품들의 근간을 형성했고, 이는 그것을 기술의 진보에 있어 중요한 단계로 만들었다.

Q: 1971년에 무슨 일이 일어났는가?
(a) IBM이 혁신적인 새로운 컴퓨터 시스템을 개발하기 시작했다.
(b) 한 휴대용 저장 장치가 널리 구매 가능해졌다.
(c) 광디스크가 데이터를 기록하는 데 사용되기 시작했다.
(d) 플로피 디스크는 더 우수한 기술에 의해 대체되었다.

19
1940년대 미국의 영화 제작자들은 이후 '필름 느와르'라는 명칭을 얻게 될 영화 장르를 창안했다. 이 장르의 영화들은 강하게 대비되는 조명과 전지적인 해설자에 의해 서술되는 회상 장면의 사용으로 특징지어진다. 필름 느와르 영화의 주인공들은 그들을 둘러싼 사람들의 행동에 대해 도덕적으로 애매모호하며 냉소적이다. 그 장르의 도입 후 60년이 지난 오늘날에도, 필름 느와르의 인기는 아직 완전히 시들지 않았다. 최근의 많은 영화들, 특히 지난 십 년을 떠올리게 하는 시대물들은 필름 느와르의 기법들을 사용했다.

Q: 지문에 따르면 필름 느와르에 대한 내용과 일치하는 것은?
(a) 엄격하게 시간 순서에 따른 줄거리로 구별된다.
(b) 과거의 사건을 조명하는 해설자가 특징이다.
(c) 도덕적으로 실망시키는 주인공들로 인해 인기가 떨어졌다.
(d) 현대 영화 감독들 사이에서 흔한 스타일은 아니다.

20
최근의 한 연구는 인터넷이 자녀들에게 해롭다는 부모들의 일반적인 믿음을 반박하며, 인터넷이 10대들의 사회적, 기술적 능력을

계발하는 데 도움이 된다고 밝혔다. 연구자들은 800명 이상의 10대들과 그들의 부모들에게 질문하고 소셜 네트워킹 사이트의 젊은이들을 관찰하는 데 1,000시간 이상을 보내며, 그들의 웹 서핑 습성을 상세히 기록했다. 그들은 젊은이들이 온라인상에서 사회적 능력을 증진시키고 새로운 정보를 받아들인다는 것을 발견했다. 그럼에도 불구하고, 많은 부모들은 인터넷은 위험하며 학업 성적을 떨어뜨린다고 주장한다.

Q: 다음 중 지문의 내용과 일치하는 것은?
(a) 1,000명 이상의 10대와 그들의 부모들이 연구를 위한 인터뷰에 참가했다.
(b) 많은 부모들은 인터넷이 자녀들의 발전을 돕는다고 생각한다.
(c) 연구원들은 온라인 활동에 관해 10대들을 인터뷰했다.
(d) 젊은이들은 온라인 활동을 통해 불건전한 사회적 습관들을 습득한다.

21

Jackson's Bistro에서 프랑스 요리를 즐기세요

보스턴의 유서 깊은 Bay Village 지역의 중심인, Jackson's Bistro는 프랑스 요리에 대한 대규모의 기념 행사를 시작할 것입니다.

2주 동안, 이 인기 많은 지역 식당은 프랑스의 다양한 지역들로부터의 와인을 친절히 곁들이고, 객원 요리사인 Jacques Papillon이 전문적으로 만든 프랑스의 진미 요리를 제공할 것입니다.

10년이 넘게 현대 프랑스 요리의 선두에 있는, Papillon 요리사는 5성급 호텔에서 근무한 인상적인 이력을 자랑합니다. Jackson's는 매우 기대되는 이 행사에서 그에게 주방을 맡기게 되어 정말 기뻐하고 있습니다.

Q: 지문에 따르면 다음 중 맞는 것은 무엇인가?
(a) 식당은 세간의 이목을 끄는 프랑스 요리사와 홍보 행사를 열 것이다.
(b) Papillon 요리사는 보스턴의 유서 깊은 지역에 새로운 식당을 열 것이다.
(c) Jackson's Bistro는 한정된 시간 동안 다시 문을 열 것이다.
(d) Papillon 요리사는 짧은 기간 동안 프랑스 요리의 선두에 있었다.

22

1938년에 만들어진 캐릭터 벅스 버니는 인기 주말 만화 프로그램의 주인공으로 남아 있다. 그는 아돌프 히틀러가 유럽을 정복하려는 시도를 시작했던 같은 해에 만들어졌다. 벅스의 인기는 제2차 세계 대전 동안 치솟았으며 그는 만화에서 히틀러, 베니토 무솔리니, 그리고 당대의 다른 악당이나 희생양들과 싸우는 것으로 묘사되었다. 전쟁 후, 새로운 전향자 세대는 벅스에 열광했으며, 그는 단편 영화뿐만 아니라, 장편 영화들에도 모습을 드러내기 시작했다. 그의 탄생 후 70년이 지난 오늘날, 벅스는 여전히 어린이와 어른 모두의 마음을 사로잡고 있다.

Q: 지문에 따르면 다음 중 벅스 버니에 대한 내용과 일치하는 것은?
(a) 그의 인기는 제2차 세계 대전 동안 일시적으로 시들해졌다.
(b) 그의 만화는 현대의 관객들에게 여전히 인정받고 있다.
(c) 1938년에 TV에서 그의 인기는 정점에 도달했다.
(d) 그는 전쟁이 종료된 후에 만들어졌다.

23

제2차 세계 대전이 끝날 무렵, 미국의 이익에 대한 구소련의 정치적 의도가 미칠 잠재적인 피해에 대한 공포가 증가되었다. 그 결과, 미국은 구소련 정보기관의 메시지를 해독하는 프로그램을 내놓았고, 이를 통해 결국 러시아가 미국의 핵 프로그램에 관한 정보를 얻고자 노력하고 있다는 것을 발견하게 되었다. 구소련의 간첩 용의자들 중에는 뉴욕에 사는 유대인 부부인 줄리어스와 에델 로젠버그가 있었다. 비록 에델이 관여한 바는 매우 적었고, 사형은 심한 보복이었지만, 두 사람 모두 간첩 행위로 유죄를 선고받고 처형되었다.

Q: 지문에서 추론할 수 있는 것은 무엇인가?

(a) 유대계 미국인들은 구소련에 대해 동조적이었다.
(b) 에델 로젠버그의 사형 선고는 부당했다.
(c) 미국 군대는 러시아인들이 정보를 입수하는 것을 방해했다.
(d) 러시아는 미국의 핵무기에 대해 전혀 알아내지 못했다.

24

더 이상 고작 자랑거리를 위해서 일하는 단독 범죄자가 아닌, 현대 해커들은 대부분의 사람들이 상상하는 것과는 훨씬 다른 유형이다. 오늘날의 해커들은 복잡하게 얽힌 범죄 생태계에 속해 있는데, 소프트웨어의 취약성을 부당하게 이용하기 위해 서로 협력하여 일한다. 더욱이, 해킹을 저지하는 데 책임이 있는 사람들은 이러한 주모자들에 의한 악의적인 침입을 점점 더 알아차리기가 어렵다는 것을 알고 있다. 이러한 정보 관리자들은 그들에게 익숙한 공격 전략을 탐지하는 것만 가능하기 때문에, 너무 늦기 전에 새롭고 창의적인 공격 방법들을 알아차리는 것은 거의 불가능하다.

Q: 글쓴이가 가장 동의할 것 같은 진술은 무엇인가?
(a) 해킹 시도를 미리 아는 것은 비교적 쉽다.
(b) 해킹 침입이 진행되는 동안 그것은 알기 쉽다.
(c) 현대 해커들은 고립되어 있고 목적이 없는 개인인 경향이 있다.
(d) 해커들의 발전하는 정교함으로 인해 대중들은 더 큰 위험에 처해 있다.

25

건강 & 의학 뉴스

모기 주의

모기는 치명적일 수 있는 질병의 매개체로 작용하기 때문에, 공중 보건 당국자들은 모기의 질병 전염력에 대해 주의를 기울여야 한다. 이 성가신 생물은 주사기 같은 부속 기관을 이용한 혈액 접촉을 통해 인간 사이에 기생충을 전염시킬 수 있다. 이 곤충은 체내 온도 조절이 불가능하기 때문에 보통 열대 지방이나 아열대 지방에서 발견된다. 그 결과, 모기로 전염되는 질병들은 전통적으로 열대 지방에 돌림병을 가져왔지만, 열대 지방 모기 몇 종이 유전적으로 온대 기후에 적응했기 때문에 이 진술의 진위 여부는 곧 문제가 될지도 모른다.

Q: 지문에서 추론할 수 있는 것은 무엇인가?
(a) 모기에 의해 유발된 대부분의 질병은 죽음에 이른다.
(b) 모기 개체 수는 유전적인 적응으로 인해 증가해왔다.
(c) 전 세계적 기후 변화는 모기가 추위를 견딜 수 있게 했다.
(d) 열대 질병들이 열대 국가 이외에서 발생할지도 모른다.

Part IV

26~27

정규직 모집:

Recovery Road 재단은 책임자급 기금 조달자를 모집하고 있습니다. 우리 조직은 장애인이 생계를 꾸리는 데 도움이 될 수 있는 기술을 가르치기 위해 1984년에 Sam Jackson에 의해 설립되었습니다. Recovery Road의 많은 수혜자들은 성공적인 사업을 시작했습니다. 다양한 공예품을 판매함으로써, 그들은 일정 수준의 재정적인 독립을 이루어냈습니다.

· 합격자는 기업들뿐만 아니라 개인들에게도 후원을 요청할 것입니다.
· 업무는 모금 행사를 기획하는 것, 현재 후원자들 및 잠재적인 후원자들과의 회의에 참석하는 것, 그리고 본사의 홍보팀을 관리하는 것을 포함할 것입니다. 기부자들과 관계를 형성하고 유지하는 것도 임무의 중요한 부분입니다.
* 모금된 기금은 선생님들을 고용하고, 수업을 위한 공예 재료와 도구를 구입하고, 운영비를 충당하는 데 사용될 것입니다.
· 디지털 마케팅 관련 경력이 필요합니다. 관련 업무들은

우리의 소셜 네트워크 사이트를 관리하는 것을 포함할 것입니다.
· 자선 단체나 비정부 기구에서 비슷한 직책을 맡아본 분들이 선호되며, 모든 지원자는 관련 분야의 석사 학위가 있어야 합니다.

26. Q: Recovery Road 재단 설립자의 의도는 무엇이었는가?
(a) 회사 경영진들이 재정적 독립에 대한 수업을 하도록 독려하기를 원했다.
(b) 장애인들에게 자활하는 데 사용할 수 있는 것들을 가르치기를 원했다.
(c) 지역 사회에서 만들어진 공예품을 위한 시장을 설립하기를 원했다.
(d) 디지털 마케터들을 위한 소셜 네트워크 사이트를 개발하기를 원했다.

27. Q: 지문에서 추론할 수 있는 것은 무엇인가?
(a) 합격자는 자원 봉사제로 일할 것이다.
(b) 수혜자들은 작은 사업을 시작하기 위한 보조금을 받는다.
(c) 재단은 인터넷을 홍보 도구로서 활용한다.
(d) 훈련 과정의 마무리를 축하하기 위한 행사들이 열린다.

28~29

동물의 세계
순록들에 대해 당신이 결코 몰랐던 것들

순록들이 북극에서의 생존을 위해 상황에 적응해왔던 여러 방식 중, 가장 독특한 하나는 그들의 눈에서 일어나는 계절에 따른 변화이다. 순록들은 높은 위도에 살기 때문에, 조도의 극심한 변화에 노출된다. 여름에, 햇빛은 수 주간 끊임없이 비치지만, 몹시 추운 겨울에는, 해가 한 번도 뜨지 않아서, 그들은 긴 기간 동안 어둠에 대처해야 한다. 빛의 부족에 대한 대응으로, 순록의 눈은 실제로 겨울에 더 민감해진다. 비록 그들의 시력이 매우 정확해지는 것은 아니지만, 그들 주변에서 일어나는 일들을 더 볼 수 있다. 이것은 그들이 포식자들로부터 달아나도록 돕는다.

흥미롭게도, 순록의 시력을 일 년 내내 예리하게 만들어주는 변화는 눈의 빛깔과 관련되어 있다. 그들 안구의 일부는 여름에는 금색이지만, 겨울에는 진청색이 된다. 그 결과, 더 적은 빛이 망막에서 반사되고 이 동물들의 주변에 대해 더 많은 정보가 얻어진다. 금색에서 파란색으로의 변화는 장시간에 걸쳐 빛의 최대 양을 받아들이기 위해 눈이 팽창할 때 발생하는 압력과 관련 있다. 이 압력은 망막 후부의 조직을 압박하는데, 이는 순록의 눈이 북극의 겨울 동안 더 짧은 파란빛의 파장을 더 잘 반사하게 만든다.

28. Q: 다음 중 지문의 내용과 일치하는 것은?
(a) 순록들은 연중 더 따뜻한 기간 동안 더 높은 위도로 이주한다.
(b) 높은 위도에 위치한 지역들은 계절에 따른 햇빛의 변화를 경험한다.
(c) 행동적 변화는 북극에 있는 종이 위험한 날씨를 피하도록 돕는다.
(d) 빛의 부족은 몇몇 동물들의 시력이 나빠지게 한다.

29. Q: 두 번째 단락에서 주로 논의되는 것은 무엇인가?
(a) 순록들이 포식자들에게서 그들의 존재를 감추게 해주는 색
(b) 북극의 겨울 동안 더 긴 파란빛의 파장
(c) 빛이 순록의 망막을 통해 반사되는 방식
(d) 순록의 시력을 적응하게 만들어주는 색 변화

30~31

Martha [오후 2:30]
안녕, Raymond.
어떻게 지냈어? 지난 주말 작문 수업에서 널 보지 못했네. 네가 이 소식을 벌써 들었는지 모르겠지만, 우리 대학의 시 경연 대회의 제출일이 바뀌었어. 시 동호회에서 참가를 원하는 사람이 있다면, 10월 1일이 아니라, 9월 28일 이전에 그들의 출품작을 제출해야 해. 교수들로 구성된 시 위원회가 제출품들을 검토할 거고, 우승자는 10월 7일에 발표될 거야. 그날 우승자들을 축하하기 위한 시 낭독 행사도 있을 거야.

Raymond [오후 2:51]
안녕, Martha.
나는 잘 지내고 있어, 고마워. 지난주에 할머니를 방문해서 오아후 섬에 있었어. 지난 주말에 동네로 돌아와서 수업에 출석할 예정이었지만, 갑작스러운 태풍 때문에 비행기가 없었어. 어쨌든, 날짜 변경에 대해 알려줘서 고마워. 9월 17일에 다음 시 동호회 회의가 있을 때 우리 조의 모두에게 그것에 대해 말할게. 우리 조원들 대부분이 경연에 참가할 예정이야. 사실은, 나도 제출품을 낼 계획이야.

30. Q: 시 낭독 행사는 언제 개최되는가?
(a) 9월 17일
(b) 9월 28일
(c) 10월 1일
(d) 10월 7일

31. Q: Raymond는 왜 작문 수업에 출석하지 않았는가?
(a) 주말 동안 동네 밖에 사는 친구를 방문하고 있었다.
(b) 갑작스러운 날씨 변화로 인해 지체되었다.
(c) 동기들과의 시 경연 대회에 대한 회의가 있었다.
(d) 대학 신문에 출판하기 위한 시들을 쓰고 있었다.

32~33

아이들이 정규 교육을 시작하는 연령은 영국에서는 5세에서 노르웨이에서는 8세까지, 세계적으로 다양하다. 늦게 학교에 다니기 시작하는 것의 이점에 대한 연구들은 대체로 결론이 나지 않았지만, 새로운 연구는 그것이 긍정적인 행동적 영향을 미친다는 것을 제시한다. 스탠퍼드 대학의 연구원들은 덴마크 아이들을 조사했고 1년 늦게 의무 교육을 시작한 아이들이 훨씬 더 나은 수준의 자제력을 가졌다는 것을 발견했는데, 이는 비구조적인 환경에서 시간을 보내는 것이 아이들의 정신 건강의 발달에 중요한 역할을 한다는 것을 암시했다.

이 연구에서, 연구원들은 두 집단의 아이들의 성장을 6세부터 추적했다. 한 집단은 정규 교육에 들어갔고, 다른 집단은 일 년간 탁아소에 보내졌는데, 그곳에서 그들은 비제한적인 놀이로 스스로를 표현하도록 장려되었다. 11살의 나이에, 후자 집단은 전자 집단보다 상당히 낮은 부주의함과 과잉 행동 비율을 보여주었다. 더욱이, 이 아이들은 교실 환경에 들어간 후 그들이 충동을 통제하고 집중하는 것을 도와주는 수준의 성숙함을 발달시켰다. 연구원들은 장기적으로 학교 입학 연령이 장래에 집중을 방해하는 것들을 무시하는 능력과 관련될 수 있다고 생각한다.

32. Q: 지문의 요지는 무엇인가?
(a) 덴마크 학생들이 보여주는 충동의 특징
(b) 어린 연령에 학교에 다니기 시작하는 것의 학업적인 이점
(c) 늦은 정규 교육의 시작이 행동에 미치는 영향
(d) 의무 교육이 평생 학습에 미칠 수 있는 영향

33. Q: 지문에서 추론할 수 있는 것은 무엇인가?
(a) 아이들은 그들이 더 통제되지 않는 놀이에 참여한다면 주의가 덜 산만하다.
(b) 집에서 교육을 받는 학생들은 대학 생활에 빠르게 적응한다.
(c) 유치원생들은 교육 시간 중에 서로를 산만하게 하는 경향이 있다.
(d) 일찍 학교에 다니기 시작한 아이들은 주의 지속 시간과 관련해 더 적은 문제를 가진다.

34~35

우연한 영웅: 알렉산더 플레밍

저명한 스코틀랜드의 과학자이자 1945년 노벨상 수상자인 알렉산더 플레밍 경은, 생물학 박사가 되기 전 런던 선박 회사의 하급 점원이었다. 그는 끝내 세인트 메리 병원 의과 대학의 교수가 되었고 그 후에 제1차 세계 대전 동안 세균학자로 근무하며, 영국 군의단에서

복무했다. 그는 병사들의 부상을 연구했고 감염을 막기 위해 처방되고 있었던 소독제가 사실 치유력이 있다기보다는 더 해로웠다는 것을 발견했다.

전쟁 이후, 그는 세인트 메리 접종과의 학과장이 되었다. 그곳은 바로 그가 첫 번째 연구 성과를 낸 곳으로, 연구는 몸에서 생성되는 약한 살균물질인, 리소자임을 발견했다.

하지만 아마도 플레밍의 의학에 대한 수많은 공헌 중 가장 널리 인정받는 점이자, 그가 세계적인 명성을 얻었던 이유는, 페니실린의 발견이었다. 이 천연 추출물은 다양한 종류의 감염을 물리치는 데 사용될 수 있는 강력한 항생제이다. 1928년에 플레밍이 페니실린을 우연히 발견한 이래로, 우리는 그것을 매독, 뇌막염, 그리고 폐렴과 같은 질병들을 치료하기 위해 사용해왔다. 오늘날, 항생제는 전 세계에서 가장 빈번하게 투여되는 종류의 의약품 중 하나가 되었다.

34. Q: 지문에 따르면 다음 중 알렉산더 플레밍 경에 대한 내용과 일치하는 것은?
(a) 세인트 메리의 교수였을 때 런던에서 선박 회사의 점원으로 부업을 했다.
(b) 제1차 세계 대전 이후에 세인트 메리 생물학과의 학과장이 되었다.
(c) 페니실린의 항생 작용의 특성의 발견으로 국제적인 인정을 받았다.
(d) 리소자임이라 불리는 강력한, 자연적으로 발생하는 방부제로 다양한 질병을 치료했다.

35. Q: 지문의 주된 목적은 무엇인가?
(a) 수백만의 생명을 구한 전쟁 영웅의 일화를 소개하기 위해
(b) 페니실린을 남용하여 발생하는 문제를 지적하기 위해
(c) 감염에 대한 전통적 치료와 현대적 치료를 비교하기 위해
(d) 의학에서 역사적인 인물의 이력을 설명하기 위해

TEST 05

LISTENING COMPREHENSION

Part I

1

M: Why didn't you send me a postcard from Jamaica?
W: _____

(a) I forgot your address.
(b) There were no envelopes.
(c) I'll go to the post office.
(d) The distance was too great.

M: 왜 자메이카에서 나한테 엽서를 안 보냈니?
(a) 네 주소를 잊어버렸어.
(b) 봉투가 없었어.
(c) 나는 우체국에 갈 거야.
(d) 거리가 너무 멀었어.

2

W: I can't believe I misplaced my keys.
M: _____

(a) Don't worry. I'll keep them for you.
(b) With your memory, I'm not surprised.
(c) Try a different door.
(d) I told you to lock it well.

W: 내가 열쇠를 둔 곳을 잊었다는 것이 믿기지 않아.
(a) 걱정하지 마. 내가 대신 가지고 있을게.
(b) 네 기억력으로라면, 놀랍지 않아.
(c) 다른 문을 열어봐.
(d) 내가 제대로 잠그라고 했잖아.

3

M: Can you contribute money to buy Anna's birthday present?
W: _____

(a) It's a complimentary gift.
(b) I'd be glad to chip in.
(c) I'm just trying to help.
(d) I'll do it in my spare time.

M: Anna의 생일 선물을 살 돈을 보탤 수 있니?
(a) 그것은 무료 선물이야.
(b) 기꺼이 낼게.
(c) 난 그냥 도우려는 것뿐이야.
(d) 여가 시간에 그것을 할게.

4

W: Why did you finish work so late today?
M: _____

(a) I got there in the nick of time.
(b) It was a pretty slow day.
(c) I had to tie up some loose ends.
(d) I left the office early due to an emergency.

W: 오늘 왜 이렇게 늦게 일을 끝냈니?
(a) 난 거기에 때맞게 도착했어.
(b) 꽤 시간이 더디 가는 하루였어.
(c) 난 몇 가지 남은 일을 처리해야 했어.
(d) 난 급한 일 때문에 일찍 퇴근했어.

5

M: How did you hurt your leg?
W: _____

(a) I overexerted myself during a workout.
(b) It didn't hurt as much as I thought it would.
(c) I should probably start exercising more.
(d) I was surprised that it's a minor injury.

M: 어떻게 다리를 다쳤니?
(a) 내가 운동 중에 너무 무리했어.
(b) 내가 생각했던 것만큼 아프지 않았어.
(c) 아마도 더 많이 운동하기 시작하는 것이 좋겠어.
(d) 이게 경상이라는 것에 놀랐어.

6

W: Did you do the laundry? My shirt is stained.
M: _____

(a) You should wear a clean one.
(b) I'll use more detergent next time.
(c) You were occupied then.
(d) I can iron out the wrinkles.

W: 너 빨래했니? 내 셔츠에 얼룩이 있어.
(a) 너는 깨끗한 것을 입어야 해.
(b) 다음번에는 세제를 더 많이 쓸게.
(c) 넌 그때 바빴잖아.
(d) 다리미질로 구김을 없앨 수 있어.

7

M: Will you be providing a standard buffet for your wedding guests?

W: _____

(a) The line's too long right now. I'll wait a bit.
(b) Actually, I opted for a simple three-course dinner.
(c) Of course, please feel free to help yourself.
(d) The guests should be hungry then.

M: 결혼식 하객들에게 일반 뷔페를 제공할 거야?
(a) 지금 줄이 너무 길어. 좀 기다릴래.
(b) 사실, 난 세 코스짜리의 간단한 저녁 식사로 선택했어.
(c) 물론이지, 마음껏 먹어.
(d) 그때쯤이면 하객들이 배고플 거야.

8

W: I find it hard to raise kids while having a full-time job.
M: _____

(a) It has been smooth sailing.
(b) Yeah, that's a bit of a bumpy ride.
(c) I'll handle them on my own.
(d) I'm usually in from 9 to 5.

W: 정규직으로 일하면서 아이들을 기르는 어려운 것 같아.
(a) 그것은 순조롭게 진행되어왔어.
(b) 맞아, 우여곡절이 꽤 많지.
(c) 난 혼자 힘으로 그들을 감당할 거야.
(d) 난 보통 9시에서 5시까지 근무해.

9

M: Do you know the way to San Marino?
W: _____

(a) It's a nice little town.
(b) It's been a long drive.
(c) Go due west for an hour.
(d) The train leaves at 5.

M: 산마리노로 가는 길을 아세요?
(a) 거긴 작고 예쁜 마을이에요.
(b) 장거리 운전이었어요.
(c) 정서 방향으로 1시간 가시면 돼요.
(d) 그 기차는 5시에 출발해요.

10

W: I can't take how hard my trainer's been pushing me lately.
M: _____

(a) Maybe it's time you got a trainer.
(b) Sounds like you need more of a challenge.
(c) Just be glad he's not making you overdo it.
(d) You could always ask him to tone it down.

W: 내 트레이너가 최근에 나를 얼마나 몰아붙이는지 견딜 수가 없어.
(a) 네가 트레이너를 구해야 할 때인 것 같아.
(b) 네가 더 많은 도전을 필요로 하는 것처럼 들리네.
(c) 그가 지나치게 시키지 않는 것을 그저 다행으로 여겨.
(d) 언제든지 그에게 강도를 약하게 해달라고 요청할 수 있잖아.

Part II

11

M: How do you like this picture I took?
W: It's very artistic.
M: Doesn't the focus seem blurred?
W: _____

(a) Yeah. You should return it.
(b) I did it on purpose.
(c) It's barely noticeable.
(d) No. It seems authentic.

M: 내가 찍은 이 사진 어때?
W: 정말 예술적이다.
M: 초점이 흐릿해 보이지 않니?
(a) 응. 너는 그것을 반품해야 돼.
(b) 내가 일부러 그랬어.
(c) 그건 거의 눈에 띄지 않아.
(d) 아니. 진짜 같아.

12

W: Do you still compete as a marathon runner?
M: Not so much. I'm swamped with work these days.
W: Really? Then how do you maintain your trim physique?
M: _____

(a) I have a medical checkup tomorrow.
(b) I try to whenever I have free time.
(c) I should take up exercise again.
(d) I abstain from processed foods.

W: 너 아직도 마라톤 선수로 시합에 나가니?
M: 그다지. 요즘 일이 넘쳐 나거든.
W: 진짜? 그럼 넌 어떻게 균형 잡힌 체격을 유지하는 거야?
(a) 내일 건강 검진이 있어.
(b) 시간이 날 때마다 하려고 노력해.
(c) 다시 운동을 시작해야겠어.
(d) 가공식품을 절제하고 있어.

13

M: Did you enjoy the musical?
W: Yes, except for one part.
M: What's that? The lead actor's performance?
W: _____

(a) I liked the critic's review.
(b) Exactly. It lacked depth.
(c) I'm glad you enjoyed it.

(d) Right. He nailed the part.

M: 그 뮤지컬 좋았어?
W: 응, 한 부분만 빼고.
M: 그게 뭔데? 주연 배우의 연기?
(a) 난 그 평론가의 비평이 마음에 들었어.
(b) 맞아. 깊이가 부족했어.
(c) 그것이 좋았다니 다행이다.
(d) 맞아. 그는 그 배역을 완벽히 해냈어.

14

W: I'm craving pizza right now.
M: Come on, let's go out and get one.
W: Let's just have it delivered.
M: _____

(a) Well, just one more slice.
(b) OK. I'll grab the number.
(c) I cooked it myself.
(d) But we got pepperoni last time.

W: 난 지금 피자가 너무 먹고 싶어.
M: 자, 어서 나가서 한 판 사 먹자.
W: 그냥 배달시키자.
(a) 음, 딱 한 조각만 더.
(b) 알았어. 내가 전화번호를 가져올게.
(c) 내가 직접 그것을 요리했어.
(d) 하지만 우린 지난번에 페퍼로니 피자를 먹었잖아.

15

M: Say, how was your slumber party?
W: There ended up being just two of us.
M: Oh. So what did you guys do?
W: _____

(a) We invited friends for a sleepover.
(b) The usual. Food and gossip.
(c) They had beds ready for us.
(d) We expected more people to show up.

M: 그나저나, 파자마 파티는 어땠어?
W: 결국 우리 둘만 남게 되었어.
M: 아. 그래서 너네 뭐했는데?
(a) 우리는 밤샘 파티에 친구들을 초대했어.
(b) 늘 하던 거. 먹고 수다 떨고.
(c) 그들이 우리를 위한 침대를 마련해뒀어.
(d) 우리는 더 많은 사람들이 올 거라고 예상했어.

16

W: Those noises coming through the floor kept me up all night! I'm exhausted.
M: What are you talking about?
W: Are you telling me you didn't hear all that creaking?
M: _____

(a) I told you they were a nuisance.
(b) It takes a lot to wake me once I'm asleep.
(c) It's not such an easy thing to fix.
(d) I'm glad you weren't too bothered.

W: 층간 소음 때문에 밤새 깨어있었어! 너무 피곤해.
M: 무슨 말을 하는 거야?
W: 그 삐걱거리는 소리를 전혀 듣지 못했다고 말하는 거야?
(a) 그것들이 골칫거리라고 말했잖아.
(b) 난 한번 잠들면 일어나는 데 오래 걸려.
(c) 그것은 그렇게 고치기 쉬운 것이 아니야.
(d) 네가 별로 성가시지 않았다니 다행이야.

17

M: Wow. You dance so gracefully.
W: Thank you. I've just started taking classes.
M: You have talent for a novice.
W: _____

(a) I took lessons for years.
(b) I need a dance teacher.
(c) I appreciate the compliment.
(d) That's not how it's done.

M: 우와. 넌 정말 춤을 우아하게 추는구나.
W: 고마워. 난 막 수업을 받기 시작했어.
M: 넌 초보치고 재능이 있어.
(a) 난 수년간 강습을 받았어.
(b) 난 무용 선생님이 필요해.
(c) 칭찬해줘서 고마워.
(d) 그렇게 하는 게 아니야.

18

W: Let's go somewhere and unwind this weekend.
M: I'd like to, but my work schedule is up in the air.
W: Oh, when will you have a clearer picture?
M: _____

(a) Our plan is to meet on Saturday.
(b) I can't blow off my job.
(c) Give me a shout when it's settled.
(d) It won't be until the last minute.

W: 이번 주말에 어디로 좀 쉬러 가자.
M: 그러고 싶지만, 내 근무 일정이 아직 미정이야.
W: 아, 언제 네 일정이 분명해지는데?
(a) 우리 계획은 토요일에 만나는 거야.
(b) 일을 땡땡이칠 수는 없어.
(c) 정해지면 나에게 말해줘.
(d) 막판이 돼서야 그럴 것 같아.

19

M: How did your internship turn out?
W: Actually, they offered me a permanent position.

M: Really? You must be elated!
W: _____

(a) It's only temporary employment.
(b) I would've turned it down anyway.
(c) Yeah, I'm working against the clock.
(d) It wouldn't be an overstatement.

M: 인턴 사원 근무는 어떻게 됐어?
W: 실은, 그들이 정규직을 제안했어.
M: 정말? 진짜 기쁘겠다!

(a) 임시직일 뿐이야.
(b) 난 어차피 거절했을 거야.
(c) 맞아, 난 시간에 맞춰 끝내려고 열심히 일하는 중이야.
(d) 그렇게 말해도 과언이 아닐 거야.

20

W: You won't believe this. I got named regional manager!
M: Get out of town! I'm so proud of you.
W: Things are finally looking up at work.
M: _____

(a) Apparently it was just a fluke.
(b) I'm not cut out for that line of work.
(c) I know you've had your heart set on this.
(d) Well, keep your head up.

W: 믿기 힘들겠지만, 나 지역 관리자로 임명됐어!
M: 어머나! 난 네가 정말 자랑스러워.
W: 직장 일이 드디어 잘 풀리고 있어.

(a) 보아하니 그건 그냥 요행수였어.
(b) 난 그런 직종에 안 맞아.
(c) 네가 이걸 간절히 원했다는 거 알지.
(d) 음, 힘을 내.

Part III

21

Listen to a conversation between two friends.

M: Courtney, are you busy this Saturday?
W: Not really. Why?
M: Could you help me pick out a gift for my sister?
W: No problem. What time should we meet?
M: After lunch. I have to be at her graduation ceremony around three.
W: OK. I'll drop by your house around one.

Q: What is the man mainly doing in the conversation?

(a) Describing his schedule
(b) Trying to find a gift
(c) Preparing for a graduation
(d) Planning a shopping trip

두 친구 간의 대화를 들으시오.

M: Courtney, 이번 주 토요일에 바쁘니?
W: 별로. 왜?
M: 내 여동생 선물 고르는 걸 도와줄 수 있어?
W: 물론이지. 몇 시에 만날까?
M: 점심 후에. 3시쯤 그녀의 졸업식에 가야 해.
W: 좋아. 1시쯤 너희 집으로 갈게.

Q: 대화에서 남자는 주로 무엇을 하고 있는가?

(a) 자신의 일정을 설명하고 있다.
(b) 선물을 찾으려 하고 있다.
(c) 졸업식을 준비하고 있다.
(d) 쇼핑하러 가려고 계획하고 있다.

22

Listen to a conversation between a salesperson and a customer.

W: Good morning. What can I do for you?
M: I would like a refund for this headset I bought.
W: What's wrong with it?
M: The microphone is on the blink.
W: Sorry, but we only offer exchanges on opened products.
M: Then please make sure there are no issues with the new one.

Q: What is the conversation mainly about?

(a) Inquiring about a return policy
(b) Replacing faulty equipment
(c) Ensuring a headset works properly
(d) Repairing a microphone attachment

판매원과 고객 간의 대화를 들으시오.

W: 어서 오십시오. 무엇을 도와 드릴까요?
M: 제가 구입한 이 헤드셋을 환불하고 싶어요.
W: 무슨 문제가 있습니까?
M: 마이크가 제대로 작동이 안 됩니다.
W: 죄송하지만, 저희는 개봉한 제품에 대해서는 교환만 해 드립니다.
M: 그렇다면 새 제품은 문제가 없도록 확실히 해 주세요.

Q: 주로 무엇에 관한 대화인가?

(a) 반품 정책에 대해 문의하기
(b) 하자가 있는 장비를 교환하기
(c) 헤드셋이 제대로 작동하는지 확인하기
(d) 마이크 부착 장치 수리하기

23

Listen to a conversation between two students.

M: I'm surprised Professor Holly got so angry in class.
W: He's usually so soft-spoken and patient.
M: What do you think got into him?
W: Maybe it's students' consistent tardiness.

M: Well, I don't want to give him any reason to get mad at me.
W: I feel the same way.

Q: What is the main topic of the conversation?

(a) Ways to avoid a temperamental teacher
(b) The unexpected behavior of a teacher
(c) The atmosphere in Professor Holly's class
(d) Justifications for the professor's reputation

두 학생 간의 대화를 들으시오.
M: Holly 교수님께서 수업 중에 그렇게 화를 내셔서 놀랐어.
W: 그분은 보통 말씨가 무척 상냥하고 참을성도 있으시잖아.
M: 그분이 무엇 때문에 화났다고 생각해?
W: 아마 학생들의 거듭되는 지각 때문일 거야.
M: 음, 난 그분이 내게 화낼 이유를 아예 만들고 싶지 않아.
W: 나도 마찬가지야.

Q: 대화의 주제는 무엇인가?
(a) 괴팍한 교사를 피하는 방법
(b) 교사의 예상치 못한 행동
(c) Holly 교수의 수업 분위기
(d) 그 교수의 평판에 대한 타당한 이유들

24

Listen to two friends discuss a financial problem.

W: I still haven't been paid due to an accounting mix-up.
M: How are you going to cover rent, then?
W: I have no choice but to pay it late and incur a surcharge.
M: Maybe accounting can call your landlord and smooth things out.
W: It's worth a shot. I'll set it up first thing tomorrow.
M: Good. The burden shouldn't rest on you.

Q: Which is correct according to the conversation?

(a) The woman will make the payment without delay.
(b) The woman will consult with the accountants.
(c) The man will contact the landlord soon.
(d) The man thinks the woman should act herself.

두 친구가 재정 문제에 관해 이야기하는 것을 들으시오.
W: 회계상 착오 때문에 아직도 월급을 받지 못했어.
M: 그러면 집세는 어떻게 해결할 거야?
W: 늦게 내고 추가 요금을 부담하는 수밖에 없지.
M: 어쩌면 회계부에서 네 집주인에게 전화해서 문제를 해결할 수 있을지도 몰라.
W: 해볼 만하네. 내일 그 일을 가장 먼저 해야겠어.
M: 좋아. 너한테 부담이 지워지면 안 되지.

Q: 대화에 따르면 맞는 것은 무엇인가?

(a) 여자는 지체 없이 납부할 것이다.
(b) 여자는 회계사들과 상의할 것이다.
(c) 남자는 곧 집주인에게 연락할 것이다.
(d) 남자는 여자가 직접 행동해야 한다고 생각한다.

25

Listen to a conversation between two acquaintances.

M: Are you still considering a new car? Do you need a helping hand?
W: Without question. I know next to nothing about mechanical things.
M: I'm willing to tag along with you to the dealership.
W: You really don't mind? That would ease my trepidation.
M: Anything to be of service. How does next week look?
W: My calendar is clear. I'll make it up to you.

Q: Which is correct about the woman according to the conversation?

(a) She already sold her previous automobile.
(b) She needs the man to repair her vehicle.
(c) She is apprehensive about going alone.
(d) She has a cramped schedule.

두 지인 간의 대화를 들으시오.
M: 아직도 새 차에 대해 고민 중이야? 도움이 필요해?
W: 물론이지. 난 기계적인 것에 대해서는 거의 아무것도 몰라.
M: 네가 대리점에 갈 때 기꺼이 따라가줄게.
W: 정말 그래 줄래? 그러면 덜 두려울 거야.
M: 도움이 된다면 무슨 일이든. 다음 주는 어때?
W: 한가해. 이 신세는 꼭 갚을게.

Q: 대화에 따르면 여자에 대해 맞는 것은 무엇인가?
(a) 이전 자동차를 이미 팔았다.
(b) 차를 수리하는 데 남자가 필요하다.
(c) 혼자 가는 것을 걱정하고 있다.
(d) 일정이 빡빡하다.

26

Listen to two colleagues discuss a business operation.

W: We've got a long way to go before we can open our restaurant.
M: But the renovations already look great.
W: I meant our menu options. I doubt that food critics will be enthused.
M: Yeah, our dishes aren't very sophisticated.
W: I think we should focus on serving exotic cuisine.
M: Maybe, but if we go that route, we'll have to hire a new chef.

Q: What is the woman concerned about?

(a) A remote location
(b) An uninspired menu
(c) A reputation for bad service
(d) An untrained kitchen worker

두 동료가 사업 운영에 관해 이야기하는 것을 들으시오.
W: 우리가 레스토랑을 개장하기까지 갈 길이 멀어요.
M: 하지만 이미 수리가 멋지게 되었는데요.
W: 우리의 메뉴 선택자 말이에요. 음식 평론가들이 열광할지 염려되어요.
M: 맞아요, 우리 음식들이 아주 세련된 건 아니죠.
W: 이국적인 요리를 선보이는 것에 집중해야 할 것 같아요.
M: 아마도요, 하지만 그 방향으로 간다면, 새 주방장을 고용해야 할 거예요.

Q: 여자가 우려하는 것은 무엇인가?
(a) 외딴 위치
(b) 평범한 메뉴
(c) 형편없는 서비스에 대한 평판
(d) 훈련받지 않은 주방 근로자

27

Listen to a conversation between two friends.

M: Kate, I need your advice. I think my wife's still upset with me.
W: Really? Did you apologize?
M: Of course, but she's still distant.
W: Well, actions speak louder than words. How about doing something out of the ordinary?
M: Do you mean like cooking dinner?
W: Why not? That will show your apology is sincere.
M: I'll give it a shot. Thanks for your help.

Q: Which is correct according to the conversation?

(a) The man has yet to apologize to his wife.
(b) The man's wife has already forgiven him.
(c) The woman suggests doing something atypical.
(d) The woman believes the man is insincere.

두 친구 간의 대화를 들으시오.
M: Kate, 네 조언이 필요해. 아내가 아직도 나한테 화나 있는 것 같아.
W: 정말? 사과는 했어?
M: 물론이지, 하지만 아내가 아직도 거리를 두고 있어.
W: 음, 말보다 행동이 중요하지. 뭔가 색다른 일을 해보는 건 어때?
M: 저녁 식사 준비 같은 거 말이야?
W: 그거 좋지. 그건 네 사과가 진심이라는 걸 보여줄 거야.
M: 한번 해볼게. 도와줘서 고마워.

Q: 대화에 따르면 맞는 것은 무엇인가?
(a) 남자는 아내에게 아직 사과하지 않았다.
(b) 남자의 아내는 이미 그를 용서했다.
(c) 여자는 이례적인 일을 해보라고 제안한다.
(d) 여자는 남자가 진실하지 않다고 생각한다.

28

Listen to a conversation between a couple.

W: So are you excited about our trip tomorrow?
M: Of course. I've been eager to check out kayaking for a while.
W: Have you packed your things yet?
M: No. I think I need to get a bigger backpack.
W: I have an extra one I can lend you if need be.
M: Thanks! The one I have is about to burst.

Q: Which is correct about the man according to the conversation?

(a) He has a planned vacation with the woman.
(b) He has recently become an avid kayaker.
(c) He broke the pack he planned to bring.
(d) He needs to leave some things behind.

커플 간의 대화를 들으시오.
W: 내일 가는 우리의 여행에 들떠 있니?
M: 물론이지. 한동안 카약을 무척 타보고 싶었거든.
W: 벌써 짐을 다 쌌어?
M: 아니. 더 큰 배낭이 필요할 것 같아.
W: 필요하다면 네게 빌려줄 수 있는 여분의 배낭이 하나 있어.
M: 고마워! 내가 가진 배낭은 터지려고 해.

Q: 대화에 따르면 남자에 대해 맞는 것은 무엇인가?
(a) 여자와 함께 휴가를 보내기로 계획했다.
(b) 최근에 카약에 열렬히 빠졌다.
(c) 가져가려던 배낭을 망가뜨렸다.
(d) 몇 가지 물건들을 두고 가야 한다.

29

Listen to a conversation at an office.

M: It's nearly 9! What are you so busy with?
W: It's the Jackson account. It's killing me.
M: Oh yes, that client is notoriously hard to please.
W: Plus, there's endless paperwork to fill out.
M: By the way, aren't you going away on Monday?
W: Yeah, that's why I'm giving up my Friday night. I want to do nothing but relax next week.

Q: What can be inferred from the conversation?

(a) The man does not think the woman should take time off.
(b) There are several mistakes to fix in the Jackson account.
(c) It is customary for the woman to work past 9.
(d) The woman intends to wrap up the Jackson account tonight.

사무실에서의 대화를 들으시오.
M: 거의 9시야! 무슨 일 때문에 그렇게 바쁜 거야?

W: Jackson 고객 건이야. 힘들어 죽겠어.
M: 아 맞아, 그 고객은 만족시키기 어렵기로 악명 높지.
W: 게다가, 작성해야 할 서류 업무가 끝이 없어.
M: 그나저나 월요일에 휴가 가는 거 아니야?
W: 맞아, 그게 내가 금요일 밤을 포기하는 이유지. 난 다음 주에 오로지 휴식만 취하고 싶거든.

Q: 대화에서 추론할 수 있는 것은 무엇인가?
(a) 남자는 여자가 휴가를 내야 한다고 생각하지 않는다.
(b) Jackson 고객 건에는 수정해야 할 여러 실수들이 있다.
(c) 여자가 9시 넘어서 일하는 것은 통상적이다.
(d) 여자는 오늘 밤 Jackson 고객 건을 마무리하려고 한다.

30

Listen to a conversation between two friends.

W: I can't get enough of Bill Bobson's *Comedy Hour*.
M: That comedy show? I'm surprised you're into it.
W: Why? I think Bill's a genius.
M: Please. Anyone can crack jokes and jump around on a stage.
W: The show is much more than that.
M: Really? In what way?
W: It's got some very poignant social commentary.
M: Huh, I guess I'll have to give it another chance.

Q: What can be inferred from the conversation?

(a) Bill Bobson recently changed his show's format.
(b) The man has a low opinion of Bill Bobson.
(c) The woman has never watched *Comedy Hour*.
(d) *Comedy Hour* is the most popular show on TV.

두 친구 간의 대화를 들으시오.
W: 난 Bill Bobson의 『Comedy Hour』를 정말 좋아해.
M: 그 코미디 쇼? 네가 그것을 좋아한다니 놀라운걸.
W: 왜? 난 Bill이 천재라고 생각해.
M: 설마. 누구나 농담을 하고 무대 위를 팔짝팔짝 뛰어다닐 수 있어.
W: 그 쇼는 그것보다 훨씬 더 대단하다고.
M: 정말? 어떤 면에서?
W: 그 쇼는 아주 신랄한 사회적 논평을 종종 해왔어.
M: 흠, 다시 한번 봐야 할 것 같네.

Q: 대화에서 추론할 수 있는 것은 무엇인가?
(a) Bill Bobson은 최근에 쇼의 구성을 바꿨다.
(b) 남자는 Bill Bobson을 과소평가한다.
(c) 여자는 『Comedy Hour』를 본 적이 없다.
(d) 『Comedy Hour』는 가장 인기 있는 TV 쇼이다.

Part IV

31

Do we need a change of direction in our lives? Research suggests that more and more people are succumbing to anxiety and melancholy. A mere 20 years ago, depression was diagnosed once in a blue moon. Now, one in every ten Americans takes antidepressant pills. This shows an increasing dependency on drugs to deal with personal issues. This psychological condition has also been linked to growing rates of divorce, obesity, and poverty.

Q: What is the main topic of the news report?

(a) The common diseases Americans experience
(b) The societal acceptance of depression
(c) The growing dependence on antidepressants
(d) The proliferation of mood disorders in Americans

우리 삶에서 방향의 변화가 필요할까요? 연구는 점점 더 많은 사람들이 불안과 우울증에 굴복하고 있다는 것을 보여줍니다. 불과 20년 전만 해도, 우울증은 극히 드물게 진단되었습니다. 이제, 미국인 10명 중 1명이 항우울제를 복용합니다. 이는 개인적인 문제들을 해결하기 위한 약물 의존성의 증가를 보여줍니다. 이 심리적 질환은 이혼, 비만, 가난의 비율 증가와도 연관되어 있습니다.

Q: 뉴스 보도의 주제는 무엇인가?
(a) 미국인들이 겪는 흔한 질병들
(b) 우울증에 대한 사회적 수용
(c) 항우울제에 대한 의존성 증가
(d) 미국인들 사이에서의 기분 장애 확산

32

Thank you for coming here and supporting our cause. Before we commence, however, I would like to inform everyone that certain qualifications must be satisfied before permission to donate blood is granted. The provided forms list those requirements and describe the procedure used to appraise your fitness as a donor. Kindly go over the forms carefully. Remember, affixing your signature at the bottom indicates your willingness to be tested.

Q: What is the announcement mainly about?

(a) Determining volunteers' interest level
(b) Organizing a blood drive
(c) Examining patients needing blood
(d) Confirming contributor eligibility

이곳에 오셔서 저희 운동을 지지해주셔서 감사합니다. 하지만 시작하기에 앞서, 헌혈에 대한 허가가 승인되기 전에 특정 조건들이 충족되어야 한다는 것을 모든 분들께 알려 드리고 싶습니다. 제공된 양식에는 그러한 필요 조건들이 나와 있으며, 기증자로서 귀하의 적합성을 평가하기 위해 사용되는 절차를 설명하고 있습니다. 부디 신중하게 양식을 검토해주십시오. 맨 아래에 서명하시는 것은 검사를 받겠다는 귀하의 의향을 나타낸다는 것을 기억하시기 바랍니다.

Q: 안내는 주로 무엇에 관한 것인가?

(a) 지원자들의 관심 수준 파악하기
(b) 헌혈 캠페인을 준비하기
(c) 혈액이 필요한 환자들을 검사하기
(d) 기증자의 적격성 확인하기

33

Let me talk about another characteristic of Hemingway's writing: he was predisposed to sentences that got to the point quickly rather than drawn-out descriptions. His economy with words was reminiscent of straight news writing, with scant use of descriptive adjectives. In fact, Hemingway expertly conveyed emotion without relying solely upon emotionally charged words. Some rejected his writing style as blunt, but they could not repudiate the fact that Hemingway's works delivered action.

Q: What is the talk mainly about?

(a) Why Hemingway disliked over-the-top narratives
(b) Hemingway's familiarity with straight news writing
(c) The conciseness of Hemingway's prose
(d) How Hemingway explored emotional tension

헤밍웨이의 글쓰기의 또 다른 특징에 대해 이야기해보겠습니다. 그는 길게 이어지는 서술보다는 빠르게 핵심에 이르는 문장을 구사하는 성향이 있었습니다. 그의 간결한 문체는 서술적인 형용사를 거의 사용하지 않는 객관적인 기사 작성을 연상시켰습니다. 사실, 헤밍웨이는 감정적으로 강렬한 단어에만 의존하지 않고도 감정을 훌륭하게 전달했습니다. 어떤 이들은 그의 문체가 직설적이라며 거부했지만, 그들은 헤밍웨이의 작품들이 이야기 속 사건을 잘 전달했다는 사실은 부인할 수 없었습니다.

Q: 담화는 주로 무엇에 대한 것인가?

(a) 헤밍웨이가 지나친 서술을 싫어했던 이유
(b) 헤밍웨이의 객관적인 기사 작성에 대한 익숙함
(c) 헤밍웨이가 쓴 산문의 간결성
(d) 헤밍웨이가 정서적 긴장에 대해 탐구했던 방법

34

WeCare, a philanthropic society that aids underage parents, will be holding a symposium this weekend designed to arm young mothers with vital knowledge and instruction they can use to support themselves and their families. Furthermore, the organization will look into the matter of unwelcome pregnancies among high school students and solicit the public's suggestions on remedies for this escalating social problem. For additional details, please contact a representative at 555-3432.

Q: Which is correct about WeCare according to the advertisement?

(a) It offers grants to adolescent parents.
(b) It provides career assistance to mothers.
(c) It teaches pregnancy avoidance strategies.
(d) It seeks feedback from the greater community.

미성년 부모를 돕는 자선 단체인 WeCare는 이번 주말에 어린 엄마들에게 본인과 가족을 부양하는 데 이용할 수 있는 필수적인 지식과 가르침을 제공하려는 취지의 학술 토론회를 개최합니다. 뿐만 아니라, 그 단체는 반갑지 않은 고교생 임신 문제에 대해 조사해보고, 이런 증가하는 사회적 문제의 개선책에 대한 대중들의 의견을 구해볼 것입니다. 추가적인 사항에 대해 문의하시려면, 555-3432로 직원에게 연락주시기 바랍니다.

Q: 광고에 따르면 WeCare에 대해 맞는 것은 무엇인가?

(a) 청소년 부모들에게 보조금을 준다.
(b) 엄마들에게 직업 지원을 해 준다.
(c) 임신 예방법을 가르쳐 준다.
(d) 더 큰 집단의 의견을 구한다.

35

Some 30,000 years ago, Arctic ground squirrels cached seeds in the Siberian permafrost that modern scientists have been able to dig up and revivify. Previously, the oldest plant matter to produce new life was a comparatively young 2,000-year-old date palm seed. The newly discovered seeds were from the Silene stenophylla plant. The cold kept the seeds in a state of suspended animation, allowing them to endure the years without disintegrating or being damaged. Researchers think it's possible that permafrost may hold much more ancient flora just waiting to be disinterred and brought back to life.

Q: Which is correct according to the talk?

(a) Date palm seeds of a similar age were discovered prior to the stenophylla.
(b) The stenophylla is the first instance of ancient seeds being rejuvenated.
(c) It is a mystery why the seeds were not damaged in the frost layer.
(d) Scientists suspect that permafrost houses other intact plant material.

약 30,000년 전에, 북극 얼룩다람쥐들은 시베리아의 영구 동토층에 현대 과학자들이 땅에서 파내서 부활시킬 수 있었던 씨앗을 저장했습니다. 이전에, 새 생명을 만들어낸 가장 오래된 식물은 비교적 어린 2,000년 된 대추야자 씨앗이었습니다. 새롭게 발견된 씨앗은 '실레네 스테노필라' 식물의 씨앗이었습니다. 추위는 그 씨앗이 분해되거나 손상되지 않고 오랜 시간을 견디도록 가사 상태로 씨앗을 유지시켰습니다. 연구자들은 영구 동토층이 발굴되어 생명이 다시 불어넣어지기만을 기다리는 더 많은 고대 식물군을 보유할 수도 있다고 생각합니다.

Q: 담화에 따르면 맞는 것은 무엇인가?
(a) 비슷한 연대의 대추야자 씨앗은 스테노필라에 앞서 발견되었다.
(b) 스테노필라는 고대의 씨앗을 되살린 첫 번째 사례이다.
(c) 씨앗이 왜 동토층에서 손상되지 않았는지는 미스터리이다.
(d) 과학자들은 영구 동토층이 다른 온전한 식물을 저장하고 있다고 추측한다.

36

On the projector, you will see the latest television ratings for the fall season. As you can see, although many of our programs are doing fairly well, the shows that we aggressively marketed have not performed as well as we had anticipated. The situation mirrors what happened last year. Obviously, there's a pattern here, and we must identify and root out the problem. I expect all of you to help rectify the situation.

Q: Which is correct according to the talk?

(a) Heavily publicized shows fell short of expectations.
(b) Last year's fall ratings were higher than this year's.
(c) The company will cut back on aggressive marketing.
(d) The network's viewership problem is unprecedented.

영사기를 통해, 여러분은 가을 시즌의 최신 텔레비전 시청률을 보시게 됩니다. 보시다시피, 우리 프로그램들 중 다수가 꽤 잘하고 있기는 하나, 우리가 적극적으로 광고했던 쇼들이 기대만큼 성과가 좋지는 않았습니다. 이 상황은 작년에 일어났던 일과 흡사합니다. 분명, 여기에는 패턴이 있으니, 우리는 문제를 파악하여 뿌리 뽑아야 합니다. 저는 여러분 모두가 상황을 바로잡는 데 도와줄 것을 기대합니다.

Q: 담화에 따르면 맞는 것은 무엇인가?
(a) 홍보를 많이 한 프로들이 기대에 미치지 못했다.
(b) 작년 가을 시청률은 올해 것보다 높았다.
(c) 회사는 공격적인 마케팅을 줄일 것이다.
(d) 방송국의 시청률 문제는 전례 없는 것이다.

Part V

37~38

Rounding out today's market report is a bit of good news for shareholders of Senoco Incorporated. Senoco Incorporated's share price gained three points yesterday, closing in positive territory for the first time since a several-week-long plunge. The drop was caused by a product recall of microwave ovens. However, the household goods maker has begun to resolve the issue, and its stock value, sustained by reports of renewed consumer confidence, is bouncing back. Linda Newhouse, an analyst from MCS Financial, expects that Senoco Incorporated's stock will continue to perform strongly in the short-term. Provided the economy remains stable, she believes its stock value could eventually return to its peak level of last year. In fact, Ms. Newhouse has recommended that investors accumulate Senoco Incorporated stock in anticipation of further rises. Stay tuned for our next market report, which will include updates on international trade, tomorrow morning at 8 o'clock.

37. Q: What is the talk mainly about?

(a) Global economic data
(b) A company's stock performance
(c) Changing consumer patterns
(d) An investor's market predictions

38. Q: What does Ms. Newhouse advise investors to do?

(a) Sell shares of stock immediately
(b) Watch a market report
(c) Disregard product recall rumors
(d) Purchase additional shares

오늘 시장 보고의 마무리는 Senoco사의 주주들에게 다소 좋은 소식입니다. Senoco사의 주가가 어제 3포인트 오르면서, 지난 몇 주간의 폭락 이후 처음으로 오름세로 마감했습니다. 이 하락은 전자레인지의 제품 회수가 원인이었습니다. 하지만, 이 가정용품 제조사는 이 사안을 해결하기 시작했으며, 새로운 소비자 신뢰의 보도로 확인된 당사의 주가는 회복되고 있습니다. MCS Financial의 분석가 Linda Newhouse는 Senoco사의 주식이 단기적으로 실적 호조를 지속할 것으로 예상합니다. 그녀는 만약 경제가 안정적으로 유지된다면, 당사의 주가가 결국 지난해의 최고치로 회복할 수 있다고 생각합니다. 실제로, Ms. Newhouse는 투자자들이 추가적인 상승을 예상하여 Senoco사 주식을 모을 것을 권고했습니다. 내일 오전 8시에, 국제 거래에 대한 업데이트를 포함할 다음 시장 보고를 위해 계속 청취해 주시길 바랍니다.

37. Q: 담화는 주로 무엇에 대한 것인가?
(a) 세계 경제 정보
(b) 한 기업의 주식 성과
(c) 변화하는 소비자 패턴
(d) 투자자의 시장 예측

38. Q: Ms. Newhouse는 투자자들에게 무엇을 하도록 권고하는가?
(a) 즉시 주식을 매각한다.
(b) 시장 보고서를 주시한다.
(c) 제품 회수에 대한 소문을 무시한다.
(d) 추가적인 주식을 산다.

39~40

Gladiatorial contests in ancient Rome are thought to have originated with an Etruscan funeral rite for nobles in which armed combatants fought to the death and the loser accompanied the deceased aristocrat into the afterlife. Over the succeeding 300 years, the ritual turned into a blood sport held for the entertainment of Roman citizens. Some gladiators were the equivalent of professional fighters, but the most substantial proportion of them was made up of slaves who had been conscripted. Prisoners of war, criminals, and other social outcasts were also often forced into the arena. Gladiators fought each other using a frightening range of deadly implements but were also pitted against wild animals. Despite all of this, they were not necessarily condemned to a life of misery. Some who prevailed in battle received small rewards. The luckiest ones, if they survived enough encounters or had otherwise proven their mettle, might even be emancipated and granted the privileges of free citizens. Frequently, all but the weakest fighters were looked up to as exemplars of bravery.

39. Q: Who formed the majority of gladiators according to the talk?

(a) Disgraced noblemen
(b) Conscripted slaves
(c) Prisoners of war
(d) Common criminals

40. Q: What can be inferred from the talk?

(a) Gladiatorial contests were staged for Etruscan entertainment.
(b) Roman citizens were prohibited from becoming gladiators.
(c) Gladiators could choose their own opponents.
(d) Some gladiators were held in high esteem by Romans.

40. Q: 담화에서 추론할 수 있는 것은 무엇인가?

(a) 검투사 경기는 에트루리아인들의 오락을 위해 개최되었다.
(b) 로마 시민들이 검투사가 되는 것은 금지되었다.
(c) 검투사들은 그들의 상대를 고를 수 있었다.
(d) 일부 검투사들은 로마인들에게 높은 존경을 받았다.

VOCABULARY

Part I

1 A: 당신은 왜 오늘 사무실이 아니라 집에 있는 거예요?
   B: 감기에 걸렸거든요.

2 A: 안녕하세요. 이번 주말에 20피트짜리 이삿짐 트럭을 빌리고 싶은데요.
   B: 가능할 거예요. 저희가 몇 대 보유하고 있거든요.

3 A: 기후 변화에 대한 그 다큐멘터리는 큰 깨우침을 주었어.
   B: 나도 동의해, 매우 유익했어.

4 A: 넌 왜 이사 가니?
   B: 대출 할부금을 내지 못해서 집을 비워야 해.

5 A: 대학에서 Derek을 그 토론 대회에 내보낼 거래?
   B: 응. 그는 결코 져본 적이 없어서, 우리는 그의 연승이 계속되기를 기대하고 있어.

6 A: 파티를 이렇게 급히 준비할 수 있는 건 Sid뿐일 거야. 파티가 노련하게 준비됐어.
   B: 맞아. 그는 경험이 많은 게 분명해.

7 A: 지난번에 해외 사이트에서 물건을 주문했을 때, 난 결국 돈을 엄청 많이 지불해야 했어!
   B: 음, 그건 정부가 최근에 수입품에 대해서 더 높은 관세를 부과하기 때문이야.

8 A: 네가 먹고 있는 식사는 양이 너무 적어. 곧 다시 배고파질 거야.
   B: 복통이 있어서 많이 먹고 싶지 않아.

9 A: Bobby가 허락도 없이 내 차를 가져갔어.
   B: 그 애는 구제 불능이군. 그와 장시간에 걸쳐 대화를 해보자.

10 A: Taylor가 아파트에서 쫓겨났니?
   B: 아니, 쫓겨난 게 아니야. 그는 자발적으로 나갔어.

Part II

11 St. Andrews 주립 교도소의 수감자들은 정부에 의해 허용된 것보다 더 가혹한 처벌을 받는다.

12 호주산 유대목 동물인 길버트쥐캥거루는 올버니에서 다시 발견되기 전까지 멸종된 것으로 알려졌던 종이다.

13 과학자 프랜시스 크릭과 제임스 왓슨은 DNA의 이중 나선 구조를 발견한 것으로 공로를 인정받았다.

14 그 병원은 심장 수술로 매년 5천여 명의 환자들을 입원시킨다.

15 한 정부 관료는 많은 양이 소비되고 있는 것을 줄이기 위해 정크푸드에 세금을 부과할 것을 제안했다.

16 성미가 고약한 그 노인은 해가 갈수록 더욱 심술궂어지는 것 같았다.

17 연구원들은 캐모마일과 같은 몇몇 허브가 배탈을 진정시키고 완화시키는 효과가 있다고 말한다.

18 평론가들에게 극찬을 받았음에도 불구하고, 그 영화는 흥행 수익에서 미미한 성공만을 거두었다.

19 빈대는 오랜 기간의 굶주림을 견뎌낼 수 있는 끈질긴 생물이다.

20 청중 앞에서 말하는 것에 대한 Penny의 긴장감은 그녀가 말을 더듬게 만들었다.

21 현재 이란의 정치적 혼란은 논란이 많았던 최근의 대통령 선거로부터 상당 부분 야기되었다.

22 영화의 저작권을 침해하는 불법 행위로 일전에 한 일당이 검거되었다.

23 불과 10년 동안 9백여 점의 그림들을 그려내어, 반 고흐는 짧은 예술 경력에 비해서 다작하였다.

24 시스템 폴더 내의 파일을 삭제하거나 함부로 변경하려고 하지 마십시오, 그렇지 않으면 컴퓨터의 운영 체제가 작동하지 않을 수 있습니다.

25 소매점들은 눈을 사로잡는 쇼윈도 진열, 가격 인하와 특별 행사들로 쇼핑객들을 유혹한다.

26 지진으로 사망한 수천 구의 시신들을 화장하는 것이 보건상 위험 요소들을 줄이는 데 가장 좋은 방법으로 여겨졌다.

27 Daryl은 프로젝트를 시작하기 전에 마지막 순간까지 늑장을 부리는 것으로 알려져 있다.

28 심사 위원들은 탈락된 참가자가 다시 한 번 기회를 달라고 성가시게 졸랐을 때 짜증이 났다.

29 월별 지출을 줄이기 위해서, Simon은 자전거로 통근하고 먹는 것을 절약한다.

30 Jim은 집안일이 있을 때 꾸물거리는 경향이 있어서, 그의 가족은 그를 게으르고 무책임하다고 한다.

GRAMMAR

Part I

1 A: 파티에 참석하는 걸 왜 좋아하지 않으시나요?
B: 글쎄요, 제가 내성적이라서 사람들과 어울리는 것보다 집에 있는 게 더 좋아요.

2 A: Brittany의 아파트는 정말 고급스러웠어, 그렇지 않았니?
B: 그녀가 장식하는 데 지나치게 너무 많은 돈을 써서 그래.

3 A: James가 오늘 밤 독서 모임에 참석할 수 있을지 모르겠다고 말하더라.
B: 그럼, 언제든지 30분 정도만 잠깐 들러도 된다고 그에게 전해줘.

4 A: 넌 왜 그 면도기를 버리니?
B: 내 피부에는 너무 거칠었어.

5 A: Ted가 벌써 휴가에서 돌아왔니?
B: 응. Julie랑 내가 오늘 공원을 산책하면서 그를 지나쳤어.

6 A: 너 지금 일어났니? 벌써 10시 30분이야.
B: 어제 하이킹을 너무 많이 하지 않았더라면, 이렇게 늦잠을 자지 않았을 거야.

7 A: 토요일에 Pete의 파티에 갈 거니?
B: 아니, 내 친구도 못 가고, 나도 파티에 혼자 가는 걸 정말 싫어하거든.

8 A: Sandra가 댄스 경연대회에 참가할 수 없다니 참 실망스러워.
B: 그러게 말이야. 1회전 직전에 발목을 삐지만 않았다면 좋았을 텐데.

9 A: 직원들이 어떤 것을 주요 기사로 실을지 토론 중이에요.
B: 그런 딜레마에 직면했을 때, 나는 어떤 것이든 대부분의 사람들이 지지하는 쪽에 동의하겠어요.

10 A: 네가 유럽으로 배낭여행을 갈 계획이라고 들었어.
B: 맞아. 여행을 끝마치는 데 4주가 걸릴 것 같아.

Part II

11 정치 스캔들 이후에, 그 주지사는 사임을 발표하기로 결정했다.

12 히포크라테스는 의료직에 대한 윤리 규범을 세운 그리스 의사였다.

13 그 해안 도시 인구의 약 5분의 2가 외국 태생이다.

14 많은 차량이 있을 것이었기 때문에, Jamie는 직장까지 택시를 타는 것이 현명하다고 생각하지 않았다.

15 『Model Gadget Magazine』은 새로운 기술을 따라가지 못하는 사람들에게 정보를 알리고 최신 정보를 갱신할 수 있도록 만들어졌다.

16 Lemonte 사의 주식이 지난 분기 이래로 약 60퍼센트만큼 올랐다.

17 지난주에 유가가 급등했음에도 불구하고, 석유 소비량은 사상 최고치에 달하고 있다.

18 경찰에 반대하는 정서가 고조되어, 항의자들은 그 부서의 위법 행위에 대한 분노를 표출하기 위해 시내에 모였다.

19 Simon의 차가 앞에 있는 차와 충돌했을 때, 그는 휴대 전화로 메시지를 입력하고 있었다.

20 이산화탄소, 물, 햇빛이 식물이 생존하는 데 필요한 기본 요소들이다.

21 수년간, 인간의 활동으로 인해 동물 수천 종이 멸종되었다.

22 연구자들은 홍역 백신이 비타민 A와 함께 투여되었을 때 면역력을 향상시키는 것을 발견했다.

23 시장이 그 스캔들에 관한 인터뷰를 실시했을 때에는, 이미 그 사건에서의 그의 역할이 널리 보도된 후였다.

24 아이작 뉴턴 경은 다양한 물체에 미치는 중력의 영향을 측정해, 처음으로 중력을 계산한 과학자였다.

25 한 회사에서 여러 직무를 관리하는 경영진들은 그들의 경영에 대한 어느 정도의 통제권을 행사하는 것이 필수적이다.

Part III

26 (a) A: 너한테서 책을 한 권 빌리고 싶은데.
(b) B: 그래, 네가 원하는 건 무엇이든 빌려줄게. 특별히 생각해둔 책 있니?
(c) A: 혹시 제인 오스틴의 작품이 있니?
(d) B: 오래되어 너덜너덜한 『오만과 편견』밖에 없지만 기꺼이 네게 그걸 빌려줄게.

27 (a) A: 너 왜 기분이 그렇게 안 좋아 보이니?
(b) B: 위층 이웃집에서 시끄러운 음악 소리가 들려서 새벽 3시에 깼거든.
(c) A: 그거 정말 신경질 나지. 나도 그렇게 깰 때 짜증나더라고.
(d) B: 응. 어떤 사람들은 정말 배려가 없어서 매너를 좀 배워야 해!

28 (a) 20세기에 사라지기 전까지, 사람들은 전염병인 천연두를 매우 두려워했다. (b) 높은 사망률과 당시 이용 가능했던 치료법이 부족했던 것을 고려하면 이것은 당연한 일이었다. (c) 그러나 1796년, 에드워드 제너가 실시한 실험은 천연두 백신을 찾아냈다. (d) 제너의 진취성이 없었다면, 세상은 치명적인 질병으로부터 자유롭지 못했을지도 모른다.

29 (a) 코뿔소라고 알려진, 다섯 종으로 구성된 포유동물은 멸종 위기에 처해 있다. (b) 뿔에 대한 수요로 인한 사냥과 밀렵은 코뿔소 수의 급락을 초래했다. (c) 그 결과, 많은 야생동물 단체들이 더 이상의 대량 살상으로부터 위협받는 종들을 보호하기 위해 노력하고 있다. (d) 그러나 인간 활동과 밀렵이 진행되는 속도로는, 코뿔소를 효과적으로 구하기란 불가능할지도 모른다.

30 (a) 터키 카파도키아 지역의 공사장 인부들은 그들이 의도하지 않았던 무언가를 발견했다. (b) 저소득층 주택단지를 공사하는 동안, 그 인부들은 지하 도시를 발굴했다. (c) 대규모의 조사는 아직 시작되지 않았지만, 그 지역의 규모와 주요 특징들은 그것이 중요한 유적지임을 나타낸다. (d) 그 지하 도시는 무려 20,000명이나 되는 거주자들을 수용했을 가능성이 있다.

READING COMPREHENSION

Part I

1 _____를 찾고 계십니까? 특별한 분을 Maiden's Hill 호텔의 Promenade로 데려가시는 건 어떨까요? 단돈 100달러에 귀하와 동반자는 개인 공간에서 호화롭고 낭만적인 단돈 100달러에 귀하와 동반자는 개인 공간에서 호화롭고 낭만적인 식사를 하실 수 있습니다. 저희 현악 4중주단이 세레나데를 연주하는 동안 도시의 멋진 석양 경관을 즐기실 수 있으며, 저희는 귀하가 사랑하시는 분께 고급 초콜릿 한 상자와 장미 꽃다발을 선물해 드릴 것입니다. 지금 전화로 예약하세요!

(a) 기억에 남을 만남의 장소
(b) 저렴한 식사 경험
(c) 귀하와 연인을 위한 숙소
(d) 도시를 바라볼 수 있는 최고의 장소

2 아일랜드 의사들은 한 실험으로부터 보행기를 사용한 유아들이 _____는 결론을 내렸다. 이 발견은, 제조업체들의 주장과는 반대로, 유아들이 자신을 도와주는 도구에 익숙해지기 때문에 보행기가 아이들이 걷는 데 도움이 되지 않는다는 일부 엄마들의 믿음을 강화한다. 전문가들은 몇몇 보육 시설에서 아이의 부모들에게 아이의 보행기 사용과 유아가 얼마나 일찍부터 걷기 시작했는지에 관한 질문에 응답하도록 요청했다. 결과는 보행기가 유아들의 보행의 시작을 지연시킬 수 있다는 것을 보여주었다.

(a) 그 기구에 정서적으로 애착을 갖는다
(b) 보다 생산적인 신체적 발달을 경험한다
(c) 다른 유아들보다 더 늦게 걷기 시작한다
(d) 다른 유아들보다 더 오래 방치된 채로 남겨진다

3 멕시코시티 주민들은 _____의 결과로 괴로워하고 있다. 2006년 말에, 멕시코 아래에서 움직이는 거대한 지각판이 갑자기 궤도를 전환했고 현재는 이전보다 네 배 더 빨리 이동하고 있다. GPS 측정이 더 정확해지면서 과학자들은 사람이 감지할 수 없는 미세한 판의 움직임을 감지하는 능력을 얻었다. 기술이 아무리 발전한 것이라 해도 이 불규칙한 운동이 증가된 지진 활동을 의미하는 것인지 규명하는 데 전혀 도움이 되지 않는데, 과학자들이 이러한 중대한 전환을 목격했던 것이 이번이 처음이기 때문이다.

(a) 지진 활동 감지의 한계
(b) 점점 더 심해지는 지진
(c) 이동하는 지각판으로 인한 심각한 위험
(d) 여전히 설명할 수 없는 지질학적 사건

4 우리의 최종 손익을 전직원의 급여와 연동시키면 직원들은 분명 _____ 것입니다. 이를 염두에 두고, 회사가 최근 실시한 이익 분배제를 설명하기 위해 다음 보고서를 나눠 드렸습니다. 이 프로그램을 시작하는 우리의 목적은 두 가지입니다. 첫째, 우리는 직원들이 회사에서 주인 의식과 책임감을 느끼기를 바랍니다. 둘째, 우리는 직원들이 회사 자원을 아껴 쓰고 수익은 극대화하면서 비용은 최소화하도록 장려하기를 바랍니다.

(a) 회사에 주된 지출이 되지 않을
(b) 회사의 성공을 도우려 노력할
(c) 서로 협력하는 것에 있어서 약해지지 않을
(d) 그들의 권리보다 더 많이 받을

5 시중에서 가장 앞선 보안 시스템, EagleVision은 절도로부터 귀하의 귀중한 재고품을 보호하기 위해 출시되었습니다. 컴퓨터로 제어되는 카메라와 자동 경보 장치로, EagleVision은 귀하가 사업 성장에 집중하는 동안 귀하의 사업장 내부를 안전하게 지켜줄 것입니다. 비상 상황에 이상적인 무선 구내전화가 구비되어 있고, 시스템은 접근하기 쉬운 데이터베이스에 보안 비디오 장면을 녹화 및 정리합니다. EagleVision이면, 귀하는 _____ 수 있습니다.

(a) 얼굴 인식을 통해 고객을 식별할
(b) 회사의 재고 시스템을 관리할
(c) 생산성을 유지하고 동시에 안전할
(d) 어떤 컴퓨터에서든 비디오 카메라를 통제할

6
고대 그리스 천문학자들은 광도와 거리를 측정하는 데 순전히 개략적인 기하학 공식과 기초적인 육안 판독에 의지했다. 이렇게 사용된 방법은 대개 부정확한 수치를 낳았지만, 그리스인들이 _____는 것을 명심해야 한다. 수학과 과학 탐구는 초기 상태의 학문 분야였고, 이 시대의 가장 위대한 지성인들이 기능면에서 부족했던 것은 독창성으로 보완되었다. 우주에 대한 그들의 급성장한 지식은 거의 2천 년 동안 천문학적 사조에 영향을 미쳤다.

(a) 제한된 자원으로 놀라운 위업을 달성했다
(b) 지적 발달의 모든 분야에 영향을 미쳤다
(c) 공간의 계산에 사용되는 기하학을 고안했다
(d) 우주의 규모에 대해 정확하게 인식했다

7
인류가 당연하게 여기는 많은 발명품들은 _____. 군은 최첨단 발전을 군대를 위해서만 사용하였고, 이러한 개발은 비밀로 가려졌기 때문에, 일반 시민들은 그것들의 존재를 알아차리지 못했다. 그러나 일단 군의 기술 하나가 대중에게 알려지면, 방위 산업체들은 종종 그것을 평시 작전을 위해 특별히 조정할 방법을 찾으려 했다. 과거에는, 마차나 손수레가 전투에서의 편리함으로 인해 처음으로 명성을 얻었고, 현대의 후기 산업 사회에서는, 위성 텔레비전과 비행 시뮬레이션 게임 같은 레저와 휴식을 위한 혁신들이 군사적 계보를 갖고 있다.

(a) 군대에서도 사용된다
(b) 고대 군사 훈련에 기원을 둔다
(c) 그러한 명성을 얻을 것으로 기대되지 않았다
(d) 처음에는 민간용으로 의도되지 않았다

8
스마트폰과 모바일 어플리케이션의 확산은 지금까지 우리의 삶에 헤아릴 수 없는 편의를 가져왔다. 그러나 이러한 과학 기술이라는 신의 선물에 결점이 없는 것은 아니다. 최신의 제품을 고객의 손에 전달하기 위해 서두르다보니, 기술 회사들은 오류와 결함이 가득한 제품들을 출시하는 경향이 있는데, 고객은 이에 대해 당연히 화를 낸다. 줄어든 배터리 수명과 느린 성능은 오류로 인한 여러 문제들 중 두 가지일 뿐이다. 회사는 _____ 책임이 있다.

(a) 고객이 가장 원하는 기능에 대한 피드백을 구할
(b) 제품의 유용성을 약화시키는 이러한 사소한 결함들을 처리할
(c) 그들의 서비스가 모바일 기기들과 호환이 되도록 조정할
(d) 기기들의 최신판을 시기적절하게 공개할

9
응원 공연에서의 안전

응원 공연단은 스포츠 위원회의 규제 관리를 거의 받지 않고 공연을 한다. 비록 동작들이 점차 더 위험하고 복잡해지고 있음에도 불구하고, 응원으로 인한 심각한 부상 발생률은 다른 스포츠에 비해 상대적으로 적었다. _____, 학교 관리자들은 응원 활동에 대한 보다 엄격한 지침을 요구해 왔다. 그들의 우려를 해결하기 위해, 국립 대학 체육 협회는 경기 도중에 수행되는 묘기의 난이도에 상한선을 승인했다.

(a) 사실상
(b) 마침내
(c) 결과적으로
(d) 그럼에도 불구하고

10
수 세기 동안, '불가촉천민', 즉 인도의 하층 카스트 계급의 힌두 집단은 많은 학교와 사원에 들어가는 것을 금지하던 사회적 제약을 받았다. _____, 1997년 코체릴 라만 나라야난이 인도 대통령으로 당선된 것은 상황이 얼마나 많이 달라졌는지를 보여준다. 그 자신이 '불가촉천민'인 나라야난은 국회와 지방 의회에 의해 선출되었는데, 그 구성원들은 보통 상위 카스트 계급 출신이었다.

(a) 그럼에도 불구하고
(b) 사실상
(c) 게다가
(d) 그 사실을 감안할 때

Part II

11
우리 집에 처음 들여놓았던 텔레비전 세트는 커다란 나무 상자로 둘러싸인 14인치의 흑백 화면이었다. (a) 우리의 시간을 차지하게 된 새로운 형태의 오락 거리가 갑자기 생겼기 때문에 우리의 생활은 급격하게 변했다. (b) 그것은 돌려서 채널을 바꿀 수 있는 커다란 플라스틱 손잡이와 음량과 화질을 조정하는 작은 손잡이들을 달고 있었다. (c) 당시만 해도 금속성의 지직거리는 소음이 나던 스피커들은 거의 화면만큼 넓적한 목각 가리개 뒤에 있었다. (d) TV 상자에는 TV 세트를 사용하지 않을 때 화면을 가릴 수 있는 두 개의 미닫이문까지 달려 있었다.

12
Communication Hub 사는 현재 12개월 미만의 휴대 전화 가입 서비스는 제공하지 않고 있습니다. (a) 연간 계약을 체결하고자 하는 고객들만 월별 청구 사양을 포함하는 저희 상품을 이용하실 수 있습니다. (b) 그러나 Communication Hub 사는 빠듯한 예산의 휴대 전화 사용자들을 위해 단기 선불 상품을 제공하고 있습니다. (c) 고객들은 소득 명세서나 양호한 신용 상태를 증명하지 않아도 3개월이나 6개월의 선불 상품을 선택하실 수 있습니다. (d) 저희의 계약 기반 상품을 신청하신 분들은 자격을 얻기 위해 점포에서 실시하는 점포 내 신용 검사를 통과하셔야 합니다.

Part III

13
공지

졸업 논문을 심사받고 있는 졸업 예정자들은 회의실을 예약하려면 대학 총무부와 조정해야 합니다. 규칙상, 미리 계획된 다른 활동들을 방해하지 않도록 하기 위해 예정 시간이 철저히 엄수되어야 합니다. 회의실은 학생들에게 무료로 이용 가능하지만, 제시간에 오지 못한 사람들과 그들에게 허용된 시간을 넘겨서 시설을 사용하는 이들에게는 요금이 부과될 것입니다.

행정실

Q: 공지는 주로 무엇에 관한 내용인가?

(a) 예약 취소에 대한 벌금
(b) 예약 시간을 지켜야 할 필요성
(c) 논문 발표를 위해 사용 가능한 장소
(d) 회의실 예약 절차

14
아프리카계 미국인 극작가 로레인 한스베리는 1959년 희곡 『태양 속의 건포도』에서 흑인 등장인물들과 주제, 그리고 갈등들을 이전까지 브로드웨이 작품에서는 볼 수 없었던 방식으로 묘사했다. 그녀는 제2차 세계 대전 이후 수년간 미국의 특징을 이루던 경제적 번영 하에서 증가하던 자국 내 긴장감과 인종 간 긴장감을 비롯한 1950년대 미국의 많은 문제들을 다루었다. 한스베리에게는, 1950년대 백인 미국

인들이 경험한 부의 상승이 흑인들을 대상으로 여전히 자행되고 있던 차별을 가릴 수 없었다.

Q: 지문의 주제는 무엇인가?
(a) 어떤 사회적 갈등을 한스베리가 예측했는지
(b) 브로드웨이 작품에서 흑인들이 어떻게 묘사되었는지
(c) 더 많은 부가 전후 미국 문학에 어떻게 영향을 미쳤는지
(d) 로레인 한스베리의 획기적인 희곡이 무엇을 논하는지

15
Mr. Alexander께,

저희는 귀하의 위성 텔레비전 서비스 취소 요청을 접수하였습니다. 하지만 귀하께서 저희 회사에 가입하신 서비스 계약은 2년으로 약정되어 있으므로, 서비스를 취소하실 경우 조기 해약금 300달러가 규정되어 있음을 알려 드립니다. 이 위약금을 지불하기 원하지 않으실 경우, 저희 회사에서는 세금과 추가 요금을 제외한 매월 약정 요금을 계속 청구할 것이며, 귀하께서는 계속 프로그램을 수신하시게 됩니다. 본 사안과 관련하여 귀하의 의향을 알려주시기 바랍니다.

진심을 담아,
William Johnston

Q: Mr. Alexander에게 보내진 편지의 주된 목적은 무엇인가?
(a) 그가 회사와의 계약서에 서명해야 한다는 것을 알리기 위해
(b) 그의 위성 텔레비전 서비스 해약 요청을 확인하기 위해
(c) 미지불 잔액을 가능한 한 빨리 지불하라고 요청하기 위해
(d) 그가 위성 텔레비전 상품을 업데이트하고 싶어하는지 묻기 위해

16
영국의 해부학자이자 고생물학자인 Richard Owen은 당시 영국에서 뼈가 발굴된 거대한 멸종 파충류를 명명하기 위해 1842년에 '공룡'이라는 용어를 제안했다. 그는 대부분의 알려진 파충류는 고관절에 2개의 추골이 있는 데 반해, 그 미지의 생물은 5개의 추골을 가지고 있다는 것을 관찰했다. 뿐만 아니라, 새로 발견된 파충류들은 사지가 도마뱀 다리처럼 몸뚱이 옆으로 뻗어 있지 않고, 몸통이 아래에 달려 있었다. 따라서 Owen은 그 생물이 그들만의 파충류군으로 분류되어야 한다고 생각했다.

Q: 지문의 요지는 무엇인가?
(a) 공룡은 시간이 지나면서 파충류로 진화한 것으로 여겨졌다.
(b) 고생물학 분야는 영국에서 정식 과학으로 발전했다.
(c) 공룡과 도마뱀은 유사한 특징을 지닌 것으로 밝혀졌다.
(d) Owen은 공룡을 별개의 파충류 범주로 인식한 최초의 과학자였다.

17
숙련된 종업원 모집

Trenton의 가장 오래된 인도 음식점 중 하나인, Mughal Palace는, 화요일부터 일요일까지 점심과 저녁 식사 시간에 교대 근무로 일할 숙련된 종업원을 찾고 있습니다.

이 직위의 주요 업무는 주문을 받고 음식을 나르는 것입니다. 하지만, 뷔페 테이블을 준비하고, 음료를 만들고, 음식 준비를 돕는 것을 포함한 추가적인 업무가 주어질 수도 있습니다. 지원자들은 고급 식당에서 종업원으로 일한 최소 6개월의 경력이 있어야 하고 인도 음식에 익숙해야 합니다.

지원하기 위해서는, 당신의 이력서를 mughalpalace@joynet.org로 보내주십시오. 이 직종 종사자의 추천서를 2부 포함해 주십시오. 임금은 지원자에 따라 다릅니다.

Q: 광고에 포함되어 있지 않은 정보는 무엇인가?
(a) 필요한 경력의 종류
(b) 종업원이 받게 될 액수
(c) 직원의 책무
(d) 식당의 연락처

18
지난 300년 동안 두 가지 주요 혁신은 농작물 수확량의 눈부신 향상을 가능하게 했다. 첫 번째 혁신은 보다 높은 수준의 유전학의 개념화로, 이 결과 교배와 선별 번식이 지속적으로 작물의 균질성과 내구성을 증대시키고 있다. 더 나아가, 콤바인과 트랙터 같은 기계의 발명은 노동 생산성을 신장시켰다. 지금은 경작자 혼자서 전례 없는 양의 곡식을 파종하고, 타작하며, 수확할 수 있다. 이러한 농업의 진보는 세계 인구에 식량을 공급하는 농부들의 능력에 중심이 된다.

Q: 다음 중 지문의 내용과 일치하는 것은?
(a) 기술의 진보는 농부들을 덜 중요하게 만들었다.
(b) 농업 과학은 약 300년 전에 발전했다.
(c) 기계화 전에는 식량 공급이 불충분했다.
(d) 유전학 연구가 보다 튼튼한 농작물을 가능하게 했다.

19
관계자 분께,

저는 귀사의 공항 지점에서 받은 서비스에 관해 불만을 제기하고자 합니다. 저녁 늦게 착륙한 뒤, 저는 렌터카 예약을 확인하고 보관소로 안내받았습니다. 그곳 직원은 자동차 바퀴 덮개가 손상된 것을 보았지만, 제가 자동차를 소유하고 있을 때 그 손상이 발생한 게 아니기 때문에 제게 비용이 청구되지 않을 거라고 확인해 주었습니다. 그런데 이게 어찌된 영문인지 약속된 시간에 차를 반납하자, 차량 검사 담당 직원이 제게 수리비 지불 책임을 지웠습니다. 제가 변호사를 구하게 되기 전에 합의를 봤으면 합니다.

진심을 담아,
Tom Johnson

Q: 다음 중 편지의 내용과 일치하는 것은?
(a) 편지를 쓴 사람은 자동차 상태에 대해 책임이 있다.
(b) 편지를 쓴 사람은 직원들로부터 서로 상반되는 진술을 들었다.
(c) 편지를 쓴 사람의 보험사는 차량 손상에 대해 변상하지 않으려고 한다.
(d) 편지를 쓴 사람은 분쟁에서 그의 편에 설 변호사와 접촉했다.

20
1990년대 이래로, 대부분의 일자리가 해외에서 외부 조달되면서, 미국인들에게 제조 및 고객 서비스 분야에서의 노동 기회가 부족해졌다. 미국인 근로자들은 유능하고 고학력이지만, 또한 높은 임금을 받기도 한다. 해외로 이전함으로써, 기업들은 새로운 시설에 대한 투자금이 빠르게 회수되는 정도로 인건비를 줄일 수 있다. 일례로, Davidson Industries는 비용에 더 민감한 일부 부서들을 인도에 두고 있다. 이러한 추세의 결과로, 미국의 노동 시장은 대대적으로 개혁되고 있다.

Q: 왜 미국 기업들은 다른 나라에 사업체들을 세우고 있는가?
(a) 해외 노동자들이 생산 공장에서 일한 더 많은 경험을 가진다.
(b) 해외의 노동 임금이 보통 훨씬 더 저렴하다.
(c) 미국 노동 시장은 필요 이상의 자격을 갖춘 노동자로 포화 상태이다.
(d) 미국의 노동 시장은 정책 변경으로 인해 불안정하다.

21
국내 > 정치

Furlong이 지지를 잃다

Rod Furlong 수상은 그의 극좌당의 몇몇 의원들이 지난 2주에 걸쳐 야당인 보수당으로 탈당한 후 입지를 약화시키는 정치적 좌절을 겪었다. 이러한 당파 관계의 변화는 여당 지도자들 간에 불화가 일어나고 있다는 말이 내부 출처에서 언론으로 흘러나온 바로 며칠 뒤에 일어났.

탈당자들 중에는 Reggie Galveston 경제 장관을 비롯한 Furlong 내각의 동료들이 있었다. 몇 개월 전에 소집된 중간 선거에서 극좌당이 경쟁 당들로부터 굴욕을 당한 뒤 정부 내에서 불만의 목소리가 높아졌다.

Q: 지문에 따르면 다음 중 극좌당에 대한 내용과 일치하는 것은?
(a) 다른 당에서의 탈당으로 새로운 구성원들을 얻게 됐다.
(b) 선거 패배 이후 혼란에 빠져 있다.
(c) Furlong 수상이 패배한 이후 해체되었다.
(d) 현재 몇몇 언론 단체와 갈등 상태에 있다.

22

James Cook 대학이 주재하는
제12회 연례 창의적 글쓰기 학회
2월 22일-24일

세부 사항:
· 학생 회관에서의 초보 작가들이 어려움을 극복할 수 있는 방법을 탐구하는 작가 Christopher Noble의 기조 연설
· 다양한 글쓰기 분야에 관한 세미나와 워크숍, 이들 모두는 캠퍼스 여기저기의 여러 건물에서 열림. 자세한 일정과 장소 목록은 www.jamescookuniversity.com/englishdept를 방문할 것
· Pottsville 주민 센터에서의 폐회식과 사교 행사

각 세미나의 좌석은 제한될 것임을 유념해주시고, 따라서 빠른 등록이 권장됩니다. 티켓 가격의 15퍼센트 할인을 받기 위해서는 2월 1일 전에 등록하세요.

Q: 다음 중 광고의 내용과 일치하는 것은?
(a) 폐회식은 저명한 작가에 의해 주최될 것이다.
(b) 여러 개의 세미나에 등록하는 사람들은 돈을 적게 낼 것이다.
(c) 학회에는 출판을 한 작가만이 참가할 수 있다.
(d) 행사는 몇몇 다른 장소들에서 열릴 것이다.

23 종종 영국 문학에서 가장 뛰어난 문필가로 여겨지는 윌리엄 셰익스피어는 희곡 작가로 가장 잘 알려져 있다. 그러나 그가 시인이자 극작가 생활을 통해서만 생계를 이어갈 수는 없었다는 사실을 아는 이들은 거의 없다. 알려진 바에 따르면 셰익스피어는 또한 영국에서 교장을 지냈고 북유럽에서 병사 생활을 했다. 많은 문학 평론가들은 셰익스피어가 그러한 다른 직업을 갖지 않고 오로지 희곡과 시를 쓰는 데만 집중했다면 어떤 다른 걸작들을 만들어냈을지 궁금해 한다.

Q: 지문에서 셰익스피어에 대해 추론할 수 있는 것은 무엇인가?
(a) 그의 희곡은 시보다 더 인정받았다.
(b) 그는 작가 생활을 시작하기 전에 군인이었다.
(c) 작가라는 직업은 충분한 수입을 제공하지 못했다.
(d) 비평가들은 다른 직업들이 그의 집필 역량을 향상시켰다고 생각한다.

24 한 새로운 연구에 따르면 인류의 초기 조상은 극한 기후에서 살아남기 위해 생리학적 변화에 적응했을지도 모른다고 한다. 이 연구를 실시한 과학자들은 1920년대에 중국에서 화석이 발견된 호모 에렉투스가 더 많은 혈액을 사지에 흘려 보내기 위해 생리학적 진화를 겪었을 지도 모른다고 한다. 전문가들은 북경 원인이라고도 알려진 이 특정 호모 에렉투스가, 아직 불이 발견되지 않았던 약 77만 년 전의 빙하기 동안 생존해 있었다고 추정하고 있다. 이 과학자들은 자신들의 가설이 어떻게 북경 원인이 그 시대의 환경에서 살아남았는지를 설명해줄 수 있다고 믿고 있다.

Q: 지문에서 추론할 수 있는 것은 무엇인가?
(a) 북경 원인은 몸을 따뜻하게 하기 위해 모피로 만든 옷을 이용했다.
(b) 중국은 빙하기 동안 지구상에서 가장 추운 곳이었다.
(c) 호모 에렉투스는 불을 일으킨 최초의 인류 조상이었다.
(d) 북경 원인은 외부의 열원 없이도 추운 기온에서 생존했다.

25 장기 이식은 도덕적, 윤리적으로 밀접하게 관련되어 있다. 그러나 노스캐롤라이나 대학의 Anthony Atala 박사가 발명한 독특한 형태의 재생 의학은 그러한 문제를 피해 갈지도 모른다. 이 창의적인 시술은 특수 젤과 함께 세포를 번갈아 분출시키는 특별히 개조된 잉크젯 프린터와 프린터 카트리지를 이용한다. 젤이 증발하면, 세포는 함께 성장하여 장기 모양의 골격을 따라 놓일 수 있다. 완전히 자란 장기는 골격 안에서 성장한 뒤, 거부 반응의 위험 없이 환자에게 안전하게 이식될 수 있다.

Q: 글쓴이가 가장 동의할 것 같은 진술은 무엇인가?
(a) 세포 생성과 프린터 기능성 사이에 유사점이 있다.
(b) 과학적 진보는 언젠가 장기 이식을 불필요하게 만들 것이다.
(c) Atala 박사의 기술은 철학적인 관심사를 조명하게 했다.
(d) 과학 기술의 적용은 어쩌면 큰 의학적 발전을 가져올 수도 있다.

Part IV

26 ~ 27

어머니의 날 기념 경연 대회:
'사랑하는 엄마에게' 영상 출품

CommunityWeb이 영상 경연 대회로 어머니의 날을 기념합니다. 어머니에게 바치는 영상 메시지를 제출할 아들과 딸들을 초대합니다. 참가자들은 어머니를 위해 노래하거나, 그녀를 위한 시를 낭송하거나, 그녀와 관련된 이야기를 할 수도 있습니다. 혹은 더 창의적인 접근을 선택할 수도 있습니다. 우리는 최고 출품작들을 우리의 '사랑하는 엄마에게' 페이지에 올릴 것이고, 가장 인기있는 영상의 창작자(들)는 최대 다섯 명의 가족 구성원(성인 두 명과 어린이 세 명)을 위한 바하마로의 유람선 여행권을 차지할 것입니다.

지침:
· 영상들은 AVI 또는 MP4 파일로 제출되어야 합니다. 25메가바이트 보다 큰 파일들은 인정되지 않습니다.
· 자녀들로부터 온 메시지여야 하지만, 자녀가 너무 어린 경우에는 부모가 도울 수 있습니다.
· 저작권의 보호를 받는 음악이나 영상 클립은 인정할 수 없습니다.
· 비속어는 허용되지 않습니다.

5월 10일까지 영상을 dearmom@communityweb.com으로 보내주세요. 파일의 크기가 10메가바이트를 초과하는 경우, 압축 프로그램을 사용해주시기 바랍니다.

26. Q: 다음 중 지문의 내용과 일치하는 것은?
(a) 모든 영상 파일들은 제출되기 전에 압축되어야 한다.
(b) AVI 파일들만이 '사랑하는 엄마에게' 페이지에 게재될 것이다.
(c) 경연 대회 참가 자격을 갖추기 위해서 영상들은 반드시 저작권을 얻어야 한다.
(d) 영상 제출품에 대한 용량 제한이 있다.

27. Q: 광고에서 추론할 수 있는 것은 무엇인가?
(a) 바하마로의 유람선 여행은 어머니의 날에 시작한다.
(b) CommunityWeb은 어린 아이들을 위해 고안된 제품들을 판매한다.
(c) 녹화 장치는 부모 중 한 사람에 의해 작동될 수 있다.
(d) 참가자들은 그들 자신의 제출품에 투표하는 것이 허용되지 않는다.

28~29

사설: 도시 경관이 변화되기 시작했다
독자의 코멘트
Peter77   4시간 전

나는 당신이 왜 초대형의 흉물스러운 것들의 건축을 허가하는 시장의 최근 결정을 지지하는지 이해할 수 없습니다. 도시의 윤곽선이, 대부분 5층 높이 이하인, 역사적인 건물들로 구성되어 있다는 사실은, 그것을 세계에서 가장 독특한 것 중 하나로 만들면서, 매일 수천의 관광객을 끌어 모읍니다. 수십 년간, 우리는 도심에 어떠한 높은 건물의 건축도 방지하는 규정들로 이 문화적 자산을 보호해왔습니다. 이런 규제들은 지난 2월에 시장 Ian Conner에 의해 통과된 새로운 정책에 의해 약화되었는데, 이 정책은 새로운 건물이 300미터 높이까지 건설되는 것을 허가했고, 이제 우리는 그 이유를 압니다.

그 새로운 정책의 결과로, 각 60층을 넘는, 총 22개의 고층건물들이 금융 지구에 건설될 것입니다. 이는 수 세기 동안 보존되어 왔던 경관을 없애면서, 우리의 윤곽선을 돌이킬 수 없게 변화시킬 것입니다. 이 고층건물들이 역사적인 건물들의 경관을 가로막지 않을 것이라는 Conner의 주장은 명백히 틀린데, 이는 300미터의 고층건물이 100미터의 교회 위에 우뚝 서지 않을 수 없기 때문입니다. 시장의 통찰력 부족은 그가 피상적인 구경거리에만 관심이 있다는 것을 보여줍니다. 우리는 너무 늦기 전에 노력하여 이 거대한 것들의 건축을 중단해야 합니다.

28. Q: 코멘트의 주된 목적은 무엇인가?
(a) 시장 Ian Conner에게 사임할 것을 요구하기 위해
(b) 계획된 건물 디자인을 변경할 것을 요청하기 위해
(c) 도시의 역사적 건물들의 형편없는 상태를 강조하기 위해
(d) 새로운 고층건물들을 건설하는 시장의 선택에 의문을 제기하기 위해

29. Q: 글쓴이는 어떤 진술에 가장 동의할 것 같은가?
(a) 새로운 정책은 도시의 자산을 보호하기 위해 폐지되어야 한다.
(b) 새로운 고층건물들은 사회의 부자들에게만 유용할 것이다.
(c) 새로운 높은 건물들을 허가하는 결정은 시장이 부패했다는 것을 보여준다.
(d) 시장은 도심의 모든 건축을 중지해야 한다.

30~31

평등주의는 대부분의 사회적 불화가 부의 불평등한 분배에서 기인한다는 믿음이다. 경제적 불평등은 보통 사회의 상류층 구성원들에게 특권을 주는 정부로 인해 발생한다. 이러한 관행은 가난한 이들의 권리에 대한 모욕으로 해석되어, 가진 이들과 가지지 못한 이들 사이에 팽팽한 대립을 초래한다. 그러므로, 평등주의자들은 특혜를 없애고 사회 계층들 사이에 더 확대된 평등을 촉진하는 것을 목표로 하고, 그렇게 함으로써 시민들에게 더 균형 잡힌 경제적 기회를 제공하고자 한다. 지지자들은 이것이 이루어질 때에만 사회가 시민 간의 갈등에서 자유로울 것이라고 믿는다.

사람들은 두 학파가 많은 기본적인 견해들을 공유하기 때문에 종종 평등주의를 공산주의와 혼동한다. 예를 들어, 이 이념들은 이용 가능한 경제적 자원의 대부분을 통제하는 사회적 엘리트의 존재에 반대하고 가난한 사람들의 수를 줄이는 것을 지지한다. 게다가, 두 이념 모두 개인들이 오직 능력에 따라 사회적 그리고 경제적 혜택을 받아야 한다는 생각에 동의한다. 하지만, 공산주의는 사회 계층의 철폐를 옹호하는 반면, 평등주의는 그것이 필수적이라고 주장하지 않는다.

30. Q: 평등주의자들의 믿음은 무엇인가?
(a) 튼튼한 경제를 이룩하는 것이 가난한 사람들의 권리가 보호받도록 보장하는 가장 좋은 방법이다.
(b) 특혜는 더 공평하고 공정한 사회를 만드는 효과적인 수단으로 여겨진다.
(c) 모든 계층의 사람들에게 동등한 경제적 기회를 제공하는 것은 사회적 갈등을 근절할 수 있다.
(d) 중산층의 성장을 촉진하는 것은 사회적 부패를 제거하는 데 도움이 될 것이다.

31. Q: 평등주의가 공산주의와 유사한 점이 아닌 것은 무엇인가?
(a) 하나의 사회 집단이 지나친 부를 갖는 것에 반대한다.
(b) 빈곤 수준이 상당히 크게 감소되어야 한다고 주장한다.
(c) 개인들이 공적에 근거하여 보상받는 것을 옹호한다.
(d) 사회 안에서 모든 계층의 완전한 철폐를 주장한다.

32~33

히스파니올라섬의 국가들

도미니카 공화국과 아이티는, 카리브해의 히스파니올라섬을 공유함에도 불구하고, 여러 측면에서 다르다. 일례로, 전자는 풍부한 목초지들과 두터운 토양을 가지고 있어서, 후자보다 농업에 더 적합하다. 그러나, 17세기 동안, 경제적 발전의 측면에서 처음에는 아이티가 상대를 앞섰다. 이에 대한 한가지 이유는 도미니카 공화국이 쇠퇴하는 스페인에 의해 식민 지배를 받았던 것에 반하여 아이티는 부유한 프랑스의 식민 지배를 받았다는 점이다. 프랑스는 아이티의 인구와 생산성을 향상시킬, 더 많은 노예를 보낼 자원들을 보유했지만, 동시에 국가의 농업 자본을 낭비한 삼림 파괴와 토양 침식을 촉진했다.

오늘날, 그것은 아주 다른 이야기인데, 도미니카 공화국이 카리브해에서 가장 큰 경제로 성장했기 때문이다. 농산물 수출에 계속 심하게 의존하는 대신에, 그 국가는 다각화했고 성장하는 서비스업과 제조업을 가진다. 이웃 나라와 다르게, 도미니카 공화국은 최근 몇 년 간 어느 정도의 정치적 안정성을 얻었고, 이는 경제를 번영하게 했다. 아이티는, 반면에, 농업적 기반을 심하게 훼손하는 일련의 굉장히 파괴적인 지진들을 겪었다. 이제 그곳은 가장 기본적인 사회 기반 시설조차 부재한, 지구에서 가장 가난한 곳 중 하나이다.

32. Q: 지문은 주로 무엇에 관한 내용인가?
(a) 식민지 시대 동안 카리브해 섬의 경제적 발전
(b) 히스파니올라가 프랑스와 스페인에 의해 점령당한 역사적 원인들
(c) 한때 유럽의 식민지였던 두 이웃하는 국가의 뚜렷하게 다른 역사
(d) 여러 카리브해 국가들에서의 농업 생산량의 감소

33. Q: 지문에서 아이티에 대해 추론할 수 있는 것은 무엇인가?
(a) 도미니카 공화국에 비하여 정치적 안정성이 부족하다.
(b) 재정적이고 인도적인 원조를 위해 도미니카 공화국에 크게 의존한다.
(c) 만연한 삼림 파괴 때문에 여러 자연재해를 겪어왔다.
(d) 최근 몇 년 간 다수의 공공 서비스를 재건했다.

34~35

속보   3시간 전 갱신됨
주 상원의원이 더 높은 공직을 노리다
Alice Merton 씀

펜실베이니아의 주 상원의원인 Jean Stein이, 주의 보수당 본부에서 그녀의 대통령 출마를 공식 선언했다. 상원의원 Stein은, 현직 대통령 Carson McCullers와 앨라배마 주지사인 Austin Bates에 뒤이어, 뉴햄프셔의 다가오는 예비선거에 등록한 세 번째 후보이다. 그녀의 두 번의 임기 동안, Stein은 혁신의 상징이 되었고 편협하고, 시대에 뒤처진 생각을 가진 정치인들에 진저리가 난 젊은 보수주의자들을 열광시켰다. 최근 여론 조사에 따르면, 그녀는 가장 가능성 있는 후보인 McCullers와 막상막하이며, 그녀의 출마는 인기와 탄력 모두를 얻고 있다.

전국적인 Stein의 인기는 현직 대통령과 행정부의 금융 추문에 대한 노골적인 비판 때문이라고 생각된다. 로비스트의 꿈으로 여겨지는 McCullers와 다르게, Stein은 기업의 연결고리가 거의 없고, 오직 개개인의 기부를 통해서만 선거유세의 자금을 대고 있다. 그녀는

또한 의회의 로비 금지법을 제의했고 정치인들이 개인적인 시민들로부터의 기부만 수용해야 한다고 제안했다. 한편, Stein의 허를 찌를 방법을 찾고 있는 McCullers는, 모든 후보자들이 각 선거 동안 같은 양의 기금을 받을 것을 제의했다. 비록 많은 이들의 Stein의 가능성에 의문을 갖지만, 그녀의 존재는 이미 현재 상태를 흔들어 놓았다.

34. Q: 기사의 주제는 무엇인가?

(a) 대통령 Carson McCullers의 재선 유세 진행 과정
(b) 예비선거에서 유력한 후보의 부정부패
(c) 전국 경선에서 지지를 얻고 있는 지역 정치인
(d) 의회 내 정치적 로비와 기업의 기부 체계

35. Q: 다음 중 기사의 내용과 일치하는 것은?

(a) Stein은 모든 로비스트들이 공직을 구하는 것이 금지되어야 한다고 제의했다.
(b) McCullers는 기득권의 영향에 대한 그의 저항으로 유명하다.
(c) Stein은 전적으로 익명의 기부를 통해 그녀의 선거유세 자금을 대고 있다.
(d) McCullers는 모든 후보자들 간의 조달 자금이 같아야 한다고 제안했다.

TEST 06

LISTENING COMPREHENSION

Part I

1

W: George, could you lend me a hand?
M: _____

(a) I already lent it to you.
(b) OK, just give me a minute.
(c) Thanks for the offer.
(d) Of course you can.

W: George, 저 좀 도와줄 수 있어요?
(a) 그건 제가 이미 빌려 드렸는데요.
(b) 알았어요, 잠시만요.
(c) 제안해줘서 고마워요.
(d) 물론 하실 수 있지요.

2

M: I wonder if Mayor Miller will get reelected.
W: _____

(a) None of us voted for that.
(b) Seems unlikely, since the current mayor is so beloved.
(c) It would come as a huge surprise to me.
(d) That's what elections are for.

M: Miller 시장이 재선될지 궁금해.
(a) 우리 중 누구도 그것에 투표하지 않았어.
(b) 그럴 것 같지 않아, 현 시장이 매우 인기 있으니까.
(c) 그건 나에게 아주 놀라운 일일 거야.
(d) 그게 선거가 필요한 이유지.

3

W: I'm sorry to hear you were laid off.
M: _____

(a) It'll be hard to make ends meet.
(b) It's a very rewarding occupation.
(c) They've agreed to adjust my wage.
(d) It's no problem. Just lay it there.

W: 네가 해고를 당했다니 유감이야.
(a) 생활하기가 빠듯해질 거야.
(b) 그건 굉장히 보람 있는 직업이야.
(c) 그들은 내 임금을 조정하기로 합의했어.
(d) 문제없어. 그냥 거기에 그걸 둬.

4

M: Would it be OK with you if I smoked?
W: _____

(a) Sure, here you go.
(b) Be my guest.
(c) I gave up smoking.
(d) I'm fine, thanks.

M: 제가 담배를 피워도 괜찮을까요?
(a) 그럼요, 여기 있어요.
(b) 그러세요.
(c) 전 담배를 끊었어요.
(d) 괜찮아요, 고마워요.

5

W: What's with the decision to drop out of school?
M: _____

(a) I'm considering changing my major.
(b) That's not my decision to make.
(c) I'm leaving right after graduation.
(d) I've been feeling burnt out.

W: 왜 학교를 중퇴하기로 결정한 거야?
(a) 전공을 바꿀까 생각 중이야.
(b) 그건 내가 내릴 결정이 아니야.
(c) 졸업하자마자 떠날 거야.
(d) 지쳤다는 느낌이 들었어.

6

M: Does the car have enough gas to get us into town?
W: _____

(a) Yes. Prices are expected to plummet.
(b) I filled the tank last night.
(c) I saw a gas station nearby.
(d) No. Electric ones are more efficient.

M: 차에 우리가 시내까지 갈 정도의 기름이 충분히 있어?
(a) 응. 가격이 급락할 거라고 예상돼.
(b) 내가 어젯밤에 탱크를 채웠어.
(c) 근처에서 주유소를 봤어.
(d) 아니. 전기차가 더 효율적이야.

7

W: Your dad really has a knack for gardening.
M: _____

(a) He's always had a green thumb.
(b) No way. He adores plants.
(c) Yeah, it's overgrown with weeds.
(d) He'll hire a landscaper to do it.

W: 너희 아빠는 정원 가꾸는 솜씨가 정말 좋으시네.
(a) 아빠는 원래 원예에 재능이 있으셨어.
(b) 그럴 리가. 아빠는 식물을 아주 좋아하셔.
(c) 응, 그곳은 잡초가 무성해.
(d) 그는 그 일을 할 정원사를 고용할 거야.

8

M: I'm not really into rock and roll.
W: _____

(a) Yeah, it soothes the soul.
(b) Hip-hop's not my thing.
(c) It's not my top choice either.
(d) You were always into that.

M: 나는 로큰롤을 그다지 좋아하지 않아.
(a) 맞아, 그건 영혼을 달래주지.
(b) 힙합은 내 취향이 아니야.
(c) 나도 가장 좋아하는 것은 아니야.
(d) 넌 항상 그것을 좋아했지.

9

W: Have you confirmed our dinner reservation?
M: _____

(a) Actually, we dined on the patio.
(b) Sure. I'll reserve us a table.
(c) It's all taken care of.
(d) Let's go out instead.

W: 우리의 저녁 식사 예약 확인했어?
(a) 실은, 우리는 안뜰에서 식사했어.
(b) 물론이지. 테이블을 하나 예약할게.
(c) 그건 모두 처리되었어.
(d) 대신에 외출하자.

10

M: If you don't accept that job offer, you'll regret it.
W: _____

(a) They said I'm overqualified.
(b) I should've sent a cover letter.
(c) It depends on the job.
(d) I want to consider all angles first.

M: 그 일자리 제의를 수락하지 않으면, 넌 후회하게 될 거야.
(a) 그들은 내가 필요 이상의 자격을 갖췄대.
(b) 난 자기 소개서를 보냈어야 했어.
(c) 그건 일자리에 따라 다르지.
(d) 난 우선 모든 관점에서 고려해보고 싶어.

Part II

11

M: Ms. Wallace, here's my revised article.
W: I was expecting it before now.
M: Sorry to keep you waiting. There were some major errors.
W: _____

(a) That's OK. I'll wait for you.
(b) I'll overlook it this time.
(c) Your report isn't due anytime soon.
(d) That means we have to edit it.

M: Ms. Wallace, 여기 제 수정된 기사예요.
W: 전 지금보다 더 일찍 줄 거라고 생각했는데요.
M: 기다리시게 해서 죄송해요. 몇 가지 중대한 오류가 있어서요.
(a) 괜찮아요. 기다릴게요.
(b) 이번에는 눈감아 드릴게요.
(c) 보고서를 당장 내셔야 하는 건 아니에요.
(d) 그럼 우리가 그걸 수정해야 한다는 거군요.

12

W: When does Peter's plane get in?
M: A few hours from now, I think.
W: So sometime this afternoon?
M: _____

(a) Barring any major delays.
(b) His plane's behind schedule.
(c) I'll meet him at the airport.
(d) I've not seen him.

W: Peter의 비행기가 언제 도착해?
M: 지금으로부터 몇 시간 뒤일 거야, 아마.
W: 그럼 오늘 오후 중으로 오는 거야?
(a) 크게 연착하는 경우만 없다면 말이지.
(b) 그의 비행기는 예정보다 늦어.
(c) 난 공항에서 그를 만날 거야.
(d) 난 그를 보지 못했어.

13

M: How was your birthday party yesterday?
W: Just OK. Only a few people showed up.
M: Sounds like it was a letdown.
W: _____

(a) We were up past midnight.
(b) Yes. I'm sorry I missed it.
(c) No, the food didn't run out.
(d) It's not the end of the world.

M: 어제 네 생일 파티는 어땠어?
W: 그저 그랬어. 겨우 몇 명밖에 안 왔었거든.
M: 실망스러웠던 것 같네.
(a) 우리는 자정 넘어서까지 깨어 있었어.

(b) 응. 나는 그것을 놓쳐서 아쉬워.
(c) 아니, 음식이 바닥나지는 않았어.
(d) 세상이 끝난 것은 아니잖아.

14

W: Do you know where the space museum is?
M: Are you familiar with Grant Park?
W: Yeah. The one with the statue.
M: _____

(a) I'm familiar with the area.
(b) It's 10 minutes from here.
(c) It's near the east entrance.
(d) It's far from the museum.

W: 우주 박물관이 어디에 있는지 아세요?
M: Grant 공원을 잘 아시나요?
W: 네. 조각상이 있는 공원 말이지요.

(a) 전 이 지역을 잘 알아요.
(b) 그곳은 여기에서 10분 거리예요.
(c) 그곳은 동쪽 입구 근처에 있어요.
(d) 그곳은 박물관에서 멀리 떨어져 있어요.

15

M: Who's that guy talking to Robin?
W: I think his name's Eric. He's from Ireland.
M: How do you know he's Irish?
W: _____

(a) That's not his nationality.
(b) He's my best friend.
(c) My family's from there.
(d) It's just what I heard.

M: Robin에게 이야기하고 있는 저 남자는 누구야?
W: 이름이 Eric이었던 것 같아. 아일랜드 출신이야.
M: 아일랜드인인 걸 네가 어떻게 알아?

(a) 그건 그의 국적이 아니야.
(b) 그는 나의 가장 친한 친구야.
(c) 우리 가족이 그곳 출신이야.
(d) 그냥 그렇다고 들었어.

16

W: Can you believe it? Some guy swiped my purse last night.
M: No way! Did you scream for help?
W: No, it happened in the blink of an eye.
M: _____

(a) At least you weren't injured.
(b) I hope your eye will be OK.
(c) You could've tried to outrun him.
(d) I'll be more careful next time.

W: 믿어지니? 어젯밤에 어떤 남자가 내 핸드백을 훔쳐간 거 있지.
M: 말도 안 돼! 도와달라고 소리는 질렀어?
W: 아니, 눈 깜짝할 사이에 일어났던 일이라서.

(a) 적어도 네가 다치진 않았잖아.
(b) 네 눈이 괜찮아지길 바라.
(c) 네가 그 사람보다 더 빨리 달려볼 수도 있었잖아.
(d) 다음번엔 더 조심할 거야.

17

M: Let's get some snacks for the bus trip.
W: No need. The bus company provides the passengers with sandwiches.
M: Really? At what point?
W: _____

(a) If you're really hungry, take two.
(b) As soon as we hit the road.
(c) I'll point it out to you, so don't worry.
(d) I'm not sure of the selection available.

M: 버스 여행을 위해 간식을 좀 사자.
W: 그럴 필요 없어. 버스 회사에서 승객들에게 샌드위치를 주거든.
M: 정말? 어느 시점에서?

(a) 네가 정말 배고프면, 두 개를 가져가.
(b) 우리가 출발하자마자.
(c) 네게 그것을 알려줄 테니, 걱정 마.
(d) 어떤 종류가 제공될지 잘 모르겠어.

18

W: Have you ever watched a 3-D movie?
M: Yeah, I saw my first one last weekend.
W: How much was it compared to a regular one?
M: _____

(a) It depends on the movie's rating.
(b) I think it was a bit overrated.
(c) Beats me. My friend paid.
(d) It was a much bigger theater.

W: 너 입체 영화 본 적 있어?
M: 응, 지난 주말에 처음으로 하나 봤어.
W: 일반 영화에 비해 가격이 얼마나 해?

(a) 영화 등급에 따라 달라.
(b) 그것은 약간 과대평가된 것 같아.
(c) 전혀 몰라. 내 친구가 돈을 냈거든.
(d) 그건 훨씬 더 큰 극장이었어.

19

M: Did you hear that Dan was shot down on his contract extension?
W: No, but that's hardly news. The writing was on the wall.
M: Well, it caught me off guard.
W: _____

(a) Right. I should have known better.
(b) Not really. I saw him earlier today.
(c) He hasn't been keeping up lately.
(d) I told him to hope for the best.

M: Dan이 계약 연장에서 거부당했다는 이야기 들었어?
W: 아니, 하지만 그건 뉴스거리도 아니지. 불길한 조짐이 있었거든.
M: 음, 난 완전히 허를 찔렸는데.

(a) 맞아. 난 더 잘 알고 있었어야 했어.
(b) 그런 건 아니고. 나 아까 그를 봤거든.
(c) 그는 요새 잘 따라가지 못했거든.
(d) 난 그에게 희망을 잃지 말라고 했어.

20

W: Dolores Auburn just released another novel.
M: Yeah, I saw it on the Internet. I might get a copy tomorrow.
W: Can I borrow it once you're done?
M: _____

(a) I intend to read it first.
(b) It's one of her best novels to date.
(c) Sorry, I don't have a copy yet.
(d) If you promise to take care of it.

W: Dolores Auburn이 최근에 소설을 또 하나 출간했어.
M: 응, 나도 인터넷에서 봤어. 난 내일 한 권 살지도 몰라.
W: 다 읽으면 나 좀 빌려줄 수 있어?

(a) 그걸 먼저 읽을 생각이야.
(b) 그건 지금까지 나온 그녀의 최고의 소설 중 하나야.
(c) 미안한데, 아직 책을 가지고 있지 않아.
(d) 네가 깨끗하게 본다고 약속하면 말이야.

Part III

21

Listen to a conversation between a salesperson and a customer.

W: Joni Automotive. How may I assist you?
M: I have some complaints about a van I bought last week.
W: Sorry to hear that, but the vehicles we sell are in mint condition.
M: If that's true, how come the heater is broken and the oil leaks?
W: As I said, the items we stock are flawless. Our cars all run like new.
M: I should have known better than to buy a lemon.

Q: What is mainly happening in the conversation?

(a) The man is returning a van he purchased.
(b) The man is questioning the quality of the dealer's stock.
(c) The woman is sympathizing with the man's vehicle problems.
(d) The woman is defending her sales tactics.

판매원과 고객 간의 대화를 들으시오.

W: Joni Automotive입니다. 어떻게 도와 드릴까요?
M: 지난주에 구입한 승합차에 대해 불만이 몇 가지 있습니다.
W: 유감입니다만, 저희가 판매하는 차량들은 새것 같은 상태입니다.
M: 만약 그게 사실이라면, 왜 히터가 고장 나 있고 기름이 새는 거죠?
W: 말씀드렸듯이, 저희가 보유한 제품들은 결함이 없습니다. 저희 자동차들은 모두 새것처럼 작동합니다.
M: 불량품을 사느니 더 알아보고 살걸 그랬네요.

Q: 대화에서 주로 무슨 일이 일어나고 있는가?

(a) 남자가 구입한 승합차를 반품하고 있다.
(b) 남자가 판매자의 상품 품질에 문제를 제기하고 있다.
(c) 여자는 남자의 차량 문제에 동감하고 있다.
(d) 여자는 자신의 판매 전략을 옹호하고 있다.

22

Listen to a conversation between two co-workers.

M: Ms. Sanders, I have a problem with my payroll statement.
W: What is it, Ron?
M: The itemized deductions are missing.
W: Well, I'm sure your net income is accurate.
M: Still, I'd like to see how things were subtracted.
W: OK, then I'll send you a revised copy.

Q: What is the conversation mainly about?

(a) The woman's failure to send a paycheck
(b) The woman's inaccurate calculations
(c) The man's concerns about his pay slip
(d) The man's unhappiness with his salary

두 동료 간의 대화를 들으시오.

M: Ms. Sanders, 제 급여 명세서에 문제가 있어요.
W: 무슨 문제인가요, Ron?
M: 항목별 공제액이 빠져 있어요.
W: 음, 당신의 실수령액은 정확하다고 확신해요.
M: 그래도, 항목들이 어떻게 공제되었는지 알고 싶어요.
W: 좋아요, 그럼 제가 수정본을 보내 드릴게요.

Q: 주로 무엇에 관한 대화인가?

(a) 여자의 급여 수표 발송 불이행
(b) 여자의 부정확한 계산
(c) 급여 명세서에 대한 남자의 걱정
(d) 급여에 대한 남자의 불만

23

Listen to a conversation about a phone plan.

W: Hello. I'm one of your subscribers, Jane Hobson.
M: Can I have your account number, please?
W: I jotted it down... here it is. It's 27-8888.
M: That's an annual phone plan, correct?
W: Yes. I'd like to discontinue it immediately.

M: OK, but you have to pay the outstanding balance on your account.

Q: What is the woman mainly doing in the conversation?

(a) Requesting her account balance
(b) Changing her subscription plan
(c) Paying her mobile phone bill
(d) Terminating her phone service

전화 상품에 관한 대화를 들으시오.
W: 안녕하세요. 저는 귀사의 가입자인 Jane Hobson입니다.
M: 고객 번호를 알려주시겠습니까?
W: 적어왔는데… 여기 있네요. 27-8888입니다.
M: 연간 전화 상품이네요, 맞습니까?
W: 네. 당장 해지하고 싶습니다.
M: 알겠습니다만, 고객님 계정의 미지불 잔금을 지불하셔야 합니다.

Q: 대화에서 여자는 주로 무엇을 하고 있는가?
(a) 계좌 잔액을 조회하고 있다.
(b) 가입 상품을 변경하고 있다.
(c) 휴대 전화 요금을 지불하고 있다.
(d) 전화 서비스를 해지하고 있다.

24

Listen to a conversation between two friends.

M: Hi, Jill. Sorry for calling you on a work night.
W: It's OK. What's the matter?
M: Can we have breakfast tomorrow? I'll swing by your house.
W: Sure. What's so pressing?
M: I need someone to talk to before my job interview.
W: No problem. I'll be ready before seven.

Q: Which is correct about the man according to the conversation?

(a) He forgot that Jill has work tomorrow.
(b) He was unsuccessful at his job interview.
(c) He wants to see Jill before his appointment.
(d) He has a job interview at seven in the morning.

두 친구 간의 대화를 들으시오.
M: 안녕, Jill. 평일 저녁에 전화해서 미안해.
W: 괜찮아. 무슨 일이야?
M: 내일 아침 같이 먹을 수 있어? 너희 집에 잠깐 들를게.
W: 물론이지. 무슨 일인데 그렇게 급해?
M: 취업 면접 전에 이야기할 사람이 필요해.
W: 좋아. 7시 전에 준비하고 있을게.

Q: 대화에 따르면 남자에 대해 맞는 것은 무엇인가?
(a) Jill이 내일 일한다는 사실을 잊었다.
(b) 취업 면접에서 잘하지 못했다.
(c) 약속 전에 Jill을 만나고 싶어 한다.
(d) 아침 7시에 취업 면접이 있다.

25

Listen to two friends discussing college.

W: I didn't get into my first-choice of university. My grades weren't up to par, apparently.
M: That happened to me too, but I got into my dream school eventually.
W: How did you pull that off?
M: Well, I enrolled at a community college, got straight As, and reapplied.
W: If it worked for you, then I'll follow suit.
M: Just be sure to hit the books.

Q: Which is correct according to the conversation?

(a) The woman will change her long-term goal.
(b) The woman suggests that the man apply again.
(c) The woman will stop studying for at least one term.
(d) The woman will keep working toward her original goal.

두 친구가 대학에 관해 이야기하는 것을 들으시오.
W: 나 1차 지망한 대학에 못 들어갔어. 아무래도 점수가 기준에 미치지 못했나 봐.
M: 나도 마찬가지였는데, 결국엔 내가 꿈꾸던 학교에 들어갔어.
W: 그걸 어떻게 해냈어?
M: 음, 지역 전문대에 입학해서 전 과목 A학점을 받고, 다시 지원했지.
W: 너한테 효과가 있었다면, 나도 따라 해볼래.
M: 열심히 공부해야 한다는 것만 잊지 마.

Q: 대화에 따르면 맞는 것은 무엇인가?
(a) 여자는 자신의 장기적인 목표를 바꿀 것이다.
(b) 여자는 남자에게 다시 지원하라고 제안한다.
(c) 여자는 최소한 한 학기 동안 공부를 쉴 것이다.
(d) 여자는 원래의 목표를 향해 계속 노력할 것이다.

26

Listen to a conversation between a couple.

M: I think the car battery is dead. What should we do?
W: Let's call a towing service. We'd need to find a number.
M: I don't have my cell phone with me.
W: Well, maybe someone at that gas station can help us.
M: I'll stop in and ask. I see someone milling about.
W: OK. I'll wait here in the car.

Q: Which is correct according to the conversation?

(a) The man needs tools to change the battery.
(b) The gas station has replacement batteries.
(c) The woman knows of a repair shop.
(d) The man is going to ask for assistance.

커플 간의 대화를 들으시오.
M: 자동차 배터리 수명이 다한 것 같아. 어떻게 해야 하지?
W: 견인 서비스를 부르자. 전화번호를 찾아야 해.
M: 난 휴대 전화를 안 가지고 있어.
W: 음, 저 주유소에 있는 누군가가 우리를 도와줄 수 있을지도 몰라.
M: 내가 들어가서 물어볼게. 서성거리는 사람이 보여.
W: 좋아. 난 여기 차 안에서 기다릴게.

Q: 대화에 따르면 맞는 것은 무엇인가?
(a) 남자는 배터리를 교체하기 위한 연장이 필요하다.
(b) 주유소에 교체용 배터리가 있다.
(c) 여자는 수리점을 하나 알고 있다.
(d) 남자는 도움을 청할 것이다.

27

Listen to a conversation between two colleagues.
W: I heard Jen Mays is being transferred to human resources.
M: I heard that too, but maybe it's hearsay.
W: Yeah. Everyone's crossing their fingers that it's not true.
M: Would Nancy Jones take over as office manager?
W: Hopefully not. She's always giving those underneath her a hard time. It's unbearable.
M: Let's hope it's only a rumor.

Q: Why is the woman unhappy about the possible transfer?
(a) She feels that she deserves to be promoted.
(b) Jen Mays's likely replacement would be disagreeable.
(c) Her department is already short-staffed.
(d) Jen Mays is known for being unkind to subordinates.

두 동료 간의 대화를 들으시오.
W: Jen Mays가 인사부로 이동될 거라고 들었어.
M: 나도 그렇게 들었는데, 아마 소문일지도 몰라.
W: 맞아. 모든 사람들이 그게 사실이 아니길 빌고 있어.
M: Nancy Jones가 부장 자리를 맡게 될까?
W: 아니라면 좋겠어. 그녀는 언제나 자기 아래에 있는 사람들을 힘들게 해. 그건 견딜 수 없어.
M: 그냥 소문이기를 바라자.

Q: 여자는 왜 발생 가능한 이동에 대해 불만스러운가?
(a) 자신이 승진될만하다고 생각한다.
(b) Jen Mays를 대신할 것 같은 사람이 마음에 들지 않는다.
(c) 그녀의 부서는 이미 직원이 부족하다.
(d) Jen Mays는 하급자들에게 불친절하기로 유명하다.

28

Listen to a couple discussing a recent flood.
M: I've been watching the news about that flood down south.
W: It's been dragging on for days, right?
M: Yeah, and it's already brought unprecedented destruction.
W: I didn't know it was causing that much havoc.
M: It's crazy. Some houses are completely submerged.
W: I'm sure that's keeping emergency crews busy with all the evacuations.
M: No doubt. Apparently, it's mass chaos.

Q: Which is correct according to the conversation?
(a) The man witnessed the chaotic scene firsthand.
(b) Emergency crews are working around the clock.
(c) The man's house was completely flooded.
(d) A flood has created unforeseen damage.

커플이 최근의 홍수에 관해 이야기하는 것을 들으시오.
M: 남부 지방의 홍수에 대한 뉴스를 보고 있었어.
W: 며칠이나 계속되고 있어, 그렇지?
M: 맞아, 그리고 벌써 전례 없는 파괴를 초래했지.
W: 그게 그렇게 엄청난 피해를 가져올 줄 몰랐어.
M: 정말 큰일이야. 일부 집들은 완전히 물속에 잠겼더라.
W: 구조 대원들은 모두를 대피시키느라 분명 하루 종일 바쁠 거야.
M: 물론이지. 보아하니 대혼란이야.

Q: 대화에 따르면 맞는 것은 무엇인가?
(a) 남자는 혼란의 현장을 직접 목격했다.
(b) 구조 대원들은 밤낮을 가리지 않고 일하고 있다.
(c) 남자의 집은 완전히 침수되었다.
(d) 홍수는 예상치 못한 피해를 초래했다.

29

Listen to a conversation between two friends.
W: I'm sorry you didn't become class valedictorian.
M: I honestly thought I would receive the honor.
W: I was shocked to learn you didn't get it.
M: Should I request that my grade point average be recalculated?
W: You should. I think you have a strong case.
M: Thanks for your support. It means a lot.

Q: What can be inferred from the conversation?
(a) The man is highly ranked in his class.
(b) The woman will graduate with the man.
(c) The man will not challenge his GPA.

(d) The woman became the class valedictorian.

두 친구 간의 대화를 들으시오.
W: 네가 졸업생 대표가 되지 못해서 유감이야.
M: 솔직히 말하면 내가 그 영광을 얻을 거라고 생각했어.
W: 네가 되지 못했다는 말을 듣고 놀랐어.
M: 내 평균 평점을 다시 계산해 달라고 요청해야 할까?
W: 그래야 해. 나는 너에게 강력한 논거가 있다고 생각해.
M: 지지해줘서 고마워. 많은 도움이 되었어.

Q: 대화에서 추론할 수 있는 것은 무엇인가?
(a) 남자의 성적은 동기생들 중에서 상위권이다.
(b) 여자는 남자와 함께 졸업할 것이다.
(c) 남자는 그의 평균 평점에 이의를 제기하지 않을 것이다.
(d) 여자는 졸업생 대표가 되었다.

30

Listen to a conversation between two friends.

M: I'm headed to the crafts fair. Care to join me?
W: Sure, I'll tag along. I planned on going anyway.
M: I'm going to look for glass ornaments. How about you?
W: Well, I'm flat broke, but some of my friends have a booth.
M: Nice. What kind of stuff are they peddling?
W: Mostly beaded accessories. They're really unique.

Q: What can be inferred from the conversation?

(a) The woman doesn't intend to buy anything.
(b) The man has little interest in beadwork.
(c) The man and woman have a common friend.
(d) The woman hopes to acquire unique crafts.

두 친구 간의 대화를 들으시오.
M: 나는 공예 장터에 가는 길이야. 너도 같이 갈래?
W: 좋아, 따라갈게. 나도 어차피 갈 계획이었거든.
M: 나는 유리 장식품들을 구하려고 해. 너는?
W: 음, 난 완전히 빈털터리이지만, 내 친구 몇 명이 판매 부스를 가지고 있어.
M: 멋진데. 그들은 어떤 종류의 물건들을 팔아?
W: 대부분 구슬로 장식된 액세서리들이야. 굉장히 독특해.

Q: 대화에서 추론할 수 있는 것은 무엇인가?
(a) 여자는 아무것도 살 생각이 없다.
(b) 남자는 구슬 세공품에 거의 관심이 없다.
(c) 남자와 여자는 서로 아는 친구가 있다.
(d) 여자는 독특한 공예품을 얻길 바라고 있다.

Part IV

31

It is generally assumed that people only get tattoos for cosmetic reasons or to show their affiliation with a group. However, in some cultures, the act of scarification represents a rite of passage or carries great religious significance. In Cambodia, for instance, yantra tattooing is considered a sacred practice. Its designs are believed to hold magical powers that can protect a person from malevolent spirits and physical harm.

Q: What is the lecture mainly about?

(a) Tattoo designs of miscellaneous cultures
(b) Tattooing as a ritualistic undertaking
(c) Religious tattooing ceremonies of Cambodia
(d) The perceived magical powers of tattoos

일반적으로 사람들은 미용상 이유로 혹은 단체에의 소속을 나타내기 위해서만 문신을 새긴다고 여깁니다. 그러나, 어떤 문화권에서는, 문신 행위가 통과 의례를 나타내거나 종교적으로 큰 의미를 지닙니다. 예를 들어, 캄보디아에서 얀트라 문신 새기기는 신성한 의식으로 간주됩니다. 그것의 도안에는 악령과 신체적 피해로부터 사람을 지켜줄 수 있는 마법적인 힘이 담겨 있다고 여겨집니다.

Q: 강의는 주로 무엇에 대한 것인가?
(a) 여러 문화권의 문신 도안들
(b) 의식 절차로서의 문신 새기기
(c) 캄보디아의 종교적인 문신 새기기 의식
(d) 문신의 감지된 마법적 힘

32

Popular vocalist Dino Johnson will be staging a concert to promote his new album and assist the Indie Songwriters Association. According to Johnson's manager, the singer is excited about putting on a show that will benefit not only his record sales, but also a group of struggling musicians. Johnson has pledged to donate the proceeds from his concert, which will be held this September, to the organization.

Q: What is the speaker mainly discussing about Johnson?

(a) His exceptional vocal abilities
(b) His own unique style of songwriting
(c) His growing charitable contributions
(d) His upcoming musical fundraiser event

인기 가수 Dino Johnson은 자신의 새 앨범을 홍보하고 독립 작곡가 협회를 돕기 위한 콘서트를 개최할 것입니다. Johnson의 매니저에 따르면, 그 가수는 자신의 음반 판매량뿐만 아니라, 어렵게 살아가는 음악가 집단에게도 이익이 될 공연을 무대에 올리게 되어 들떠 있다고 합니다. Johnson은 올 9월에 열릴 콘서트의 수익금을 그 단체에 기부하겠다고 약속했습니다.

Q: 화자는 Johnson에 대해 주로 무엇을 논의하고 있는가?

(a) 그의 특출한 발성 능력
(b) 그만의 독특한 작곡 방식
(c) 늘어나는 그의 자선 기부금
(d) 다가오는 그의 기금 모금 음악 행사

33

Few people know what an assistant director does on set. No wonder, because the position is less glamorous than being a head director or cinematographer. However, an assistant director plays a pivotal role in filmmaking. The AD prepares the shooting schedule and oversees the duties of the cast and crew. Several ADs, like Alfred Hitchcock, have transitioned to the post of director, but now they're more likely to end up as producers because of their penchant for management.

Q: Which is correct according to the lecture?

(a) The director assesses the shooting schedule.
(b) ADs take charge when directors are not present.
(c) Most ADs eventually become directors.
(d) The skills of ADs are suited to producing.

조감독이 촬영장에서 무슨 일을 하는지 아는 사람은 드뭅니다. 그도 그럴 것이, 그 자리는 감독이나 촬영 감독보다 덜 화려하기 때문입니다. 그러나, 조감독은 영화 제작에 있어서 중심적인 역할을 합니다. 조감독은 촬영 일정을 준비하고 출연진과 팀의 업무를 감독합니다. 알프레드 히치콕과 같은 몇몇 조감독들은 감독 직책으로 옮겨 갔으나, 조감독들은 관리하는 것을 좋아하기 때문에 요즘엔 제작자가 되는 경우가 더 많은 편입니다.

Q: 강의에 따르면 맞는 것은 무엇인가?

(a) 감독은 촬영 일정을 평가한다.
(b) 조감독은 감독이 없을 때 책임을 맡는다.
(c) 대다수의 조감독은 결국 감독이 된다.
(d) 조감독의 능력은 제작에 적합하다.

34

Marine biologists are reporting that a particular jellyfish-like organism has a sizeable effect of ocean CO_2 levels. Salps, which swarm in abundant quantities across the globe, devour vast numbers of carbon-producing phytoplankton. Phytoplankton are also consumed by other marine animals, but only salps produce waste that sinks directly to the bottom of the ocean. This means that carbon becomes sequestered in the salps' waste, which prevents it from being recycled back into the water.

Q: Which is correct according to the lecture?

(a) Phytoplankton produce most of the world's CO_2.
(b) Phytoplankton prey upon other marine animals.
(c) Salps outnumber phytoplankton in sheer quantity.
(d) Salps remove carbon dioxide from seawater.

해양 생물학자들은 해파리와 비슷한 특정 생물이 해양 이산화탄소 수치에 상당한 영향을 끼친다고 보고하고 있습니다. 전 세계에 걸쳐 많은 수로 떼를 지어 다니는 살파는 탄소를 내뿜는 많은 양의 식물성 플랑크톤을 먹어 치웁니다. 식물성 플랑크톤은 다른 해양 동물들에 의해 먹히기도 하지만, 살파만이 바다 밑바닥으로 곧장 가라앉는 배설물을 생산합니다. 이는 살파의 배설물에서 탄소가 격리되며, 수중에서 재이용되는 것을 막는다는 것을 뜻합니다.

Q: 강의에 따르면 맞는 것은 무엇인가?

(a) 식물성 플랑크톤은 전 세계 이산화탄소의 대부분을 생산한다.
(b) 식물성 플랑크톤은 다른 해양 동물들을 잡아먹는다.
(c) 살파는 절대적인 양에서 식물성 플랑크톤보다 수가 많다.
(d) 살파는 해수에서 이산화탄소를 제거한다.

35

For tonight's offbeat music news, the Gringers' front man Kirk Helms was upstaged during the band's concert last night after asking an audience member to join him on stage. Helms is known for his exceptional vocal ability, but when the newcomer began to belt out one of the band's most famous singles, his voice proved to be of superior quality. The band wasn't fazed by the incident and in fact, they commended the man identified only as "Jon."

Q: What was Jon commended for?

(a) Proving his loyalty as a fan
(b) Singing better than Kirk Helms
(c) Writing a single for the Gringers
(d) Helping to set up a stage

오늘 밤의 색다른 음악 뉴스입니다. Gringers의 리더 Kirk Helms가 어젯밤 밴드의 콘서트 중 관객 한 명에게 무대로 올라와 함께 해달라고 요청한 뒤에 관심을 빼앗겼습니다. Helms는 특출한 노래 실력으로 유명하나, 그 무대에 올라온 사람이 밴드의 가장 유명한 싱글 중 한 곡을 큰 소리로 노래하기 시작했을 때, 그의 음색이 더 뛰어나다는 것이 드러났습니다. 밴드는 그 사건으로 당황하지 않았으며 사실, 그들은 'Jon'이라고만 알려진 그 남자를 격찬했습니다.

Q: Jon은 무엇에 대해 격찬받았는가?

(a) 팬으로서 그의 충성심을 증명한 것
(b) Kirk Helms보다 노래를 잘 부른 것
(c) Gringers를 위해 싱글을 쓴 것
(d) 무대 설치하는 것을 도운 것

36

The Mazzkani Adjustable is the latest addition

to our therapeutic sleep product line. It may look like a conventional bed, but its features resemble those found in medical sleep systems. Although the Mazzkani Adjustable will initially be distributed solely to hospitals, it will debut with the public by the year's end. It's been our practice to get customer feedback before product releases, so we are requesting volunteers to test the Mazzkani Adjustable.

Q: What can be inferred about the Mazzkani Adjustable from the talk?

(a) It lets patients avoid long hospital stays.
(b) It comes with attributes absent in ordinary beds.
(c) Its sale will be confined to medical institutions.
(d) It has undergone testing by volunteers.

Mazzkani Adjustable은 저희의 수면 치료 제품 라인에 추가된 최신 제품입니다. 평범한 침대처럼 보일 수도 있지만, 이것의 특성은 의료용 수면 장치의 특성과 유사합니다. Mazzkani Adjustable은 처음에 병원에만 유통될 것이나, 연말 경 대중에게 소개될 것입니다. 제품 출시 전에 고객의 의견을 받는 것이 저희의 관행이기에, Mazzkani Adjustable을 시험 삼아 써 보실 지원자 분들을 구합니다.

Q: 담화에서 Mazzkani Adjustable에 대해 추론할 수 있는 것은 무엇인가?

(a) 환자들이 병원에 장기 입원하는 것을 막아준다.
(b) 평범한 침대에는 없는 특성이 있다.
(c) 그것의 판매는 의료 기관에 한정될 것이다.
(d) 지원자들의 테스트를 거쳤다.

Part V

37~38

Are you the proud owner of a truck or sedan? You might not be aware that roughly 10 million accidents happen each year on our nation's roads. Sure, this includes everything from parking lot scrapes to pileups, but how confident are you about the odds of avoiding even one? Cars are expensive enough to maintain without having to worry about the skyrocketing cost of accident coverage. That's why you need CarSure. CarSure can guarantee comprehensive auto coverage at an affordable price. Choose from our range of economical plans. We don't turn anybody down. We understand accidents happen to everyone, even to responsible motorists. So why not give us a call? Dial 1-800-CAR-SURE to speak to a CarSure representative today. CarSure is available in all 50 US states. Terms and conditions apply.

37. Q: What is mainly being advertised?
(a) A car dealership
(b) A repair shop
(c) An insurance provider
(d) An auto accident attorney

38. Q: Which is correct about CarSure?
(a) It maintains a national database of accident records.
(b) It charges different rates according to driver histories.
(c) It promises to beat the lowest price of its competitors.
(d) It provides coverage across the entire US.

당신은 트럭이나 세단형 자동차의 자랑스러운 주인이십니까? 당신은 전국의 도로에서 매년 약 천만 건의 사고가 발생한다는 사실을 알지 못할지도 모릅니다. 물론, 이는 주차장에서 긁힌 자국부터 연쇄 충돌 사고에 이르는 모든 것을 포함하지만, 이 중 하나라도 피할 확률에 대해 얼마나 확신하십니까? 자동차는 사고 보험의 치솟는 비용에 대해 걱정해야 할 필요 없이 유지하는 것만으로도 충분히 돈이 많이 듭니다. 이 때문에 당신은 CarSure가 필요합니다. CarSure는 저렴한 가격으로 종합 자동차 보험을 보장해 드릴 수 있습니다. 저희의 다양한 실속 있는 제도 중에서 선택하십시오. 저희는 누구도 거부하지 않습니다. 저희는 모든 사람, 심지어 책임감 있는 운전자들에게도 사고가 발생한다는 것을 알고 있습니다. 그러니 저희에게 전화 주시는 것이 어떠신가요? 오늘 1-800-CAR-SURE로 전화해 CarSure 상담원과 이야기하십시오. CarSure는 미국의 모든 50개 주에서 이용 가능합니다. 이용 약관이 적용됩니다.

37. Q: 주로 광고되고 있는 것은 무엇인가?
(a) 자동차 영업소
(b) 수리점
(c) 보험 제공업체
(d) 자동차 사고 변호사

38. Q: CarSure에 대해 맞는 것은 무엇인가?
(a) 사고 기록에 대한 전국적 데이터베이스를 가지고 있다.
(b) 운전자 기록에 따라 다른 요금을 청구한다.
(c) 경쟁사들의 최저가를 능가한다고 장담한다.
(d) 미국 전역에 걸쳐 보험을 제공한다.

39~40

Although the Cold War between the United States and the Soviet Union created deep distrust between the two superpowers, it also had some positive outcomes. One of these was the so-called space race, in which the countries engaged in one-upmanship to see who could make the furthest advancements into space. The Soviets launched both the first satellite and first man into orbit. Not to be outdone in the pursuit of national prestige, the Americans became the first to reach the moon. As stunning as these achievements were, the Soviet and US rivalry also prompted substantial and well-funded research into various aspects of space exploration, expanding our knowledge of the cosmos. If not for the nations' tumultuous relationship, our knowledge of the universe would be decades behind its current state. Today, the two countries continue to vie for supremacy in space, but their endeavors are decidedly more collaborative.

39. Q: What is the lecture mainly about?

(a) How the Cold War was instrumental to space exploration
(b) The United States' ulterior motives for space exploration
(c) How the Soviet Union spurred on the space race
(d) The short-term repercussions of the Cold War

40. Q: How do the two countries approach space exploration now?

(a) They focus more on practical technology than on impressive feats.
(b) They are no longer concerned with moon landings.
(c) They engage in more cooperation regarding space exploration.
(d) They provide funding to international research organizations.

미국과 소련 간의 냉전이 두 초강대국 사이의 깊은 불신을 자아내기는 했으나, 몇 가지 긍정적인 결과도 낳았습니다. 이 중 한 가지는 이른바 우주 개발 경쟁이었는데, 여기서 이 국가들은 누가 우주에 대해 가장 많은 발전을 이룩할 수 있을지 보기 위해 상대보다 한발 앞서기 위한 경쟁에 참여했습니다. 소련인들은 최초의 인공위성과 최초의 사람을 모두 궤도에 진입시켰습니다. 국위를 추구하는 데 지지 않기 위해, 미국인들은 최초로 달에 도달했습니다. 이러한 업적이 놀라운 만큼, 소련과 미국의 경쟁은 우주 탐사의 다양한 측면에서의 실질적이고 풍부한 자금을 지원받은 연구를 촉구하여, 우주에 대한 우리의 지식을 확장했습니다. 이 국가들의 격동의 관계가 아니었다면, 우주에 대한 우리의 지식은 현재 상태보다 수십 년 뒤처졌을 것입니다. 오늘날, 양국은 계속해서 우주에서의 패권을 위해 경쟁하지만, 그들의 노력은 확실히 더 협력적입니다.

39. Q: 강의는 주로 무엇에 대한 것인가?
(a) 냉전이 우주 탐사에 어떻게 주된 역할을 했는지
(b) 미국의 우주 탐사에 대한 숨은 동기
(c) 소련이 어떻게 우주 개발 경쟁에 자극을 주었는지
(d) 냉전의 단기적인 영향

40. Q: 두 국가는 현재 우주 탐사에 어떻게 접근하는가?
(a) 눈부신 업적보다 실질적인 기술에 더 집중한다.
(b) 달 착륙에 더 이상 관심이 없다.
(c) 우주 탐사에 관하여 더 많은 협력을 한다.
(d) 국제 연구 기관에 자금을 제공한다.

VOCABULARY

Part I

1 A: 조만간 또 날 보러 와, 알았지?
   B: 그럴게. 오늘 초대해줘서 고마워!

2 A: 네 차고 바닥에 있는 이 물건은 뭐니?
   B: 신경 쓰지 마. 그 쓰레기 전부 갖다 버릴 거야.

3 A: 넌 항상 수업에 늦더라.
   B: 나도 알아. 좀 더 시간을 잘 지켜야겠어.

4 A: 왜 이사 간다고 내게 얘기하지 않았니?
   B: 미안해. 그 얘기를 꺼낼 시간이 없었어.

5 A: 여기서 1주 더 머물면 안 될까?
   B: 나도 그러고 싶지만, 우리에겐 선택의 여지가 없어.

6 A: Sam이 왜 화가 났지? 난 그의 예술에 대해 내 솔직한 의견을 얘기했을 뿐인데 말이야.
   B: 글쎄, 비방이 그가 발전하도록 격려해 주지는 않을 거야.

7 A: 시간을 절약하기 위해서, 우리는 모든 이메일 서신을 간결하게 유지해야 해요.
   B: 알겠어요, 제가 직원들에게 알릴게요.

8 A: 사회 변화에 대한 Robert의 기사를 이해했니?
   B: 그랬다고 말하고 싶지만, 그건 이해하기 어려웠어.

9 A: 단식 투쟁을 하고 있는 노조 지도자들이 안쓰러워.
   B: 맞아. 그들의 얼굴이 정말 수척해 보이더라.

10 A: 그 부장님은 직원들의 존엄성을 노골적으로 무시해.
   B: 정말 그래. 그를 해고시켜야 해.

Part II

11 성수기에는, 원하는 항공편의 좌석을 확보하기 위해서 사전 예약이 권장된다.

12 운동선수와 아마추어의 훈련 방식을 구별하는 특징은 강도이다.

13 소송을 피하기 위해서, 미시간 주민들은 분쟁을 해결하려고 지역 사회 중재인들에게 도움을 청하고 있다.

14 구호 단체로의 기부금이 줄어들었지만, 자원봉사자들의 수는 줄지 않았다.

15 그 기관은 대학 교육을 계속하기를 원하는 형편이 어려운 학생들에게 장학금을 수여한다.

16 Daphne는 잡티를 가리기 위해 결점을 감춰주는 크림 소량을 얼굴에 발랐다.

17 그 호텔의 귀빈실은 여러 수공예 가구들로 장식되어 있다.

18 연방 지출을 줄이기 위해 다음 달부터 노동자 연금에 대한 정부 기여금의 상한이 정해질 것이다.

19 매운 음식을 먹는 것은 궤양이 있는 이들에게 극심한 복통을 일으킬 수 있다.

20 Tony는 심장병 때문에 군복무에서 면제되었다.

21 항공 교통 관제사들은 비행 중 사용되는 암호화된 메시지들을 판독하는 데 도움이 되는 훈련을 받는다.

22 브라질의 약 15만 킬로미터에 해당하는 열대 다우림이 불법 벌목으로 인해 없어졌다.

23 명예가 실추된 일부 정치인들은 그들의 카리스마 때문에 아직도 용케 유권자들의 환심을 사고 있다.

24 그 환자는 팔을 너무 심하게 다쳐서 의사들은 회복하는 데 2년이 걸릴 것이라고 생각한다.

25 변호사들은 투자자들로부터 수백만 달러를 횡령했다는 의뢰인의 혐의가 무죄임을 성공적으로 밝혀냈다.

26 Carl은 중요한 프로젝트를 하고 있을 때는 덜 중요한 일들은 회피해도 괜찮다고 생각한다.

27 그 정직한 기업은 사업상의 거래를 하는 데 있어서 굉장히 격식을 따지고, 모든 것을 규칙대로 한다.

28 고등학교 교사들은 다루기 어려운 기이한 행동을 보이는 학생들과 흔히 마주친다.

29 그 신문 칼럼니스트는 자원봉사 단체들조차 사기 행위로 부패되어 가는 추세를 폭로했다.

30 뉴스 방송사는 저작권 분쟁에 말려든 두 기업에 대해 과도하게 보도를 할 애했다.

GRAMMAR

Part I

1 A: 금요일에 점심 먹을래?
B: 나도 그러고 싶은데, 그날 치과 진료 예약이 있어.

2 A: 새 드레스 쇼핑은 어떻게 됐어?
B: 아무것도 마음에 들지 않아서, 대신 핸드백을 하나 샀어.

3 A: 제 자동차의 바람 빠진 타이어를 교체하셨나요?
B: 네, 교체했습니다.

4 A: 내가 LA를 방문한 건 이번이 처음이야.
B: 차를 타고 도시를 돌아보는 게 어때?

5 A: 너희 가족은 아직도 차고를 작업실로 개조하려고 계획 중이니?
B: 응, 하지만 5월까지는 개조하지 않을 거야.

6 A: 네가 관심이 있는지 모르겠지만, 나한테 비엔나행 표가 한 장 더 있어.
B: 관심이 있고말고. 난 올해 아직 아무 데도 못 갔어.

7 A: 조심해요. 벤치의 페인트가 아직 완전히 마르지 않았어요.
B: 고마워요, 하마터면 앉을 뻔했어요.

8 A: 아무도 이 꽃들을 사지 않아요. 그것들이 정말 너무 비싼가 봐요.
B: 혹시라도 우리가 가격을 내리면, 훨씬 더 잘 팔릴 텐데요.

9 A: 어떻게 프렌치토스트를 이렇게 맛있게 만든거야?
B: 풍미를 더하기 위해 설탕 가루를 약간 뿌렸어.

10 A: 새로 발매된 앨범에 왜 이 곡을 넣지 않았나요?
B: 그 곡은 평범하기 그지없어서, 버려져야 하는 잘 맞지 않은 곡이었어요.

Part II

11 기자의 대 피라미드는 틀림없이 가장 놀라운 고대 건축물 중에 하나이다.

12 Jamaican Blue Mountain 커피의 새로 나온 맛은 다른 커피 맛보다 덜 쓰다.

13 이 모듈이 끝날 즈음에 Jean은 석사 학위를 받는 데 필요한 요건들을 충족할 것이다.

14 사람들은 보통 어린 시절에 또래들과의 관계를 발전시키기 시작한다.

15 학자들에 따르면, 초기 한시는 고대의 가장 뛰어난 문학의 일부로 언급된다.

16 Cliff Davis는 표절 소송에 맞서 자신을 변호하기 위해 얼마가 들더라도 지불할 준비가 되어 있었다.

17 Durham의 시장은 시의회의 고위 당국자 여러 명과 함께, 지역 의료 보험 혜택을 확대하겠다는 계획을 선언했다.

18 음주 운전으로 여러 차례 징계받은 뒤, Steve는 면허가 무기한 취소되었다.

19 판사는 부모 중 어느 쪽이 자녀의 양육권을 얻을지 중재하는 것은 문제가 있다고 생각했다.

20 사람의 행동과 비슷하게, 암컷 벌은 집을 지을 장소를 찾을 때 가장 까다롭다.

21 어젯밤, 스포츠 분석가들이 말하길 리그 역사상 가장 의외의 승리 중 하나였다는 경기에서 Hawks가 Pirates를 이겼다.

22 기술적인 어려움을 알리거나 문의하실 때, 내선 번호 952로 전화를 거시면 시스템 관리자에게 연결됩니다.

23 고객들의 유행하는 취향과 계속 발을 맞추려는 의도로, Bradford의 제품들은 정기적으로 갱신된다.

24 역사를 통틀어, 메뚜기 떼는 농작물과 목초지를 전멸시킨다고 알려져 왔다.

25 시 금고 침입 사건의 수사가 너무 철저해서 경찰은 몇 주 동안 구내를 봉쇄해야 했다.

Part III

26 (a) A: 너 『모리와 함께한 화요일』이라는 책 읽어봤어?
(b) B: 공교롭게도 그 책은 내가 읽어본 최고의 책 중에 하나야.
(c) A: 나도 동의해. 이야기에 그렇게 감동받은 적이 예전에는 한번도 없

었거든.
(d) B: 이야기도 상당히 감동적이지만, 나를 사로잡은 건 이야기가 쓰여진 방식이었어.

27 (a) A: 주방 수도꼭지가 제대로 잠겨 있는데도, 물이 계속 뚝뚝 떨어지네요.
(b) B: 아, 배관공이 지난번에 수도꼭지를 수리하려 한 이후로 그게 멈추지 않더라고요.
(c) A: 원하시면 제가 한번 살펴보고 도와 드릴 수 있는지 볼 수 있어요.
(d) B: 괜찮아요. 다음 주 중에 전체 장치를 수리받으려고 하거든요.

28 (a) 최근의 연구는 서구적인 식단을 채택하는 사람들이 심장병에 걸릴 위험이 높아진다는 것을 보여준다. (b) 이 종류의 식단은 주로 가공된 육류 및 지방과 나트륨 함량이 높은 음식으로 이루어져 있다. (c) 이와 같은 건강에 해로운 음식은 고혈압을 일으킬 수 있고 동맥을 막을 수 있다. (d) 이를 막기 위해서, 보건 전문가들은 사람들이 자신의 식단을 변경하고 섬유질을 더 많이 섭취해야 한다고 강조한다.

29 (a) 1971년에 발사된 Mariner 9호는 다른 행성의 궤도를 돈 최초의 우주선이 되었다. (b) 그 우주선은 화성을 조사하고 그 행성의 대기를 연구하기 위해 만들어졌다. (c) 우주 탐사선 Mariner 9호를 통해, 과학자들은 이른바 붉은 행성의 자연 경관의 특징들을 확인할 수 있었다. (d) 가장 주목할 만한 발견 중 하나는 화성의 모래 언덕이었는데, 그것은 북아프리카의 것과 유사한 특성을 보였다.

30 (a) 아이와 함께 비행기 여행을 하는 것은, 특히 장거리 비행인 경우에, 부모에게 아주 힘들 수 있다. (b) 여행 중에는 아이가 쉽게 지루해하기 때문에, 부모는 아이를 몰두시킬 방법을 생각해내야 한다. (c) 전문가들은 책, 장난감, 그리고 소형 게임기처럼 오락과 재미를 제공하는 물건을 가져갈 것을 권한다. (d) 또한 비행 중에 식사가 제공되기는 하지만, 간식으로 여분의 음식물을 챙겨 가는 것이 바람직하다.

READING COMPREHENSION

Part I

1 고(故) 다이애나 왕세자비의 진기한 사진과 그녀가 아끼던 옷들을 선보이는 박물관이 _____, 목요일에 개관했다. 그녀의 아들들은 어머니의 추억을 이용하여 돈을 번다고 박물관을 비난했다. 박물관 관장은 자선 단체에 기부되지 않는 모든 수익금은 건물 유지비와 직원의 급여에 사용될 것이라며, 그 비난에 반박했다. 관장에 따르면, 입장권 판매액의 절반은 다이애나가 좋아했던 자선 단체들을 재정 지원할 것이다.
(a) 그녀 유산의 지원을 받아서
(b) 사람들에게 왕실 가족에 대해 알리는 것을 도우면서
(c) 그녀의 자식들의 항의를 받으면서
(d) 자선 단체의 비용으로 박물관의 질을 높이면서

2 신문 기사를 쓸 때, 당신은 _____ 해야 한다. 당신이 원하는 대로 쓸 수 있는 어휘는 제한되어 있는데, 그 이유는 글이 다양한 독자에 맞춰져야 하기 때문이다. 전문 용어의 사용은 선택 가능한 대안이 아니므로, 이는 더욱 창의적이고 흥미로운 접근을 요한다. 당신이 말하고자 하는 요점으로 관심을 끄는 정확하고 명료한 단어를 사용함으로써, 독자들이 당신이 쓴 것을 반드시 이해하도록 할 수 있다. 이러한 방식으로, 독자들은 당신의 이야기를 당신이 원하는 방법으로 해석할 것이고, 그 결과 그들에게 당신이 쓴 다른 기사들도 읽어보도록 설득할 수 있다.
(a) 편집자가 동의하는 줄거리를 추구
(b) 정중한 학술적 어조를 유지
(c) 적절한 수준의 어휘를 사용
(d) 다양한 독자층의 관점을 고려

3 Handyman Tools께,
저는 16번째 생일에 아버지께서 Handyman 래칫 세트를 선물해 주신 이후로 귀사의 공구를 열심히 사용해왔습니다. 제 생각에, 귀사는 물건을 손수 만드는 사람들을 위해 튼튼하고, 실용적인 공구를 만들어내는 것으로 좋은 평판을 얻어 왔으며, 바로 그렇기 때문에 저는 귀사가 생산 공장을 방글라데시로 이전할 것이라는 소식을 듣고 매우 심란했습니다. 국내 제조업과 미국 노동자의 자랑스러운 지지자로서, 저는 양심상 _____ 수 없습니다. 저는 귀사의 결정을 다시 검토하시길 강력히 권고합니다.
존경을 담아,
Elmer Boyle
(a) 귀사를 계속 애용할
(b) 저의 가장 소중한 공구를 교체할
(c) 귀사 제품이 장수하리라 믿을
(d) 경쟁사로부터 구매할

4 _____ 하려면 Henan 강화수를 마셔보세요. Henan 강화수는 비타민 및 칼슘과 칼륨 같은 식이 미네랄이 주입된 정제수입니다. 이 제품은 섭취하는 음식만으로 영양 권장량을 충족시킬 수 없는 분들께 이상적입니다. Henan 강화수에 든 비타민과 미네랄은 바이러스와 박테리아에 대한 방어를 강화하고, 감염될 위험을 낮추어 신체의 면역 체계를 개선합니다.
(a) 수인성 질병을 예방
(b) 매일의 영양분을 확실히 섭취
(c) 몸에서 해로운 미네랄을 제거
(d) 몸에 수분을 유지하고 건강을 유지

5 다큐멘터리는 장편 영화와 달리, 보통 '영화'의 일반적인 정의에 부합하지 않는다. 장편 영화는 종종 허구적이고 제작사의 재정적 성공만큼이나 관객의 즐거움에 맞춰진다. 반면, 다큐멘터리는 작품들이 _____는 점에서, 장편 영화와 완전히 반대이다. 대부분의 다큐멘터리는 논란이 되는 정치적, 역사적 또는 사회적 문제를 제시하고 감독의 관점에 기반을 둔다. 그들의 비상업적 접근에도 불구하고, 다큐멘터리는 재정적으로 성공할 가능성을 보이기 시작하고 있다.
(a) 실제 상황과 사건을 분석한다
(b) 수익성을 항상 염두에 둔다
(c) 관객을 끌기 위해 평론가들의 호평에 의존한다
(d) 덜 매력적인 등장인물에 기반을 둔다

6 로봇이 출현하기 전에는, 실패 가능성 때문에 심해 탐사와 같은 과학적 임무를 수행하는 것이 가능하지 않았다. 그러나, 원격 로봇, 즉 무선 네트워크나 유선 접속을 통해 멀리서도 조정이 가능한 전문적인 로봇의 도움으로, 전문가들은 이제 무언가 잘못 되더라도 안전 거리에 머물면서 수중 화석을 발굴하고, 화산성 원소를 검출하며,

우주를 탐구하는 데 의존할 수 있는 수단이 생겼다. 과학자들은 로봇들의 _____ 능력에 열광하고 있다.

(a) 복잡하고 위험한 작업을 수행하는
(b) 연구실에서 혁신 기술을 개발하는
(c) 심해 탐사 지원을 보장하는
(d) 제조사에서 새로운 로봇을 입수하는

7

_____, 비잔틴 제국은 로마 제국의 마지막 자취를 중세까지 보존시켰다. 로마 제국의 계승자로서, 비잔틴 사람들은 고대 로마 사회의 법적, 문화적 토대의 많은 부분을 유지했지만, 이러한 요소 중 일부는 그리스 문화의 여러 면에 의해 무너졌고, 그리스 문화는 아주 널리 보급되어 결국 그리스어가 라틴어를 대신하여 공식적으로 승인된 제국의 언어가 되었다. 이러한 영향력의 융합은 비잔틴 제국의 독특성에 기여했다.

(a) 주로 라틴 문화에서 영향을 받아
(b) 고대 로마 유산에 대한 아무런 암시 없이
(c) 자기만의 독특한 문화를 발전시켰지만
(d) 로마의 정치적 권위를 앗아갔지만

8

정치인 Tom Blackford는 최근에 _____ 시도했다. 그의 소셜 미디어 플랫폼은 그가 갓난 아들을 안고 있는 사진들로 가득 차 있었고, 그를 헌신적인 가장으로 그리고 있었다. 이것은 결코 가족 친화적이지 않은 법안을 계속해서 제안해온 공무원에게서 나왔다. 이 전략은 대중에게 받아들여지지 않았는데, 이들은 그 사진들을 미디어 책략으로 생각했고 Blackford를 약해진 대중적 이미지를 부활시키려는 책략이라고 비난했다. Blackford는 처음으로 아버지가 된 어떤 사람이라도 똑같이 행동했을 것이라고 주장하면서, 어떠한 숨은 의도도 부인했다.

(a) 부모로서의 새로운 지위를 통해 평판을 개선하려
(b) 그의 사생활에 대한 사진이 온라인에 공개되는 것을 막으려
(c) 가정에 영향을 주는 정치적 문제에 대한 그의 입장을 명확하게 하려
(d) 그의 경력을 위해 가족을 등한시해온 것을 부인하려

9

전기 요약

에바 페론의 정치적 포부는 그녀가 아르헨티나에서 방송 연기자 노조 조합장으로 재임하는 동안 불붙었다. 주재하는 동안, 그녀는 개인 라디오 프로그램에서 당시 노동부 장관이었던 후안 페론의 업적을 자주 칭찬했고, 정치적 반대 세력이 페론을 감금시켰을 때 그를 해방시키는 집회를 조직화하는 일에서 대중적으로 신임을 얻었다. 에바의 모습은 워낙 인기를 끌어서 1946년 선거에서 그녀가 후안의 선거 운동에 연대하자 그의 승리로 이어졌고, 곧이어 두 사람은 결혼했다. _____, 에바는 남편의 정권에 대한 대중의 지지를 강화하는 활동에 몰두했다.

(a) 그럼에도 불구하고
(b) 마찬가지로
(c) 그 후에
(d) 이에도 불구하고

10

지난 수십 년간 수집된 인구통계학 자료는 미국인들이 20대에 더 나은 고용 기회를 찾아 교외의 가정을 떠나 더 발달한 도시 지역으로 모인다는 것을 보여준다. 그러나 그들이 30대가 될 무렵에는, 정착해서 아이들을 기르기 위해 교외로 되돌아가는 전반적인 경향을 보여준다. _____, 인구 이동에 대한 장기적인 통계 자료는 젊은이들이 교외에서 도시로 이동했다가 되돌아오는 정해진 패턴을 보여준다.

(a) 게다가
(b) 그렇기는 하지만
(c) 반면에
(d) 즉

Part II

11

소설이 문학의 한 형태로 떠오른 것은 대중에게 사회적 기회가 확산된 시점과 일치했다. (a) 영국에서, 소설가 다니엘 디포와 찰스 디킨스는 점진적으로 개방되는 사회에서 사는 것의 이점에 대해 논의했다. (b) 인도에서, 소설은 상대적으로 진보적인 국가들로부터 받은 평등주의의 영향이 인도 사회에 침투하기 시작한 영국 통치 시기에 꽃을 피웠다. (c) 당대의 많은 소설가들은 산업화의 등장에 매료되었다. (d) 따라서, 소설의 내용은 그 시대의 진보적인 사회적 감성과 문화적 감성을 반영하면서 발전했다.

12

세부 사항에 대한 주목과 제안에 대한 열린 마음은 훌륭한 영상 편집자들이 내재해야 할 두 가지 자질이다. (a) 그러므로, 최종 작품에 무엇이 배제되고 포함되어야 하는지 철저하게 검토하라. (b) 프로젝트에 관련된 다른 사람들과 의견을 주고받으며 당신의 주관을 유지하면서도 그들의 충고도 기꺼이 받아들이라. (c) 시간을 들여 새로운 기술들을 살펴보고 그것들을 자신만의 스타일로 통합시키는 것 또한 당신의 성장을 도울 것이다. (d) 결국, 당신이 제시한 건설적인 비판이 독특한 시각의 이점을 제공할 것이다.

Part III

13

CashFlow Plus: 경제적 성공을 위한 길

편안한 은퇴 생활 자금을 마련하기 위해 필요한 추가 수입을 보장받고 싶으십니까? 부동산 투자는 여러분이 경제적으로 자유를 얻으실 수 있는 가장 빠른 길이며, 저희 CashFlow Plus 시스템은 여러분께 시작하는 방법을 알려 드립니다.

몇 시간만 수고하시고 수천 달러를 버십시오. 확신, 추진력, 그리고 CashFlow Plus DVD와 책 세트만 있으면 됩니다. 여러분은 즉시 시장의 동향을 분석하고 은행에 저당이 잡히거나 압류된 부동산이 지닌 가치를 발견하시게 될 것입니다.

CashFlow Plus가 여러분의 풍요로운 미래의 열쇠가 되어 드리겠습니다!

Q: 광고는 주로 무엇에 관한 내용인가?

(a) 주식 시장에 돈을 투자하기
(b) 주식 중개인이 되는 법 배우기
(c) 부동산을 구매하여 돈 벌기
(d) 부동산을 구매하기 위해 은행에 담보 잡히기

14

책임감 있는 애완동물 소유자들의 모임(SRPO) 회장인 Amy Beck은 모든 애완동물이 생후 6개월이 되면 번식을 막기 위해 불임 수술을 받아야 한다고 생각한다. 왜냐하면 불임 수술을 받은 동물들은 원치 않는 새끼들을 갖지 않아도 되고, 덜 공격적이고 텃세가 덜하며, 대부분의 주인들이 선호하는 아기 같은 행동을 하며, 생식기 계통 암에 걸릴 확률이 낮기 때문이다. Beck과 다른 SRPO 회원들은 애완동물 주인들과 일반 대중들에게 불임 수술의 이점을 교육하기 위한 운동을 벌이고 있다.

Q: 지문은 주로 무엇에 관한 내용인가?
(a) 동물들의 개체 수 과잉을 둘러싼 논의
(b) SRPO 소속 수의사들에게 수술을 받은 동물들
(c) 애완동물에 불임 수술을 하는 동기
(d) 애완동물 불임 수술에 대한 도덕적 고찰

15 현재 우리 행성을 둘러싼 대기는 수십억 년 전의 대기와 매우 다르다. 지구가 아직 팽창하던 녹은 맨틀과 암석 덩어리였을 때는 헬륨과 수소로 이루어진 유해한 물질로 덮여 있었다. 지구의 표면 온도가 낮아지자, 화산 폭발이 대기에 이산화탄소, 수증기, 질소 구름이 형성되게 했다. 그 이후, 시아노 박테리아가 출현했고 대기에 산소를 제공하기 시작했다. 대기 중에 산소가 축적되어 결국 오늘날 우리가 들이마시는 생명 유지에 필요한 대기 혼합물을 생성했다.

Q: 지문의 주제는 무엇인가?
(a) 지구 대기 내 산소의 중요성
(b) 지구 대기의 형성
(c) 생명 유지에 필요한 대기의 필수 성분
(d) 지구 대기의 현재 구성 요소

16 심리학자들은 유아들이 손에 잡히는 거리에 있는 장난감보다 손에 잡히지 않는 거리에 있는 장난감에 더 매료된다는 점을 오랫동안 주목해왔다. 어린이를 대상으로 한 이 관찰 결과는 어른 응답자들이 쉬운 일을 해냈을 때보다 어려운 일을 해냈을 때 성취감이 더 크다는 평가를 내렸다는 설문 결과와도 일치한다. 이러한 연구 결과는 지속적인 노력의 결과로 달성한 목표가 특별한 의미를 지니게 된다는 사실을 드러낸다.

Q: 지문은 주로 무엇에 관한 내용인가?
(a) 사람들이 호기심을 유지하는 방법
(b) 사람들이 어려운 일을 극복하도록 동기를 부여하는 방법
(c) 가치를 부여하는 인간의 기준
(d) 효과적으로 어린이의 관심을 끄는 데 사용되는 방법

17 사원 여러분들께,

오늘 아침 부서장 회의에서, 모든 사원들이 유니폼을 입어야 한다는 결정이 내려졌으며, 해당 유니폼의 디자인이 첨부되어 있습니다. 과거에 회사의 복장 규정이 엄격했던 적이 없었기에 많은 분들이 이 방침에 놀라실 것을 알지만, 새로 부임하신 최고 경영자께서 보다 일관되고 전문적으로 보이는 모습이 우리 이미지를 증진시킬 것이라고 강력히 주장하고 계십니다. 사원 여러분들에게는 한 달 후에 유니폼이 지급될 것입니다.

진심을 담아,
Travis Howe

Q: 다음 중 이메일의 내용과 일치하는 것은?
(a) 사원들에 의해 예전 유니폼은 폐기 처분될 것이다.
(b) 새로운 유니폼 디자인은 아직 공개되지 않았다.
(c) 새로운 유니폼이 이번 달에 사원들에게 지급될 것이다.
(d) 유니폼 규정이 오늘 오전에 제정되었다.

18 화산이 폭발하면, 마그마라고 불리는 액체 상태가 된 암석이 화산 꼭대기에 있는 구멍을 통해 땅에서 분출된다. 그러나 때로, 용암은 지표면 아래의 암석층들 사이에 갇혀 나갈 곳이 없어진다. 이러한 현상을 병반이라고 하는데, 이는 결과적으로 와이오밍 주에 있는 악마의 탑같이 하늘로 수백 피트 솟아오른 거대하고 놀라운 구조가 된다. 병반은 처음에 그것을 감싸고 있던 퇴적물이 시간의 흐름에 따라 침식되면, 남아 있던 용암이 굳어진 후에 형성된다.

Q: 다음 중 지문의 내용과 일치하는 것은?
(a) 병반은 퇴적물이 충분히 쌓였을 때 형성된다.
(b) 와이오밍 주는 화산 활동으로 유명하다.
(c) 위로 솟아오르는 마그마가 항상 밖으로 빠져나갈 수 있는 것은 아니다.
(d) 병반은 화산 폭발의 과학적 명칭이다.

19
특별 사진 전시

9월 1일 – 11월 30일
독일 국립 평화 박물관, 전시실 4
제2차 세계 대전 중 강제 수용소 내부에서 나치 군인들에 의해 촬영된 200장이 넘는 사진들

이 전시는 독일 강제 수용소의 현실을 탐구하는데, 이곳은 나치당이 바람직하지 않게 여긴 유대인들과 그 밖의 사람들을 구금하는 수단으로 1933년에 처음 설립되었습니다.

입장료
일반: 15달러
학생/노인: 10달러
20명 이상의 단체: 1인당 7달러
박물관 회원: 무료

Q: 다음 중 광고의 내용과 일치하는 것은?
(a) 전시물은 봉쇄 지역 내에서 찍은 사진들을 포함한다.
(b) 학생들로 구성된 단체는 요금 없이 전시회에 들어갈 수 있다.
(c) 사진들은 제2차 세계 대전 이전 몇 년간 촬영되었다.
(d) 노인들에게는 박물관 회원권이 인하된 가격에 이용 가능하다.

20 고대 그리스인들은 모든 물질이 흙, 물, 공기, 그리고 불의 혼합으로 이루어져 있다고 생각했다. 인류의 물질에 대한 이해는 1600년대까지는 이를 넘어 발전하지 못했는데, 그 당시 인의 발견은 과학자들로 하여금 원소의 특징을 철저하게 규정하도록 했다. 오늘날, 원소는 더 단순한 물질로 쪼개질 수 없는 물질이며 전하를 띤 입자로만 구성된 물질이라고 받아들여지고 있다. 17세기 이후로, 100개 이상의 다른 원소들이 발견되었고, 그 중 94개는 지구상에서 자연적으로 발생하며 합성 물질이 아니다.

Q: 다음 중 지문의 내용과 일치하는 것은?
(a) 94개의 확인된 원소가 있다.
(b) 인은 발견된 최초의 반론의 여지가 없는 원소였다.
(c) 전하를 띤 입자들이 원소를 구성한다.
(d) 기본 원소들은 고대 그리스인들에 의해 발견되었다.

21 제1차 아편 전쟁은 영국과 중국의 무역 불균형에 의해 발생되었다. 그 당시, 차와 같은 중국 제품들은 영국에서 인기 있는 상품이었다. 하지만, 그 반대는 사실이 아니었다. 영국은 수출한 9백만 파운드의 제품들로, 중국에서 2천 7백만 파운드를 샀다. 영국 동인도 회사는 인도의 농장에서 재배한 아편을 상인들에게 판매함으로써 일을 그들에게 유리하게 만들었는데, 상인들은 은으로 아편을 사서 이것을 중국으로 운송했다. 이러한 은의 유출과 아편 중독자의 증가에 놀란 중국 관리들은 대량의 아편 수송품을 압수했고, 이는 영국과의 전쟁을 촉발했다.

Q: 지문에 따르면 다음 중 맞는 것은 무엇인가?
(a) 영국인들은 중국으로부터 제품들을 구입하는 데 관심이 거의 없었다.
(b) 중국의 수출은 영국의 수출을 크게 능가했다.
(c) 영국은 인도에서 재배한 아편의 대부분을 수출하는 것을 꺼렸다.
(d) 분실된 아편 수송품이 중국 관리들을 화나게 했고 전쟁을 일으켰다.

22

Robert Kilner께,

저희 Magna Corporation은 직원의 전문성 개발에 전념하고 있습니다. 따라서, 저희는 매년 모든 직원들이 최소 3개의 공인된 리더십 강의를 이수하기를 요구합니다. 상환을 받기 위해 영수증을 제출하시면, 이것은 경영진에 의해 전부 보상됩니다. 올해가 끝나가기 때문에, 귀하께서 어떠한 강의도 등록하지 않았다는 것이 저희의 주의를 끌게 되었습니다. 등록하지 않기로 선택하는 것은 귀하의 현재 계약이 지금으로부터 6개월 후에 만료될 때 저희와의 고용 관계를 끝내는 것을 의미하기 때문에 저희는 귀하께서 이를 즉시 바로잡으시기를 권고합니다.

진심을 담아,
Beverly Driscoll
인사부

Q: 지문에 따르면 다음 중 맞는 것은 무엇인가?
(a) 진행 중인 교육은 지도부 역할을 맡은 직원들에게 요구된다.
(b) 직원들은 그들 스스로의 전문성 개발을 위해 대금을 지불하도록 기대된다.
(c) 고용주는 Robert Kilner가 리더십 교육을 받기를 요구하고 있다.
(d) 강의 등록을 거부하면 바로 해고될 것이다.

23

경제
요트 회사가 격변을 마주하다

Fantasy Yachts 주식회사는 올해 1분기에 막대한 손해를 전한 이후 회사의 몇몇 제조 시설을 폐쇄해야 할 위기에 처했다. 회사 대변인은 부채 급증과 판매 감소로 인해 공장이 폐쇄되는 상황을 막기 위해 Fantasy Yachts 사가 정부 대출을 받을 수도 있다고 밝혔다.

이사회에서는 또한 기금을 마련하기 위한 기업 공개와 불필요한 지출을 피하기 위한 인력 간소화를 계획하고 있다.

Q: 지문에서 추론할 수 있는 것은 무엇인가?
(a) 사원들이 직업을 잃을 가능성이 있다.
(b) 생산을 늘리기 위해 새 제조 공장이 건설될 것이다.
(c) 회사를 살리기 위해서는 정부가 인수해야 한다.
(d) 경쟁사와의 합병이 회사의 문제를 해결할 것이다.

24

오스트리아 연구자 Friederike Range와 그의 비엔나 대학 동료들이 수행했던 연구에서, 개도 인간과 마찬가지로 추상적인 개념을 형성하는 능력이 있다는 결론이 내려졌다. 연구의 처음 단계에서, 연구원들은 개가 터치스크린에 비친 풍경 사진이 아닌 개 사진을 선택할 때마다 먹이를 보상으로 주었다. 그 개들은 또한 먹이를 받지 않고도 앞에서 보지 않았던 일련의 사진들 중에서 개들을 식별해내는 법도 배웠다. 마침내, 그 개들은 풍경만 있는 사진 말고 개와 풍경이 함께 있는 사진을 선택했다.

Q: 지문에서 추론할 수 있는 것은 무엇인가?
(a) 개는 먹이를 받으면 사물을 더 잘 분류할 수 있다.
(b) 대부분의 개들은 개 사진보다 풍경 사진을 더 좋아한다.
(c) 시각 자료는 개의 지능을 발달시키는 것을 도울 수 있다.
(d) 개는 복잡한 사진 속에 있는 요소들을 구별한다.

25

빛의 속도보다 빠른 이동에 대한 가능성은 우리의 현대 물리학의 개념으로는 불가능하다. 즉, 적어도 인접 관찰자의 시각에서 보면, 일상적인 환경에서 물체가 빛의 속도보다 빠르게 움직일 수 없기 때문에, 일반 상대성 이론에 위배된다. 그러나, 만일 충분한 양의 중력이 이용된다면, 시공의 구조가 구부러질 수 있기 때문에 물체는 광속의 한계를 넘을 수 있다. 그러한 조건은 안정적인 체제 안에서는 재현될 수 없기 때문에, 그러한 유사한 상황이 실제로 발생할 가능성은 거의 없다.

Q: 지문에서 추론할 수 있는 것은 무엇인가?
(a) 일반 상대성 이론은 이상적인 조건하에서만 적용된다.
(b) 빛의 속도에 가깝게 움직이는 물체를 관찰하기란 불가능하다.
(c) 시공의 구조는 물체가 움직이는 속도에 영향을 미친다.
(d) 안정적인 체제는 빛의 속도를 뛰어넘기 위한 전제 조건이다.

Part IV

26~27

San Fernando 신문
채용 공고: 칼럼니스트

'San Fernando 신문'에서 지역의 쟁점과 국내 정치 모두에 대해 특유의 견해를 제공할 수 있는 경력직 칼럼니스트를 찾고 있습니다. 칼럼니스트는 또한 지역사회 모임에서 우리를 대표하고 지역의 독자들과 관계를 맺으면서, 신문의 공식적인 얼굴이 될 것입니다.

자격요건:
- 언론계에서 최소 5년의 업무 경력이 필수적이고, 지역 신문사에서의 경력이 있는 사람들이 선호됨.
- 언론학 또는 관련 분야의 학사 학위가 있어야 함.
- 한 주에 최소 두 번 특유의 목소리와 관점을 나타내는 칼럼을 쓰는 능력.
- 기삿거리, 특히 지역사회를 기반으로 하는 이야기를 찾고 조사하는 우수한 능력.
- 지역과 거주민들의 다민족 문화와 사회 경제적 차이점에 대한 견고한 이해는 필수적임.
- 기사 편집과 교정 기술은 필수적이고, 멀티미디어 관련 경력은 이점으로 고려됨.

지원자들은 그들의 이력서, 두 명의 최근 추천인의 연락처 정보, 세 부의 작문 견본, 그리고 두 부의 칼럼 기획안을 제출해야 합니다. 지원서를 늦어도 5월 7일까지 recruiting@sfchronicle.com으로 보내주십시오.

26. Q: 다음 중 지문의 내용과 일치하는 것은?
(a) 칼럼니스트는 오로지 San Fernando 지역의 정치적 쟁점에 대해서만 글을 쓸 것이다.
(b) 이 신문은 지역 언론 학교의 최근 졸업자들을 고용하는 것을 선호한다.
(c) 칼럼니스트는 지역 행사에 참여하도록 요구될 것이다.
(d) 지원자들은 San Fernando와 관련된 두 부의 완성된 칼럼을 제출해야 한다.

27. Q: 이 신문의 칼럼니스트는 어떤 자질을 필수적으로 갖춰야 하는가?
(a) 시청각 미디어를 편집하는 높은 수준의 전문 기술
(b) 지역 신문이나 매스컴에서 기자로 활동한 경력
(c) 지역 주민들의 소득과 배경의 다양성에 대한 이해
(d) 신문 특집 기사를 위해 지역민들을 인터뷰하는 능력

28~29

Kirkwall 여객선 회사
하버 가 29번지, 브라이건타인,
뉴저지 주, 미국, 07109

지출 승인 요청 양식
요청 일자: 5월 7일
요청자: Ross Shearer   직급: 페리 관리자

지출 요청 세부 사항:
5월 5일에, 안전 기준을 강화하려는 회사의 노력에 대해 안내받았습니다. 새로운 정책에 따라, 저는 갑판 승무원들이 WaveCharger

연락선에 대한 전면적인 검사를 수행하게 했습니다. 이 과정을 통해, 저는 저희에게 몇 개의 새로운 구명조끼가 필요하다는 결론에 도달했습니다.

선상에 보유하도록 요구되는 250개의 구명조끼 중, 20개가 수년간 갑판 위에서 햇볕과 바다 물보라에 노출되어 왔습니다. 결과적으로, 천은 색이 바랬고 몇몇 줄들은 해졌습니다. 저는 이 부유 장치들이 비상시에 믿을만하지 못할까 봐 염려스럽습니다. 반면에, 저희의 주 승객 객실에 보관된 230개의 구명 조끼는 여전히 좋은 상태에 있으므로, 그것들은 얼마간 유지할 수 있을 것이라고 생각합니다. 저희의 최대 관광 성수기의 시작인 6월 1일 전까지, 새 구명조끼를 구입한다면 가장 좋을 것입니다.

예상 비용: 950달러

28. Q: 다음 중 지문의 내용과 일치하는 것은?
(a) Kirkwall 여객선 회사는 몇몇 정부 기준을 충족하는 데 실패했다.
(b) 관리자는 250개의 구명조끼를 주문했다.
(c) 여객선의 갑판 승무원들은 새로운 안전 조치에 관한 교육을 받을 것이다.
(d) WaveCharger의 몇몇 안전 장비들은 야외에 보관되어 있다.

29. Q: 지문에서 추론할 수 있는 것은 무엇인가?
(a) 6월에 여객선 승객의 수가 증가할 것이다.
(b) 선상의 직원들은 각 항해 전에 비상 지침을 설명한다.
(c) WaveCharger는 현재 전력으로 작동할 수 없다.
(d) Ross Shearer는 월 주기로 검사를 수행한다.

30~31
소금과 후추는, 요리의 필수적인 재료뿐만 아니라 테이블에 놓인 뿌리는 용기의 형태로서도, 서양 요리에서 아주 흔하다. 그러나, 소금과 후추가 요리의 역사 내내 유행 타기를 반복해 왔기 때문에, 항상 이런 것은 아니었다. 중세 시대 동안, 유럽의 귀족들이 먹던 음식은 강하게 양념이 되었고, 음식이 요리되는 동안 소금과 후추가 첨가되었다. 소금이 식탁 위에 있는 경우에, 그것은 소금 통에 들어있거나 고기를 자르는 사람에 의해 뿌려졌다. 그러나, 양념이 비쌌기 때문에, 대부분의 인구는 훨씬 더 담백한 음식을 먹었다.

16세기와 17세기 동안, 유럽의 귀족 요리는 점점 덜 강하게 양념이 되었다. 요리 사학자들은 이것이 양념이 널리 이용 가능해졌기 때문이라고 생각하며, 이는 그것들이 더는 부유한 사람들만 향유할 수 있던 사치스러운 것으로 여겨지지 않았다는 것을 의미한다. 향신료가 유익한 건강 특성을 가졌다는 관념도 줄어들기 시작했다. 한편, 프랑스 요리에서는, 식사의 주요 재료가 강하게 드러나야 한다는 개념이 양념에 대한 더 적은 강조로 이어졌다. 그럼에도 불구하고, 소금과 후추는 결코 완전히 사라지지 않았고 20세기 초에 뿌리는 용기가 흔해졌을 때 새 출발의 기회를 얻었다.

30. Q: 지문의 주제는 무엇인가?
(a) 음식 보존 시 소금과 후추의 이용
(b) 중세 시대 동안의 소금과 후추의 무역
(c) 유럽 요리에서 양념 사용의 역사
(d) 현대의 소금 사용 관습에 관한 개관

31. Q: 지문에서 추론할 수 있는 것은 무엇인가?
(a) 중세 시대의 대부분의 평범한 시민들은 소금과 후추를 살 형편이 안 됐다.
(b) 소금과 후추는 16세기와 17세기에 교역된 주요 상품들이었다.
(c) 중세 시대 동안 프랑스 요리법은 유럽에서 선구적인 요리 분야였다.
(d) 의학의 진보는 향신료의 인지된 건강상의 이점이 근거 없음을 증명했다.

32~33

과학 노트

'호모 사피엔스'의 진화 이전 몇 세기 동안, 또 다른 인간과 비슷한 종인 네안데르탈인이, 유럽 도처와 아시아 일부에 살았다. 대부분의 초기 고고학자들은 이러한 고대인들은 현대인과 같은 지적 능력이 없이, 더 원시적이었다고 결론내렸다. 그러나, 그들이 잡식성이었고, 장신구를 착용했고, 미술품을 만들었다는 증거와 함께, 네안데르탈인의 더 복잡한 양상이 드러나기 시작했다. 이 가장 최근의 발견은 스페인에서 나왔는데, 그곳에서 국제적인 고고학자 단체는 초기 인간에 의해 그려졌다고 생각되었던 많은 고대 동굴 벽화가 네안데르탈인에 의해 그려졌음을 발견했다.

방사성 탄소 연대 측정법을 사용하여, 이 단체는 몇몇 동굴의 고대 미술작품 위로 생긴 방해석 표면을 분석했고, 그것들이 최소 6만 5천 년 전에 그려졌다는 것을 밝혔다. 인간은 불과 4만 년 전에 유럽으로 진출했기 때문에, 이 작품들은 약 12만 년 전부터 유럽에 살았던, 네안데르탈인에 의해 만들어졌음이 틀림없다. 손자국과 기하학적인 모양들을 포함하는 이 그림들은, 네안데르탈인이 가지고 있을 것으로 생각되지 않았던 복잡성의 정도를 보여주는데, 이는 우리의 진화적 친척이 인지력, 지각 작용, 그리고 창의성 측면에서 기존에 상상했던 것보다 훨씬 더 인간에 가까웠다는 것을 제시한다.

32. Q: 지문은 주로 무엇에 관한 내용인가?
(a) 네안데르탈인의 행동의 복잡성에 관한 새로운 고고학적 증거
(b) 네안데르탈인과 인간 사이의 진화적 연관성에 대한 반박
(c) 최근 고고학에서 탄소 연대 측정법의 적용
(d) 아시아 대륙에 걸친 네안데르탈인 사회의 발달

33. Q: 네안데르탈인에 대해 지문에서 추론할 수 있는 것은?
(a) 호모 사피엔스가 진화하기 약 6만 5천 년 전쯤에 먼저 유럽에서 살기 시작했다.
(b) 약 12만 년 전에 인간 활동으로 인해 완전한 멸종에 처했다.
(c) 서아시아와 북아프리카에서 유럽의 다양한 지역으로 이주했다.
(d) 6만 5천 년 전에 유럽 대륙의 몇몇 지역에 존재했다.

34~35

Ogdan이 더 푸르러질 준비가 되다
Max Cooper 씀

4월 1일부터 Ogdan의 도시 쓰레기 매립지에 모든 폐기물을 처리하는 비용이 더 비싸진다. 의회는 도시의 폐기물 처리 체계의 개선을 위한 기금을 모으고 도시의 쓰레기 매립지의 과용을 막는 수단으로서 새로운 쓰레기 매립 요금을 도입하기로 결정했다.

현재, 쓰레기 매립지에 어떤 물건이든 처리하는 것은 1톤당 10달러의 고정 요금을 발생시키는데, 이것은 쓰레기 매립지를 관리하는 비용을 충당하려고 의도된 것이다. 새로운 세금 하에서, 각 쓰레기의 비용은 대체로 폐기물의 종류에 달려있다.

나무, 배관, 관, 그리고 플라스틱을 포함한, 활성 폐기물은, 1톤에 50달러가 부과될 것이다. 반면에, 흙, 콘크리트, 그리고 유리와 같은, 불활성 폐기물은 1톤에 2.5달러가 부과될 것이다. 이 차이는 전자의 폐기물 종류를 처리하는 데 있어서의 어려움을 반영한다. 무게가 4분의 1톤 이하인 작은 쓰레기는 기존의 고정 요금이 부과될 것이다.

정부는 새로운 요금으로 얻을 대부분의 기금이 더 포괄적인 재활용 체계에 쓰일 것이며, 이는 근본적으로 처리되는 폐기물의 양을 감소시키고 쓰레기 매립지에 대한 Ogdan의 의존도를 낮출 것이라고 주장한다. 그러나, 많은 주민들은 요금 인상이 폐기물 처리를 그들에게 너무 비싸서 할 수 없는 것으로 만들 것이라고 주장하면서, 그것에 반대의 목소리를 내고 있다.

34. Q: 다음 중 가장 비싼 요금이 부과될 것은 무엇인가?
(a) 10톤의 콘크리트 쓰레기

(b) 4분의 1톤의 유리 쓰레기
(c) 3분의 1톤의 흙
(d) 1톤의 플라스틱 폐기물

35. Q: 기사의 주된 목적은 무엇인가?
(a) 더 나은 재활용 체계의 도입에 찬성하기 위해
(b) 쓰레기 매립지에 폐기물을 버리는 것의 문제를 서술하기 위해
(c) 폐기물 처리에 관한 새로운 요금이 어떻게 운영될 지 설명하기 위해
(d) 쓰레기 매립지 폐기물 처리에 더 많은 세금이 부과되어야 한다고 제안하기 위해

시험에 나올 문제를 미리 풀어보는
텝스 적중예상특강
해커스텝스 HackersTEPS.com

해커스 텝스 최신기출유형 실전모의고사 문제집

ANSWER KEYS
OMR 답안지

TEST 01

LISTENING COMPREHENSION

1	(a)	2	(a)	3	(b)	4	(d)	5	(d)
6	(c)	7	(b)	8	(d)	9	(a)	10	(c)
11	(a)	12	(b)	13	(c)	14	(d)	15	(d)
16	(d)	17	(d)	18	(b)	19	(b)	20	(b)
21	(c)	22	(d)	23	(b)	24	(c)	25	(b)
26	(c)	27	(b)	28	(a)	29	(d)	30	(b)
31	(a)	32	(a)	33	(d)	34	(a)	35	(b)
36	(c)	37	(b)	38	(b)	39	(b)	40	(d)

VOCABULARY & GRAMMAR

VOCABULARY

1	(a)	2	(c)	3	(a)	4	(b)	5	(c)
6	(b)	7	(a)	8	(a)	9	(b)	10	(b)
11	(d)	12	(c)	13	(d)	14	(b)	15	(c)
16	(b)	17	(d)	18	(d)	19	(b)	20	(a)
21	(d)	22	(d)	23	(c)	24	(b)	25	(a)
26	(c)	27	(d)	28	(b)	29	(c)	30	(d)

GRAMMAR

1	(b)	2	(d)	3	(b)	4	(b)	5	(d)
6	(c)	7	(c)	8	(d)	9	(c)	10	(a)
11	(c)	12	(d)	13	(b)	14	(a)	15	(c)
16	(c)	17	(c)	18	(c)	19	(c)	20	(c)
21	(b)	22	(d)	23	(a)	24	(b)	25	(b)

26 (c) Never I have → Never have I
27 (c) astonishing → astonished
28 (b) of which → which
29 (a) are → is
30 (b) can infect → can be infected

READING COMPREHENSION

1	(d)	2	(d)	3	(a)	4	(b)	5	(c)
6	(a)	7	(a)	8	(a)	9	(b)	10	(a)
11	(d)	12	(b)	13	(a)	14	(d)	15	(d)
16	(c)	17	(a)	18	(c)	19	(a)	20	(c)
21	(c)	22	(d)	23	(c)	24	(b)	25	(d)
26	(a)	27	(c)	28	(b)	29	(b)	30	(d)
31	(a)	32	(d)	33	(b)	34	(b)	35	(b)

TEST 02

해커스 텝스 최신기출유형 실전모의고사 문제집

LISTENING COMPREHENSION

1 (c)	2 (d)	3 (b)	4 (a)	5 (d)
6 (c)	7 (c)	8 (d)	9 (d)	10 (b)
11 (a)	12 (d)	13 (d)	14 (a)	15 (d)
16 (c)	17 (d)	18 (c)	19 (d)	20 (b)
21 (d)	22 (a)	23 (d)	24 (d)	25 (c)
26 (c)	27 (b)	28 (c)	29 (c)	30 (d)
31 (b)	32 (c)	33 (b)	34 (b)	35 (c)
36 (a)	37 (c)	38 (d)	39 (a)	40 (d)

VOCABULARY & GRAMMAR

VOCABULARY

1 (b)	2 (b)	3 (a)	4 (d)	5 (c)
6 (b)	7 (c)	8 (a)	9 (c)	10 (a)
11 (b)	12 (b)	13 (b)	14 (d)	15 (c)
16 (b)	17 (c)	18 (b)	19 (d)	20 (a)
21 (d)	22 (d)	23 (c)	24 (b)	25 (b)
26 (c)	27 (c)	28 (a)	29 (b)	30 (d)

GRAMMAR

1 (b)	2 (b)	3 (a)	4 (b)	5 (b)
6 (b)	7 (c)	8 (c)	9 (d)	10 (c)
11 (b)	12 (c)	13 (b)	14 (d)	15 (d)
16 (a)	17 (b)	18 (c)	19 (b)	20 (b)
21 (b)	22 (d)	23 (b)	24 (b)	25 (a)

26 (c) you'll figure → you figure
27 (d) Reading → While I was reading
28 (d) act → act on(upon)
29 (d) helped her make → helped (to) make her
30 (c) which → in which 또는 where

READING COMPREHENSION

1 (b)	2 (d)	3 (c)	4 (c)	5 (a)
6 (a)	7 (b)	8 (a)	9 (a)	10 (d)
11 (c)	12 (d)	13 (c)	14 (b)	15 (c)
16 (c)	17 (d)	18 (c)	19 (a)	20 (c)
21 (c)	22 (a)	23 (c)	24 (a)	25 (a)
26 (c)	27 (b)	28 (a)	29 (b)	30 (b)
31 (a)	32 (a)	33 (d)	34 (d)	35 (d)

TEST 03

LISTENING COMPREHENSION

1	(b)	**2**	(d)	**3**	(b)	**4**	(a)	**5**	(d)
6	(d)	**7**	(c)	**8**	(b)	**9**	(c)	**10**	(b)
11	(d)	**12**	(b)	**13**	(b)	**14**	(c)	**15**	(c)
16	(c)	**17**	(c)	**18**	(b)	**19**	(a)	**20**	(d)
21	(d)	**22**	(a)	**23**	(b)	**24**	(c)	**25**	(b)
26	(c)	**27**	(c)	**28**	(b)	**29**	(b)	**30**	(a)
31	(b)	**32**	(c)	**33**	(b)	**34**	(a)	**35**	(b)
36	(c)	**37**	(b)	**38**	(d)	**39**	(b)	**40**	(c)

VOCABULARY & GRAMMAR

VOCABULARY

1	(b)	**2**	(c)	**3**	(a)	**4**	(b)	**5**	(d)
6	(d)	**7**	(c)	**8**	(b)	**9**	(c)	**10**	(b)
11	(c)	**12**	(a)	**13**	(c)	**14**	(a)	**15**	(b)
16	(a)	**17**	(a)	**18**	(b)	**19**	(b)	**20**	(a)
21	(c)	**22**	(b)	**23**	(c)	**24**	(c)	**25**	(d)
26	(a)	**27**	(b)	**28**	(a)	**29**	(c)	**30**	(a)

GRAMMAR

1	(b)	**2**	(c)	**3**	(d)	**4**	(a)	**5**	(d)
6	(c)	**7**	(b)	**8**	(b)	**9**	(d)	**10**	(c)
11	(d)	**12**	(a)	**13**	(c)	**14**	(c)	**15**	(a)
16	(c)	**17**	(b)	**18**	(c)	**19**	(b)	**20**	(d)
21	(a)	**22**	(c)	**23**	(c)	**24**	(b)	**25**	(a)

26 (c) fail → failing
27 (c) Don't get wrong → Don't get me wrong
28 (d) consistent → consistently
29 (c) are needed → he needed
30 (c) he did → did he

READING COMPREHENSION

1	(c)	**2**	(b)	**3**	(d)	**4**	(d)	**5**	(c)
6	(d)	**7**	(d)	**8**	(b)	**9**	(a)	**10**	(d)
11	(c)	**12**	(c)	**13**	(b)	**14**	(b)	**15**	(d)
16	(b)	**17**	(d)	**18**	(c)	**19**	(b)	**20**	(d)
21	(b)	**22**	(b)	**23**	(d)	**24**	(a)	**25**	(b)
26	(b)	**27**	(c)	**28**	(a)	**29**	(c)	**30**	(b)
31	(d)	**32**	(b)	**33**	(c)	**34**	(b)	**35**	(d)

TEST 04

해커스 텝스 최신기출유형 실전모의고사 문제집

LISTENING COMPREHENSION

1 (c)	2 (b)	3 (c)	4 (c)	5 (b)
6 (c)	7 (a)	8 (a)	9 (c)	10 (b)
11 (c)	12 (d)	13 (c)	14 (b)	15 (c)
16 (c)	17 (d)	18 (a)	19 (d)	20 (a)
21 (d)	22 (c)	23 (c)	24 (c)	25 (d)
26 (d)	27 (a)	28 (b)	29 (b)	30 (a)
31 (b)	32 (c)	33 (c)	34 (c)	35 (d)
36 (c)	37 (c)	38 (b)	39 (d)	40 (a)

VOCABULARY & GRAMMAR

VOCABULARY

1 (c)	2 (c)	3 (d)	4 (b)	5 (d)
6 (d)	7 (b)	8 (b)	9 (d)	10 (a)
11 (c)	12 (a)	13 (b)	14 (c)	15 (a)
16 (d)	17 (d)	18 (d)	19 (b)	20 (b)
21 (c)	22 (a)	23 (d)	24 (a)	25 (d)
26 (b)	27 (a)	28 (c)	29 (b)	30 (a)

GRAMMAR

1 (b)	2 (a)	3 (a)	4 (c)	5 (b)
6 (b)	7 (c)	8 (d)	9 (b)	10 (d)
11 (a)	12 (d)	13 (c)	14 (a)	15 (a)
16 (c)	17 (c)	18 (c)	19 (b)	20 (d)
21 (d)	22 (c)	23 (a)	24 (b)	25 (d)

26 (b) for → in
27 (c) are → is
28 (b) in which → of which
29 (c) To function → Functioning
30 (c) are expected → they expected

READING COMPREHENSION

1 (a)	2 (b)	3 (a)	4 (c)	5 (a)
6 (d)	7 (c)	8 (c)	9 (d)	10 (a)
11 (b)	12 (c)	13 (d)	14 (c)	15 (c)
16 (d)	17 (b)	18 (b)	19 (b)	20 (c)
21 (a)	22 (b)	23 (b)	24 (d)	25 (d)
26 (b)	27 (c)	28 (b)	29 (d)	30 (d)
31 (b)	32 (c)	33 (a)	34 (c)	35 (d)

TEST 05

LISTENING COMPREHENSION

1	(a)	2	(b)	3	(b)	4	(c)	5	(a)
6	(b)	7	(b)	8	(b)	9	(c)	10	(d)
11	(c)	12	(d)	13	(b)	14	(b)	15	(b)
16	(b)	17	(c)	18	(d)	19	(d)	20	(c)
21	(d)	22	(b)	23	(b)	24	(b)	25	(c)
26	(b)	27	(c)	28	(a)	29	(d)	30	(b)
31	(d)	32	(d)	33	(c)	34	(d)	35	(d)
36	(a)	37	(b)	38	(d)	39	(b)	40	(d)

VOCABULARY & GRAMMAR

VOCABULARY

1	(a)	2	(c)	3	(d)	4	(a)	5	(b)
6	(b)	7	(d)	8	(c)	9	(b)	10	(d)
11	(d)	12	(b)	13	(d)	14	(a)	15	(b)
16	(a)	17	(b)	18	(a)	19	(a)	20	(a)
21	(a)	22	(c)	23	(c)	24	(b)	25	(a)
26	(c)	27	(c)	28	(d)	29	(b)	30	(c)

GRAMMAR

1	(c)	2	(b)	3	(c)	4	(b)	5	(c)
6	(d)	7	(c)	8	(d)	9	(a)	10	(c)
11	(d)	12	(a)	13	(a)	14	(d)	15	(c)
16	(d)	17	(d)	18	(a)	19	(b)	20	(a)
21	(d)	22	(a)	23	(b)	24	(a)	25	(a)

26 (d) lend to you → lend it to you
27 (c) awaken → am awakened
28 (d) It had not been for → Had it not been for
29 (c) threatening → threatened
30 (a) intend to do → intend to

READING COMPREHENSION

1	(a)	2	(c)	3	(d)	4	(b)	5	(c)
6	(a)	7	(d)	8	(b)	9	(d)	10	(d)
11	(a)	12	(d)	13	(b)	14	(d)	15	(b)
16	(d)	17	(b)	18	(d)	19	(b)	20	(b)
21	(b)	22	(d)	23	(c)	24	(d)	25	(d)
26	(d)	27	(a)	28	(d)	29	(a)	30	(c)
31	(d)	32	(c)	33	(a)	34	(c)	35	(d)

TEST 06

LISTENING COMPREHENSION

1 (b)	2 (c)	3 (a)	4 (b)	5 (d)
6 (b)	7 (a)	8 (c)	9 (c)	10 (d)
11 (b)	12 (a)	13 (d)	14 (c)	15 (d)
16 (a)	17 (b)	18 (c)	19 (c)	20 (d)
21 (b)	22 (c)	23 (d)	24 (c)	25 (d)
26 (d)	27 (b)	28 (d)	29 (a)	30 (a)
31 (b)	32 (d)	33 (d)	34 (d)	35 (b)
36 (b)	37 (c)	38 (d)	39 (a)	40 (c)

VOCABULARY & GRAMMAR

VOCABULARY

1 (b)	2 (a)	3 (d)	4 (a)	5 (d)
6 (a)	7 (c)	8 (d)	9 (b)	10 (b)
11 (c)	12 (c)	13 (d)	14 (d)	15 (a)
16 (c)	17 (a)	18 (d)	19 (a)	20 (c)
21 (c)	22 (c)	23 (a)	24 (a)	25 (b)
26 (d)	27 (b)	28 (d)	29 (c)	30 (d)

GRAMMAR

1 (b)	2 (d)	3 (c)	4 (b)	5 (b)
6 (d)	7 (a)	8 (a)	9 (c)	10 (b)
11 (a)	12 (c)	13 (d)	14 (b)	15 (c)
16 (b)	17 (b)	18 (d)	19 (b)	20 (a)
21 (c)	22 (b)	23 (d)	24 (d)	25 (a)

26 (c) such → so
27 (a) proper → properly
28 (d) modify → to modify
29 (d) between → to
30 (c) to bring → bringing

READING COMPREHENSION

1 (c)	2 (c)	3 (a)	4 (b)	5 (a)
6 (a)	7 (c)	8 (a)	9 (c)	10 (d)
11 (c)	12 (d)	13 (c)	14 (c)	15 (b)
16 (c)	17 (d)	18 (c)	19 (a)	20 (c)
21 (b)	22 (c)	23 (a)	24 (d)	25 (c)
26 (c)	27 (c)	28 (d)	29 (a)	30 (c)
31 (a)	32 (a)	33 (d)	34 (d)	35 (c)

시험에 나올 문제를 미리 풀어보는
텝스 적중예상특강
해커스텝스 HackersTEPS.com

시험에 나올 문제를 미리 풀어보는
텝스 적중예상특강
해커스텝스 HackersTEPS.com

TEPS

Test of English Proficiency
developed by
Seoul National University

OMR 답안지

시험에 나올 문제를 미리 풀어보는
텝스 적중예상특강
해커스텝스 HackersTEPS.com

TEPS

Test of English Proficiency
developed by
Seoul National University

OMR 답안지

시험에 나올 문제를 미리 풀어보는
텝스 적중예상특강
해커스텝스 HackersTEPS.com

TEPS

Test of English Proficiency
developed by
Seoul National University

OMR 답안지

시험에 나올 문제를 미리 풀어보는
텝스 적중예상특강
해커스텝스 HackersTEPS.com

TEPS

Test of English Proficiency
developed by
Seoul National University

OMR 답안지

시험에 나올 문제를 미리 풀어보는
텝스 적중예상특강
해커스텝스 HackersTEPS.com

TEPS

Test of English Proficiency
developed by
Seoul National University

OMR 답안지

시험에 나올 문제를 미리 풀어보는
텝스 적중예상특강
해커스텝스 HackersTEPS.com

텝스 고득점을 위한
최종 마무리 모의고사

**해커스
텝스
최신기출유형
실전모의고사
문제집**

초판 11쇄 발행 2024년 3월 25일
초판 1쇄 발행 2018년 6월 25일

지은이	해커스 어학연구소
펴낸곳	(주)해커스 어학연구소
펴낸이	해커스 어학연구소 출판팀
주소	서울특별시 서초구 강남대로61길 23 (주)해커스 어학연구소
고객센터	02-537-5000
교재 관련 문의	publishing@hackers.com
동영상강의	HackersIngang.com
ISBN	978-89-6542-259-4 (13740)
Serial Number	01-11-01

저작권자 ⓒ 2018, 해커스 어학연구소
이 책 및 음성파일의 모든 내용, 이미지, 디자인, 편집 형태에 대한 저작권은 저자에게 있습니다.
서면에 의한 저자와 출판사의 허락 없이 내용의 일부 혹은 전부를 인용, 발췌하거나 복제, 배포할 수 없습니다.

텝스 전문 포털, 해커스텝스
HackersTEPS.com
해커스 텝스

- 매달 업데이트 되는 스타강사의 **텝스 무료 적중예상특강**
- 문법, 독해, 어휘, 청해 문제를 꾸준히 풀어보는 **매일 실전 텝스 문제**
- **텝스 기출 보카 TEST 및 텝스 단어시험지 자동생성기** 등 다양한 무료 학습 콘텐츠

외국어인강 1위, 해커스인강
HackersIngang.com
해커스 인강

- 실제 시험과 동일한 성우 음성의 **교재 MP3 무료 다운로드**
- 텝스 시험에 나올 어휘를 정리한 **단어암기장 및 단어암기 MP3**
- 해커스 스타강사의 **본 교재 인강**

헤럴드 선정 2018 대학생 선호브랜드 대상 '대학생이 선정한 외국어인강' 부문 1위

1위 해커스의 노하우가 담긴
해커스텝스 무료 학습 자료

[해커스어학원] 2015 대한민국 퍼스트브랜드 대상 외국어학원 부문(한국소비자포럼)

1 매일 업데이트되는 텝스 실전문제로 시험 대비
매일 텝스 풀기

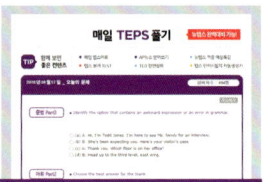

2 16년 연속 베스트셀러 1위 해커스텝스의 비법 수록
텝스 리딩 무료강의

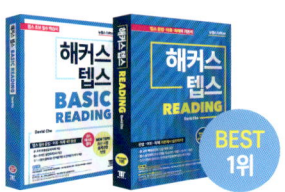

3 1위 해커스 스타 강사진의
텝스 적중예상특강으로 고득점 달성
텝스 적중예상특강

청해 **강로사** 문법 **설미연** 독해 **손승미**

4 텝스 필수 기출 어휘 학습
매일 텝스 어휘

5 텝스 최신 기출 어휘를 꼼꼼하게 복습
해커스 텝스 기출 보카 TEST

[16년 연속 베스트셀러 1위] [해커스어학연구소] 알라딘 외국어 베스트셀러 텝스 분야 Reading/Listening 부문 1위
(2008.11.~2024.9. 월별 베스트 기준, READING 154회, LISTENING 191회, 구문독해 37회)

더 많은 텝스 무료자료는 **해커스텝스** **검색** 에서 확인하세요.   해커스텝스 바로가기 ▶